The World of Salt Shakers, Volume III

ANTIQUE & ART GLASS VALUE GUIDE

by Mildred & Ralph Lechner

COLLECTOR BOOKS

The current values in this book should be used only as a guide. They are not intended to set prices, which vary from one section of the country to another. Auction prices as well as dealer prices vary greatly and are affected by condition as well as demand. Neither the Authors nor the Publisher assumes responsibility for any losses that might be incurred as a result of consulting this guide.

Searching For A Publisher?

We are always looking for knowledgeable people considered to be experts within their fields. If you feel that there is a real need for a book on your collectible subject and have a large comprehensive collection, contact Collector Books.

On the cover:
Chick Head condiment set: Opaque blue and tan colored glass shakers, mold blown with HP floral sprays on the back and sides of the egg-shaped dispensers. Each shaker is 1¾" tall; the holder measures 3⅝" between the most distant supporting feet (tip-to-tip); it is 1⅝" between the end supporting feet. Circa 1890. Extremely rare as a complete set. No price determined due to extreme rarity.

Cover design by Beth Summers
Book design by Beth Ray

COLLECTOR BOOKS
P.O. Box 3009
Paducah, Kentucky 42002-3009

Contents

Acknowledgments

Thoughts of writing this book began after the publication of our Volume II, 1992, salt shaker book. We began our evaluation of feasibility by viewing several advanced collections of the Antique and Art Glass Salt Shaker Collectors' Society members throughout various parts of the country and being encouraged by numerous collectors, friends, and readers to consider authoring another antique glass salt shaker book.

Obviously the involved technical writing and assembly requires continuous hours of dedication and enjoyment of the stimulus associated with the challenges involved. The principal challenge is the closeup photography involving relatively small glassware pieces, much of which had to be done at various collectors' homes under widely varying conditions.

Because of the personal interest and consideration provided by the following AAGSSCS members who took the time to make their salt shakers collections available to our camera, we have been able to bring this book to a meaningful completion.

Victor Buck, California. Our mentor, loyal friend, and wise advisor throughout our many years of antique glassware collecting and researching. His knowledge of art glass from the Art Nouveau era ranks among the best in the country. We owe him much!

Harold and Ila Coalmer, Ohio. Personal friends. Advanced and knowledgeable collectors. Very down-to-earth folks who went out of their way to help in any way that they could to make our visits both meaningful and enjoyable. Harold is a very skilled photographer. His personal assistance provided some of the excellent photos taken by him that are part of this book. He is also a member of the AAGSSCS Board of Directors.

Richard and Mary Ann Krauss, Ohio. Good friends and gracious hosts in their beautiful home. Advanced art and pattern glass collectors and dealers. As the reader peruses this book, it will become obvious their collection has provided a lot of beauty and knowledge to the antique glassware universe. Richard is a past President of the AAGSSCS and he worked very hard to provide membership interest and growth. He is a good photographer and contributed a number of photos from their collection.

Marilyn and Charles Lockwood, New York. Marilyn was our first AAGSSCS president. Under her dedicated leadership the society got off to a great start. She is a fine lady and a very knowledgeable collector and researcher that has written excellent articles for the society's membership publication *The Pioneer* and *Glass Collectors Digest* magazine. As he did in our previous book, Charles (Chub) provided voluntary photographic backup from their collection. Their friendship and help have been much appreciated throughout our many years of acquaintance. We were deeply saddened to learn that Marilyn passed away in June 1997.

Stan and Shirley McElderry, Iowa. If we need assistance or help they have always been there. The special acknowledgment that we highlighted in our Vol. II book still applies to them both. Our special study involving the Mt. Washington Tomato pattern reproductions is an outstanding example of their interest and thoughtfulness.

Phil and Faye Rathbun, Tennessee. As our AAGSSCS 1997 president, Phil is a low key, soft spoken person that just moves ahead in an efficient, dedicated manner while trying to show consideration for everyone. Faye is chairperson of the society's ID committee. Her efforts and committee decision coordination are reflected in each issue of *The Pioneer*. The personal help they have provided is reflected throughout the book.

Maralyn and Bill Ridgway, West Virginia. Good friends, thoughtful and advanced collectors and researchers who entrusted us to take care of their quality glassware for photographing and book inclusion. Maralyn is vice president of the AAGSSCS.

Barbara and Bob White, New York. Knowledgeable advanced collectors, good friends and advisors. Barbara's technical knowledge and advice is much appreciated. She has served on the club's ID committee for many years.

A lot of additional AAGSSCS folks and institutions deserve our thanks and gratitude for their assistance in the research and production of this book. Past president Scott Arnold, Geraldine Tognetti, Janice Eldridge, Tom Neale, Dean Armstrong, Lorrie Vit, and Bette Howard plus the various AAGSSCS members whose submittals of many rare and heretofore undocumented patterns to the society's ID committee have been made available for our study and publication.

A special thank you to Frank M. Fenton who willingly made himself available to us when we visited him in 1994 relative to Fenton glassware and production processes.

Finally, a particularly large gesture of appreciation must go for the numerous long distance telephone calls made to us by caring individuals so that we could accurately record and establish various technical details associated with their various salt shakers.

Abbreviation Key

aka — also known as
Circa — estimated year, about
Dia. — diameter (in inches)
H-1 – 9 — Heacock Book 1 thru 9 (his Encyclopedia of Pattern Glass books)
HP — hand painted
OMN — original manufacture's name (pattern name)
IVT — Inverted Thumbprint
p. — page number
UV — ultraviolet (radiation with black light)
Vol. — volume
NPD — No price determined due to extreme rarity.

Foreword

The Lechners have done it again! When their last book came out, I was certain that there wouldn't be enough different salt shakers found to fill another book. —WRONG— I failed to take into account the hard work, tenacity, perseverance, and penchant for details they are capable of. When I talked to Ralph about the "next book," he was fairly certain that he could come up with enough to make another completely different showing of colored glass salt shakers; I was sure he pulling my leg, but….

When the old time collectors who had sort of "kept in the background" until his last edition was released apparently decided he was doing it the way it should be done; they opened up their collections and gave him carte blanche to photograph, describe, value, and list their treasures in his straight forward, detailed, and honest style. That's how this book is written.

If Ralph and Mildred have uncovered data on a shaker that was previously unknown, or additional updated information on present listings, you can bet it is so listed in this treatise. There are another 800 or so shakers in this book and a true education to the rest of us who let somebody do the work so we can have it at our fingertips and know we are getting the complete story. Perusing the introduction will give the reader an idea of the thoroughness of the Lechners' research.

There are other good authors around who have given us reference books on various subjects; Chris Revi (art glass), Paul Evens (art pottery), Henry Kaufman (pewter, tin ware, copper and brass, etc.), Dorothy Rainwater (silver)… just to mention a few, and the Lechners have entered into that world. If you look around your personal library or your friends' libraries you will see these basic "solid foundation" books on the shelf that are constantly referred to as *the* reference book in a particular category.

I won't say there will not be a fourth volume on salt shakers by the Lechners, but I can feel safe to say, this is the most complete treatise to date on this subject.

Many thanks to the Lechners and the members of the Antique and Art Glass Salt Shaker Collectors' Society who have contributed to this book's success.

I am very proud to have been asked to contribute my opinion.

Victor W. Buck
Upland, California

The Antique and Art Glass Salt Shaker Collectors' Society Inc. is a group of people who enjoy collecting, studying, and trading shakers, but not necessarily in that order.

We have a yearly convention at which time we meet new members, renew friendships, and acquire new or rare shakers. The conventions usually feature two or three speakers knowledgeable in the field of glass collecting.

This year the board of directors comprised of Rick Hess, vice president; Joan Richardson, secretary; Joe Richardson, treasurer; Dorothy Maxfield, past president; Bette Wasson, director; Maralyn Ridgway, director; and Harold Coalmer, director voted to give Mildred and Ralph Lechner any assistance we could with their new publication *World of Salt Shakers, Volume III.* This assistance included the use of over 300 unknown shakers from the ID project which had been put together by 22 members and the ID committee. These shakers have been published in our quarterly newsletter, *The Pioneer*, edited by Bill Avery.

Several of our members have invited Mildred and Ralph to their homes for a two or three day photo session to include many of the better collections in this new book.

The board of directors were available and helpful to Mildred and Ralph and I am pleased to have been able to assist in this publication.

Phil Rathbun, president 1995 – 1997
Faye Rathbun, chairperson ID Project

Pertinent Thoughts from the AAGSSCS First President

The Antique and Art Glass Salt Shaker Collectors' Society owes much to its founders, members, and its honorary president, Dr. Arthur G. Peterson. Dr. Peterson's first book, *Salt and Salt Shakers*, planted the seed of an idea. His second book, *Glass Salt Shakers, 1,000 Patterns*, fed that seed which germinated in the minds of founders, Dottie and Bill Avery. Their hard work and enthusiasm brought the idea to fruition in the form of a society dedicated to promoting the collection and study of Victorian and art glass salt and pepper shakers. Their perseverance has made it bloom and bear fruit beyond even their expectations, we suspect. The society continues to grow as a perennial, not just an annual.

The group was first organized as the Salt Shaker Collectors' Club and subsequently held its first convention in 1986 in Hornell, NY. At its second convention, recognizing that the membership fell into two divergent areas of interest, the Club was formally divided. As the parent group, we take pride in our "child," The Salt and Pepper Novelty Shakers Club whose membership and achievements have soared. The parent group continued as the Antique and Art Glass Salt Shaker Collectors' Society and its newsletter acquired a name, *The Pioneer.*

The Averys had published the newsletter informally for over three years until Neila Bredehoft agreed to fulfill that task in December 1986. With her experience as a writer and editor, *The Pioneer* matured as a source of information and education for members. In 1993, Bill Avery accepted editorship and continues the standards set for this invaluable part of the organization. Under his initiative the publication has been enhanced by the introduction of pictures in color. The names of members who contribute to *The Pioneer* include many who have published books and articles in current glass literature.

At first members depended primarily on the illustrations and meticulous research in the books of Dr. Peterson mentioned above and his *Glass Patents and Patterns* and *400 Trademarks on Glass.* Other sources, such as the books of William Heacock, began to appear. Knowledgeable members added to the growing store of information. Finally, the first book published by members Mildred and Ralph Lechner provided the incentive to add the society's bit. The Lechners' second book was the icing on the cake. We are sure this third book will be the a la mode.

Collectors have discovered the chase for the favorite objects of their desire and its success is not the whole story. To many that is just the beginning of identification and research to know and appreciate their collections. That idea captured the fancy of the members of the Antique and Art Glass Salt Shaker Collectors' Society and spawned its Identification Project.

The society established an I.D. Committee and during the last decade it has been led successively by Neila and Tom Bredehoft, Bill and Dottie Avery and, currently, Faye Rathbun. Committee members Laura and Harry Sine, Marilyn and Charles Lockwood, Nancy and Harry Ware, Carole and Bob Bruce, Barbara and Bob White, Bette Wasson, and Dorothy Maxfield have served at various times through the years. Equally valuable has been the essential input of many society members to identify patterns with prior publication and to name those not found in existing glass literature.

Society members have learned so much beyond patterns, colors, kinds of glass, and attributions:

- Cooperation leads to advancement in knowledge.
- Sharing information takes planning and organization.
- Choosing names for shakers is difficult—avoiding names that limit by color, decoration, etc. or those names already used. This brought an added respect for authors who have done this; authors such as Peterson and the Lechners.
- Admiration for those who have pioneered research on which we all build.
- Pride in our predecessors, the Victorians, who designed the myriad patterns and crafted the glass with imagination and artistry.
- Amazement at the variety of patterns and art glass.
- The knowledge that there is so much more to discover.

The society takes pride in continuing to cooperate and share information with the Lechners. This assistance should benefit all of us. We are assured that our contributions, constructive criticism, and active support have been of value to Mildred and Ralph during the tribulations of writing this book. We know their books are enjoyed and used by collectors and dealers in many areas of Victorian glass.

We also anticipate the ongoing work of the society's Identification Project as more patterns and shakers come to light.

Marilyn Lockwood
Antique and Art Glass
Salt Shaker Collectors' Society

The society welcomes new members who share its goals of promoting the collection and study of Victorian pattern and art glass. For membership information write to Antique and Art Glass Salt Shaker Collectors' Society, 6832 Rapidan Trail, Maitland, FL 32751.

Introduction

This book (Volume III), used in conjunction with our second book (Volume II) is not solely for the collector or dealer of glass salt and pepper shakers. Both are an excellent guide for the identification of art and pattern glass items that were produced in other shapes and forms.

This is the third volume in our series of books on antique art and pattern glass salt and pepper shakers that continues to document the many additional patterns and forms that this type of ware was produced in during the Victorian era, circa 1870–1915. As was the case with our previous volume, this book, wherever possible, continues to generally concentrate on the colored glassware shakers due to their higher collectibility (popularity) factor and monetary value in the antique glassware market place.

A Few Comments About Book Content and Format

The vast majority of the shakers contained in this book have not been illustrated in our two previous books. However, some of the more popular shakers published in our 1976 book have been reintroduced into this book due to the fact that the book has been out of print and unobtainable for at least a decade. There have been numerous reader requests that we take this action if another book was ever published. Regardless, in most instances the reader will find that new or updated information has been added to most of any republished items.

We wish to highlight the fact that our previous 1992 (updated 1996) book has been redesignated as *The World of Salt Shakers Vol. II* by our publisher. As you can see on the front cover, this book is designated as Vol. III. The reasoning behind the two books redesignation is proper as previously explained.

The general layout and format of this book remains the same as in our two previous publications since it has been so well received by our readers. In general, the book content flows in alphabetical order by glass factory of manufacture and pattern name. Those shakers that could not be positively attributed will be found in a Potpourri section with each salt shaker listed in alphabetical order by pattern name. Any annotations pertinent to individual shaker forms (text) will be found consolidated within a Notes section at the back of the book and this section is identified within the book Table of Contents listing to enhance easy reader access. The book Index contains a detailed alphabetical listing of all shakers by pattern name and the individual page(s) upon which each item has been documented.

A comprehensive chapter that addresses the various aspects and types of Victorian glassware imitations, reproductions, and look alikes has also been included along with appropriate illustrations. We believe this important addition will be of considerable help to our readers. New art glass shakers never before published have also been included within a special book section; many in the form of rare condiment sets.

Whenever possible, the individual shakers have been documented by pattern names that have become nationally recognized by the trade. Much of today's existing pattern name recognition is the result of material published by previous authors such as E. G. Warman, Ruth Webb Lee, Minnie Watson Kamm, Arthur G. Peterson, and William (Bill) Heacock, etc.

It has required a time-consuming effort on our part to research previous antique glassware publications in order to establish whether an already existing collector-accepted pattern name may have been inadvertently reused by us in conjunction with what we believed to be a new, unidentified, recently discovered shaker pattern.

Despite all of the aforesaid cross-checking efforts, there always remains the possibility that an occasional name may have been unintentionally reused, thus, resulting in pattern name duplicity. In this respect, we realize that perfection is seldom achieved by any author that is involved in the formulation of a new comprehensive technical art and pattern glass book. However, every effort has been made to avoid such occurrences.

Photographing Glass Salt Shakers

We have added this short scenario to perhaps help the many collectors who like to maintain a photographic record of their collection for both personal and business reasons such as insurance records or selling intercommunication.

No one is more aware than we are of the frustrations that are involved with photographing glass. We first started pointing a quality 35mm camera at this ware during the mid-1960 time frame. Nevertheless, there are times that we have felt that our picture taking results seemed to have gotten worse instead of better. Despite many years of practical experience, we have never completely mastered the technique of obtaining consistency; especially with clear glass.

Clear colored and opaque glass presents a somewhat different setup technique; primarily relative to deciding the proper type of colored background to be used in conjunction with the photographic lighting involved. With some exceptions, a neutral opaque gray or tan generally works best because it does not impart a false coloration into the pieces being photographed.

There are many reasons for the aforementioned problems; most dominant is photography lighting reflections (highlights) that obscure part of the pattern details. Also, the ability to achieve an acceptable "compromise focus" is another; meaning... when you use close-up or macro lenses, your depth of photographic field becomes very sharp and limited; and, if you focus specifically on either the inner or outer edges of an embossed or intaglio pattern you will many times loose clear focus of the other portion. This, in turn, obviously affects total pattern clarity. It requires a careful, meticulous effort of checking and rechecking the focus before snapping the picture.

Despite the fact that we are aware of all of these anomalies, at times, we still end up revisiting the same problems each time we have a photographic session. In reality, we often had to do the major portion of our photography in each individual collector's home which often restricted the photographic setup that could be used. The bottom line is if you want a challenge, glassware photography will provide it. Fortunately, there are many excellent books at your local photography store that will provide excellent basic guidance so you can get started.

Salt Shaker Physical Characteristics and Measurements

The reader will find that in some instances certain shakers will have more detailed physical dimensions presented other than just a height measurement. There are generally two reasons for this occurrence: (1) We deemed it to be important as an aid to help the collector in positive identification of a more complex type of shaker since we had been able to personally verify measurement accuracy. (2) In the majority of instances, the shaker being presented will be an item that was submitted to us for publication by the AAGSSCS identification committee involving their standardized form that calls for each member's shaker submitted to include the width and base diameter measurements. However, any sixteenth of an inch measurements that had been submitted are not germane! We are presenting all received data in terms of plus or minus one eighth of an inch accuracy.

As a first thought, it may appear to our readers that such additional measurements as width and base diameter are of significant importance. However, we ask that our readers keep in mind that the method of measurement that was employed by the various individuals involved could have been (and no doubt was) accomplished in several different ways, involving various types of measuring instruments. The result is that such data presented lacks uniformity and is therefore subject to an unknown margin of error.

When you couple this with the fact that the glass factory manufacturing process and producibility tolerances that could be controlled during the Victorian era were subject to various manufacturing variables, it is our personal experience that shaker width and base diameter dimensions often lack consistency from one shaker to another involving the same pattern.

It is because of the aforesaid facts that, as was done in our previous Vol. II salt shaker book, we normally only provided a shaker height measurement, and even then, consider our measuring accuracy to be within plus or minus ⅛ of an inch. All of the recorded height measurements (measured by us) are taken with an ordinary desk type ruler with the shaker top removed. Where a two-piece type metal top is involved, our measurement is taken to the top edge of the permanently attached part of the top after the screw-on portion has been removed.

Why the Beginning Collector Needs Guidance (Based upon our own personal experience)

We first became interested in antique glassware in the mid-1950s. At that time our most pressing problem was that we had no guidance as to how and where to begin. As a result, we became random collectors.

Our collecting interest was initially aroused when we attended an auction in California and purchased a dozen Bohemian wine goblets. They were absolutely beautiful and we acquired them at $2.00 each. Today, one of these goblets is worth at least $200.00.

Having become addicted to collecting antique glass, we spent the next several years acquiring antique glass lamps, vases, table settings, pitchers, tumblers, goblets, sugar shakers, etc. It soon became apparent that our collecting approach was consuming too much living space, and it was getting difficult to display our glassware so that we could enjoy it. Also, it became obvious that we had finally reached a point where some collecting stability decisions along with specialization had to be made.

During 1961, while attending an antique glassware show, we met and subsequently became friends with two art glass dealers who changed our collecting ways forever. Victor and Mary Buck of Upland, California, showed us some Mount Washington salt and pepper shakers from the early 1890s that were absolutely lovely. The couple further pointed out that such quality types of antique salt and pepper shakers had been produced in the majority of American pattern glass as well as many of the rare trade-accepted art glass designs.

Thus, the Bucks convinced us that by collecting this type of ware we could essentially cover the entire Victorian glassware era and acquire something of quality that was both small and beautiful at a reasonable cost. Also, this ware is relatively easy to display, and provides great potential for future monetary appreciation.

By making us aware of the pattern glass books published by Minnie Watson Kamm and Arthur G. Peterson, we were able to obtain valuable insight that guided us along the antique collecting trail. Fortunately, today's collector has a myriad of specialty books that are available to them that can provide excellent collecting guidance.

Additional Reasons to Collect Glass Salt Shakers

Many collectors like to show and tell about their antiques. Glass salt and pepper shakers lend themselves very well to mutual interest and conversation among friends and collectors when linked with the characteristics and history of the various types of glass shakers that can embody a collection. With some exceptions, good color pictures of salt shakers provide a very effective method for quick identification of glass patterns. We can absolutely stipulate that this ware is available in a large variety of shapes, colors, and patterns including animal designs.

Cost Considerations

Many times price doesn't seem to be an absolute purchasing determinate to the true collector. On various occasions we have paid prices above what some might consider market value for shakers that appealed to us for one reason or another. It is often very difficult to walk away from a desirable item that has been sought after for many years, especially when it is known that the chances are slim-to-none that a future purchasing opportunity is likely to present itself.

Of course, all collectors love bargains, but the *true collector* is often willing to pay the seller's asking price. The real acquisition urge is the love of the glass itself, coupled with the desire to seekout and own that which we cherish. Obviously, the final purchasing decision is up to each individual!

We believe that the guidance and knowledge provided by specialized books does assist the beginner, as well as the more advanced collector, from making serious collection mistakes. Little, if any, such guidance was available to us during our beginning collector years. In addition, it is our personal belief that collection enjoyment amounts to much more than collecting only for the purpose of monetary satisfaction. The many antiquing sojourns, along with any resultant acquisitions, are all part of fond memories and collecting satisfaction.

The Pattern Name Debate

As additional antique glassware text books continue to be written by various authors, there appears to be an abundance of alternative pattern glass names that over time have been assigned to the identical pattern configuration. Such occurrences are the result of good intentions by the authors involved; they usually occur as a consequence of their research efforts to further educate and communicate with collectors, dealers, and other glass researchers. Unfortunately, this type of effort often hinders more than it helps by creating collector/dealer "communications confusion."

To augment our point by way of example: the reader's attention is directed to the pattern currently known as "Snail" (see our Vol. II, p.195). This pattern was originally produced by George Duncan & Sons as their No. 300 Line, which represents the original manufactures name (OMN). However, Kamm named it "Double Snail," Ruth Webb Lee named it "Compact," and S. T. Millard named it "Small Comet." Obviously you can't change what was published years ago! Modern authors should use common sense!

There are some current authors and collectors that advocate the obliteration of all existing alternate pattern names by replacing them with only the original manufacturers name (OMN). Based upon experience, it is our belief that implementing such a resourceful step would only create additional collector/dealer confusion by severely restricting the trade's ability to clearly communicate and interact in the antique glassware market place. Such action would also seriously impact previously published antique glass literature.

While not a perfect solution, it is our position that well established pattern names that have been previously published and accepted for decades should be retained within current and future antique publications. Therefore, we shall continue to follow this philosophy in our various articles and publications. Enough confusion already exists without our deliberately adding to it.

Documentation of Colors that Were Originally Produced

As a continuation of our previous policy, we have only listed those pattern colors that we have been able to verify as to the initial factory of origin. Our reason for following this rule is quite simple! We do not want to cause our readers to search for colors that may not exist by promoting the availability of pattern colors that have not been confirmed.

When our second book was updated in 1996, we inserted a special Color Addendum that documents the existence of additional factory original colors for many of the illustrated patterns that have been discovered and verified subsequent to the aforesaid book's initial publication in 1992. This additional color data was obtained from a 2½ year study conducted by various dedicated AAGSSCS members and collectors. Their efforts were coordinated, compiled, and verified by Stan and Shirley McElderry who initiated the original idea and followed through until the color project was completed. All salt shaker collectors are indebted to the folks that participated and made publication of the verified additional color data possible.

Still another factor that supports our conservative color publication approach, is that some of the old glass patterns have been reproduced, copied and/or reissued in colors that were never made by the originating glass factory.

Clear vs. Colored Glass Shakers

Definitive studies conducted during the past two decades have satisfied us that the antique clear, uncolored pattern glass shakers continue to lose popularity (collectibility) with today's collectors. While there are some exceptions, particularly with respect to figural and mechanical agitator shaker forms, the collector will be well advised to collect as many of the patterns as possible in colored glass rather than their clear counterparts.

Of course, some of the early pattern glass shakers produced prior to (and after) 1880, were not manufactured in colored glass; therefore, it becomes obvious that any such desired patterns must be acquired in their clear form; particularly if the collector is trying to complete a full tableware setting. However, our study data positively shows that even many of the later dated Victorian patterns that were produced only in clear glass continue to have a lower monetary market place collectibility factor when compared and analyzed over time.

As we have met with various collectors of antique glass shakers during our travels around the country, we have made it a point to ask about the percentage of clear shakers that they have collected versus the colored glass types. In the majority of instances our questions were answered by the disclosure that most collectors had either sold off their clear shakers, or had put them away in boxes for (hopefully) future monetary disposal. Additional discussion usually revealed that the majority of such shakers had been acquired early on when they first began collecting this type of ware.

Value Guide Discussion

KEEP IN MIND...Value is established by how many individuals with how much money want a particular item how badly!
The trade calls this "collectibility."
A William Heacock quotation

All of our comments involving the compiling and use of a value guide that are published on pages 13 and 14 of the *The World of Salt Shakers, Vol. II* are still valid. However, various letters of correspondence and telephone calls from our readers have shown that our value guide has often been incorrectly used, or simply not properly understood. Perhaps highlighting proper value guide usage by way of example will help to better enhance reader comprehension. Therefore, please consider the following:

1. The prices listed in our value guides apply only to the shakers listed/illustrated in each individual book. Example—if an opalware (milk glass) shaker pattern is illustrated, the suggested monetary value applies only to this type of glass. Any other type of glass, crystal or colored, will have an entirely different value.

2. The reader should assume that an illustrated shaker's value is based upon chip free condition unless otherwise stated in the written text that apply to it. Example—If the reader has an identical shaker that contains chipping or cracks, the shaker will have little, if any, monetary value on the retail market. No knowledgeable collector will buy it! Don't make the mistake of attaching our listed book value to it. There is no logical reason for a collector to invest in damaged glassware with any expectations of future monetary appreciation.

3. Where external painted decoration is involved, our value guide assumes that the decorative paint(s) on that shaker is intact with some noticeable fading present; and, that the subject piece does not have portions of the painted motif design missing or obliterated. Example—Look closely at the book illustration of each subject shaker that has been priced. If abnormal decorative wear is present, our descriptive text will so stipulate; the monetary worth listed in our value guide will have been adjusted accordingly. Obviously, if an identical shaker that a reader is attempting to evaluate is in better or poorer decorative condition, the assigned value should be adjusted up or down to fit the existing situation. Please be cognizant of the fact that very few decorated antique glass salt shakers will be found to be in mint condition due to the harsh kitchen soaps that were often used by the Victorian housewife.

The value of all antique glass salt shakers and other glassware, is contingent upon collectibility, color, and condition. In the case of art glass types that are color dependent upon a heat-sensitive glass batch that has been reheated by the gaffer at the glory hole, the more surface color that is present as a result of the refiring process, the higher value such a shaker will have. Examples—Agata, New England, Wheeling, and Mt. Washington Peachblow, Amberina, Plated Amberina, and Burmese, etc. These are all outstanding examples of heat-sensitive art glass that commands premium prices at today's shops and auctions and by knowledgeable selling individuals.

In some instances, the reader will find that a few of our listed prices represent the best estimates of experts regarding certain shakers that seldom appear on the market and therefore, have insufficient pricing data available to establish a definitive value base line. Mt. Washington/Pairpoint "Napoli" shakers are a good example of estimated pricing, since very few are known to exist. The same holds true for the Mt. Washington/Pairpoint "Cockel Shell" condiment set with its original companion Pairpoint metal holder.

Outstanding Salt Shaker Rarities

We are very grateful to all of those individuals that provided extra effort to make this section of the book possible. Detailed written text for each illustrated item can be found by using our alphabetically arranged pattern index where the appropriate page number will be listed.

There are many rare and beautiful shakers in this book. This quick look at rarities should motivate the reader to either start collecting this type of ware or provide an advanced collector with incentive to continue the salt shaker acquisition search. We only hope that our readers receive enjoyment and knowledge from the material presented. Without the help and interest of the names mentioned in our acknowledgments section, the following rare pieces could not be illustrated.

Eldridge collection

Condiment Set
Chick Head, Mt. Washington

McElderry collection

Bead Work Cruet Set

Krauss collection

Bead Work Condiment Set

Findlay Onyx Art Glass

Krauss collection

Purple Mustard, Orange Shaker, Amber Mustard

Harris collection

Harris collection

Torquay Condiment and Single Salt Shaker

Rathbun collection

Krauss collection

Bird in Flight Condiment Set

Bird in Flight Shaker

Krauss collection

Pillar, Ribbed Mt. Washington Peachblow satinized (left) glossy (right))

Neale collection

Fig Condiment Set

Krauss collection

Burmese Glossy Cruet Set

Harris collection

MOP Diamond Quilted Cruet Set

Harris collection

Crown Condiment Set

Harris collection

Crown Salt Shaker

Krauss collection

Brownie Salt, Pepper, and Toothpick Condiment Set

Krauss collection

Puzzle, Mt. Washington "Napoli" decorated

Krauss collection

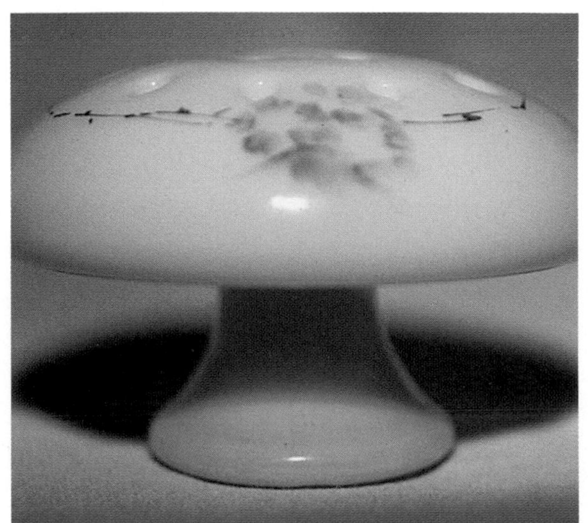

Krauss collection

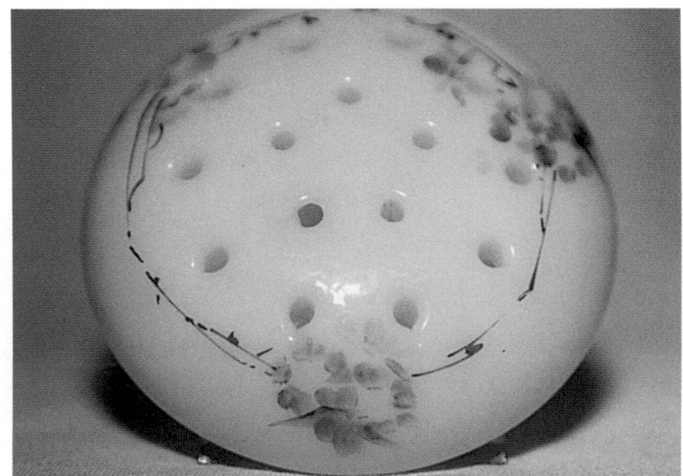

Mushroom, Mt. Washington/Pairpoint Salt Shaker

Krauss collection

Puzzle, Mt. Washington/Pairpoint "Verona" decorated

Rathbun collection

Egg, Flat End Varient, "Verona" decorated

Rathbun collection

Chevarie Pillar, Salt and Pepper Shakers

Authors' collection

Flying Saucer, Pairpoint Delft decorated

Krauss collection

Curved Ribbing
Plated Amberina (left) Amberina (right)

Krauss collection

Opaque Green, New England's Cruet Set

Krauss collection

Agata Cruet Set

Krauss collection

Cylindrical Plated Amberina Condiment Set

Lockwood collection

Iverene, Steuben Salt and Pepper Shakers by Frederick Carder (Each panel has hand cut/etched floral designs.)

Krauss collection

Chrysanthemum Sprig Cruet Set

Fostoria's Beaded Triangle

Krauss collection

3½" tall with original top

Rathbun collection

Note chocolate glass color variation.

Krauss collection

Loetz of Austria Art Glass
Silver Overlay Glass

Double Bulged, Loetz

Krauss collection

Mustard, Open Salt, Pepper, Loetz Condiment Trio

Krauss collection

Double Bulged, Loetz, Salt, Pepper, Mustard

Outstanding Historical Glass Salt Shaker Rarities

This section of the book has been created to illustrate and discuss a group of rare shakers that were made to depict historical American events.

There were several Victorian glass factories that produced souvenirs of various historical events such as the Spanish-American War, Christopher Columbus's expeditions, etc. For example: during 1898 – 99, The McKee Glass Co. made a two stack warship labeled "Remember the Maine." In the latter part of 1898 the U.S. Glass Co. turned out plates showing busts of Admiral Dewey. The Indiana Tumbler and Goblet Co. produced a Dewey pattern that was kept in production until around 1903. A Dewey pitcher with Capt. Charles V. Gridley, who was Master of Admiral Dewey's flagship *Olympia*, decorates one side of the pitcher. In bust form these two naval officers have a similar likeness because they both wore handle-bar mustaches. A white opalware salt shaker of both Admiral Dewey and General Shafter was made circa 1898 – 1902. Our research indicates that these two shakers were probably produced by the Beatty-Brady Glass Company of Dunkirk, Indiana. Both Columbus and Isabella salt shakers were produced circa 1892 by the Novelty Glass Co., Fostoria, Ohio. The detail associated with each illustrated shaker type follows.

Krauss collection

General Shafter (left), Admiral Dewey (right), with identical metal tops

Krauss collection

Columbus (pair)

Krauss collection

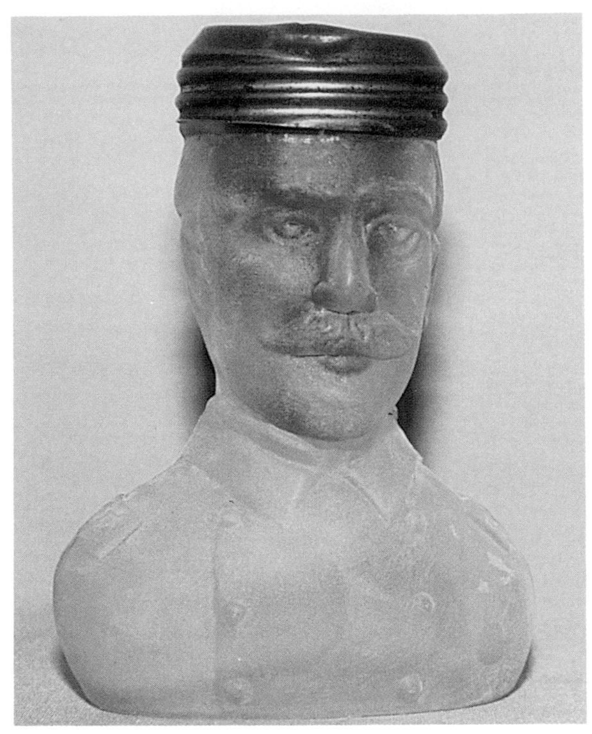

General Shafter
Top is not original.

Krauss collection

Columbus, bearded

Krauss collection

Columbus, bearded; punch cup

Maxfield collection

Maxfield collection

Globe, Columbian: Opaque white opalware glass, mold blown and pressed. Actually, this is a globe-shaped two-part condiment set. The upper half of the globe consists of a fully enclosed shaker with a perforated metal top. When lifted off, the remaining lower portion becomes an open salt dish. The upper part is embossed with an 1492 date; the bottom piece has a 1892 date. Obviously, this unique condiment set design was created to recognize the 400th anniversary of the discovery of America by Christopher Columbus. For purposes of pattern clarity we temporarily colored the dates in red and outlined the banner ribbons in blue. Circa 1892 – 1893. 2" tall x 2¼" wide. Very rare! **NPD.**

Krauss collection

Krauss collection

***Clermont*, Robert Fulton's Steamboat, 100th Anniversary (1807–1907)**

Harris collection

Texas Centennial: Clear mold blown and pressed glass. This shaker was undoubtedly created in celebration of the freedom of (then) Territory of Texas from Mexican domination (Remember the Alamo) etc. One side contains an embossed 1836 date; the other side 1936. The shaker base is encircled with the embossed words "TEXAS CENTENNIAL." Because this ware was produced relative to a historical occasion, production quantities were no doubt limited. Circa 1936. 2⅜" tall. Very scarce! **$70.00 – 90.00.**

Krauss collection

Krauss collection

Little Boy Blue: Clear pressed glass. In order to bring out the outline and shape of this figure we temporarily coated the inside surface with a washable coloring. Several colors were tried. The best photographic results were obtained with a light blue color. The embossed pattern shows Little Boy Blue emerging from beneath a haystack with his horn. The opposite side of the shaker portrays the bottoms of his bare feet. As the Mother Goose Rhyme indicates…"Under the Haystack…Fast Asleep." Considerable time and effort was spent by Dick Krauss and ourselves trying to ascertain who the author of "Little Boy Blue" was. The results indicated that the author is unknown. Circa 1890 – 1905. 3⅛" tall. Rare! **$115.00 – 130.00.**

Admiral George Dewey: Opaque white satin opalware glass, mold blown. Considerable research has been done by Dick Krauss and ourselves on these two bust (figural) shakers (Gen. Shafter and Admiral Dewey).[1] Our analysis has concluded that both illustrated items were produced by the same glasshouse. We could not find any previous existing antique glass literature that records their existence in the form being presented. Our photo provides a side-by-side comparative view to highlight to the reader some of the obvious pattern similarities. Dewey was born December 26, 1837, in Montpelier, Vermont. He graduated from the U.S. Naval Academy in 1858. He held the rank of lieutenant in the U.S. Navy at the outbreak of the American Civil War. In 1862, while in the command of the sloop *Mississippi*, he participated in the capture of New Orleans during the operation led by Admiral Faragut. By 1872 he was a commander; in 1884 he made captain; by 1896 he was a commodore. When the U.S. declared war on Spain in 1898, he was ordered to capture or destroy the Spanish squadron based in Manila. In the ensuing battle he completely destroyed the Spanish fleet without the loss of a single American. As a result, he was ultimately promoted to the special rank of Admiral of the Navy. He passed away in Washington, D.C., on January 16, 1917. Estimated time of shaker production is 1898 – 1905. Dewey is 3⅜" tall; each shaker metal top is identical and original. The Dewey shaker is extremely rare! General Shafter[2], very rare! No current market value exists. Each shaker is worth whatever a purchaser is willing pay.

Clermont, Robert Fulton: Opaque white opalware glass, mold blown using a three part mold. The shaker pattern was apparently created to commemorate the 100th anniversary of the design of the first commercially successful American steamboat *The Clermont;* which is credited to Robert J. Fulton. Historical research by Dick Krauss and ourselves has revealed that various line drawings of the aforesaid boat differ in terms of the boat's actual appearance. *The Clermont's* functional operation is dated circa 1807. Apparently, no black and white photograph of the boat has been published since the event precedes the availability of photography. The illustrated (flared-out) shaker design was obviously created to provide an embossed portrayal of this sail and steam-driven paddl-wheel boat. The backside of one shaker is shown so the reader will realize that an embossed anchor is present on the back of each shaker. This ware is circa 1907 – 1908. 2¼" tall x 3" at widest point. Very rare! $260.00 – 300.00 pair.

Columbus: Opaque white opalware, mold blown. This is a non-bearded figurine bust of Christopher Columbus that contains a perforated metal top for dispensing condiments such as salt and pepper. The base of the shaker is embossed with the word "Columbus." Today, this ware is sought after by both figural bottle and antique salt and pepper shaker collectors. An almost identical Columbus shaker is illustrated in our Vol. II, p. 213; the principal difference being that a so-named "Columbus, Bearded" comprises the principal pattern, and the glass color is opaque Nile green. Author Melvin Murray of Fostoria, Ohio, attributes this ware to the Novelty Glass Co. at Fostoria, Ohio, circa 1892 – 1893.[3] 3⅝" tall. Rare! $850.00 – 900.00 pair.

Columbus, Bearded: Opaque white opalware, mold blown and pressed. Two items are illustrated. One of our photographs has the reader looking at a very rare embossed clear pressed glass punch cup containing a gilt painted bust of Columbus. Beneath him is the embossed inscription "1492 COLUMBUS 1892." Obviously if there is a punch cup, somewhere there is a punch bowl. The curators at the Fostoria Glass Museum at Fostoria, Ohio, are still trying to locate one. If any of our readers can help, please let us know. Also illustrated herein is an authentic "Bearded Columbus" shaker in opalware as it was originally produced by Novelty Glass circa 1892. Within the Imitation Glass section of this book we expose the existence of a fake Bearded Columbus shaker with appropriate explanatory details. The opalware shaker is 3½" tall. This ware was also produced in homogeneous Nile green. Current retail value for the rare opalware shaker, $650.00 – 700.00. Punch cup, whatever a purchaser is willing to pay for it.

General Shafter: We are illustrating two shakers: One is opaque white opalware and the other is translucent frosted glass; both are mold blown. These shakers are a bust of Spanish American War Major General William Rufus Shafter. Both photos display his head, shoulders and upper chest.[4] He was born on October 16, 1835, in Galesburg, Michigan. He died November 12, 1906, on his ranch (after retirement) near Bakersfield, California. General Shafter began his military career as a first lieutenant in the 7th Michigan Infantry in August 1861 during the Civil War. He distinguished himself in both wars and was promoted periodically as the result of such continuous recognition.[5] 3¼" tall x 1½" dia. The metal top on the frosted shaker is not original; the opalware shaker top (shown beside Admiral Dewey) is original. Circa 1898 – 1902. Very rare! Due to extreme rarity no current market value exists! Each shaker is worth whatever another purchaser is willing to pay for it!

Glass Manufacturing Firms

ADAMS COMPANY
Pittsburgh, Pennsylvania
(1851 – 1891)

An old line glass manufacturing firm. First established by John Adams in 1851 who headed the factory until his passing away in 1886. The factory remained in operation until it joined the U.S. Glass Co. in 1891.

Harris collection

Hidalgo (OMN): A clear amber stained glass, mold blown. The bulbous pattern consists of four individual large shaped leaves containing beveled blocks in raised relief. Each principal motif is amber stained. Prior to joining U.S. Glass, this pattern was produced in many clear glass forms only. Circa 1890 – 1898.[1] Also can be found in ruby stained glass. According to Kamm, the pattern name is Spanish. There are counties in Texas and Mexico called Hidalgo. 3⅛" tall. Very scarce in this color. **$20.00 – 25.00** due to condition.

AKRO AGATE COMPANY
Akron, Ohio
(1911 – 1914)
Clarksburg, West Virginia
(1914 – 1951)

The Akro Agate Co. of Akron, Ohio, was established in 1911. The company was initially established to make marbles and games. During early October 1914, the company moved to Clarksburg, West Virginia, to take advantage of cheap natural gas fuel and the fine. West Virginia sand for making glass marbles.

As a result of heavy competition, Akro began to produce limited types of glassware in the early 1930s. However their lines of glass products really expanded after the Westite factory division of the Brilliant Glass Co. burned down on July 16, 1936, which resulted in all of their molds, materials, etc. being sold to Akro Agate. Also, the Westite plant superintendent John A. Henderson went to work for Akro Agate, thus solidifying their subsequent glass production. The Akro factory went out of business in 1951 primarily as a result of competition from foreign imports. For details of Akro glassware we recommend the book *The Collector's Encyclopedia of Akro Agate Glassware* by Gene Florence from Collector Books.

Authors' collection

Hobnail, Akro Footed: Opaque marbleized (variegated) opalware, mold blown. As the pattern name indicates, this shaker pair is entirely covered with circular shaped hobnails in raised relief except for a plain ring shaped supporting foot. The color term "marbelized" is used throughout the Akro book regardless of what the actual glass color mixtures may be. Circa 1941 – 1945. 4" tall with original metal tops. Rare! **$105.00 – 125.00** pair.

ATTERBURY & CO.
Pittsburgh, Pennsylvania
(1859 – 1893)

Established by Thomas B. Atterbury in 1859. He remained the president of the factory until it ended during 1893 when the firm became known as The Atterbury Glass Co. There are 110 patents relative to glass and manufacturing processes and machinery that are credited to his name. Many of the Atterbury design patents resulted in lowering glass manufacturing costs as a result of his value engineering. The Atterbury white opalware glass has become highly collectible in the various designs that he innovated.

Harris collection

Corset, Atterbury's: Opaque white opalware glass, mold blown. This is an eight vertical paneled shaker divided by narrow interspersed concave panels from the shoulder to the horizontal flanged base. The bottom is deeply concave for one inch (up to the narrowest part of the shaker waist). Inside this hollow area, embossed in reverse, it is inscribed "Pat'd July 16th, 1872." The top of the shoulder has been flattened to accommodate top edge threading. The Atterbury catalog shows that a special metal top, having an inserted glass center, was an original part of the shaker as it was sold to the Victorian consumer.[1] Circa 1872. 3" tall; 2⅛" wide at the shoulder; 2¼" base diameter. Rare! NPD.

Rathbun collection

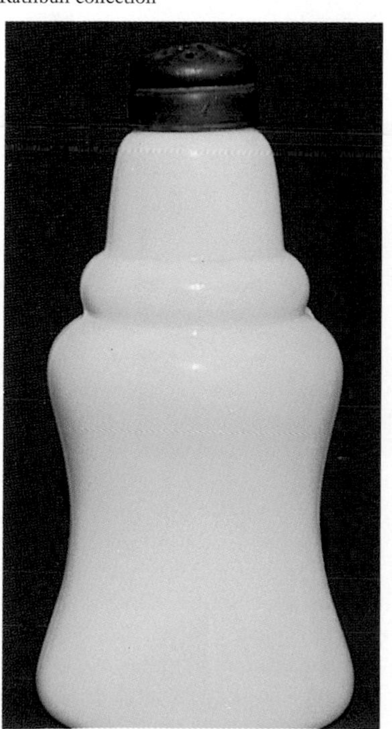

Rathbun collection

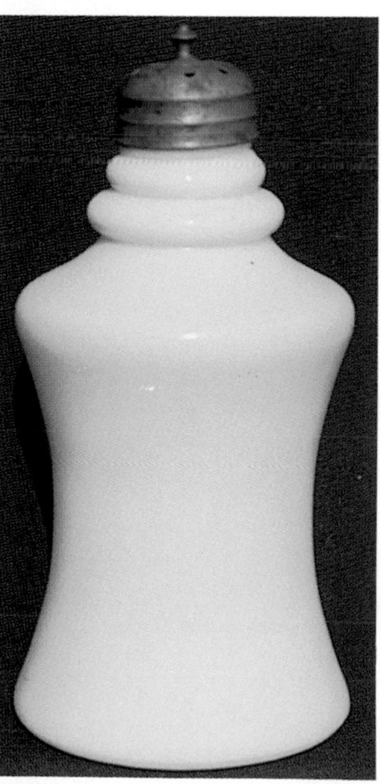

Curved Body, Atterbury's: Opaque white opalware, mold blown into a two-piece mold. Each shaker has basically the same pattern shape with the exception of neck length and the location of the neck ring(s). These are both saloon shakers; and Atterbury seemed to have an established market for this type of ware. Circa 1877 – 1882. The long neck shaker with the single protruding ring is 5¼" tall with an original two-piece top; the other shaker is 5" tall and the top is not original. Rare! **$85.00 – 105.00** each.

BEAUMONT GLASS COMPANY
Martins Ferry, Ohio
(1895 – 1902)
Grafton, West Virginia
(1902 – 1906)

Rathbun collection

McElderry collection

Aster & Leaf: Clear emerald green glass, mold blown. The pattern name describes the principal exterior motif of this shaker. This is a bulbous shaped shaker that narrows toward the top that contains a prominent neck ring. Originally designated as "Beaumont's No. 217."[1] This ware is also being shown in blue. There was also production in cranberry. Circa 1895. 3" tall. Rare! **$90.00 – 110.00.**

Rathbun collection

Rathbun collection

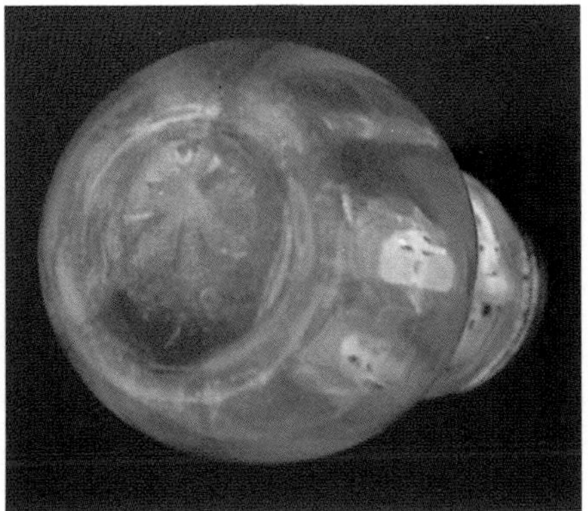

Beaumont #101 (aka – "Inside Ribbing"): Clear vaseline glass, dual mold blown. The basic shape consists of a bulbous based body. The exterior surface is smooth; the inside has seven vertical optic panels. A "Pressed Optic" pattern name was created by Bill Heacock.[2] Kamm called it "Inside Ribbing."[3] Circa 1900 – 1901. 3⅛" tall; 2⅛" at widest point; 1⅝" base diam. The bottom of the illustrated shaker has an embossed poinsettia on it; some shakers are decorated with three HP gold rings encircling the outside body surface. Rare in this color! **$60.00 – 75.00.**

Krauss collection

Barrel, Windows: Translucent blue opalescent glass, dual mold blown. The varying sized clear oval-shaped windows are inside molded; the opalescence was achieved by coating the surface with a sensitive crystal glass containing bone ash and arsenic which was blown into a pattern mold to create the desired surface decoration. Thc windows design was acquired by reheating the slightly cooled shaker to bring out the desired opalescent coloring. Circa 1896 – 1899. 3" tall; 2¾" wide; 1⅜" base diameter. Rare! **$150.00 – 170.00.**

Coalmer collection

Seaweed, Opalescent: Clear opalescent vaseline glass, mold blown. This is a bulging base shaker with an extensive opalescent pattern design that defies verbal description. Perhaps that is why it was designated by author Ardelle Taylor as being reminiscent of seaweed. According to Heacock[4] this pattern was initially a Hobbs design with the molds subsequently acquired by Beaumont. Also produced in white, blue, and cranberry opalescent colors. 3½" tall; circa 1890s. Very scarce! **$75.00 – 90.00.**

Krauss collection

Yarn: Opaque red/white/blue and brown/white spatter glass, dual mold blown. Has a cylindrical shape with swirls running from left to right. Actually this ware falls within the pattern parameters of a "Reverse Swirl." Both shakers have a relatively flat shaped shoulder. Circa 1895 – 1896. Also produced in clear cased, frosted brown/white cased, and cranberry. 3" tall x 1⅝" wide. Very scarce in the colors illustrated! **$235.00 – 260.00** pair.

THE BELLAIRE GOBLET COMPANY
Bellaire, Ohio (1876 – 1888)
Findaly, Ohio (1888 – 1891)

This glasshouse moved from Bellaire, Ohio, to Findlay, Ohio, in 1888, and joined the U.S. Glass Co. during 1891, where it operated as Factory M. U.S. Glass turned on factory operations during August 1891, and factory production continued to produce many of the original pattern designs that were sold prior to the merger. The last glass made at the factory was on December 8, 1892, and on January 12, 1893, the City Gas Trustees had all gas shut off at the factory. The factory buildings were sold during May 1894, and were subsequently torn down with salvageable building materials being sold to various building contractors.

Ridgway collection

Authors' collection

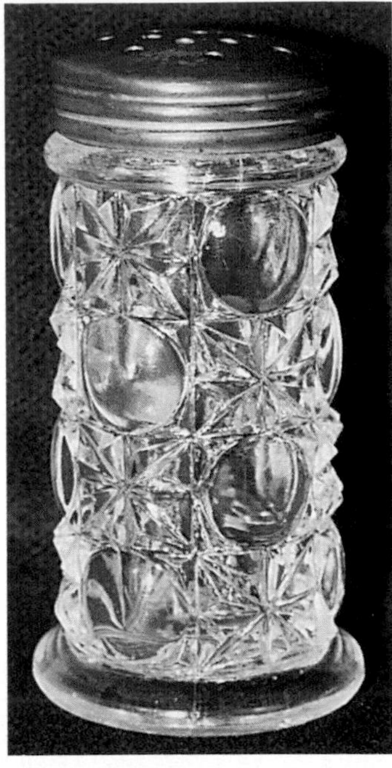

Currier & Ives: Clear and amber and canary (vaseline) glass, mold blown and pressed. The pattern name was originally created from a comic scene that was impressed in the bottom of a water tray that is somewhat reminiscent of some of the old Currier & Ives prints. This pattern is one of the best known by the Bellaire Goblet factory; it was made in a full table setting.[1] Clear and blue colors were also produced. Circa 1889 – 1891. 3" tall. Very scarce! Rare in canary! Amber **$45.00 – 55.00;** Canary **$80.00 – 95.00.**

Krauss collection

Authors' collection

Log & Star (cruet set): Clear amber glass, mold blown and pressed. Pattern name by Kamm. This pattern is also referred to as "Milton" since only a slight difference appears on the cruet only.[2] The pattern amounts to alternating plain and starred cubes in raised relief. Circa 1890. Each shaker is 2⅞" tall; the cruet with an original stopper is 5½" tall to the top of the pouring spout. The amber matching glass holder is 8" in length. We are also illustrating an earlier version castor set with clear 4¼" tall pressed glass shakers and a 4½" tall oil bottle (with stopper removed) in a matching clear pressed glass circular-shaped glass holder. The clear set is believed to have been produced prior to Bellaire joining the U.S. Glass Company. Both sets are very scarce! Amber set **$350.00 – 380.00;** clear set **$185.00 – 210.00.**

BELMONT GLASS COMPANY
Bellaire, Ohio
(1866 – 1888)
BELMONT GLASS WORKS
(1888 – 1890)

In addition to producing glass, this factory chipped molds for the Crystal, Gillinder, and Fostoria glass factories. Additionally, the factory produced various blown ware patterns such as Belmont #100, which was a Daisy & Button pattern, opalescent ware, and their No. 444 line which was first released during July 1888. This factory also created "Dewberry" and a pattern called "Royal" which comprised a woman's-head figure.

Vit collection

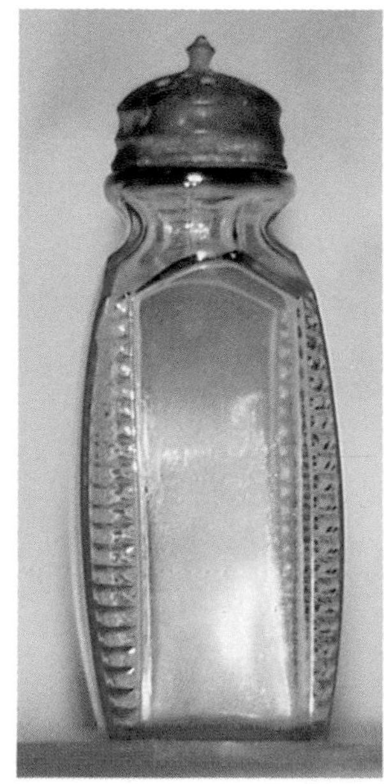

Zipper, Belmont: Clear aqua colored glass, mold blown. A bulging shaker with a zipper pattern down the sides. There is a small intaglio star (or maybe it's a many petaled flower) in the center of the bottom. According to AAGSSCS member Lorrie Vit (who researched it) this is Belmont's #104 pattern which was used in a castor set. Circa 1888 – 1890. 3⅞" tall x 1⅜" wide; 1¼" base diameter. Very scarce! **$65.00 – 80.00.**

Rathbun collection

Stripe, Opalescent (castor set): Translucent striped opalescent glass, mold blown. The castor set consists of four pieces (salt, pepper, mustard, and stoppered oil bottle). This set is shown in an 1888 catalog ad pictured in Heacock's Book 9, page 35 where it is listed as a "Regal Castor Set." The fact that this ware is attributed to this Ohio glass factory was a surprise revelation. The set is also pictured in Heacock 2, page 37, fig. 189; where no positive attribution is made, only speculative possibilities. Peterson called the pattern "Opal Stripe, Tall" in his salt shaker book. The condiment holder is clear with opalescent tipped feet attached to a metal frame that comprises a metal framework with a lifting handle. All of Heacock's color illustrations show the oil bottle in translucent opalescent blue with a clear glass stopper. The stopper of the oil bottle in our illustrated set is not believed to be original. The salt, pepper, and mustard bottles are 3¾" tall; the oil is 4½" tall. It is 8" to the top of the metal lifting handle. Circa 1888 – 1890. Rare as a complete set! **$390.00 – 415.00** set.

BOSTON & SANDWICH GLASS COMPANY
Sandwich, Massachusetts
(1825 – 1888)

Authors' collection

Cabin in the Snow Decoration: We are illustrating a very rare salt, pepper, and a sugar shaker (muffineer) combination containing HP bleak winter scenes that have been positively attributed to the Sandwich factory by way of a circa 1880 catalog distributed by Boston distributors Morey, Churchill & Morey that illustrates this ware in caster frames. Authors Barlow & Kaiser point out that one of several Sandwich artists could have done the painting, one of which is Mary Gregory. The authors date the shakers circa 1870 – 1887. The salt and pepper are 4" tall (measured with the original two-piece metal tops in place); the sugar shaker is 5¾" tall with the screw-on portion of the two-piece metal top removed.

In our 1976 book on p. 66 we presented an identical salt shaker in the "Creased Neck" pattern and named the shaker "Cabin in the Snow" due to the HP winter snow scene. However, all three of these shakers meet the decorative research criteria established by Barlow & Kaiser, and we concur with their Boston & Sandwich Glass Co. attribution.[1] Also, it is interesting to note that both a toothpick and "Christmas Barrel" salt shaker were also produced with identical HP "Cabin in the Snow" decoration.[2] While various condiment dispensers differ in shape/form, a mutual decorative commonality has been established by the outstanding documented research done by the aforementioned authors in their four books *The Glass Industry in Sandwich*. Salt and pepper pair, **$700.00 – 750.00;** sugar shaker, **$1,500.00 – 1,700.00.**

Lockwood collection

Fine Rib: Clear thin glassware, mold blown in a three-part mold. The narrow fine vertical ribs extend upward to a horizontal neck ring. This globe-shaped shaker has a concave bottom. Barlow & Kaiser present the thought that the neck ring prevented the perforated metal cap from being screwed on too tightly;[3] an interesting theory. Circa 1870 – 1880. 2⅛" tall x 1⅛" wide at base. Rare! **NPD.**

Lockwood collection

Greek Border (OMN): Clear thin glassware, mold blown. This shaker has a ring neck and tapers to an expanded middle where the Greek Border design surrounds the body. Greek Border (aka "Greek Key") was a popular design when engraved into the thin blown Sandwich glass known (at that time) to the industry as bubble glass. This design also adapted well to pressed glass and with very little labor could be "dressed" by roughing the surface of the border in the cutting shop. By doing so, two Sandwich patterns were added to the inventory; "Greek Key" and "Frosted Greek Key."[4] It was very interesting to learn that the Greek Border design appears in an 1874 Boston & Sandwich catalog.[5] Whereas, the "Roman Key" pattern did not appear in that catalog and was probably a substitute in later years for the more difficult to produce Greek Border.[6] Circa 1874 with continued production into the 1880s. 3" tall x 2⅝" wide. Rare! **NPD.**

Krauss collection

Marble Shaped: Opaque white opalware, mold blown. This is a small shaker. As the pattern name implies, the overall shape is reminiscent of a child's glass "shooting" marble. The HP bleak winter scene with snow on the ground containing a foreground leafless tree has been confirmed as Sandwich decoration by Barlow & Kaiser.[7] 1¾" tall with a two-piece metal top. Circa 1780 – 1887. Rare! **$130.00 – 150.00.**

Authors' collection

Pillar, Spangled: Translucent cobalt blue silver mica glass, mold blown. As the pattern name indicates this shaker was produced by first coating flakes of mica with nitrate of silver and then rolling a partially blown bubble of hot glass over the silvered particles. The bubble was then reheated to integrate the silvered particles into the inside glass surface. According to Barlow & Kaiser this blue glass shaker containing silver flakes was produced by both the Boston & Sandwich Glass Co. and the Vasa Murrhina Art Glass Company.[8] Circa 1884. 3½" tall with a two-piece metal top. Very rare! **NPD.**

Krauss collection

Tapered Shoulder Variation (cruet set): Opaque white opalware, mold blown. The HP decoration on this set's four pieces contains the same bleak winter scene with snow on the ground and the same foreground leafless tree that is present on the small Marble Shaped shaker. While this type decoration has been attributed to Sandwich by Barlow & Kaiser via credible research documentation, our research finds that there is more detail involved relative to this type of decoration.[9] Similar (if not identical) decoration is attributable to the Smith Brothers during their decoration involvement at Mt. Washington Glass at New Bedford, Massachusetts. The aforementioned winter scene decoration tie-in between Sandwich and Mt. Washington has been related by author George Avila in his book *The Pairpoint Glass Story* involving William L. Smith, the father of Alfred E. and Harry A. Smith (better known as the Smith Bros.) who began his decorating career in America at Sandwich.[10] After several years the elder Smith left Boston & Sandwich to establish The Boston & China Decorating Works. It is of significance to note that both Harry and Alfred were trained and employed by their father and thus acquired considerable skill in various HP glass decorative techniques.[11] The condiment set consists of salt, pepper, mustard, and a handled cruet. Salt and pepper are 3⅝" tall; mustard 2½" tall; cruet 5" tall. The silver-plated metal holder is marked "E. G. Webster & Bro. N.Y." who operated from 1859 to 1873 when the name changed to E.G. Webster & Son with continuous operation through 1886. In later years this independent firm became part of the International Silver Co. conglomerate. Rare as a complete set. **$700.00 – 750.00** set.

BRYCE, HIGBEE & COMPANY
Homestead, Pennsylvania
(suburb of Pittsburgh)
(1879 – 1906)

Krauss collection

Fleur-de-Lis, Arched (Higbee's): Clear ruby stained glass, mold blown and pressed. The pattern consists of four large clear fleurs-de-lis outlined by a ruby stained arch. Just below the metal top are four additional clear fleurs-de-lis outlined in ruby stain. Circa 1898 – 1906.[1] 2⅝" tall. Very scarce! **$65.00 – 75.00.**

Spiraea Band: Opaque blue opaline glass, mold blown. This is a tall, narrow shaped, footed cylinder containing a shelf on the base foot.[2] The shaker center is encircled with small raised vertical ribs that are formed between the upper and lower ringed bands. 3⅞" tall. Circa 1891. Made in all basic colors including clear transparent. Rare in this color! **$70.00 – 85.00.**

Neale collection

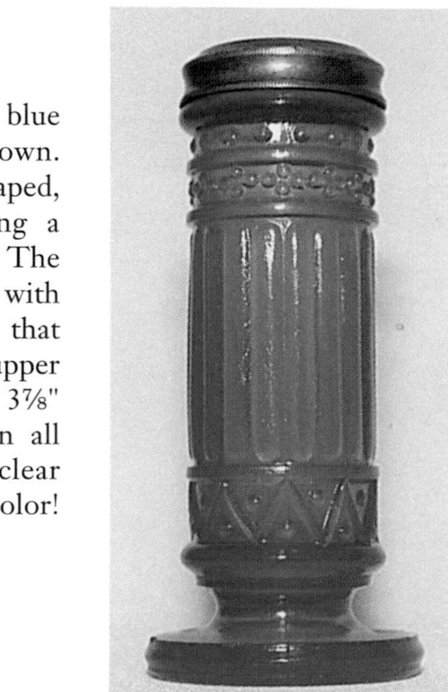

BUCKEYE GLASS COMPANY
Martins Ferry, Ohio
(1878 – 1896)

Established in 1878 by Henry Helling and associates. A majority of this factory's art and opalescent glassware was created by John F. Miller and the influence of Harry Northwood. Buckeye went out of business during February 1896 as the result of a major fire.

Krauss collection

Reverse Swirl (cruet set): Clear blue, cranberry, vaseline, and white opalescent glass, dual mold blown. The pattern name describes the basic pattern configuration. This colorful four-piece cruet set is completely original and was marketed by Buckeye circa 1890.[2] The metal holding stand is marked "Barbour Bros Co"; it measured 8⅞" to the top of the lifting handle. Red and white shakers 2¼" tall; white colored opalescent mustard 2¾" tall; blue cruet 4¼" to top of the pouring spout. Rare as a complete set! **$675.00 – 710.00 set.**

Harris collection

Chrysanthemum Base Variant: Translucent cranberry opalescent glass, mold blown. This is an embossed ribbed base pattern; the remainder has white swirling opalescent stripes. Taller, but essentially the same pattern is illustrated in our Vol. II.[1] Also made in white, canary, and blue opalescent glass; some are satinized and speckled. Circa 1888 – 1891. 3⅛" tall. Very scarce! **$120.00 – 135.00.**

Ridgway collection

Reverse Swirl, Tall: Opaque blue and white spatter glass, mold blown. This is a bulbous shaped shaker that is widest in the middle and tapers at both ends containing complete reverse swirl coverage.[3] Also produced in speckled and opalescent glass colors. Circa 1887 – 1890. 3" tall. Very scarce! **$75.00 – 90.00.**

Lockwood collection

Reverse Swirl, Optic: Translucent blue and clear white speckled glass, dual mold blown. This type of glass was patented by Northwood in 1888 while he was associated with Buckeye. Apparently the patent rights were left with John Miller after Northwood departed since production of this glass continued. These are small bulbous shakers 2½" tall. Circa 1888 – 1890. Very scarce! **$180.00 – 205.00 pair.**

CAMBRIDGE GLASS
Cambridge, Ohio
(1902 – 1957)

Cambridge factory production began during 1902; having been built by the National Glass Corporation to become their new and modern production facility. While under control of the corporation, from time to time, molds were moved in from other National factories in what was viewed as "needs of the business" efficiency to meet various production requirements.

After the National breakup, around 1904, the plant was leased by the factory manager Mr. Bennett, until he was able to purchase it from stockholders around 1907; thereafter making it an independent facility.

Cambridge produced both high quality handcrafted blown ware and pressed glass pieces. The aforesaid type of blown ware appears to have dominated production after 1917. The Cambridge factory had to close during 1957; the molds were subsequently sold to the Imperial Glass Co.

Coalmer collection

Ball Shaped Line, No. 3400: Clear royal blue glass, mold blown and pressed. These shakers look like the pattern name; a ball-shaped body with an attached clear pressed glass foot and clear glass threaded tops. According to a 1930 issued Cambridge catalog with subsequent supplements[1] this ware is circa 1933. 2¾" tall with the threaded top edges polished-off smooth. Rare in this color! **$130.00 – 150.00** pair.

Coalmer collection

Cambridge #1207: Translucent ruby red glass, mold blown. This is a busy pattern that consists of an allover diamond point within three panels that tapers toward the top. Each panel is separated by double columns of notches that end in an Inverted Fan motif. Circa 1918 – 1925. 2⅞" tall; also produced in amber glass. Very scarce! **$28.00 – 37.00.**

Coalmer collection

Cambridge #1266 Variant: Translucent ruby red glass, mold blown. This is a multi-vertical paneled shaker with clear glass tops which appears in a 1930 Cambridge catalog.[2] Due to their size, it appears that Cambridge used a modified etched flower and leaf motif shown in catalog pictures 3400/6 on a cheese and cracker piece and 1349 bowl.[3] 2¼" tall. Rare pair in this color! **$85.00 – 110.00** pair.

Lockwood collection

Wheat Sheaf: Clear heavy pressed glass embossed "Near Cut" on the inside bottom. Each sheaf motif sprays upward with a central vertical slash and teardrop shape on each upper side. Each sheaf is also bordered by vertical beading and topped by a beveled arch. There are arched panels between the sheave that have two six-sided medallions filled with six flat-topped buttons around a faint petaled flower. In total, a very intricate pattern.[4] Circa 1910 – 1920. 2¾" tall x 1⅝" wide. **$13.00 – 21.00.**

Harris collection

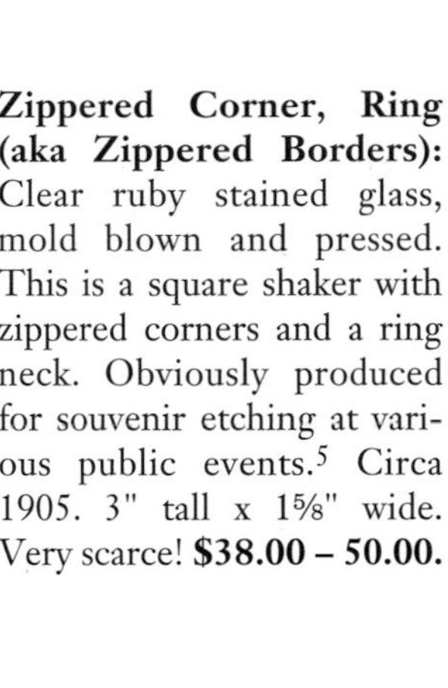

Zippered Corner, Ring (aka Zippered Borders): Clear ruby stained glass, mold blown and pressed. This is a square shaker with zippered corners and a ring neck. Obviously produced for souvenir etching at various public events.[5] Circa 1905. 3" tall x 1⅝" wide. Very scarce! **$38.00 – 50.00.**

THE CENTRAL GLASS COMPANY
Wheeling, West Virginia
(1863 – 1891)

Began as Osterling & Henderson Co.; joined U.S. Glass in 1891. U.S. Glass closed the factory in 1893; it was reopened as an independent in 1896 and moved to Summitville, Indiana. Joined the National Glass Company in 1899. The West Virginia factory was reopened as new company sometime after 1900 again carrying the name Central Glass Company. For additional information, refer to our Vol. II, page 35.

Authors' collection

Diamond, Pressed: Clear vaseline pressed glass. The shaker body is cylindrical-shaped and has a brief ringed base. The body is covered with embossed rows of diamonds, each split down the middle and also crosswise. Pattern name by Ruth Webb Lee. Originally designated as the factory's No. 775 pattern.[1] Circa 1885 – 1891. 2¾" tall. Very scarce in vaseline! **$65.00 – 85.00.**

CHALLINOR, TAYLOR & COMPANY
Tarentum, Pennsylvania
(1866 – 1891)

Began production on the south side of Pittsburgh in 1866. Moved to Tarentum in 1884. Became a part of the United States Glass Company in 1891 as Factory C. The factory was destroyed by fire shortly after the U.S. Glass merger and it was never rebuilt. This glasshouse specialized in variegated colored and hand-painted glassware along with numerous pressed/blown novelties.

White collection

Barrel, Challinor 14 Variant: Opaque opalware glass, mold blown. This is very similar to the Challinor & Taylor #14 except for height and width dimensions; also top thread count. The HP decoration contains brown leaves and twigs within a white band that encircles the shaker. Circa 1888 – 1891. 2⅜" tall x 1⅝" wide. Very scarce! **$25.00 – 30.00.**

Roland collection

Challinor & Taylor #14: Opaque opalware glass, mold blown. This is a barrel-shaped shaker produced from a two part mold.[1] The glass top threading count is only 1½ threads. The HP decoration amounts to a cattail type plant. Circa 1888 – 1891. 2½" tall; 1¼" wide at the top; 1⅛" base diameter. Very scarce! **$25.00 – 30.00.**

Authors' collection

Beaded Oval Mirror, etc: Opaque yellow opalescent and pink and green variegated shakers; each have the same basic square-shaped pattern. We are picturing three pattern colors not shown in our Vol. II book. Beginning on the left is a pink and white variegated shaker we initially named "Slag"; in the center is a variegated brown/white and green "Beaded Oval Mirror"; on the right is an opalescent yellow "Square S" shaker. All are desirable pieces for a collection and they are getting more and more difficult to acquire. Circa 1890. 3¼" tall. Very scarce! Pink and white Slag, **$90.00 – 100.00;** Beaded Oval Mirror, **$120.00 – 135.00;** Square, **$75.00 – 95.00.**

Rathbun collection

Concave Panel: White opaque opalware glass, mold blown. This is a pattern of multiple concave panels separated by prominent sharp vertical ribs containing multicolor floral sprays. This is the Challinor & Taylor #18 pattern.[2] Circa 1890 – 1891. 1¾" tall; 2½" wide. Very scarce. **$28.00 – 37.00.**

Ridgway collection

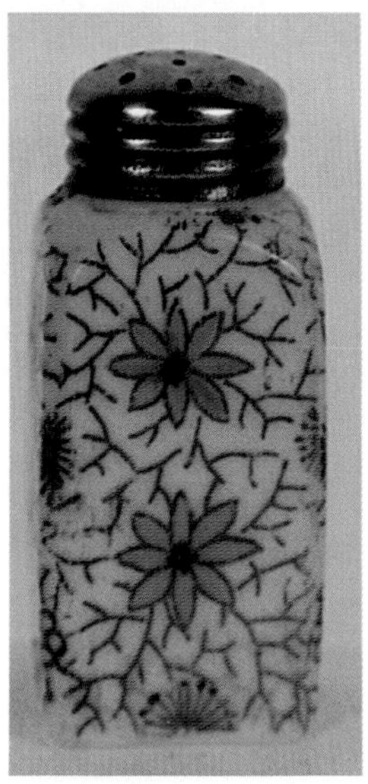

Cube, Narrow: Opaque white opalware, mold blown. This ware has a short cube shape with each vertical panel containing HP eight-point petaled blue flowers among dense brown stems. Circa 1889 – 1891. 2⅞" tall. Very scarce! **$40.00 – 50.00.**

Rathbun collection

Forget-Me-Not: A rare opaque variegated butterscotch shaker that is darkest at the bottom and shades to a lighter color near the shaker top. The embossed floral pattern with large bulging lobes is also shown on page 37 of our Vol. II. Circa 1887 – 1891. This shaker is rare in this color; probably an experimental factory color that had limited production. 2" tall. **$105.00 – 115.00.**

Rathbun collection

Marble Glass Box: Opaque shaded blue glass, light blue near the top to a darker blue color at the bottom; not a variegated glass in the true definition of the word. This pattern name was established by A.G. Peterson in his 1970 salt shaker book; to avoid reader confusion, the pattern name is being retained. A true Marble Glass Box colored shaker is shown in our Vol. II, p. 38. However, the shaker pattern does have a boxy form. 2¾" tall. Circa 1890 – 1891. Very scarce! **$125.00 – 140.00.**

Krauss collection

No. 16 (Challinor's): Opaque opalware glass, mold blown. This is a plain milk glass shaker shaped in the form of a cube; similar to "Cube, Rounded Off" illustrated in our Vol. II, p. 120 but taller. The front panel contains a red and green floral sprig. Circa 1890 – 1891. 2⅞" tall. Scarce! **$20.00 – 30.00.**

Lockwood collection

Challinor & Taylor's #15: Opaque white opalware glass, mold blown. The pattern amounts to a square with rounded corners; each corner is tapered from a round neck to the square shape. The decorative motif consists of transfer designs of leaves, branches, and flowers, touched with HP colors and tiny enameled dots on some flowers. Circa 1888 – 1893. 2¾" tall x 1¼" wide. Scarce! **$65.00 – 85.00** pair.

CONSOLIDATED LAMP & GLASS COMPANY
Corapolis, Pennsylvania
(1895 – 1964)

The factory was established in 1893 at Fostoria, Ohio. Production continued well into 1895. The Fostoria factory was relocated to Coraopolis, Pennsylvania, where operations were permanently established. For additional historical details see our Vol. II, page 40.

Rathbun collection

Bulging 3 Petal: Translucent dark green glass, mold blown. The pattern motif consists of a total of 12 bulging petals (in groups of three) as illustrated in our Vol. II, p. 42. After careful examination of the shaker, we concluded that this item is a look-alike [1] circa 1960 era. It is not an authentic shaker that was produced by the Consolidated Lamp & Glass Co., circa 1894 – 1900. Also, original factory catalogs and trade ads do not indicate that this shaker pattern was produced in this color. However, enough years have now passed that collecting this pattern as a complete condiment set with companion glass holder would be very desirable. We don't price imitation pieces.

Authors' collection

Cosmos (condiment): Opaque white opalware glass, mold blown. Some collectors get this pattern confused with Northwood's Apple Blossom pattern due to similarities. Both patterns have a netted background and similar looking flowers in raised relief; also they were both produced in white opalware. One of the main differences is the fact the Apple Blossom pattern has a ribbed swirl effect similar to what is present on Northwood's Royal Ivy pattern pieces.[2] Each of the bulbous shaped "Cosmos" condiment dispensers are divided into three rounded segments by a single recessed vertical rib. Each segment contains a single HP blue, yellow, or pink flower in high raised relief. The salt, pepper, and mustard are 2½" tall. However, the mustard has a larger top opening and requires a special threaded metal top. The matching glass base is 7⅛" tall to the top of the metal lifting handle. Being glass, the base is relatively fragile and difficult to find chip-free. Rare in undamaged condition as a set! **$450.00 – 500.00** set.

Krauss collection

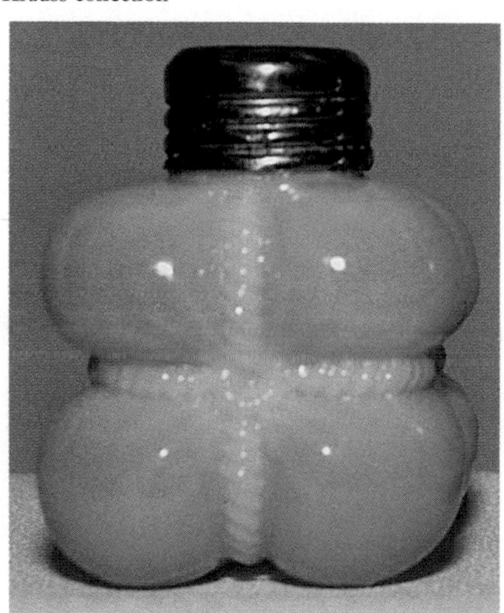

Cotton Bale: Translucent variegated butterscotch colored glass, mold blown. The pattern name provides an adequate physical description of the shaker.[3] While this ware has been produced in a wide range of solid colors, our illustrated shaker is a rarity in this color. Circa 1894 – 1895. 2⅝" tall. **$165.00 – 180.00.**

Krauss collection

Leaf, Gaudy: Translucent red homogeneous glass, mold blown. A bulbous shaped shaker containing three large leaves in raised relief. Pattern name by Peterson. Circa 1894 – 1902. 2¾" tall. Rare! **$160.00 – 175.00.**

Krauss collection

Leaf, Twisted (condiment): Pink opaque triple cased glass, dual mold blown. The pattern consists of four large vertically twisted leaves in raised relief that run from the base to within approximately ¼" of each dispenser's top. A single shaker is shown in our Vol. II, p. 66 and was mistakenly attributed to Dithridge & Co. whose factory was also located in the Pittsburgh, Pennsylvania, area. The salt and pepper are 2⅞" tall; oil/vinegar bottle 3⅝" tall without stopper; mustard 2⅞" tall. The unique frosted glass base contains four glass cups for retention of the aforesaid pieces; the metal lifting handle is 6⅝" tall. A complete set is on display at the Fostoria Museum, Fostoria, Ohio. This set is circa 1894 – 1900. Rare! **$800.00 – 850.00** set.

Steiger collection

Leaning: Opaque pink and white variegated glass, mold blown. The pattern name pretty much describes these shakers. The unusual design was created by Nicholas Kopp Jr. 3¼" tall. Also produced in opaque white, blue, and pink. Very scarce! **$105.00 – 125.00** pair.

Rathbun collection

Rib, Bulbous Twenty-Four: Opaque pink homogeneous glass, mold blown. First illustrated in opaque blue in our 1976 book. The pattern name describes this spheroid shaped shaker that consists of 24 vertical raised ribs. Circa 1894 – 1900. 2½" tall. Very scarce! **$50.00 – 65.00.**

Rathbun collection

Opera Glasses (condiment set): Opaque creamy white opalware glass, mold blown. In our Vol. II, p. 241, we were unable to fully illustrate what this condiment set looked like due to an incomplete metal holder. Therefore, this illustration provides a correct total view. Thanks to the Fostoria Museum and author Melvin Murray, we now have positive attribution that this ware was produced by Consolidated. The HP decoration on each shaker, along with the companion metal holder, is in exceptional condition. The shakers are 3" tall. Rare as a complete set! **$450.00 – 480.00** set.

Authors' collection

Rib, Triple: Opaque green variegated cased glass, dual mold blown. The variegated outer layer has been blown over a thin, white inner glass layer created by a dual mold process. Probably factory created as an experimental color. Circa 1894 – 1900. 3¼" tall. Rare in this color. **$160.00 – 185.00.**

Authors' collection

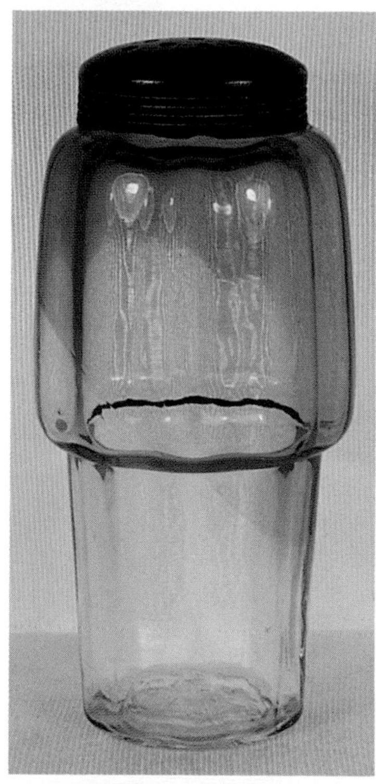

Rib, Vertical Optic (condiment): Clear Rubina glass, dual mold blown. The complete set consisting of salt, pepper, mustard, and vinegar/oil within a clear (uncolored) pressed glass holder is illustrated in our Vol. II, p. 250. The set has been attributed to Consolidated Lamp & Glass Co. by author Mel Murray and the Fostoria Museum at Fostoria, Ohio, where a complete set is on display. We are illustrating a single 4½" tall shaker to provide the reader with a clear view of the unusual pattern motif of the glass pieces. This set was produced circa 1891 – 1896. Rare as a complete set! **$700.00 – 750.00** complete set.

Ridgway collection

Torquay, Bulging Short: Opaque opalware, mold blown. This is a short bulging example of the "Torquay" pattern containing a HP pink and green floral spray with an extended glass base for condiment set use. It would be interesting to find out what the set's mustard looked like? Our illustrated bulging pattern version was also made in two different night lamp styles named "Paris."[4] Circa 1898 – 1900. 2¼" tall; 1⅞" base diameter. Very scarce! **$35.00 – 40.00.**

Torquay: Among the various glass pieces illustrated, the single opalware shaker is a rare and unusual form of this pattern (named by Heacock) because it contains eight intaglio yellow HP stripes. Also shown are Torquay glass dispensers with red painted stripes in a complete condiment set with a matching companion glass holder. In addition, we are illustrating a very rare complete ruby stained glass salt, pepper, and mustard condiment set. The companion holding tray has a unique matching pattern shape with varying ruby stain coloration that is readily apparent in our photo illustration. While exposed to natural sun light, we perceived a small clear rim chip on the tray bottom that verified that this set's coloration was achieved by a ruby staining process. Similar stain color variation is also present on the set's mustard piece. All of our illustrated ware is circa 1898 – 1901. Shakers 3⅛" tall x 1¼" base diameter; bulbous mustard 2⅛" tall x 1¼" base diameter. Ruby stained holding tray 5½" diameter as measured across the bottom. Overall ruby stained condiment set height is 7¼" to the top of the metal lifting handle. Yellow striped shaker **$120.00 – 130.00;** red striped opalware set **$375.00 – 420.00.** The very rare ruby stained glass condiment set **NPD**.

Rathbun collection

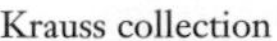

Krauss collection

Harris collection

Harris collection

THE BEAVER FALLS CO-OPERATIVE GLASS COMPANY (1879 – 1889) COOPERATIVE FLINT GLASS COMPANY Beaver Falls, Pennsylvania (1889 – 1937)

The Co-Operative Flint Glass Company appeared as the result of a reorganization of The Beaver Falls Co-Operative Glass Co. The factory produced both pressed and mold blown glass tableware some of which were ruby or amber stained by their own decorating department. The factory remained an independent; never joining with either the U.S. Glass or National Glass corporations. This glasshouse remained in business until its closing in 1937.

Lockwood collection

Co-op's #1901: Clear glass, mold blown and pressed. The pattern has radiating ribs filling an upside-down heart bordered by a zippered inverted V, which in turn is bordered by a second zippered V. The pattern is repeated three times around the shaker with each middle V curving at the bottom up to the next. Upper Vs converge between the hearts at a small bull's eye below a diamond shape filled with smaller diamonds.[1] Circa 1901. 3" tall x 2¾" wide. Scarce! **$17.00 – 25.00.**

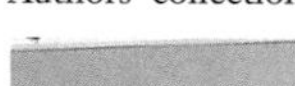

Authors' collection

Dice, Double (aka "Dice"): Opaque white homogeneous opalware (milk) glass, mold blown. Peterson called this pattern "Dice." We referred to this ware as "Double Dice" on page 221 of our Vol. II book. The shape consists of a pair of fused together dice forming a midsection twist in such a manner that the number of spots on the upper die cannot be directly related to the lower die. Attribution substantiation happened as a result of a 1921 factory catalog obtained through the efforts of Maralyn Ridgway and Earl Autenreith. 3⅛" tall with a top opening of ¾" in diameter. Earl, Maralyn, and ourselves believe that this ware was first produced earlier than 1921 as popular novelties. Circa 1900, with availability through 1921 (perhaps even later). Very scarce! **$195.00 – 225.00** pair.

Rathbun collection

Dice Stacked: Opaque white homogeneous opalware (milk) glass, mold blown. As the pattern name indicates, the motif consists of a pair of stacked dice containing intaglio black painted dots. We consider this ware to be similiar to the shaker entitled "Domino" shown on page 222 of our Vol. II. Differences being that the top opening is ¾" in diameter; the Domino opening measures 1" in diameter. Additionally, each side of the four-sided stacked dice adds up to seven. This is not the case involving the Domino shaker. Attribution of this ware was obtained through the research efforts of Maralyn Ridgway and Earl Autenreith from a 1921 catalog published by the Co-operative Flint Glass Co., Beaver Falls, Pennsylvania. 3¼" tall. Circa 1915 – 1921. Rare! **$105.00 – 125.00.**

Harris collection

Douglass: Clear ruby stained glass, mold blown and pressed. A very simple flared out paneled shaker containing an etched fleur-de-lis and star that alternate from panel to panel. This pattern was named after the factory president. Circa 1903.[3] 2⅞" tall. Very scarce! **$35.00 – 40.00** due to panel edge roughness.

Authors' collection

Regina (OMN): Opaque homogeneous blue glass, mold blown using a four-part mold. The shaker pattern consists of a smooth shoulder that tapers to a pointed bulge above eight vertical panels; four plain panels alternate with four panels that have six deep vertical ridges. The base flaring contains 28 wider pleats. Also produced in clear glass.[2] Circa 1901. 3" tall x 2¼" wide. Very scarce! **$40.00 – 50.00.**

Rathbun collection

Dogwood Paneled (aka "Art Novo"): Two shakers are illustrated, ruby stained and clear, both are mold blown. As the pattern name implies, the principal motif is an intaglio Dogwood flower on each of the two large panels. The ruby stained shaker has gold painted floral decoration; the other contains clear flowers. Circa 1905 – 1918. 2⅞" tall. This is a rare pattern in salt and pepper shakers! **$175.00 – 200.00** pair.

CRYSTAL GLASS COMPANY
Pittsburgh, Pennsylvania
(1868 – 1890)

The Crystal Glass Co. was established at Pittsburgh in 1879. It initially produced tumblers, jelly glasses, fruit jars, and smoke bells. During the first year this factory made a #350 pattern called "Pinafore" which is today's "Actress"/"Annie" pattern. Various table pieces contained embossed busts that portrayed popular actresses and actors that were publicly recognized during their popularity period in time. At least 26 different pieces were produced that depict several favorite actresses and actors (Annie Pixley, Maud Granger, Kate Claxton, Fanny Davenport, Lotta Crabtree, etc.). Other patterns produced by this factory were Frosted Eagle, Polar Bear, and Swan.

Krauss collection

Authors' collection

Annie (aka "Actress"): Clear amber colored pressed glass, two-part mold. Pattern name for the salt shaker is by Peterson.[1] The front and back of the shaker portrays a head view of Annie Pixley in raised relief. Previous pattern glass authors state that this pattern was produced in clear and frosted.[2] As the reader can see our illustrated shakers are in a very rare amber color. Circa 1879 – 1883. We are illustrating two views; one of which has a black cloth placed inside each shaker in an effort to enhance pattern clarity. 2⅞" tall x 1⅝" wide at the shoulder; 1⅝" base diameter. **$400.00 – 450.00** pair.

DALZELL, GILMORE, and LEIGHTON COMPANY
Findlay, Ohio
(1888 – 1901)

This factory began operations in early September 1888, at Findlay. The factory became involved with the National Glass Co. in October 1899. The plant closed at the end of November 1901. More historical detail is available in our Vol. II.

Lockwood collection

Teardrop-Clear: Clear glass, mold blown. A cylindrical-shaped shaker with a horizontal row of teardrops in high relief; below each teardrop is a wide pointed rib at the top and bottom.[1] Circa 1899. 3¼" tall x 1⅞" wide. Scarce! **$23.00 – 30.00.**

Authors' collection

Robbins: Opaque white opalware glass, mold blown. This is a spheriod-shaped shaker containing four bulging lobes that are present from the top to the bottom of the shaker. About one inch from the top of each shaker lobe there is a very small protruding round peg. Apparently, these shakers were produced without HP decoration. The shaker illustrated as Robbins on page 57 of our Vol. II is incorrect since it illustrates a six lobe shaker. Circa 1895 – 1900. The correct height dimension is 2¾". Scarce! **$20.00 – 25.00.**

Krauss collection

Findlay Onyx Glass: Opaque onyx glass, dual mold blown. Patented on April 23, 1889. Onyx glassware was made from a sensitive mixture containing metallic substances capable of producing silver, ruby, and various other colored lusters. Coloration was produced while the still glowing mixture was subjected to heat and gaseous fumes. Two molds were used, one to produce the raised pattern; the other mold brought the article to full size and final shape. The patent wording leads the reader to conclude that onyx ware embodied a homogeneous mixture since there is no mention of casing or plating. However, chemical analysis of countless shards of various types of onyx glass, obtained from the original factory site at Findlay disclosed that this was not always true. Silver/platinum lustred onyx glass is indeed homogeneous;[2] the other colored onyx lusters such as ruby/rose, cinnamon/amber, orange, purple, and black were cased. Many collectors believe that silver lustered onyx pieces are cased. This is understandable because visual inspection imparts a cased-like appearance. In the actual manufacturing process, the gaffer dipped his blowpipe into a pot of fluid metal (glass); and in order to develop opalescence, the bulb was rapidly cooled and then reheated at the glory hole. Two and sometimes three additional platings were added over the original glass bulb; all from the same pot of fluid metal mix. What the gaffer created was several successive platings. Due to the fact that the inner plating had been heated higher than the successive platings, it developed a denser looking color giving the finished article the appearance of cased glass. Since the same mix of opal glass was involved, the glassware by accepted technical definition has to be called "homogeneous." True cased glass is made of two or more contrasting layers involving more than one glass mixture.

The factory produced various lusters and other effects by gaseous reaction upon metals that permeate glass mixtures; not only by sulfurous fumes but also by reducing gaseous actions which would bring the various metals in the glass to the surface and allow leeway for producing different effects. The level of heat and mixture strength also allowed modification of color shades. The principal problem associated with this type of production process, as it applies to glass, was the difficulty encountered in obtaining consistent color results. This obstacle was prevalent at the Dalzell firm and it was a principal reason why several shades of rose, amber, and orange onyx are encountered by the collector. These types of color deviations have resulted in the reporting of color variants that were really produced due to lack of manufacturing process control. Color inconsistency was one of the main reasons why onyx glass was made by the factory for less than a year. Another reason was high cost of production. This glassware was produced before the principles of the coefficient of expansion were really understood. Also, it is a fact that the various layers of onyx glass expanded and contracted at different rates during the factory annealing process, which resulted in a high percentage of this glass being fractured or having annealing cracks. The cost of production became so expensive that it had to be dropped as a marketable line! Collectors should use a magnifying device to ascertain if annealing cracks are present prior to making a purchase. The onyx shakers and mustards shown in our Outstanding Salt Shaker Rarities Section are excellent examples of the aforesaid color and manufacturing problems discussed. This ware is circa 1889. 2⅝" tall. Very rare! **NPD.**

DALZELL – VIKING CORPORATION
New Martinsville, West Virginia
(1986 – Present)

This corporation is the successor to the Viking Glass Company. We have yet to investigate the history of this firm. We are presenting shakers primarily acquired during the late 1980s containing a Dalzell-Viking paper label. In reviewing the patterns of New Martinsville and Viking, one of our illustrated patterns resembles the New Martinsville "Curved Body" form. Arthur Peterson picked up a shaker produced by Viking which we are also illustrating.

Authors' collection

Barrel, Small Block: Clear homogeneous cranberry pressed glass. As the pattern name indicates this is a round, symmetrical barrel containing 10 vertical embossed rows of small square blocks that encircle the shaker. The pattern is also present upon the bottom. Circa 1986 – 1991. 2½" tall. The top edge is fire polished smooth. **$15.00 – 20.00** pair.

Authors' collection

Curved Body (Dalzell-Viking's): Clear cobalt blue glass, mold blown. A plain shaker that curves into a flared-out base. The factory paper label is visible in our illustration. Circa 1986 – 1990. 3⅛" tall with a silver colored plastic top. Also produced in ruby. **$6.00 – 9.00.**

Authors' collection

Diamond Thumbprint (Dalzell-Viking's): Clear homogeneous cranberry pressed glass. The pattern consists of a series of embossed diamonds with an intaglio thumbprint in the center of each diamond. This is a heavy shaker with fire polished top edges. Circa 1987 – 1993. 3¾" tall with silver colored plastic tops. **$20.00 – 28.00** pair.

Coalmer collection

Eye-Winker Variant: Clear homogeneous red cranberry glass, mold blown and pressed. As the pattern name implies, the center is configured with what can be described as a lidded (half-closed) eye above a series of eight raised bubbles that surround the base of this shaker. Circa 1985 – 1993. This pattern may have been created prior to the change in corporate name to Dalzell-Viking. 3⅝" tall with chrome-plated top that is believed to be original. **$12.00 – 18.00.**

Coalmer collection

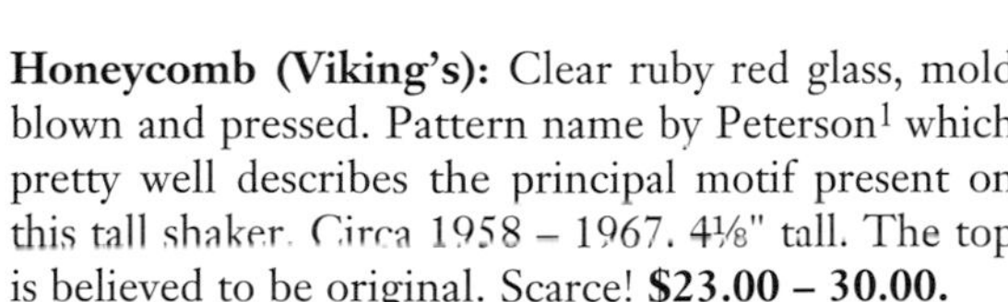

Honeycomb (Viking's): Clear ruby red glass, mold blown and pressed. Pattern name by Peterson[1] which pretty well describes the principal motif present on this tall shaker. Circa 1958 – 1967. 4⅛" tall. The top is believed to be original. Scarce! **$23.00 – 30.00.**

DITHRIDGE & COMPANY
Pittsburgh, Pennsylvania
(1863 – 1903)

This factory was an outgrowth from the Fort Pitt Glassworks and the name was changed to Dithridge & Co. in 1863 under the ownership of Edward D. Dithridge. In 1903 it merged with the Pittsburgh Lamp & Brass Co. In terms of glass produced, it operated as a serious competitor to the Consolidated Lamp & Glass Co. The novelties and ware that were produced have a great similarity to Consolidated Lamp.

Coalmer collection

McElderry collection

Rathbun collection

Beaded Bulb: We are illustrating three unique shakers: opaque lavender, opalescent blue, and variegated white/butterscotch glass, mold blown. A relatively plain shaker pattern containing four large lobes; each lobed panel is separated by 14 small glass beads running consecutively from top to the bottom. A large glass ring is present just below the metal top. Pattern name by Peterson. These colors are not normal production colors used by Dithridge & Co. However, it is an established fact that limited market testing of experimental colors were pursued by them from time to time.[1] 3⅜" tall. Circa 1894 – 1901. Rare in these colors! **$125.00 – 160.00** each.

Authors' collection

Corn: Opaque pink triple cased glass, dual mold blown. The motif is the same as that illustrated in our Vol. II, page 61. It is being presented because of its rarity and high collectibility factor in this color. The pattern is in the form of a tapered ear of corn. 3⅛" tall. Circa 1894 – 1901. **$135.00 – 150.00.**

McElderry collection

Dithridge Princess Swirl (condiment): Opaque custard glass, mold blown. Consisting of four pieces, salt, pepper, mustard, and matching glass holder. Photographing and examining this condiment group permits us to present the visual pattern detail that we lacked relative to this set within our Vol. II. Both shakers and the mustard are 2⅛" tall. However, additional discussion is in order relative the C.F. Monroe "Erie Twist"/(Helmschmied Swirl), "Fenton Swirl,"[2] and the "Dithridge Princess Swirl"[3] patterns. Despite the fact that a complete record of our research involving these pattern similarities is covered within our Vol. II; during 1997, a couple of incomplete and speculative articles were published, relative to the aforesaid swirl patterns, that failed to address all the recorded research facts involved.[4] As a result, these articles are a classic example of a presentation of incorrect assumptions and half-truth conclusions. A number of years of research and cross checking were conducted before we published our data and we can find no reason to change it. The "Dithridge Princess Swirl" condiment set was also produced in opaque pink. Rare in custard! **$550.00 – 575.00** set.

Coalmer collection

Fleur-De-Lis, Skirted: Opaque blue homogeneous glass, mold blown. The upper portion of this pattern is encircled by a series of embossed fleurs-de-lis. The lower portion of the shaker flares outward in the form of 18 vertical ribs positioned below an encircling series of embossed beads. 2¾" tall x 2¾" wide; 1⅜" base diameter. Also produced in opaque pink and white. Circa 1894 – 1900. Very scarce! **$33.00 – 45.00.**

Rathbun collection

Floral Sprig: Opaque blue homogenous glass, mold blown. This pillar-shaped shaker with a bulbous base and a small protruding glass bottom extension is part of a condiment set. An identical (complete) HP condiment set in white opalware is illustrated in our Vol. II, Page 63. It has been our experience that this type of plain surfaced ware was produced with a simple HP decoration that is dedicated to colored foliage. Circa 1896 – 1900. 2⅞" tall. Very scarce in opaque blue! **$28.00 – 35.00.**

McElderry collection

Net & Scroll: Opaque green homogeneous glass, mold blown. The pattern name given this shaker by Warman describes the overall motif very well. The factory mold detail is of outstanding quality; thus creating the centrally located scrolling in high raised relief. Circa 1894 – 1900. 2⅞" tall; 2⅛" base diameter. Very scarce in this color! Also produced in white opalware and probably other solid colors. **$40.00 – 55.00.**

Rathbun collection

Diamonds with Ribs: Opaque homogeneous green glass, mold blown. The physical shape amounts to a short sphere containing 12 vertical ribs in high raised relief. Two encircling rows of miniature diamond bumps at the top and base of the shaker complete the motif description. Circa 1894 – 1900. 2⅝" tall. Very scarce! **$35.00 – 45.00.**

Rathbun collection

Sunset: Opaque yellow and green glass, mold blown. This pattern configuration is fully detailed in our Vol. II, page 67. However, the two shakers that we are illustrating are in colors that (for some reason) are seldom seen. The bright yellow shaker is not custard and does not react when exposed to black light radiation. The green is a very warm and bright color. Circa 1894 – 1897. Very scarce! **$55.00 – 65.00** each.

Rathbun collection

Scalloped Fan Condiment: Opaque HP opalware glass, mold blown and pressed. This is a three-piece condiment set with a scalloped fan-shaped milk glass holder that has three deep recessed openings to accommodate retention of a salt, pepper, and mustard. Each condiment piece contains HP orange poppies supported by green leafed branches. The top of the scalloped fan base has similar small HP floral decoration. Shakers, 3½" tall; mustard, 3⅛" tall. The complete set is 7⅞" to the top of the lifting handle. Circa 1895 – 1901. Very scarce! **$165.00 – 180.00** set.

Krauss collection

Swirl, Multi: Blue opaque homogeneous glass, mold blown. The motif consists of a series of grooved embossed swirls with a large neck ring. This is a variation of the "Swirl, Wide Diagonal" shaker illustrated in our Vol. II, p. 68. Also produced in pink and white opaque. Circa 1894 – 1900. 2⅝" tall x 2½" wide; 1" base diameter. Very scarce! **$39.00 – 50.00.**

DOYLE & COMPANY
Pittsburgh, Pennsylvania
(1866 – 1891)

The factory was located on the south side of Pittsburgh. The first owners were Joseph and William Doyle. The factory joined the U.S. Glass Co. in 1891 as Factory P. Many of the old Doyle patterns that were created during the late 1870s and 1880s were reissued by U.S. Glass and appeared in a trade catalog around 1891. If the reader wants a comprehensive history of this company refer to Kamm 8, page 90.

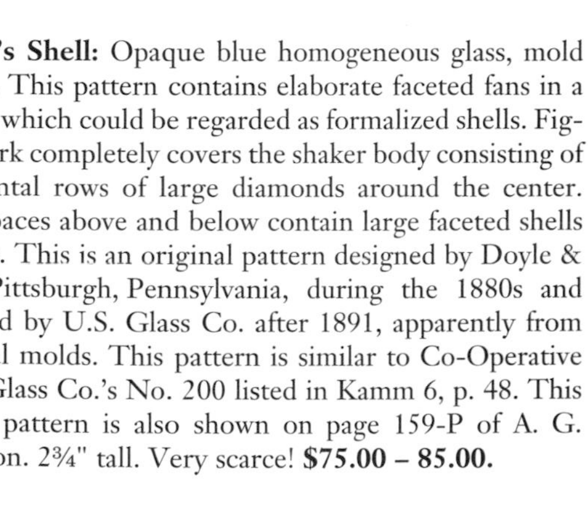

Doyle's Shell: Opaque blue homogeneous glass, mold blown. This pattern contains elaborate faceted fans in a design which could be regarded as formalized shells. Figure work completely covers the shaker body consisting of horizontal rows of large diamonds around the center. The spaces above and below contain large faceted shells or fans. This is an original pattern designed by Doyle & Co., Pittsburgh, Pennsylvania, during the 1880s and reissued by U.S. Glass Co. after 1891, apparently from original molds. This pattern is similar to Co-Operative Flint Glass Co.'s No. 200 listed in Kamm 6, p. 48. This Doyle pattern is also shown on page 159-P of A. G. Peterson. 2¾" tall. Very scarce! **$75.00 – 85.00.**

Coalmer collection

DUNCAN & MILLER GLASS COMPANY
Washington, Pennsylvania
(1900 – 1955)

This company was formed during 1900 when the George Duncan's Sons Co. name change came about as the result of J. Ernest Miller sharing company ownership of the Washington, Pennsylvania, factory. Some of what we call today's Duncan purist collectors like to factory separate the patterns that were marketed by the various Duncan family factories from their beginning in 1866. Then there are other collectors that are quite content to just call the various patterns by their trade accepted name and refer to them under the general term "Duncan Glass." A. C. Revi in his book *American Pressed Glass & Figure Bottles* was content to list the various factory names but did not specifically tie down by date when each factory name change took place. The reader can glean still further detail of the Duncan family factories by referring to our Vol. II, p. 71.

Lockwood collection

Blocked Thumbprint Band: Clear ruby stained glass, mold blown and pressed. This is a cylindrical-shaped shaker that is completely plain except for a band of eight arched thumbprints with concave surfaces on the base portion. Each arch abuts the next by way of a raised pointed rib as a common delineator.[1] The stained portion has been souvenir engraved. Circa 1904 – 1913. Scarce! **$35.00 – 45.00.**

GEORGE DUNCAN & SONS
Pittsburgh, Pennsylvania
(1866 – 1892)

This factory joined the U.S. Glass conglomerate in 1891. For additional historical facts the reader is referred to our Vol. II, page 71.

Krauss collection

Beveled Buttons: Clear translucent glass, mold blown and pressed. The pattern consists of an overall series of royal blue stained buttons within intaglio clear diamonds that covers the entire exterior. This is an original Duncan & Sons, Pittsburgh, Pennsylvania, pattern originally cataloged as their No. 320. However, when Duncan joined the U.S. Glass conglomerate as Factory D, there was continued production of this ware.[1] The "Beveled Buttons" pattern name was created by William Heacock.[2] Circa 1890 – 1892. 3" tall with two-piece metal tops. Very scarce! **$90.00 – 110.00** pair.

Authors' collection

Clover, Duncan's: Clear vaseline glass, mold blown and pressed. There is more than one Clover pattern, hence the reference to the factory of manufacture to avoid confusion.[3] A pillar-shaped paneled shaker with alternating panels of clover; the plain vertical panels can sometimes be found in amber or ruby stained. Black light exposure resulted in a high illumination. Circa 1890. 3⅛" tall. Very scarce in vaseline! **$60.00 – 75.00.**

Lockwood collection

Zippered Block: Clear ruby stained glass, mold blown and pressed. A cylindrical-shaped shaker with zippered bands at the top and bottom above a ringed base. Three oblong blocks are divided by vertical ribbed zippers with deep grooves on each side. Originally listed as the No. 90 line. This design was patented on March 15, 1887, by John E. Miller.[4] At least 40 forms for the table were all illustrated in the company's 1887 catalog. Heacock has indicated there was continued production after the factory joined U.S. Glass. Also produced in clear glass. Circa 1887. 2⅞" tall x 1½" wide. Very scarce! **$60.00 – 70.00.**

EAGLE GLASS & MANUFACTURING COMPANY
Wellsburg, West Virginia
(1894 – 1937 glass producing years)

As described in our Vol. II, page 73, this is a family owned and operated business that celebrated their 100th anniversary in 1994. This is one of the few Victorian companies that continues to operate today by virtue of product diversification and good management. Simply stated, when glass manufacturing became unprofitable, they ceased producing it and turned to various commercial products that sell. Our questions and research of Eagle's glass production were greatly enhanced by both personal communications with Margaret Carmichael Paull and a 1994 historical book written and published by her entitled *Eagle Manufacturing Company One Hundred Years*. The book contains wide variety of the glass patterns and other products that this company has produced.

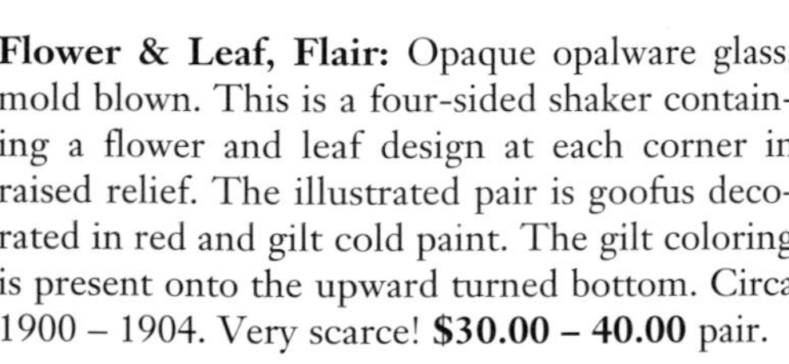

Flower & Leaf, Flair: Opaque opalware glass, mold blown. This is a four-sided shaker containing a flower and leaf design at each corner in raised relief. The illustrated pair is goofus decorated in red and gilt cold paint. The gilt coloring is present onto the upward turned bottom. Circa 1900 – 1904. Very scarce! **$30.00 – 40.00** pair.

Authors' collection

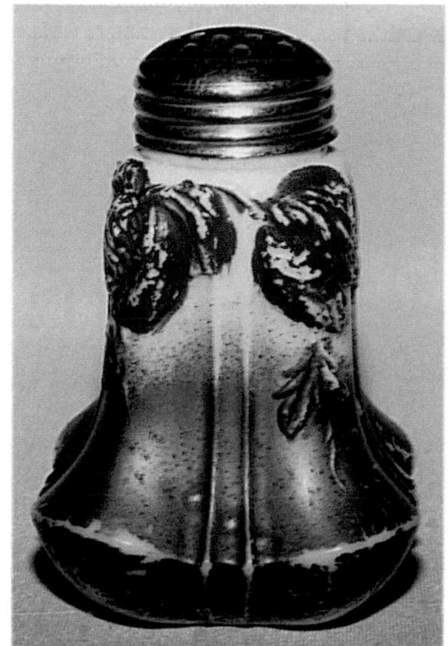

Coalmer collection

Flower, Open: Opaque white opalware glass, mold blown. The pattern consists of an elaborate red centered flower with associated gilt decorated foliage in raised relief on a tapered pillar. The flower is hand decorated in what is known to today's collectors as goofus decoration. Circa 1903 – 1908. 3⅛" tall with an original metal and celluloid center screw-on top. Very scarce with goofus decoration still present! **$28.00 – 37.00.**

Krauss collection

Flower Tracery: Opaque goofus (red and gilt) decorated opalware, mold blown. A somewhat dome-shaped shaker that is divided into segments by a single embossed horizontal band and five raised vertical bands. The principal motif amounts to a large petaled flower and leaves that cover one entire side. 2⅜" tall x 2⅞" wide. Circa 1899 – 1905. Very scarce! **$20.00 – 30.00.**

Lockwood collection

Ribbed Base with Flower: Opaque white opalware glass, mold blown. A bulbous shape with four embossed flowers and leaves divided by upright scrolled panels. Has a band of embossed slightly curved ribs that completely encircle the base. Decoration amounts to blue and yellow on the embossed figures. This shaker is very similar to those in Eagle's "Cosmos Scroll" condiment set.[2] Pattern name by Warman.[3] Circa 1899 – 1906. 2⅝" tall x 2" wide. Very scarce! **$28.00 – 35.00.**

Lantern, Eagle's: Clear green glass, mold blown. This is one of the glass candy container types shaped in the form of a lantern. This highly popular ware was also produced in clear and blue. These items were made in several sizes and covered by design patents 37,268 and 37, 269, patented December 20, 1904, by James Paull. Our illustrated shaker has the wrong type of top.[1] The original top contained a flexible wire carrying handle to simulate the type used by railroad brakeman and conductors to pass directive signals to their locomotive engineer, etc. 4⅜" tall. Very scarce in this color! **$15.00 – 20.00** due to improper top and base chipping.

Harris collection

S. W. FARBER, INC.
Brooklyn, New York

The S. W. Farber firm did not manufacture glassware. However, they are quite well known for their Farber Ware metal products. During the late 1920s and for a number of years thereafter, they purchased American and imported quality glass for selling along with their various household chromium-plated metal holders. Many salt and pepper collectors are very aware of the shakers, cruets, etc. that Farber purchased from Cambridge Glass. But, a series of glass animal shakers that they sold in gift boxes were imported from Europe. Our collection has one of the "Bird" salt shakers with a paper label marked Czechoslovakia. As far as we have been able to ascertain, various metal Farber Ware products are still being marketed today for the American housewife.

Krauss collection

Dog, Standing Ear: Translucent amethyst, lime green, and cranberry mold blown and pressed glass. We are illustrating a matched figural trio consisting of a "Standing Ear Dog" with glass eyes. The salt and pepper are 2⅛" tall; the sugar shaker is 3½" tall. This glass dog pattern was previously shown and discussed in our 1976 book on page 84 where it is portrayed in a dark green colored glass. Circa 1928 – 1934; longer production is probable. Rare as a complete set! **$780.00 – 825.00** set.

Krauss collection

Elephant Trio: Translucent cranberry and green mold blown and pressed glass. Illustrated is a glass-eyed matched trio comprising an elephant salt, pepper, and sugar shaker that were originally sold in a gift box. A 1930 Farber catalog that made positive attribution possible was discovered and made available to AAGSSCS members by author Neila Bredehoft. The salt and pepper are 2⅛" tall; the elephant sugar shaker is 3½" tall. Circa 1928 – 1934 (perhaps longer production). Rare as a complete combination set (trio)! **$850.00 – 900.00** set.

Krauss collection

Owl: Translucent cranberry and purple mold blown and pressed glass salt and pepper shakers. Each shaker is configured in the form of a feathered owl. The metal heads contain glass eyes. No doubt a matching owl sugar shaker was also produced. Each shaker is 2¼" tall. Due to physical body configuration, each shaker is slightly taller than the other Farber figurals that are illustrated. Circa 1928 – 1934 with later production probable. Very scarce! **$180.00 – 210.00** pair.

Krauss collection

Rabbit, Standing: Translucent cranberry and pale green mold blown and pressed glass salt and pepper. The shakers measured 2⅛" tall. A matching sugar shaker was also made to comprise a complete trio. Circa 1928 – 1934. Rare. **$220.00 – 245.00** pair.

FENTON ART GLASS COMPANY
Williamstown, West Virginia
(1905 – Present)

This factory began actual glass manufacturing in January 1907 at Williamstown. Early production of iridescent (carnival), chocolate, and opalescent glass resulted in a profitable operation in Williamstown where the factory is still functioning today.

Fenton has always been known for the production of quality glass and has demonstrated they are capable of producing any form/type of glass throughout its many years of operation. In addition to the three Fenton books that were written by William Heacock with technical backing by Frank M. Fenton, there is a very comprehensive book published by The Fenton Art Glass Collectors of America (FAGCA) that is edited by Ferill J. Rice. The book is entitled *Caught in the Butterfly Net.*

This publication is a collection of the best articles and notes that were published in the club's membership newsletter from 1977 to 1991. We highly recommend that any collector/dealer interested in Fenton glass identification be aware of the book. It contains considerable detail and illustrations not provided in the aforementioned Heacock books.

Authors' collection

No. 1906 Daisy & Button: Clear olive colonial green glass, mold blown and pressed. The glass is essentially translucent due to the surface congestion caused by the Daisy and Button pattern that covers ¾ of the surface. The bottom quarter of the shaker has vertical ribbing rising upward from a clear green foot. 3" tall. This shaker was also produced in a rare chocolate opaque glass by Fenton. Circa 1976.[1] Very scarce! **$25.00 – 35.00.**

Cactus, Fenton's: Two types of shakers are illustrated — clear canary (vaseline) and opaque pale satinized off-white glass. Both types are mold blown and pressed and are a reproduction of the "Caramel Cactus" pattern that was originally produced by the Indiana Tumbler & Goblet Co., Greentown, Indiana, circa 1902.[2] Of course the authentic pattern was not produced in vaseline glass. These Fenton shakers are circa 1959 – 1963. Fenton called the clear vaseline color "topaz opalescent."[3] Both shaker types illuminate brightly when exposed to black light. 2⅞" tall. Very scarce! Opaque pair, **$45.00 – 55.00**; single clear, **$28.00 – 35.00.**

Authors' collection

Authors' collection

Flower Panel condiment set (aka -#6206 White Milk Glass): Opaque white mold blown glass. This is a reproduction of an old McKee pattern that Peterson called "Flower Panel" which is shown on page 42 of our 1976 book. We are also illustrating a shaker pair in the difficult to obtain transparent "James Town Blue." Circa 1957 – 58. Shakers and open topped mustard 2¼" tall. Very scarce! complete condiment set, **$80.00 – 100.00;** James Town Blue, **$65.00 – 80.00** pair.

Woolley collection

Authors' collection

Authors' collection

Fenton No. 4409: Opaque black glass, mold blown with very large intaglio thumbprints. A heavy shaker that is supported upon three curving glass legs as illustrated on page 88 of *Fenton Glass: The Third Twenty-five Years.* Circa 1968 – 1976. 3⅝" tall. Very scarce! **$38.00 – 45.00.**

Authors' collection

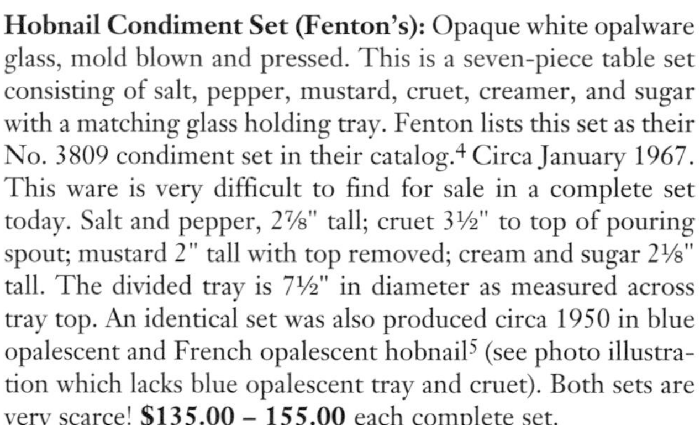

Hobnail Condiment Set (Fenton's): Opaque white opalware glass, mold blown and pressed. This is a seven-piece table set consisting of salt, pepper, mustard, cruet, creamer, and sugar with a matching glass holding tray. Fenton lists this set as their No. 3809 condiment set in their catalog.[4] Circa January 1967. This ware is very difficult to find for sale in a complete set today. Salt and pepper, 2⅞" tall; cruet 3½" to top of pouring spout; mustard 2" tall with top removed; cream and sugar 2⅛" tall. The divided tray is 7½" in diameter as measured across tray top. An identical set was also produced circa 1950 in blue opalescent and French opalescent hobnail[5] (see photo illustration which lacks blue opalescent tray and cruet). Both sets are very scarce! **$135.00 – 155.00** each complete set.

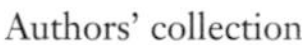

Authors' collection

Authors' collection

Authors' collection

Optic Rib: Clear green opalescent glass, mold blown. If the reader wants a challenge, try and collect this illustrated pair in the green opalescent color. We show a pair of cranberry opalescent in our Vol. II, page 84. Circa 1953 – 1969. Salt 5", pepper 4" tall. Rare! **$175.00 – 190.00** pair.

Harris collection

Polka Dot Variant: Translucent dark blue glass, dual mold blown. This shaker was produced from the same Fenton mold referred to as "Polka Dot"[6] except that the chemical mixture used to create an opalescent effect was not included in the glass batch that was used. An external surface area is outlined in miniature HP gold scrolls that contains a HP green and white floral spray. Because this shaker became available during the final stages of our manuscript, we did not have the time to check with Frank Fenton to ascertain if this decoration was done by Fenton decorators or elsewhere. We can find nothing in published Fenton literature that verifies that this ware was hand painted at the Fenton factory. The basic pattern is circa 1955 with probable later production in blue as illustrated. The silver metal top is not believed to be a Fenton Factory original. 2⅞" tall. Very scarce! **$50.00 – 60.00.**

Authors' collection

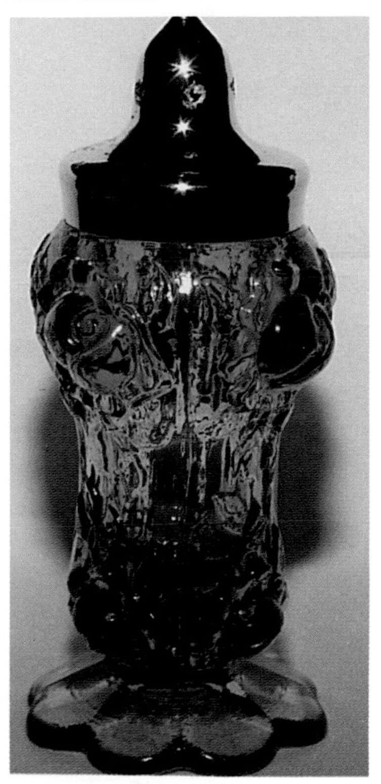

Rose: Clear homogeneous colonial amber glass, mold blown and pressed. The pattern has eight roses in high raised relief; four at the top and four at the base. All "Rose" shakers are supported by a foot containing eight scallops. Circa 1962 – 1980; a more detailed history of this pattern is related in our Vol. II, page 84. Also produced in colonial blue and green. 3⅜" tall with original metal finial top. Scarce! **$16.00 – 22.00.**

Krauss collection

Spatter Glass Swirl: Opaque cased spatter art glass, mold blown. The pattern consists of 10 vertical spiraling swirls that encase the inside spatter decoration. If collectors want a challenge, the following scenario will explain why! This shaker is one of six that Dr. A. G. Peterson's wife Ruby had made for him for his 60th birthday by Frank Fenton.[7] The "Fenton Swirl" mold was used to produce the basic pattern.[8] Circa 1959. 3⅛" tall with an original screw-on top. Extremely rare! Since there is no monetary market base line, the shaker is worth whatever another purchaser is willing to pay for it.

Authors' collection

Swirl: Opaque black homogeneous glass, mold blown. This pattern is fully addressed in our Vol. II book under the Fenton section.[9] It is being highlighted again to illustrate the latest 1995 black glass production of a reproduced form that began at the Fenton factory circa 1954. 2⅛" tall with a silver colored plastic top. **$8.00 – 12.00.**

Authors' collection

Teardrop, Bulging (Fenton's): Translucent turquoise iridescent glass, mold blown. This is a reproduction of the "Teardrop, Bulging" Dithridge pattern that we purchased at the Fenton Factory gift shop in 1995. Of course, Dithridge never made shakers in this color. Fenton has produced this pattern in various colors for many years.[10] 2¾" tall. **$8.00 – 13.00.**

THE FINDLAY FLINT GLASS COMPANY
Findlay, Ohio
(1888 – 1891)

This glasshouse didn't last very long. It was organized during November 1888; glass production began on August 12, 1889; the factory was destroyed by fire on June 6, 1891. While operational, it is known to have produced Findlay #19, Pillar, Findlay's "Dot," Spur Hobnail, Elephant Head mustard with lid, Squash Caster set, Pichereau's ink well and Butterfly toothpick patterns.[1]

Krauss collection

Squash Castor Set: Clear uncolored glass, mold blown and pressed. The assigned pattern name appears to have been based upon the shape of the metal handled glass castor set holder. The four-piece set consists of a salt, pepper, pumpkin-like lidded mustard, and glass condiment holding stand with metal lifting handle.[2] Salt and pepper are 2½" tall; mustard 2⅛" tall with glass lid removed. Each of the three condiment pieces have 1¼" diameter extended bases to assure their retention within the glass holder. The castor set holder is 7½" across. Circa 1890. Rare as a complete set. **$325.00 – 350.00** set.

FOSTORIA GLASS COMPANY
Moundsville, West Virginia
(1887 – 1983)

This glass factory commenced operations on December 15, 1887, at Fostoria, Ohio. Lucien B. Martin was the first president. In 1891, the factory was moved to Moundsville, West Virginia. Many examples of the glassware that was produced while the factory was located at Fostoria, Ohio, can be viewed today at the Fostoria Museum in downtown Fostoria, Ohio. Factory production ended during 1983, and the remaining inventory and molds were subsequently sold off.

Authors' collection

Artichoke, Fostoria's (aka "Valencia"): Clear partially frosted glass, mold blown and pressed. The pattern consists of an external triangular-shaped formation of frosted overlapping leaves in high relief. The overlapping leaves have a lateral curvature. A.G. Peterson expressed the opinion that relatively few artichoke shakers were made.[1] Circa 1891. 2⅝" tall. Rare! **$65.00 – 80.00.**

Fostoria Glass Company

MANUFACTURERS OF

FLINT GLASSWARE AND

DECORATED LAMPS

We have surpassed all former years in the quality and variety of our lines for 1902

Krauss collection

Rathbun collection

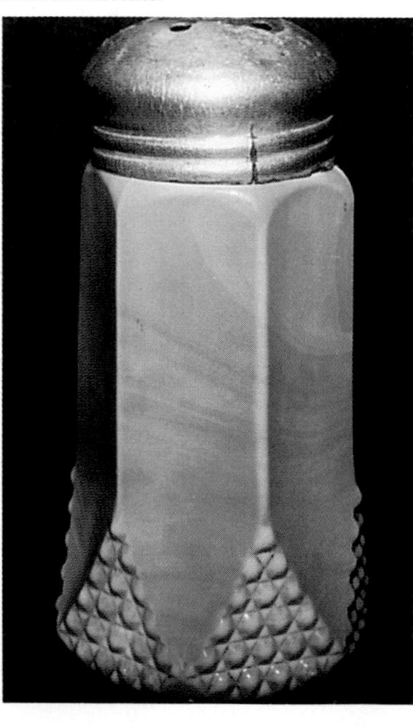

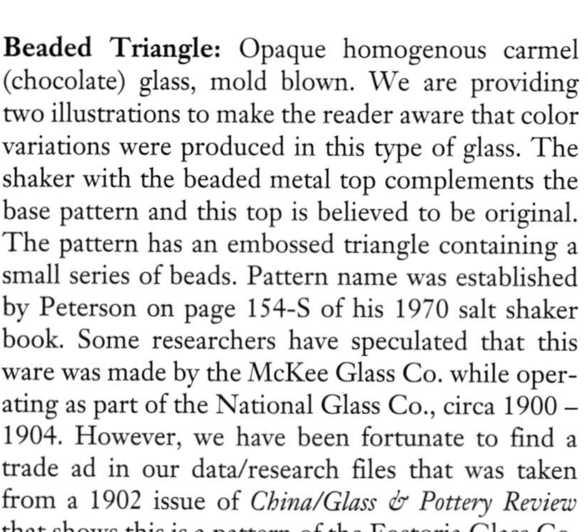

Beaded Triangle: Opaque homogenous carmel (chocolate) glass, mold blown. We are providing two illustrations to make the reader aware that color variations were produced in this type of glass. The shaker with the beaded metal top complements the base pattern and this top is believed to be original. The pattern has an embossed triangle containing a small series of beads. Pattern name was established by Peterson on page 154-S of his 1970 salt shaker book. Some researchers have speculated that this ware was made by the McKee Glass Co. while operating as part of the National Glass Co., circa 1900 – 1904. However, we have been fortunate to find a trade ad in our data/research files that was taken from a 1902 issue of *China/Glass & Pottery Review* that shows this is a pattern of the Fostoria Glass Co. Of course, we are fully aware that Fostoria Glass is not credited with being a chocolate glass producer; also, they never became a part of the National Glass Co. conglomerate. It is interesting to note that our illustrated 1902 Fostoria ad is coincident with the time frame that chocolate glass production was at the height of its popularity in America. However, it makes no sense to disregard a trade ad published in such a well recognized Victorian era publication. After all, most of today's principal art and pattern glass books have used this type of research material to make positive factory attributions. To say it another way, such ads provide the chief support of art and pattern glass written credibility identification. Each illustrated shaker is 3½" tall. Circa 1902. Very rare! **NPD.**

Lockwood collection

Fostoria's #956: Clear, heavy, fire-polished glass, mold blown. The shaker is square with rounded corners. The center square of the pattern is divided by an X and the two side triangles, formed by the X, are filled with tiny diamond point. Each lower corner is a rounded point with radiating ribs in a circle.[2] Circa 1901. 3¼" tall x 1¾" wide; 2¼" base corner-to-corner. Scarce! **$13.00 – 20.00.**

Coalmer collection

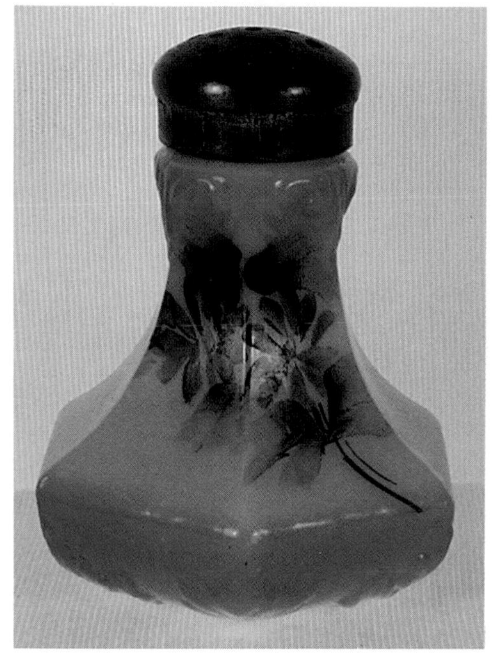

Hexagon, Leaf Base: Opaque opalware glass, mold blown. As the pattern name implies, this is a hexagon shaker that has swooping panels that have been decorated with a fairly large HP spray of violets over a light blue background. The shaker base has been embossed with small leaves. Circa 1901 – 1907. 3¼" tall. Scarce! **$27.00 – 35.00.**

Long Buttress: Clear ruby stained glass, mold blown and pressed. The pattern form has deep-pressed U's near the base, adjacent to very thick buttresses that flare out and provide extra width to the shaker. Also made in transparent clear glass. Listed in the Fostoria catalog as their No. 1299 pattern. 2¾" tall. Circa 1904 – 1910. Very scarce! **$65.00 – 75.00.**

Krauss collection

Harris collection

Lorraine, Fostoria's (aka "Flat Diamond Box"): Clear ruby stained glass, mold blown and pressed. The shaker body is curved inward through the middle creating a flared out top and bottom. The primary pattern consists of a uniform diamond block pattern. The two sides have an elliptical concave clear space to which ruby stain has been applied. Circa 1893. Also produced in clear glass.[3] 3⅛" tall. Very scarce! **$55.00 – 70.00.**

Lockwood collection

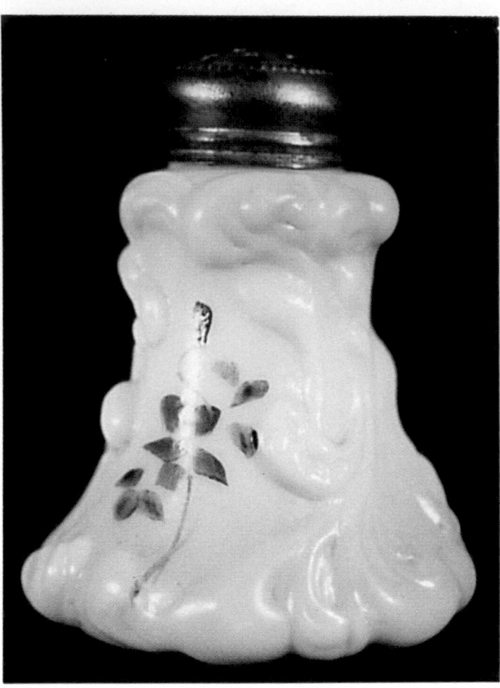

Scroll, Bold: Opaque heavy opalware glass, mold blown. A rather complicated flared-out shape consisting of embossed scrolls around the top and bottom and up two sides. The principal decorated motif amounts to a red and green floral sprig on the front and back between the upper and lower yellow painted wash. Circa 1900.[4] 3¼" tall x 2¾" wide. Very scarce! **$48.00 – 60.00.**

Lockwood collection

Wild Rose (Fostoria's): Opaque opalware glass, mold blown. The physical pattern amounts to an embossed long scroll-bordered oval shape that encloses embossed wild roses and leaves. This same pattern is repeated on the opposite side. Unfortunately, the decoration is badly worn on this piece but it amounted to gilt on the scrolls and yellow on the flowers. Circa 1900 – 1905.[5] 3½" tall x 2¼" wide. Scarce! **$3.00 – 5.00.**

FOSTORIA SHADE AND LAMP COMPANY
Fostoria, Ohio
(1890 – 1894)

This company was established by Nicholas Kopp and Charles Etz. Due to a merger, this factory was reestablished during 1894 as the Consolidated Lamp & Glass Co. and subsequently moved to Coraopolis, Pennsylvania. If the reader desires in-depth details regarding both these factories, we recommend *Fostoria Ohio Glass II* by Melvin L. Murray beginning on page 133.

Krauss collection

Pink Rose (condiment): Opaque pink satinized glass, mold blown. As the pattern name indicates, each shaker consists of a delicate individually petaled rose. The two-piece metal top is almost identical to the type of top used on the Mt. Washington/Pairpoint "Tomato" shakers. The showy silver-plated condiment holder is marked "Toronto SP Co." and is 7½" tall to the top of the lifting handles. Each shaker is 1⅝" tall. A patent was awarded to Kopp for this unique shaker design on March 10, 1891.[1] Rare as a set! **$710.00 – 730.00** set.

Witt collection

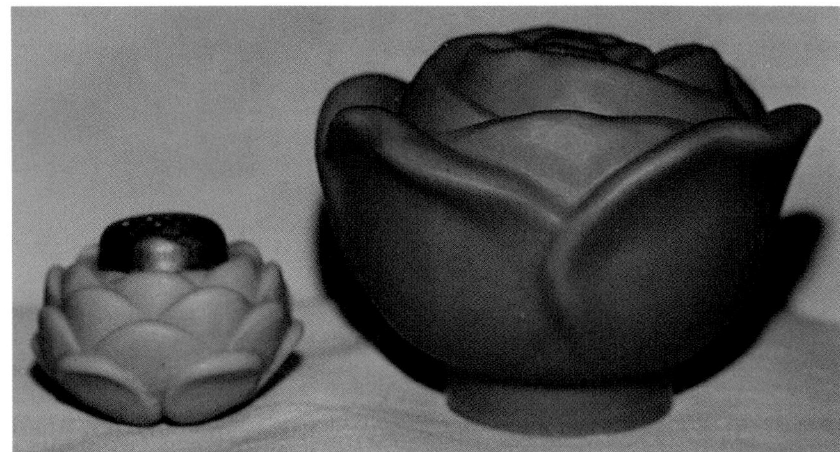

Pink Rose Shaker & Shade: We are also illustrating a pink rose shaker beside a pink rose petaled lamp shade. The homogeneous glass design and coloring are the same. Thus far, we have not been able to find any confirming back-up documentation that Kopp designed and produced this bedside lamp shade, but it is our opinion that he did. We invite comments and written documentation from our readers relative to this piece. We have also gotten an opinion from a knowledgeable advanced lamp collector that this may be a shade that was used on a type of Perfume Lamp? Rare! **NPD.**

GILLINDER AND SONS
Philadelphia, Pennsylvania
(1861 – 1905)

This factory started as The Franklin Flint Glass Company in 1861, at Philadelphia, Pennsylvania. After 1867 Gillinder's sons joined the factory and the name was changed to Gillinder and Sons. A second factory located at Greensburg, Pennsylvania, joined the U.S. Glass Co. in 1891, as Factory G. If the reader would like a comprehensive overview of the various Gillender operations we highly recommend *American Pressed Glass & Figure Bottles* by Revi, pages 163 through 165.

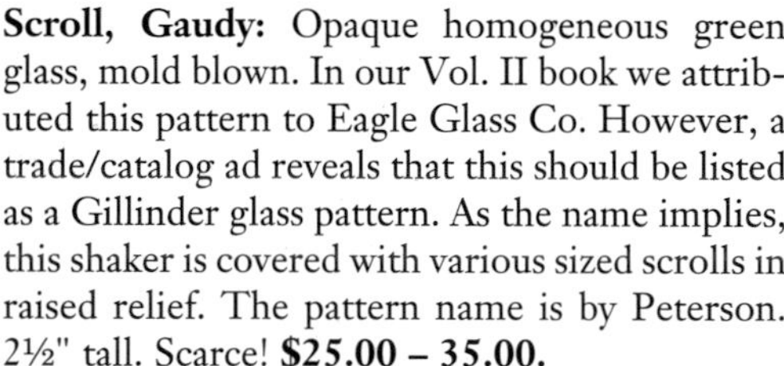

Scroll, Gaudy: Opaque homogeneous green glass, mold blown. In our Vol. II book we attributed this pattern to Eagle Glass Co. However, a trade/catalog ad reveals that this should be listed as a Gillinder glass pattern. As the name implies, this shaker is covered with various sized scrolls in raised relief. The pattern name is by Peterson. 2½" tall. Scarce! **$25.00 – 35.00.**

Coalmer collection

Authors' collection

Authors' collection

Melon, Gillinder: Opaque homogeneous opalware, mold blown. This pattern is illustrated in our Vol. II, p. 92. We are presenting a different version to highlight the special patented celluloid top that was originally used with these shakers; the outside center reads "Pat.FEB.23-04." This was an obvious sales convenience that was supposed to avoid the unpleasant salt corrosion associated with metal perforated tops. Few of these tops survived because their thin celluloid material lacked durability; once cracked they became useless. Each of the six glass lobes contains HP flowers and leaves in red, orange, and blue with green leaves. 2⅝" tall. Circa 1903 – 1905. Rare with original tops! **$75.00 – 90.00.**

GREENSBURG GLASS COMPANY
Greensburg, Pennsylvania
(1890 – 1892)

The factory was formed in 1890 with Julius Proeger as the chief executive officer. The factory ceased operations in 1892 and was reorganized to become the Greensburg Glass Co. Limited which then operated until 1898. It was reopened for production by the National Glass Corporation in 1899.

Krauss collection

Melrose: Ruby stained glass, mold blown and pressed. The ruby stained portion contains an etched floral pattern; the clear lower half has a band of six bevelled diamonds set side by side around the body with fans above and below the points of contact. This pattern originated with the Brilliant Glass Works, Brilliant, Ohio. Circa 1887 – 1888.[1] The pattern was continued after the creation of the new Greenburg Glass Co. at Greensburg, Pennsylvania.[2] 2⅞" tall. Very scarce! **$55.00 – 65.00.**

Rathbun collection

Stanley Condiment Set (aka "Jumbo"): Electric blue and clear mold blown and pressed glass. The principal pattern consists of a glass holder in the form of a three elephant head design to accommodate three condiment pieces. Our illustrated set consists of a blue salt and mustard with a clear pepper. However, these sets were originally produced with all pieces the same color. The set we are illustrating has to be considered incomplete with the pepper in clear glass. These sets were also produced in clear and amber glass. The "Stanley" set is illustrated in an October 28, 1891, issue of *China, Glass & Lamps* as a product of the Greensburg Glass Co., Greensburg, Pennsylvania. 8½" tall to the top of the metal lifting handle, the shakers are 3" tall, mustard 2⅝" tall. Circa 1891. Very rare! **NPD.**

T. G. HAWKES & COMPANY
Corning, New York
(1868 – ?)

Krauss collection

Hawkes, Multiple Ring: Clear amber stained glass, mold blown. As the pattern name indicates, this is a multiple ring pattern in which every other protruding ring is amber stained. Printed on the bottom is the Hawkes signature/trademark. 2¾" tall with a threaded clear glass top. Quality glass. Circa 1940. Very scarce! **$55.00 – 60.00** pair.

HAZEL ATLAS GLASS COMPANY
Washington, Pennsylvania
(1886 – 1956...became part of Continental Can Co.)

White collection

Newport: Opaque white platonite glass, mold formed. Also referred to by collectors as the "Hairpin" pattern. This is a so-called Depression glass pattern consisting of 12 scallops on the footed base. This pattern was also made in pink, amethyst, and cobalt blue. Fully pictured and discussed in the various issues of *Collector's Encyclopedia of Depression Glass* by Gene Florence. Circa 1936 – 1940. 3½" tall x 1⅝" wide; 1⅛" base diameter. **$14.00 – 18.00.**

THE A.H. HEISEY GLASS COMPANY
Newark, Ohio
(1893 – 1957)

First established by Augustus H. Heisey in 1893. Factory production started in 1896. The factory produced high quality glassware. A large proportion of their ware was trademarked by a "Diamond H." Heisey also produced considerable ruby stained items and considerable custard glass. One of their most popular patterns was their "Ivorina Verde" in custard, called "Winged Scroll" when clear glass is involved.

Paneled Cane, Heisey's #315: Clear heavy pressed glass. This shaker has a concave arched vertical plain panel on each of the four sides. The principal motif is two vertical columns of flat topped buttons. Each corner has a shorter arched vertical panel filled with cane. Circa 1900 – 1908.[1] 2⅞" tall x 1¾" wide. **$14.00 – 22.00.**

Lockwood collection

Ridgeleigh, Heisey No. 1469½ (OMN): Clear glass, mold blown. Referred to as "Ridgeleigh Double Cone" to differentiate it from the standard round shaped "Ridgeleigh" shakers.[2] Sometimes it can be found marked with a Diamond H on the bottom; also with a Diamond B (Bryce) who purchased the machine and made some salt shakers in this shape; often in a yellow similar to Heisey's Sahara color. The metal top illustrated was not used by Heisey, but may have been added by a mounting company. There are five perforated holes in the front of the bird for dispensing salt. This pattern was also made by Heisey in clear amber; other colors were made by Bryce. Circa 1935 – 1944. 2½" tall x 2" wide with a 1¼" base diameter. Very scarce! **$15.00 – 25.00.**

White collection

Winged Scroll: Clear emerald green glass, mold blown. The pattern amounts to a small round cylinder containing three large tapering scrolls, equally spaced in raised relief, that are usually decorated by hand-applied gold paint. This is a difficult shaker to acquire in clear green due to its high collectibility factor with today's collectors. Also illustrated is an "Ivorina Verde" custard shaker with HP decoration.[3] Circa 1901 – 1902. 2¾" tall. Both shakers are rare! **$135.00 – 150.00.**

Lockwood collection

Lockwood collection

THE HELMSCHMIED MANUFACTURING CO.
Meriden, Connecticut
(1904 – 1907)

Upon leaving C.F. Monroe, Carl V. Helmschmied formed his own decorating company at Meriden. A major portion of his decorative ware involved his very comprehensive "Bell-Ware" line. In reviewing the Helmschmied factory catalog republished by A.C. Revi,[1] many of his glass forms and decoration techniques employed look identical to products that were also advertised in various C.F. Monroe catalogs.

There is little doubt that various pieces sold in today's antique market place as Monroe factory ware are actually Helmschmied. One of the principal reasons for this occurrence is simply because many of today's collectors/dealers don't realize the amount of decorated glass Carl Helmschmied produced. This was no doubt one of the reasons that many of the Helmschmied items are found with either a "Bell Ware" signature or are embossed with his initials "CVH." For additional details see our Vol. II, page 95.

Rathbun collection

White collection

Cartouche: Opaque opalware glass, mold blown. The shaker shape is in the form of a squatty cylinder. The decoration consists of an allover fired-on background wash except for the front portraying panel. The illustrated pair contains HP red and yellow flowers on green leafed stems against a white background. The single shaker has a pink rose sprig and white background. The aforesaid floral designs are encircled by a series of either green or brown stained scrolls which create a visual framing effect. The use of various color-enclosed scrolling shapes is a principal identifying artistic motif of the "Bell-Ware" line. 2⅝" tall x 1⅝" wide; 1½" base diameter. Circa 1904 – 1907. Rare! **$225.00 – 250.00** pair; **$95.00 – 110.00** single shaker.

Rathbun collection

Scroll, Beaded: Opaque white opalware, mold blown. The main motif consists of three individual HP floral sprigs separated by elaborate beaded scroll panels. This is another unusual scrolling design using yellow and pink staining to create a unique framing effect around the flowers. The shaker form has a large protruding base with small round supports to fit within a condiment holder. This pattern was first documented in our 1976 book on p. 104. 3¼" tall. Circa 1904 – 1907. Very scarce! **$175.00 – 190.00** pair.

Rathbun collection

Krauss collection

Rathbun collection

Slender Neck (Helmschmied's): Opaque opalware, mold blown. The shaker pattern consists of a slender form with a bulging base. The exterior surface is shiny smooth with HP floral sprigs on the base portion. The shaker bottom has a mold embossed signature "CVH" and the written words "Belle Ware" (see our illustration). Circa 1905 – 1907. 3⅜" tall. Rare! **$140.00 – 160.00** single; **$285.00 – 315.00** pair.

HOBBS, BROCKUNIER & COMPANY
Wheeling, West Virginia
(1863 – 1891)

Krauss collection

Barrel, Spangled Glass Variant: Translucent tortoise shell colored spangled glass containing random spaced micro flecks on the inside surface, dual mold blown. This is a very heavily flecked art glass shaker. The motif (but not the color) is similar to the shaker illustrated in our Vol. II, p. 97. This type of ware was the result of experiments by Wm. Leighton Jr. who secured a patent for the process on January 29, 1884. It should also be noted that John Charles Devoy's similar patent for this type of ware was issued to him on July 1, 1884, which he ultimately assigned to the Vasa Murrhina Art Glass Company of Sandwich, Massachusetts.[1] Unfortunately, vast amounts of the Vasa Murrhina-produced spangled ware cracked in the annealing ovens.[2] Extensive research by Barlow & Kaiser has verified that very little finished Vasa Murrhina glass in salable condition was produced at this Cape Cod glass company's site. The vast majority of quality antique spangle glass found by collectors in the United States was produced by Hobbs, Brockunier & Co.[3] As a result of their process problems, by late 1883, the financial condition of Vasa Murrhina became unstable and production ceased in late 1884. Our illustrated Hobbs shaker is circa 1884 – 1889. 3⅛" tall with a two-piece metal top. Rare! **$350.00 – 400.00.**

Ridgway collection

Bulbous Base, Opalescent: Translucent opalescent frosted glass, dual mold blown. The shaker has a bulged out base with a small creased ring just above the base bulge. It is an unusual motif having white opalescent random scrolling on the inside surface. 3" tall with a two-piece metal top. Circa 1887 – 1891. No doubt produced in other opalescent colors. Rare in this color! **$85.00 – 100.00.**

Rathbun collection

Bulbous Base Variant: Clear crystal glass with intaglio amber stained vertical ribs, dual mold blown to produce an optic ribbing effect. The overall physical shape is similar to the "Bulbous Base" shaker shown in our Vol. II on page 97. Circa 1889 – 1891. 2⅞" tall. Very scarce! **$65.00 – 85.00.**

Lockwood collection

Hobb's Block: Frosted amber stained glass, mold blown. A busy pattern with six vertical sections composed of alternating portions of plain and beveled star squares. Pattern name from Kamm 3, page 95.[4] Also produced in clear. Circa 1890. 3" tall x 1½" wide. Very scarce. **$65.00 – 80.00.**

Bacon collection

Honeycomb, Rubina Opalescent: Translucent Rubina opalescent glass, dual mold blown. The exterior is smooth with the inside containing a continuous honeycomb pattern. This ware was produced by utilizing the smaller Hobbs Wheeling Peachblow shaker molds. The upper two thirds have inside cranberry staining with the remaining portion having a white opalescence. 2⅝" tall with matching two-piece metal tops. Circa 1886 – 1888. Rare! **$325.00 – 350.00** pair.

Rathbun collection

Leaf and Flower: Amber stained clear and frosted glass (one of each type), mold blown and pressed. The principal motif consists of intaglio flowers and leaves; the flower pattern on the frosted shaker is different from the one on the unfrosted. There is also an intaglio flower on the bottom of each. The center has raised scallops that are present on both the clear and frosted pieces. The pattern name was created by Ruth Webb Lee. Heacock attributes this ware to Hobbs, Brockunier in his Book III, page 30. Circa 1888 – 1892. A. G. Peterson illustrates this shaker type on page 164 of his 1970 salt shaker book and indicates that the shaker is rare! 2⅝" tall. **$190.00 – 215.00** pair.

Krauss collection

Mario: Clear amber stained glass, mold blown. The upper portion of this cylinder shaped shaker is amber stained, the lower part is clear. Production of this pattern continued after Hobbs became U.S. Glass, Factory H. Also produced in clear and ruby-stained. An etched version of this shaker is illustrated in our Vol. II, page 192. Circa 1890 – 1895.[5] 2⅝" tall. Rare! **$75.00 – 90.00**

Rathbun collection

Pillar, Sixteen: Cranberry opalescent (somewhat translucent) glass, dual mold blown. The principal motif consists of 16 embossed vertical ribs in the form of a pillar shape containing an overall white lattice that forms a diamond pattern. Pattern name by Peterson. Being illustrated to disclose the existence of two sizes, 2⅞" tall with a 1⅝" diameter, and 3⅜" tall with a 1½" diameter. Both produced by Hobbs, Brockunier & Co. Circa 1885 – 1890. Also produced in blue, white, and cranberry spatter opalescent colors. However, the reader should refer to our opening presentation of the Harry Northwood glass section of this book regarding an attribution controversary involving this pattern. The illustrated shakers are very scarce! **$130.00 – 150.00** per single in either size.

Rathbun collection

Ring Neck Variant: Clear blue opalescent swirls, dual mold blown to create the inside raised optic swirls over which the opalescent striping is present. A similar shaped shaker is shown on page 99 of our Vol. II in a spangled glass motif that was produced by Hobbs, Brockunier & Co., Wheeling, West Virginia. This shaker is 3" tall. Circa 1887 – 1890. Very scarce! **$75.00 – 90.00.**

Lockwood collection

Satina Swirl: Translucent frosted vaseline glass, dual mold blown. A fairly tall shaker containing swirls from top to bottom. It is interesting to note that the direction of the swirls in our illustrated shaker are swirled in the opposite direction from that shown on various forms pictured in the Hobbs factory catalog.[6] Circa 1885 – 1890. 3½" tall x 1⅝" wide. Very scarce! **$170.00 – 190.00.**

Rathbun collection

Rathbun collection

Seaweed, Opalescent: Translucent white and blue opalescent glass shakers, mold blown. The pattern name indicates the motif formed by the white opalescent Rococo colored placement on these bulbous base shakers. Circa 1890 – 1891. There was production of some other forms by Beaumont Glass Co., circa 1900.[7] Shakers were also produced in cranberry opalescent. 3" tall. Very scarce! White, **$70.00 – 85.00;** blue, **$120.00 – 140.00.**

Krauss collection

Krauss collection

Spangled Glass, Hobbs' (cruet set): Opaque pink cased spangled glass with silver embedded mica flakes, dual mold blown. The manufacturing process for producing this type of art glass is described on page 198 of *Nineteenth Century Glass* written by A.C. Revi. There is no external HP decoration on any of this set's pieces which consists of salt, pepper, mustard, and a frosted crystal handled cruet with a clear crystal, faceted stopper. The stopper appears to be original, since it meets the descriptive criteria outlined on page 6 of Heacock's Book 6 relative to the types of cruet stoppers used by Hobbs, Brockunier (we have provided two illustrations). Circa 1881 – 1891. The shakers are 3⅝" tall with two-piece metal tops; mustard is 2¾" tall; the cruet is 4⅛"tall to the top of the pouring spout with stopper removed. Circa 1885 – 1891. The highly ornate silver-plated condiment holder was produced by the Meriden B. Co., Meriden, Connecticut, which became part of the International Silver Co. during 1898. Rare as a complete set! **$950.00 – 975.00**

Rathbun collection

Stripe, Hobbs' Wide: Clear cranberry opalescent glass, dual mold blown, with 12 vertical opalescent stripes; the top of the shaker contains a large raised neck ring. Considered to be a variant of the Opal Ribbon, Vertical that is illustrated in our Vol. II page 98. Circa 1888 – 1891. 2¾" tall. Very scarce! **$140.00 – 155.00.**

Krauss collection

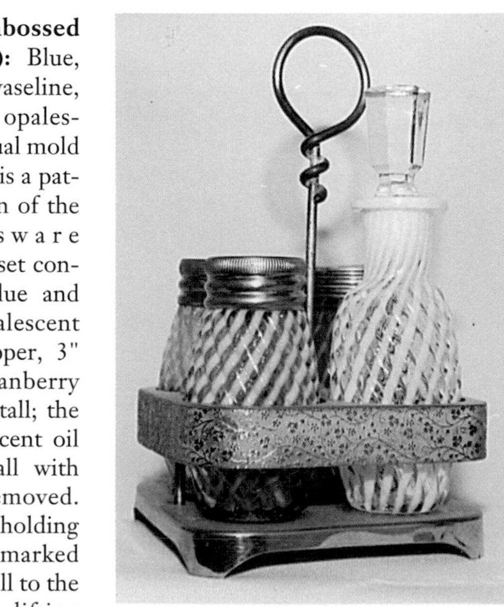

Swirl, Embossed (condiment): Blue, cranberry, vaseline, and white opalescent glass, dual mold blown. This is a pattern variation of the "Francesware Swirl." The set consists of a blue and vaseline opalescent salt and pepper, 3" tall; the cranberry mustard, 3" tall; the white opalescent oil bottle, 4" tall with stopper removed. The metal holding stand is unmarked and is 6½" tall to the top of the lifting handle. Circa 1889 – 1891. Rare as a complete set! The vaseline shaker has a ¾" length crack extending downward from the top so, current retail value **$130.00 – 160.00** set.

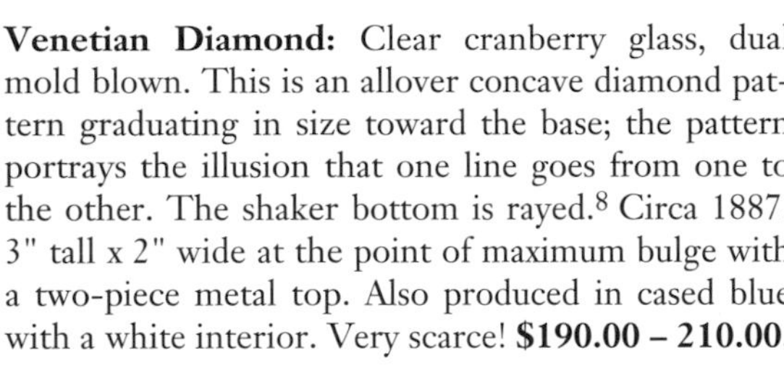

Venetian Diamond: Clear cranberry glass, dual mold blown. This is an allover concave diamond pattern graduating in size toward the base; the pattern portrays the illusion that one line goes from one to the other. The shaker bottom is rayed.[8] Circa 1887. 3" tall x 2" wide at the point of maximum bulge with a two-piece metal top. Also produced in cased blue with a white interior. Very scarce! **$190.00 – 210.00.**

Lockwood collection

THE IMPERIAL GLASS COMPANY
Bellaire, Ohio
(1904 – 1984)

Factory glass production began during January 1904. Formed by Mr. Edward Muhleman, this glasshouse ultimately became an unprofitable operation and closure took place in 1984. During the many years of operation, the factory produced quality art and pattern glassware and did considerable private mold work for L.G. Wright. Additional detail is provided in our Vol. II salt shaker book.

Authors' collection

Dewdrop Opalescent: Clear opalescent vaseline glass, mold blown and pressed. A heavy, short bulbous shaker with opalescent round hobnails in high raised relief; called "Dewdrops" in the Imperial Glass catalog. Gives off a strong illumination when exposed to UV black light radiation. The bottom supporting foot is embossed with the Imperial IG trademark. Circa 1965 – 1969. 2¾" tall. Scarce! **$20.00 – 30.00.**

Lockwood collection

Imperial's #68: Translucent ruby stained glass, mold blown. A bulb shape shaker with a band of vertical concave ribs that encircles the lower half inch of the base perimeter; has a narrow gilded line around the neck. The plain smooth surface of this shaker contains souvenir lettering marked "Bradford, Pa." Circa 1915.[1] 3¼" tall x 2¼" wide with a partially oxidized metal top in need of replacement. Scarce! **$18.00 – 25.00.**

Authors' collection

Soda Gold: Translucent carnival glass, mold blown. The carnival glass collectors refer to our illustrated color as "smoke." The shakers are most difficult to collect; over the years we have seen very few. The advanced carnival collectors have convinced us that we were way-off in our estimated time of first production[2] so we are revising it to circa 1927 – 1931. 3" tall. Rare! **$85.00 – 100.00.**

INDIANA TUMBLER & GOBLET COMPANY
Greentown, Indiana
(1894 – 1903)

Began operations in June 1894 with D.C. Jenkins Jr. as president. This factory was always a profitable one. In 1899 it joined the National Glass Co. and subsequently became well known for the production of both holly amber (golden agate) and chocolate glass; both due to the innovation and design guidance of Jacob Rosenthal. Unfortunately the factory was destroyed by fire in 1903 and never rebuilt.

Harris collection

Dewey: Opaque "Nile green" glass, mold blown and pressed. Created to commemorate Admiral Dewey. This is an embossed shaker containing medallions near the base and on each peaked-scalloped foot. 2⅞" tall. Very difficult to obtain in this color...more-so than in chocolate glass. Circa 1900 – 1901. Rare in this color! **$625.00 – 700.00.**

Rathbun collection

Krauss collection

Pleat Band (aka "Panel, Ten"): Clear blue, amber, and chocolate glass, mold blown and pressed. A tapered shaker containing ten vertical panels with a footed base that contains an encircling series of intaglio ribs on the underside. Circa 1898.[1] 3⅛" tall. Very scarce! Also illustrated is a rare chocolate glass shaker. Blue and amber pair, **$90.00 - 110.00;** chocolate glass single, **$850.00 – 900.00.**

Neale collection

Teardrop & Tassle: Opaque homogeneous "Nile green" glass, mold blown and pressed. The pattern name is a good general description of this embossed shaker. In the last two decades we have only seen one of these shakers for sale in the Nile green color. Circa 1900.[2] 2⅞" tall x 1⅝" wide. Rare in this color! **$500.00 – 550.00.**

THE JEFFERSON GLASS COMPANY
Steubenville, Ohio
(1901 – 1907)
Follansbee, West Virginia
(1907 – 1920s)

Established in 1901 at Steubenville, Ohio, and relocated at Follansbee, West Virginia, in 1907. The factory produced a considerable quantity of custard glass as well as pressed and blown ware including opalescent patterns in stripes, polka dots, and floral designs. The factory ceased operations and went out of business sometime in the 1920s.

Krauss collection

Bead and Panel: Clear green opalescent glass, mold blown. The pattern consists of six plain panels that are established by six vertical rows of beads in raised relief. The base and some of the larger beads are opalescent. This is a very difficult color for a collector to acquire. Consists of heavy quality glass that has been finished off by fire polishing. Circa 1901 – 1903. 3" tall; the top in the illustration is contemporary (not the proper type).[1] Rare in this color! **$85.00 – 100.00.**

Rathbun collection

Idyll (Jefferson #251): Clear blue glass, mold blown. With a curved body, the shaker design has a series of scrolls and dots for a total of four pattern repeats around the circumference. The scrolls are gold decorated. Circa 1907. 3" tall. Produced in many forms and colors.[2] Rare! **$285.00 – 300.00** pair.

Krauss collection

Jefferson Optic (cruet set): Clear amethyst glass, mold blown. This illustrates the physical configuration of a complete cruet set with the special designed tray containing recessed circular cut-ins for retaining the salt, pepper, and cruet. Circa 1910 – 1912. Salt and pepper, 2⅞" tall; cruet, 5¾" tall to the top of the spout; tray, 6" long and has bottom hobnails for support/rigidity. Rare in a complete set! **$480.00 – 520.00** set.

Coalmer collection

Harris collection

Jefferson Optic: Clear electric blue, mold blown. A clear shaker with HP floral sprigs. The bottoms have been configured for use with a companion condiment set base. 2⅞" tall. Circa 1905 – 1910. Rare in this color with decoration! We have also included a very scarce opaque custard souvenir example containing a string of wall-eyed pike fish. Other versions of this shaker pattern are illustrated in our Vol. II, p. 107. **$190.00 – 220.00** pair; souvenir fish, **$45.00 – 65.00.**

Rathbun collection

Krauss collection

Ribbed Drape (aka Jefferson #2501): Opaque pale yellow custard glass, mold blown. The motif consists of embossed fine vertical ribbing graduating in length around the base. 3¼" tall x 2" wide. The configuration displays a drape effect as a result of being outlined in gold. The shaker body has HP rose floral decoration. This is a rare shaker produced by the Jefferson Glass Co. Circa 1904 (see H4, fig. 319). Also, known production in clear glass with gold trim. **$485.00 – 500.00** pair; **$195.00 – 215.00** single.

Lockwood collection

Swag with Brackets, Variant: Two known versions of this pattern are shown. The first is translucent opalescent green with protruding brackets that are synonymous with other forms of this Jefferson pattern. The second is clear amethyst with gold decoration on the swags and leaf forms at the bottom corners. Its brackets are rosettes which do not protrude, but are embossed the same as the swags. When our book Vol. II was published we were not aware of the aforementioned variation in the salt shakers. 3" tall. Circa 1904. Rare! **$175.00 – 200.00** pair.

KANAWHA GLASS COMPANY
Dunbar, West Virginia
(1955 – 1988)

Founded by D.P. Merrit and began by producing cut/etched crystal and milk glass lighting fixtures. Colored glass was introduced circa 1960. They produced various novelty forms in colored crackled ware. In our Vol. II, p. 109 we featured a clear amberina shaker in this type of ware. In 1988 the factory was sold to the Raymond Dereume Glass Co. of Punxsutawney, Pennsylvania, along with the right to continue use of the Kanawha tradename.

Authors' collection

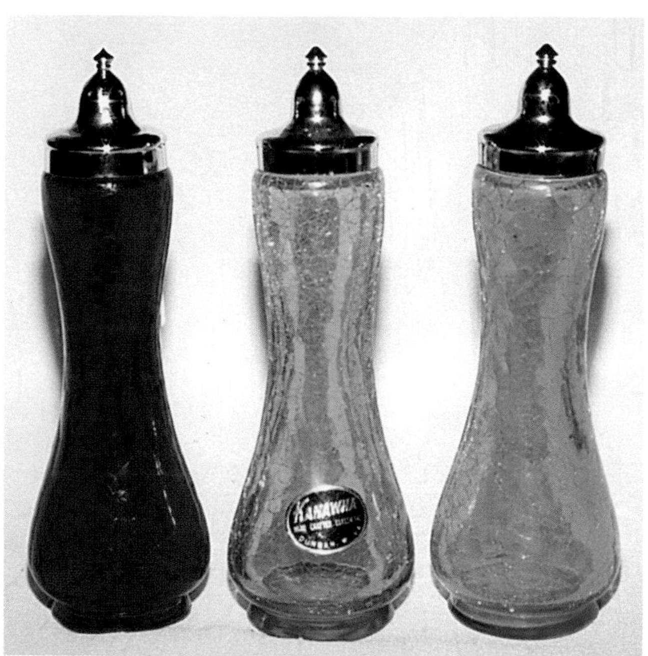

Crackle, Bulbous Base: Clear ruby, amber, and green mold blown glass with a crackle motif. These are tall shakers that have smooth, undecorated exteriors. With the publication of these additional colors we have established that this ware was produced in a family of colors. The glass quality is excellent. A Kanawha paper label is present on the amber shaker. Circa 1965. 5⅝" tall with original tops. Scarce! **\$20.00 – 30.00** each.

THE KOKOMO GLASS COMPANY
Kokomo, Indiana
(1900 – 1905)
D.C. JENKINS GLASS COMPANY
(1906 – 1932)

The Kokomo Glass Co. was built by D.C. Jenkins in 1900. The factory burned down in 1905. It was reopened in 1906 as the D.C. Jenkins Glass Company.

Lockwood collection

Gibson Girl: Opaque white molded porcelain. This same shaker has been seen by us in white opalware with identical HP decoration. The Gibson Girl became popular as the result of sketches that appeared in *Life* magazine from 1899 to 1905.[1] Her HP adornment consists of a high pompadour with velvet bow at the top and on the shoulder. Circa 1904. This shaker has a cylindrical shape with a slight ring neck that has a gold stripe. 3⅜" tall. The illustrated top is not original. Very scarce! **\$50.00 – 65.00.**

W.L. LIBBEY AND SONS COMPANY
Toledo, Ohio
(1888 – 1892)
LIBBEY GLASS COMPANY
(1892 – Present)

This glass factory represents a continuation of the New England Glass company after it was moved from Cambridge, Massachusetts, to Toledo, Ohio, and changed its name to W.L. Libbey & Sons Company. During 1892 the board of directors changed the corporate name to the Libbey Glass Company and the factory remained at Toledo. A detailed and more chronological history of both factories are delineated in our Vol. II, pages 111 and 157.

Authors' collection

Maize, Libbey Iridescent: Translucent iridescent glass, mold blown. The principal motif consists of embossed small kernels of corn. Since our illustration of the four-piece Maize condiment set that was design patented by Joseph Locke shown in our Vol. II, p. 111, we have verified that an identical set was also produced in clear crystal that has been treated (while the glass was still hot) with an appropriate chloride spray so that each individual piece radiates a white iridescent coloration that causes the condiment dispensers to appear somewhat translucent. Our research has been unable to establish in what time frame that this type of iridescent/white carnival ware was produced. It has been clearly established that the opaque white and pale yellow Maize condiment sets were produced during the 1888 – 1890 time period at both the New England and Libbey Glass factories.[1] As we have stipulated elsewhere in this book, "There is ample evidence that at least experimental pieces of carnival glass (doped ware) was made by various glass factories prior to the 1907 date that generally credits the Fenton Art Glass Company with the carnival glass innovation.[2] Our illustrated pieces (salt, pepper, and mustard) were acquired at an estate auction during 1994. We have also viewed and handled a complete iridescent Maize condiment set that was offered for sale at a Harrisburg, Pennsylvania, antique show during the spring of 1995. However, we did not purchase it because the set contained too much chipping damage and the asking price was $900.00. The salt and pepper are 3¾" tall; mustard, 2¾" tall. Our illustrated three pieces are rare! A complete condiment set is very rare! Current retail values could not be established since no value base line exists in the antique glassware market place. **NPD.**

LOETZ WITWE, KLOSTERMUHLE
Austria

During their Art Nouveau prime, Loetz of Austria was primarily known for their iridescent glass which is contemporary with Tiffany's similar lustered art glass. Loetz also produced some outstanding pieces of cameo glass during this same period.

Krauss collection

Loetz, Double Bulged: Blue iridescent art glass within silver overlay, free blown finished glass. This is high-quality glass of the Art Nouveau period. The Loetz glass factory operated in the western part of Austria known as the Bohemian Woods. Formerly known as Lotz' Witwe, Klostermuhle (Loetz of Austria). Our illustrations reveal special noteworthy dark blue iridescent glass with splashes of silver-blue iridescent overlaying the darker color. A clear view of the aforesaid coloration was revealed by our examination of the bottom ground/fire polished pontil area. Photography was very difficult due to highlight reflections from the silver overlay. We could find no Loetz signature on these salt and pepper shakers. However, when a signature is present on a piece, it will be identified as "Loetz," "Loetz-Austria," or "Austria" with a pair of crossed arrows in a circle. The salt and pepper and mustard physical motif consists of double-bulged iridescent art glass beneath elaborate, hand-engraved silver overlay containing flowers, leaves, and vines.[1] Loetz only produced salt and pepper shakers by way of special customer orders. It was interesting to discover the fact that one shaker weighed in at 5 oz. and the other weighed 4 oz; a specific result of the difference in each metal (glass) gather blown and used by the factory gaffer to produce the pair. There was no florescence under long wave black light (UV) exposure. The two-piece tops are of a special design; containing slit-like openings for dispensing the condiments. The tops are of a pressure-fit design configuration with a metal collar (bezel) cemented onto the glass to which the tops press fit (adhere tightly) onto each bezel. 3" tall. Very rare! **NPD.**

Krauss collection

Loetz Condiment Trio: Blue iridescent art glass encased in silver overlay. The trio consists of a pepper, open salt, and double bulging mustard. The set was a special purchase since each piece contains the same (difficult to read) engraved initials in fancy block lettering. All the two-piece silver tops are of the press fitting type. The dimensions of each are mustard, 2⅞", tall; 2½" diam. bottom bulge, 2¼" diam. top bulge; open salt, 1⅛" tall, 2⅛" diam. base bulge, 1¼" diam. top opening; pepper, 2⅞" tall, 2⅛" diam. single base bulge. This set is from the Art Nouveau era. Very rare! **NPD.**

McKEE GLASS CO.
Jeannette, Pennsylvania
(1899 – 1904 as part of National Glass Co.)

Things get a little confusing in terms of a company name after the National Glass conglomerate lost/relinquished control during 1904. As a result, many of National's larger glass factories were leased to their various managers and were operated as independent factories. The McKee factory became the McKee Jeannette Glass Co. with its former manager A.J. Smith as president. By 1908 the factory was again incorporated as the McKee Glass Co., an independent that was no longer under the influence of National Glass.

Authors' collection

Champion (aka "Fan with Cross Bars"): Clear with ruby stained crossbars, mold blown. Some collectors consider this to be a variation of the "Diamond and Sunburst" pattern. The pattern consists of a series of inverted Gothic arches; each arch has convexed bars with diamonds at the crossings. Heacock reported that this pattern was purchased by Beaumont Glass who then decorated it and sold it as their own product. First made by McKee circa 1894, it appeared in their catalog as late as 1917. 2⅞" tall. Very scarce! **$65.00 – 75.00.**

Krauss collection

Doric: Clear green homogeneous glass, mold blown and pressed. According to Kamm[1] this is a variant of the "Feather" pattern and was produced by McKee & Bros. while they were still located at Pittsburgh, circa 1896. The upper part of this shaker is evenly scalloped with the panels being swirled. 2½" tall. Very scarce! **$32.00 – 40.00.**

Harris collection

Eureka Variant (National's): Clear ruby stained glass, mold blown and pressed. This basic pattern is illustrated in our Vol. II, p. 114. However this shaker, a more bulbous, flared-out version, was produced by National with the same basic embossed pattern and ruby stained design application. Circa 1901 – 1904. 2¾" tall. Rare! **$60.00 – 75.00.**

Rathbun collection

Geneva: Opaque chocolate (carmel) glass, mold blown. Produced by McKee while under control of National Glass. The pattern amounts to three embossed shell panels symmetrically spaced around the shaker body. Just below the neck are three intricate scrolls. Not a hard pattern to find except in the case of chocolate glass which is very rare! Circa 1902 – 1903. Also produced in clear green and custard.[2] 3" tall. **$950.00 – 1,000.00** pair.

Harris collection

Gothic, McKee's (aka "Spearpoint Band"): Clear ruby stained glass, mold blown. A cylindrical-shaped column containing nine spear points around the lower part of the shaker in raised relief. The base contains an intaglio rayed star. Also produced in clear glass. Circa 1904 – 1905.[3] 3⅛" tall. Very scarce! **$50.00 – 60.00.**

White collection

McKee's 401: Opaque opalware glass, mold blown. The central part of this shaker consists of an embossed scroll type pattern with a tied-on ribbon.[4] The base has 24 ribs containing one pinhead bump on each rib. The scrolls have a partial rust color; probably because most of the paint has worn off. Circa 1904 – 1910. 2⅞" tall x 2⅝" at widest point; base is 1¾". Scarce! **$5.00 – 10.00.**

Lockwood collection

McKee's #550: Translucent ruby stained glass, mold blown. A four-sided, paneled, bulging shaker with protruding ribs separating arched panels. Embossed fans are present at the top of each arch; an embossed shell motif is at the base of each panel.[5] Circa 1904 – 1908. 3½" tall x 2¼" wide. Also produced in clear glass. Scarce! **$50.00 – 65.00.**

Lockwood collection

Paneled Hexagons: Clear apple green glass, mold blown and pressed. A straight-sided cylinder with a ring at the neck and base. Has nine vertical panels, each containing three six-sided flat top buttons in a diamond.[6] The bottom is rayed. Circa 1886. 2¾" tall x 1½" wide with 1½" base. Also made in clear and vaseline. Scarce! **$20.00 – 28.00.**

Authors' collection

Paneled Icicle: Clear blue glass, mold blown. This is a four flat paneled shaker with thin narrow verticle ribbing that is reminiscent of icicles. This pattern is similar to the McKee "Appolo" and "Vulcan" patterns; it is one of several Colonial types that were produced by McKee circa 1900 – 1910. 3¼" tall. Very scarce! **$30.00 – 40.00.**

Battertons collection

Scroll, McKee No. 402: Clear glass, mold blown. This is a low bodied, three mold, bulging based shaker with neck scrolling. The principal body design has a series of scrolls with three horizontal lines inside that connects each scroll pair. This shaker pattern is listed in a McKee catalog among miscellaneous salts and peppers.[7] Circa 1904 – 1910. 2" tall x 3" wide. Scarce! Our apologies for the AAGSSCS furnished picture! **$12.00 – 17.00.**

Sultan (aka "Wild Rose with Scrolling"): Opaque opalware glass, mold blown. The principal motif is a five-petaled rose nestling within rosette foliage. Different catalogs from this glasshouse indicate that certain patterns (such as this one) would often be reissued and appear in McKee catalogs during various time frames; sometimes in additional added forms.[8] Our illustrated shaker has been hand painted in pink, yellow, green, and gray. Unfortunately the ravages of kitchen washings have resulted in worn and faded decoration causing the pattern detail, seen by the camera, to be somewhat obscured. We are unaware of these shakers having been produced in other colors. This pattern was first recorded by Kamm, but the factory of origin was not identified.[9] While other forms of this pattern were produced as late as 1925, this shaker appears to be circa 1905 – 1910. 4¼" tall. Very scarce! **$25.00 – 30.00** due to worn decoration.

Musgrave collection

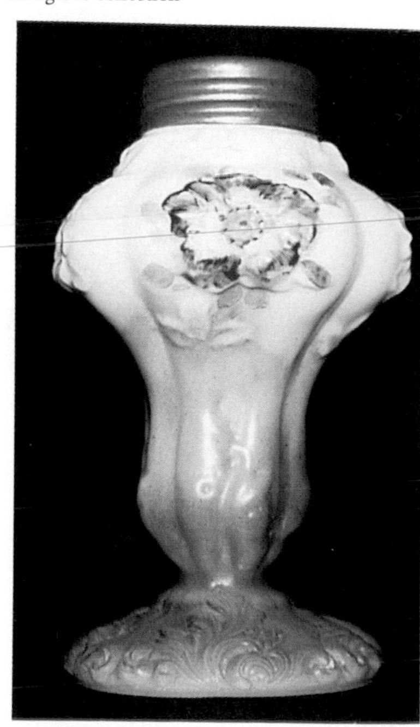

MODEL FLINT GLASS CO.
Albany, Indiana
(1893 – 1903)

Authors' collection

Collared Reverse Swirl (aka "Reverse Swirl")[1]: Translucent opalescent vaseline glass, mold blown. Very similar to "Reverse Swirl" and "Chrysanthemum Swirl." According to Heacock[2] this is the third pattern made under a patent held by John F. Miller who managed this Albany factory. Mr. Miller earlier managed the Buckeye factory. Unfortunately, our illustrated shaker contains an improper top that obscures a portion of the protruding top collar. When exposed to ultraviolet black light, this shaker radiates a very high yellow illumination. Pattern name is by Heacock. Circa 1900 – 1902. 3" tall. Rare! **$190.00 – 215.00.**

Krauss collection

Collared Reverse Swirl, Variant: Translucent pale blue opalescent glass, mold blown. This is an ornate shaker containing 15 reverse swirls in raised relief which provide an artistic motif. Produced by Model Flint Glass Co., Albany, Indiana, circa 1893 – 1899. 3⅛" tall; 2" wide; 1⅜" base dia. Very scarce! **$100.00 – 115.00.**

C. F. MONROE
Meriden, Connecticut
(1892 – 1916)

This factory was an elaborate opalware (milk glass) decorating firm that obtained its ware in the form of glass blanks that were supplied by various American and European glass manufactures. Mt. Washington/ Pairpoint was certainly a principal supplier as many of the glass forms that they manufactured appear in some of the Monroe catalogs containing various Monroe hand-painted and transfer-type motifs. Likewise Dithridge and Co. had on-going supplier contracts with the Monroe factory.

The three principal decorative categories used were "Wave Crest," "Nakara," and "Kelva." Monroe's most outstanding designer decorator was Carl V. Helmschmeid who withdrew from the factory in 1903 to open his own decorating business. While Monroe sold decorated and cut clear glass forms, it is not considered to be a major portion of their business; it certainly is not predominate in their factory catalogs and seems to lack a high collectibility factor in the antique glassware market place.

Collectors have become cognizant of a painted decorative transfer technique used by Monroe beginning around 1898. This chromolithograph (transfer) process was used to cut factory production costs thus making them more competitive in the market place. To tell the difference between transfer and hand-painted work, examine the decoration closely using 10 power magnification. If the decoration or picture is made up of many tiny dots, it is a transfer. The use of chromolithograph decorating was employed by many American glasshouses commencing in the 1890s for similar reasons.

Krauss collection

Bulging Stopper, Wave Crest: Opaque opalware glass, mold blown. As the pattern name indicates, this is a small shaker whose shape is reminiscent of a glass stopper. The exterior surface has been satinized and contains a transfer decorated hunting dog walking among a field of undergrowth. The background has a pale blue color. 2" tall. Circa 1899 – 1904. Rare! **$210.00 – 235.00.**

Rathbun collection

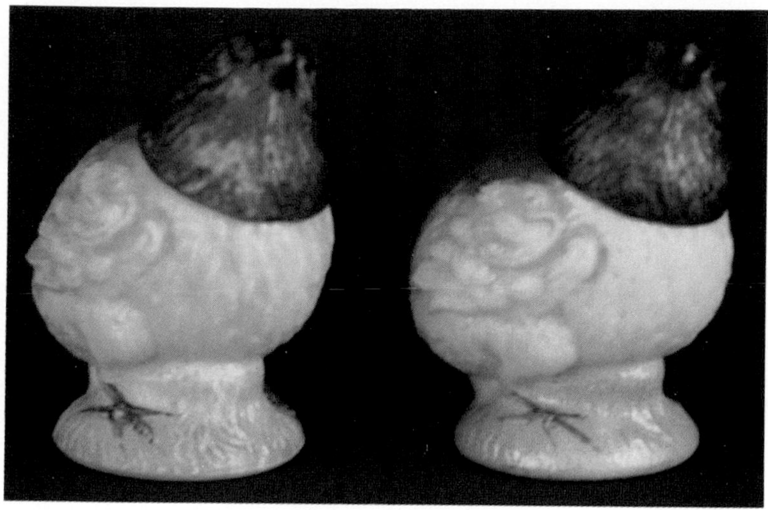

Chick on Pedestal: Opaque pale yellow and brown shading with a light green painted pedestal over white milk glass, mold blown. The shakers contain a special metal chick head (screw-on) type metal top.[1] A matched pair is illustrated. We want collectors and dealers to be aware that these shakers are being reproduced in undecorated white opalware; no doubt due to the rarity and the high collectibility factor associated with this ware. So beware of undecorated milk glass shakers; the tops are not interchangeable with old authentic shakers; ask any seller for certification of authenticity and right of return in writing. The illustrated pair are circa 1903. Very rare as a matched pair! **$1,050.00 – 1,100.00** pair.

Coalmer collection

Creased Neck, Special Threaded: Opaque opalware glass, mold blown with pink HP apple blossoms and associated brown stemmed and green leaves. This version of the Creased Neck shaker contains extensive top threading and therefore uses a special single piece metal top. This matched pair is "Wave Crest" decorated and is illustrated on page 88 of Monroe catalog No. 65 dated 1900 – 1901. 3⅝" tall. Circa 1900. The basic opalware blanks were no doubt produced by Mt. Washington/Pairpoint and purchased by C.F. Monroe for subsequent "Wave Crest" decoration. Rare! **$375.00 – 400.00** pair.

Bette Howard collection

Creased Neck, Matching Floral: Opaque opalware glass, mold blown with a tall matching HP pink flowered motif. Another one of the various "Wave Crest" decorated shakers shown in the C.F. Monroe catalogs in this basic opalware form. 2⅞" tall. Circa 1894 – 1898. Very scarce as a matched pair! **$190.00 – 215.00** pair.

Bette Howard collection

Creased Neck, Expanded (condiment): Opaque satin finished opalware, mold blown. The physical parameters of these shakers have a larger circumference than the normal "Creased Neck" shaker; hence, the reason for the term "expanded." As the picture shows, the transfer-type floral decoration is in excellent condition. The very ornate silver-plated holder is 6⅜" tall to the top of the center lifting handle and contains no silver manufacturer marking; overall width (as illustrated) is 5¾". This is an outstanding example of C.F.Monroe "Wave Crest" ware. Circa 1898 – 1902. 3¼" tall. Rare as a complete set! **$950.00 – 1,100.00** set.

Lockwood collection

Creased Neck, Short: Opaque white opalware, mold blown. A short round pillar-shaped version of the "Creased Neck" pattern. Shown are "Wave Crest" shakers containing a transfer process decorated kitty standing below a large spider web. This design is shown in the 1900 – 1901 C.F. Monroe catalog No. 6, on page 89, motif No. 79-DD that was published by Elsa Grimmer. 2¾" tall. Circa 1900 – 1903. Rare! **$200.00 – 220.00** pair.

Neale collection

Cube, Shortened Kelva: Opaque white "Kelva" decorated opalware, mold blown. This shaker is the same physical cube type shown in our Vol. II, p. 119. However, this is a "Kelva" decorated shaker portraying an apple blossom flower surrounded by green foliage. 2½" tall; 1¼" wide. Circa 1897 – 1902. Rare! **$110.00 – 125.00.**

Bruce collection

Elongated Bulb Variant: Opaque "Wave Crest" opalware glass, mold blown. A tall bulbous-shaped shaker containing pink and brown floral transfer type decoration. This is a variation of the shaker illustrated in our Vol. II, p. 120. The base of this shaker is more flared and slightly shorter. Circa 1901 – 1904. 3⅛" tall x 2⅛" wide. Very scarce! **$78.00 – 90.00.**

Bruce collection

Monroe #79: Opaque satin-finished "Wave Crest" opalware glass, mold blown. A cylindrical-shaped shaker containing HP floral sprays. This condiment dispenser is listed in an 1895 – 1896 Monroe catalog as their #79 shaker pattern.[2] Circa 1895 – 1901. 3⅝" tall with a two-piece metal top. Very scarce! **$165.00 – 180.00.**

White collection

Nakara: Opaque C. F. Monroe "Nakara" glass, mold blown. This is a short smooth surfaced shaker that widens into a bulging base. The motif consists of HP enameled daisy flowers upon a light brown stained background. Circa 1898 – 1902. 2⅜" tall x 1⅞" wide; 1⅝" base diameter. Rare! **$160.00 – 175.00.**

Krauss collection

Panel, Tapered (condiment): Opaque C.F. Monroe "Wave Crest" opalware, mold blown. The pattern consists of six bulbous vertical ribbed panels with ring neck and ring footed base. Each shaker has a HP pink and green floral spray encircling the center panels. The decoration has been applied over a pale blue background. The ornate silver-plated holder is unmarked. Each shaker is 2⅞" tall. Circa 1898 – 1903. A single shaker is illustrated in our Vol. II, p. 122. Rare as a set! **$650.00 – 700.00** set.

Neale collection & Krauss collection

Parker Non-corrosive Salt: Opaque "Wave Crest" opalware, mold blown. This is a bulging shaker containing 16 smooth vertical ribs in raised relief. The transparent clear version of this salt is identical except that the vertical ribs have small cuts or slots that have been molded in. Patented July 4, 1899, Monroe produced three physical versions of this shaker.[3] The opaque "Wave Crest" illustrated version contains HP apple blossoms. Salt is loaded in the shakers by removal of a screwed-on metal bottom thus allowing the salt to be dispensed through a perforated glass top and avoiding the salt against metal corrosion action. Monroe claimed to have the sole patent rights to manufacture and decorate this ware. Circa 1899. 2½" tall; 1¾" wide. Rare! **$325.00 – 350.00;** clear transparent, **$125.00 – 140.00.**

Krauss collection

Scroll & Leaf, Hexagon: Opaque off-white "Wave Crest" opalware, mold blown. This is a hexagon-shaped shaker containing embossed scrolls primarily in the shaker's lower half section. First illustrated (but not attributed) in our 1976 book on p. 106. Subsequently shown in *Wavecrest, The Glass of C.F. Monroe* by Wilfred Cohen. Three of the six vertical panels contain HP floral decoration. 3" tall. Circa 1898 – 1904. Very scarce! **$165.00 – 190.00.**

Scroll, Wave Variant: Opaque "Nakara" decorated opalware, mold blown. This is a bulbous tapered shaker that contains a dense complicated scrolled base in raised relief. The main body has specific formed scrolling designed to surround and cause a smooth surface to stand out so that it can be used for various types of HP or transfer colored scenes. This ware is usually found with "Wave Crest" decoration. Our illustrated shaker contains a dark olive drab paint surrounding a pink, white, and light green floral spray scene. This basic pattern form is shown in a C. F. Monroe 1901 catalog supplement.[4] 3⅝" tall. Circa 1901. Very scarce. **$155.00 – 175.00.**

Neale collection

White collection

Simplicity: Opaque "Wave Crest" opalware glass, mold blown. A slim expanded simplistic type shaker. With the exception of a small blue stained neck ring, the motif amounts to a violet and green colored floral spray. Circa 1896 – 1900. Known to have been produced in various floral decorations.[7] 2½" tall x 1⅝" wide; 1⅛" base diameter. Very scarce! **$125.00 – 140.00.**

Shasta Daisy, Single & Double: Opaque "Wave Crest" opalware, mold blown. When A.G. Peterson named this ware[5] he stated there are two types; we are illustrating both a top view and side view of this ware. The shaker on the left is the "Single Shasta Daisy"; the one on the right is the "Double Shasta Daisy." The only difference is that the design of the floral-shaped petals alternates in length on the "Single Shasta Daisy" whereas they are all the same length on the "Double Shasta Daisy." Each of these shakers may be found with either a transfer or HP motif on top of the daisy flower. Since this design was patented in June 1891,[6] it seems to have been produced by the Monroe factory for a number of years because the use of colored transfers was primarily employed beginning with the late 1890s to reduce production costs. The earlier produced shakers will be found with an embossed patent date on the bottom. Circa 1890 – 1898. Each shaker type has equal monetary value. Rare! **$185.00 – 200.00** each depending upon painted motif (transfer or hand applied).

Krauss collections

Lockwood collection

MOSER MEIERHOFEN WORKS
Karlsbad, Bohemia
(1895 – 1933)

The factory was founded by Ludwig Moser in 1895, at Karlsbad, Bohemia (Czechoslovakia). It became world famous for its outstanding hand-painted decoration that continues to be highly sought after by discriminating collectors. This glasshouse is one of the few that would take a basic batch of colored glass and by the application of heavy enameled decorative colored hand painting turn a form into a very luxurious appearing piece of art glass. The factory went into bank receivership in 1933.

Harris collection

Barrel, Arabesque, Moser: Opaque basic opalware glass, mold blown. The reader is viewing a complex and elaborate design of intertwined flowers and foliage surrounding an eight-pointed star geometrical pattern; all of the aforesaid was created by heavily applied HP enameled paint of many colors over a solid pink colored background. Circa 1897 – 1906. 3⅛" tall with a two-piece metal top. Rare! **$510.00 – 540.00.**

Harris collection

Cylinder, Moser (condiment): Opaque basic opalware glass turned into art glass by elaborate HP decoration. These mold-blown shakers have essentially the same decoration as the condiment shakers illustrated in our Vol. II, page 127. It consists of solid hand-applied gold coloring over basic white opalware with the addition of heavy enameled blue flowers and shaded green and pink vines and leaves. The shakers have an embossed floral appearance due the very liberal application of enameling by the factory decorating artist. The shakers have a cylindrical form and are 3½" tall with two-piece metal tops. The bottom of the silver-plated condiment holder is marked James W. Tufts Boston and is 7⅛" tall to the top of the lifting handle. There is some gold background paint wear on the shoulder of each shaker which is distinguishable in our illustrative photo. Circa 1897 – 1906. Rare as a complete set! **$350.00 – 400.00** set due to decorative wear.

Rathbun collection

Rathbun collection

Fish Pond Array: Clear cranberry, translucent blue and frosted glass shakers with HP heavy enameled paint by the factory artists. Each complete scene depicts a pair of swimming fish beneath the surface plant foliage. Similar type blue glass Fish Pond shakers are illustrated in our Vol. II, page 127. The separately illustrated mold blown cranberry glass shaker is a real rarity. Over the years we have viewed numerous advanced collections, and discussed the availability of cranberry Fish Pond shakers with many art glass dealers. There is no doubt that the chance of finding one for sale is relatively remote. Each shaker is 3¾" tall with a two-piece metal top. Circa 1900 – 1910. Blue shaker is very scarce! Frosted is rare! Cranberry is very rare! Blue, **$235.00 – 260.00;** Frosted, **$350.00 – 375.00;** Cranberry, **$1,100.00 – 1,200.00.**

Maxfield collection

Maxfield collection

Rectangularity, Moser: Blue two layer cased art glass, dual mold blown. Two views of the shaker are being shown to reveal the continuous and delicately enameled floral forms that have been created. After the beginning of the twentieth century, decorative motifs dominated by flowering plants were pursued on colored or shaded glass blanks by Moser. Typical backgrounds are composed of finely leafed foliage which comprises part of the makeup of our subject shaker. Circa 1910 – 1925. 3¼" tall x 1½" wide with a two-piece metal top. Rare! **$575.00 – 600.00.**

Investigated Facts Relative to "Verona" Art Glass Produced by Mt. Washington/Pairpoint, circa 1894

The purpose of this scenario is intended to alert the reader to the realization that considerable effort and knowledge are involved in order to make a correct identification of an unsigned form of decorated "Verona" art glass. A final identification must be based upon personal knowledge and experience associated with the glass characteristics, plus actual inspection of each form in question. Of great significance is the fact that the absolute identification of an authentic "Verona" signature has not been positively established. It is also a true fact that in today's antique glassware arena, the presence of a signature (by itself) should never form the basis for purchasing any piece of antique art glass![1]

Considerable confusion abounds among collectors/dealers relative to the identification of Mt. Washington/Pairpoint "Verona" glass. During 1993 and 1994 we wrote and published a series of feature articles in *Antique Week* involving some of the more obscure and rare art glasses produced by these glass factories.[2] Our main objective was to assist and clarify, for today's less experienced art glass collectors/dealers, the appearance and characteristics pertinent to the identification of these wares.

Rathbun collection

Puzzle, Intaglio Verona: Frosted translucent "Verona" art glass, mold blown. This shaker pair is identical in shape and mold design to the "Napoli" decorated shakers. The principal difference is that the frosted front surface (left) contains a gleaming pink and yellow pansy with a lengthy green stem. The back-side (right) has a HP yellow/white floral sprig. Of significance is the fact that pansy decorations were often used by Mt. Washington/Pairpoint on their various crystal and translucent frosted "Verona" form decorated items. Circa 1894. 2¾" tall. The tops, while old, are not believed to be original. As was the case with the "Napoli" shakers, one weighed 1½ oz.; the other 2 oz. The weight difference no doubt was caused by the amount of glass (metal) gather used by the gaffer. Also, in consonance with the "Napoli" shakers, the glass threaded top rims have been ground-off smooth after their removal from the pontil rod. Rare! **NPD.**

The reader should keep in mind that "Verona" art glass is an exterior surface hand-painted decorative process that is relatively rare. It was never patented! Hence, there is no known patent verbiage detailing the explicit decorative processes that were involved. The resultant research conducted by ourselves, as well as other antique glassware authors has verified that production was limited. No doubt this was due to low volume sales due to lack of acceptance by the Victorian consumer. The rare salt shakers that we are illustrating are "Verona"-style decorated pieces.

Only one art glass book mentions the presence of a signed piece, but provides no illustrated signature example(s).[3] Despite this fact, there are a couple of art glass collector/dealers that have published articles claiming that all authentic "Verona" pieces were signed. This is quite an amazing stance, since any collector or dealer that is knowledgeable of Mount Washington/Pairpoint practices is fully aware that the preponderance of the various types of art glass produced by this factory will not be found with a signature. So! Why should "Verona" be an exception? Our experience has shown that most Victorian era glass factories randomly signed their wares. It is unfortunate that many collectors ferret out only signed examples rather than learning to recognize them through shapes, glass quality, type of pontil, weight, and so forth.

In the case of "Verona" art glass, our total research effort comprised more than one year of detailed investigation in order to ascertain what various art glass collectors, dealers, authors, museum curators, leading auction houses, plus more than 20 years of published price guides recognize as authentic "Verona art glass that has been, and is sold by, "the trade."

To be more specific, our research involving this rare art glass uncovered numerous descriptive listings in leading trade recognized price guides published by the Kovels, Warman, The Antique Trader, and Wallace/Homestead.

After reading the price guide extrapolations that we are presenting, which represents descriptions gathered from the finest dealers and auction houses throughout the United States, the reader should have no problem in accepting that not all art glass dealers can be incorrect in their evaluation of what "Verona" is and is not. The various publishers involved did not go out of their way to fool or deceive the collecting public.

The aforementioned price guide analysis has been researched all the way back (in time) to the early 1970s. The resultant data gathered enabled us to verify that 1. The majority of "Verona" art glass pieces are not signed. 2. Three types of clear and colored "Verona" glass blanks were produced at Mt. Washington/Pairpoint. 3. The various exterior hand-painted motifs produced are of great extent, range, and widely varied.

Rathbun collection

Egg, Flat End Variant (Verona): Translucent frosted art glass, mold blown. The physical make-up of this ware is shown in our Vol. II, p. 137 with hand-decorated red satin glass. The plug-in top contains the small spring-loaded metal tapered fingers that push into the shaker opening. The HP decoration is done in the Mt. Washington/Pairpoint "Verona" art glass style which has pink, blue, and yellow pansy flowers on the front and back of the shaker. "Verona" art glass is very rare due to the fact that it was produced for only a very short time during 1894. Because this ware was apparently unpopular with the Victorian consumer, the unique exterior surface decorative process was never patented; patent office research has verified that no patent exists. The illustrated shaker is 2⅜" tall. Circa 1894. **NPD.**

Examples

The Antique Trader Price Guide to Antiques, Winter 1973, page 69: Vase, 4½"h., "Verona," flared and ruffled top, violets and leaves outlined in gold.

The Antique Trader Price Guide to Antiques, Summer 1974, page 71: Vase, 6"h., "Verona," raised gold iris and leaf decor, gold rim.

The Antique Trader Price Guide to Antiques, Spring 1975, page 72: Vase, 14"h., "Verona," enameled poppies and leaves outlined in coin gold on pale rose to green ground.

The Antique Trader Price Guide to Antiques, Summer 1978, page 79: Vase, 8"h., "Verona," enameled blue and gold florals, gold outlines and dusting.

The Antique Trader Price Guide to Antiques, Fall 1978, page 78" Pitcher, 8¼"h., applied shell handle, "Verona," lily-of-the-valley decor w/leaves outlined in gold.

The Antique Trader Antiques & Collectibles Pride Guide, 1985, page 595: Vase, 16"h., "Verona," dusty rose ground, front w/scene of page boy in formal court regalia & ornate blossoms & foliage reverse.

The Antique Trader Antiques & Collectibles, 1994, page 594: Vase, 11"h., jack-in-the-pulpit form, "Verona," clear mold-blown rib design decorated w/heavy enameled gold ribbons, scrolls, roses & leaves.

Kovels' Complete Antiques Price List, 1976 – 1977, page 317: Mt. Washington, Vase, "Verona," Daisies, 10½"x 6¾".

Kovels' Antiques & Collectibles Price List, 1993, page 493: Vase, "Verona," Pale Florals, Ruffled Top, Signed, 14".

The Complete Antiques Price List — Ralph & Terry Kovel, page 356.

Mt. Washington, Vase, Verona, Mums outlined in Gold Coin, Panel Ribbed.

Mt. Washington, Vase, Verona, Panel Ribs, White &Wine Mums, Gold Outline.

Mt. Washington, Vase, Verona, Paneled Crystal, Enamel Iris & Foliage.

Mt. Washington, Vase, Verona, Rose & White Mums, Outlined in Gold, Clear.

Mt. Washington, Vase, Verona, Violets, Coin Gold Outline, Flared, Ruffled.

Warman's Glass by Ellen Tischbein Schroy, Wallace-Homestead Book Company, 1992:

Jug, 6"h, 5½"w, Verona, yellow, gold and purple spider mums and buds, green leaves dec.

Pitcher, 5"h, 5"w, Verona, gold fish swimming among coral, rust, purple, and green plants on handle, gold trim spout & rim.

Pitcher, 8"h, Verona, bulbous, maiden hair fern dec, gold highlights, applied clear reeded handle.

Warman's Antiques and their Prices, 1988, page 340: Vase, 5½", cylindrical, clear, Verona, day lily dec., outlined in gold.

Warman's Antiques and their Prices, 1991, page 362: Pitcher, 6"h x 5½"w, Verona, four yellow, gold, and purple spider mums, six buds, green leaves.

In conclusion, "Verona" decoration was used on three types of glass blanks: crystal, transparent colored, and pastels, accomplished through the use of the wax removal system. As the reader should note, only a few price guide examples are listed as decorated on a colored ground; therefore, it is logical to deduce that the rest of the descriptions are speaking about crystal blanks.

MT. WASHINGTON/PAIRPOINT CORP.
New Bedford, Massachusetts
(1869 – 1938)

Established in 1869 as the Mt. Washington Glass Works under the ownership of Wm. L. Libbey, who resigned in 1872 to become an agent for the New England Glass Co. The factory was reorganized in 1874 with A.H. Seabury as president and Frederick S. Shirley as manager. In 1876 the company name was changed to the Mt. Washington Glass Co. In July 1894 Mt. Washington merged into the Pairpoint Mfg. Co. which in 1900 changed its name to Pairpoint Corporation until it closed in 1938.[1]

Krauss collection

Maxfield collection

McElderry collection

Bale, Pairpoint: Clear blue glass, mold blown. Very similar to the "Cotton Bale" Consolidated Lamp & Glass Co. pattern. The primary difference is the effect of the cord that divides the shaker into eight lobes. Each lobe contains HP quality leaf and flower sprigs. Circa 1894 – 1900. 2⅜" tall; 1½" wide at the base with a two-piece metal top. We are also illustrating a pair produced in cranberry. Very scarce! **$125.00 – 140.00.**

Coalmer collection

Barrel, Ellipse Oval Variant: Clear blue shading to crystal, dual mold blown. The interior surface contains a series of varying sized ellipses in raised relief. The exterior surface has been decorated with four HP sunflower sprigs that are colored pink and white. The physical configuration is that of a convex barrel tapering toward the base. Circa 1884 – 1890. 3¼" tall with matching two-piece metal tops. Very scarce! **$260.00 – 280.00** pair.

Arnold collection

Barrel, Footed Optic: Clear cranberry glass, dual mold blown. The pattern name pretty much reflects the style and shape of this shaker. The interior surface has swirled (curved) optic ribbing. The exterior surface contains a HP white, pink, and shaded green floral spray. Circa 1887 – 1891. 3½" tall; 2" at widest point; 1¼" base diameter. Very scarce! **$175.00 – 190.00.**

Bette Howard collection

Columned Ribs: Opaque white satinized glass, mold blown. Shown are salt and pepper shakers and the companion sugar shaker in this pattern which is very similar to the "Ribbed Pillar" motif. This ware contains "Crown Milano" type decoration (see our Vol. II, page 135 and Peterson 26-H for the decorative appearance and artistic technique details; also Padgett's *Pairpoint Glass* page 56 illustrates this pattern in toothpicks and mustards). The salt and pepper are 2½" tall with two-piece metal tops; the sugar shaker is 5⅝" tall. Very rare as a table condiment group. **$1,500.00 – 1,700.00** set of three.

Arnold collection

Barrel, Quilted Diamond: Clear blue glass, dual mold blown. The inside surface contains a quilted diamond motif; the smooth exterior contains an elaborate white, orange, and yellow HP floral spray. Because of the inside and outer motifs, the shaker is almost translucent. Circa 1885 – 1890. 3¼" tall x 2" wide; 1⅜" base diameter with a two-piece metal top. Very scarce! **$195.00 – 225.00.**

Krauss collection

Rathbun collection

Rathbun collection

Chevarie Pillar: Illustrated are four clear optic ribbed shakers in cranberry and blue glass, mold blown. The pattern amounts to a round-shaped pillar that is smooth on the outside with six inside wide optic ribs. The two illustrated bottom views reveal that the aforesaid inside ribbing forms a hexagon shape. The smooth circular exterior of each shaker contains a quality HP nature scene involving a deer, single long beaked bird and a pair of ground feeding birds. While similar, these shakers are shorter than the "Game Bird, Tall" type shakers.[2] Mt. Washington produced a series of this type ware decorated with various HP nature scenes involving various plants and animals. The shakers are of excellent fire polished quality glass. Circa 1885 – 1890.[3] 3½" tall with two-piece metal tops. Rare and very difficult to collect today! **$550.00 – 600.00** each.

Roland collection

Column, Supreme: Opaque satinized opalware glass, mold blown. A round column shape with a ringed top very similar to the Creased Neck patterns used by this glasshouse. The HP red dots form a rather intricate floral spray. Black light examination revealed no return florescence. Circa 1887 – 1894. 2⅞" tall x 1½" wide. Rare in this decoration! **$160.00 – 180.00.**

Krauss collection

Creased Neck, Brownie Decorated: Opaque white opalware, mold blown. This is a tall pillar-shaped shaker containing three painted Palmer Cox Brownie elves in group discussion. This type of decoration was accomplished by use of a transfer technique which was a decorating process designed to cut factory production costs. To tell the difference between chromolithograph (transfer) and HP work, examine the decoration closely using 10 power magnification. If the decoration or picture is made up of many tiny dots, it is a transfer. The use of transfers began during the late 1890s in the decorating departments of many of the leading glasshouses to enhance their competitive sales position in the market place. This ware was produced circa 1898 – 1904. 3¼" tall. Rare. **$200.00 – 220.00.**

Coalmer collection

Creased Neck, Tapered: Opaque opalware glass, mold blown. Smooth cylinder shaped with a small cabin with snow on the roof. At the shaker base is a small, HP leafy branch in brown and yellow; colors are reminiscent of late fall/winter. The reader is referred to our Vol. II, page 217 for additional details regarding this type of shaker. Circa 1890 – 1894. 3½" tall. Excellent condition. Very scarce with this type of motif! **$50.00 – 60.00.**

Authors' collection

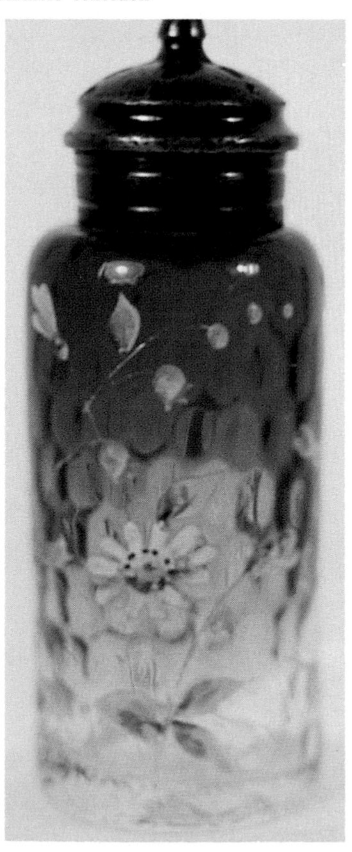

Cylinder, Plain Neck: Clear rubina stained glass, dual mold blown. In terms of external decoration, shape, and basic pattern configuration, this item is identical to an AAGSSCS shaker they named "Cylinder, Craquelle." It consists of a cylinder shape with a plain rounded neck and small IVT on the inside surface; essentially smooth on the outside with numerous HP florals. Circa 1885 – 1891. 3¾" tall x 1½" wide with a two-piece metal finial top. Very scarce! **$190.00 – 215.00.**

Lockwood collection

Neale collection

Egg, Flat End: Opaque satinized opalware, mold blown with a HP hen on one egg and a rooster on the other. The basic "Flat End Egg" was patented by Mt. Washington Glass Co. in 1889. Since that time they produced many circumference dimensional variations to their egg-shaped shakers; many of the variants took place in the late 1890 time frame. Some of their eggs require two-piece metal tops, while others only required a single piece metal top due to threading of the glass at the top of the shakers (see our Vol. II, p. 138). The Hen and Rooster shakers have top threaded glass, thus, eliminating the need for the metal bezel and a companion threaded metal top. We are also illustrating three additional opalware "Flat End Eggs" to document the HP decorative variances employed by the factory. Circa 1889 – 1899. Acquiring these particular shakers is a real challenge to the collectors of today. 2¼" tall. All these shakers are rare! Hen and Rooster, **$350.00 – 400.00,** pair; Pairpoint Delft, **$300.00 – 325.00;** extensive gold decorated Flat End Egg, **$300.00 – 325.00.**

Neale collection

Neale collection

Egg, Flat End Variant (Verona): Translucent frosted art glass, mold blown. The physical make-up of this ware is shown in our Vol. II, p. 137 with hand-decorated red satin glass. The plug-in type top contains the small spring-loaded metal tapered fingers that push into the shaker opening. The HP decoration is done in the Mt. Washington/Pairpoint "Verona" art glass style which has pink, blue, and yellow Pansy flowers on the front and back of the shaker. "Verona" art glass is very rare due to the fact that it was produced for only a very short time during 1894. Because this ware was apparently unpopular with the Victorian consumer, the unique exterior surface decorative process was never patented; patent office research has verified that no patent exists. (See our extensive "Verona" write-up as part of the Mt. Washington/Pairpoint section). The illustrated shaker is 2⅜" tall. Circa 1894. **NPD.**

Authors' collection

Coalmer collection

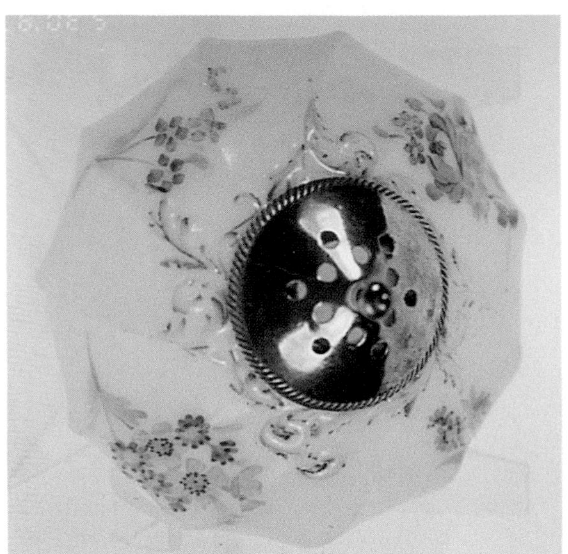

Tognetti collection

Flying Saucer: Opaque white opalware glass, mold blown. The pattern name describes this shaker's physical form. A most unusual thick set (squatty) pattern containing 11 swirled panels and embossed curlicue scrolling at the neck. The bottom has a receding circle with the outer edge having four short supporting feet. (We are illustrating three shakers.) The "Delft" shakers have HP surface decoration in various shades of blue and contains a windmill. Many of today's experienced art glass dealers call this "Pairpoint Delft" type decoration. Various glass forms including small oil lamps were produced with the blue Delft type motif. The other two opalware shakers contain various HP red, yellow, and green floral sprays. Circa 1894 – 1899. Each shaker is 1½" tall with an original special two-piece metal top containing a finial. The presence of any other type top has a negative monetary impact on retail value. Rare! Pairpoint Delft, **$425.00 – 450.00;** HP flora, **$295.00 – 320.00** each.

Krauss collection

Game Bird: Opaque pink triple cased, mold blown glass with two HP speckled-brown game birds feeding within an area containing a number of grasses containing jointed hollow stems (perhaps a marsh land). The physical configuration consists of a slightly tapering barrel shape that is narrower at the base. A slightly smaller shaker is shown in our Vol. II p.142. Produced circa 1885 – 1890. 3" tall with a two-piece metal top. Rare in this color! **$275.00 – 300.00.**

Coalmer collection

Honeycomb, Intaglio Pillar: Clear blue glass, dual mold blown. The exterior surface contains elaborate, HP orange berries and white flowers over an intaglio honeycomb motif. The inner surface of the shaker is smooth. Circa 1884 – 1890. 3⅝" tall with a two-piece metal top. Rare! **$275.00 – 300.00** pair.

Inverted Thumbprint, Maralyn: Clear blue glass, dual mold blown. We are showing two shakers, each has slightly different tri-leaf coloring. The inside surface of both shakers has IVT, and the smooth outer surface of one contains an outstanding HP white and brown, vertically placed, floral design supported by very thin stems; the other has a green and black tri-leaf. The shakers taper downward from a bulging top. Their physical shape is similar to the shaker shown in our Vol. II p. 149. Circa 1887 – 1891. 3" tall; 1⅝" top diameter; 1¼" bottom diameter with a two-piece metal top. Rare! **$190.00 – 210.00.**

Krauss collection

Ridgway collection

Lockwood collection

Inverted Thumbprint, Sphere Variant: Translucent cobalt blue glass, dual mold blown. With the exception of a height and HP floral decoration difference, this is the same shaker illustrated in our Vol. II, page 142 where this ware is present within a Mt. Washington/Pairpoint two-piece condiment set. Circa 1887 – 1894. 2" tall x 2" wide. Very scarce! **$135.00 – 160.00** pair.

Krauss collection

Lobed Heart: Clear cranberry glass, dual mold blown. The shaker resembles four heart-shaped oval panels with baby thumbprint on the inside. Each panel is separated by a protruding rib. Each smooth panel surface has a HP floral decoration of either a blue or white flower. The shaker bottom contains ⅛" of clear (uncolored) glass. Circa 1894. 2¼" tall; 1⅞" wide with a two-piece metal top. Rare! Excellent condition. **$160.00 – 175.00.**

Lockwood collection

Rathbun collection

Melon, Six Lobe: Clear reverse and regular "Rose Amber" (amberina) glass, and clear blue and cranberry. Each are dual mold blown with some free-hand finishing. The physical motif amounts of six irregular bulging lobes that contain inside IVT with a smooth outside/exterior surface. This ware was also made in "Diamond Quilted Mother-of-Pearl" (MOP) art glass utilizing an air trap type of production process. All of the aforementioned items contain two-piece metal tops and were produced circa 1885 – 1890. These shakers are being illustrated to document the various colors that were produced. 2⅝" tall. Rare! **$295.00 – 325.00.**

Krauss collection

Mother of Pearl Diamond Quilted Barrel: Opaque satinized ivory colored cased glass containing a Diamond Quilt type air trap pattern on a symmetrical squared-off shoulder having a barrel shape. This pattern is a variation of the pattern illustrated in our Vol. II, p. 145. This is a unique MOP coloration in this pattern. Circa 1886 – 1888. The bottom has a partially ground off pontil. 3" tall with a two-piece metal top. Rare in this color! **$370.00 – 410.00.**

Krauss collection

Mother of Pearl Pinched-in Diamond Quilt: Deep pink/rose MOP satinized cased glass containing a small Diamond Quilted air trap pattern with a fire-polished bottom that has a circular recessed (intaglio) center. Each of the four sides has been pinched in, causing the shaker body to reflect a somewhat rectangular shape. Circa 1882 – 1887. 2¾" tall with a two-piece metal top. Rare in this color! **$350.00 – 400.00.**

Bette Howard collection

Optic Ribs, Bulging: Clear cranberry glass, dual mold blown. The shaker contains a series of inside optic ribs and has a bulging shape with a short narrow ringed neck. Similar in shape to one of the "Daisy Sprig" and also the "Starlet" shakers shown in our Vol. II except this shaker contains optic ribbing and is taller. The exterior surface has HP daisy sprigs in two parallel rows that encircle the entire shaker. 2¾" tall with a small two-piece metal top. Circa 1886 – 1890. Rare! **$195.00 – 215.00.**

Krauss collection

Krauss collection

Pillar, Ring Neck: Clear blue glass, dual mold blown. These shakers have the same physical shape as the "Mayfly" and "Tall Game Bird" illustrated in our Vol. II, pages 143 and 145. Their inside surface contains six vertical optic ribs. The smooth outer surface of one has a HP red-beaked white stork on the wing. The exterior surface of the other shaker contains HP red and blue daisy flowers that are randomly distributed around the entire shaker body. Each shaker radiates a yellow fluorescence when exposed to long wave UV black light. Circa 1886 – 1891. 3⅞" tall with two-piece metal tops. Very scare! **$145.00 – 160.00** each.

Krauss collection

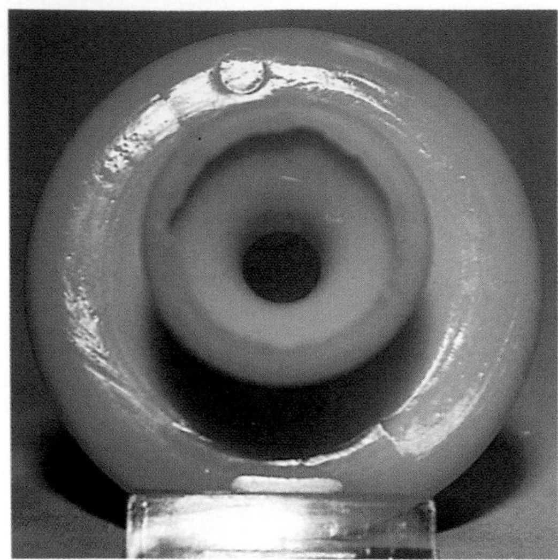

Krauss collection

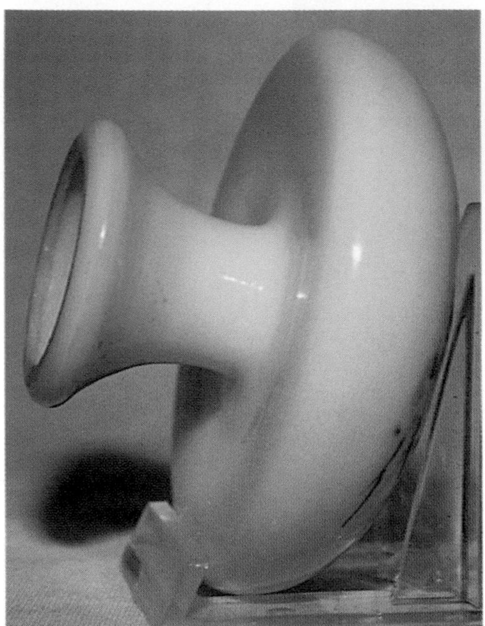

Krauss collection

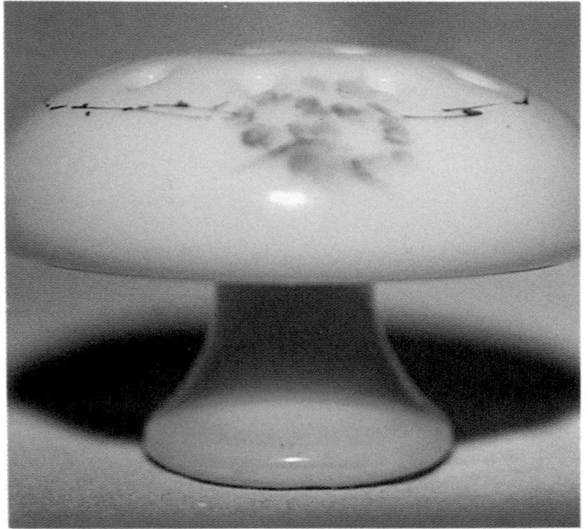

Krauss collection

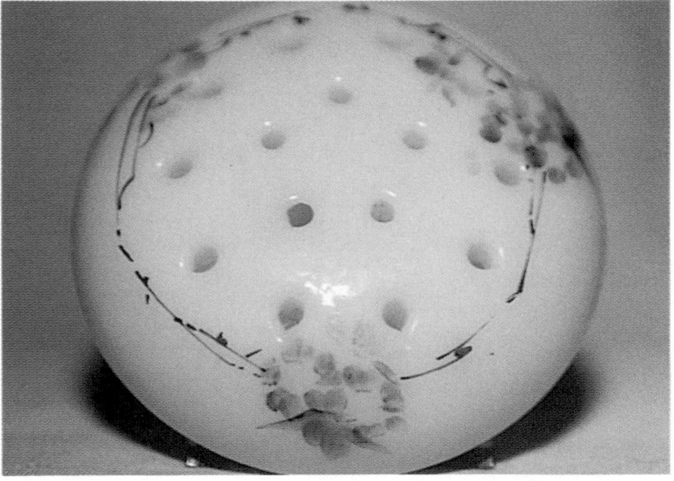

Mushroom: Opaque off-white opalware, mold blown. The pattern name fully describes the physical shape of this ware. This is the smaller size of two shakers that was produced in this motif. The design was patented by Andrew Snow, Jr. who was awarded patent No. 496,013 on April 25, 1893. He assigned this patent to the Mt. Washington Glass Co., New Bedford, Massachusetts. As part of the technical, descriptive wording contained in the awarded patent, Mr. Snow stipulated that the top surface openings project into the interior and "not only hold the stems of flowers straight" but "in the case the receptacle is used for condiments, the projections serve to break up and powder the condiments, when the receptacle is shaken." Mention is also made that the bottom "is fitted with a stopper." The patent makes it clear that the shaker was originally intended as a dual-use article. A side, top, support foot, and bottom view are illustrated. Past AAGSSCS President Scott Arnold did the patent research involving this shaker. Circa 1893. The shaker measures 1⅞" tall; 2¾" wide; ⅞" holder thickness; 1" length of the foot; 1½" base diameter of the foot. The bottom condiment (salt) insertion hole size is 5/16". The top surface of the shaker contains HP pink and green floral sprigs encircling the perimeter. Very rare! **$750.00 – 800.00.**

Krauss collection

Krauss collection

Krauss collection

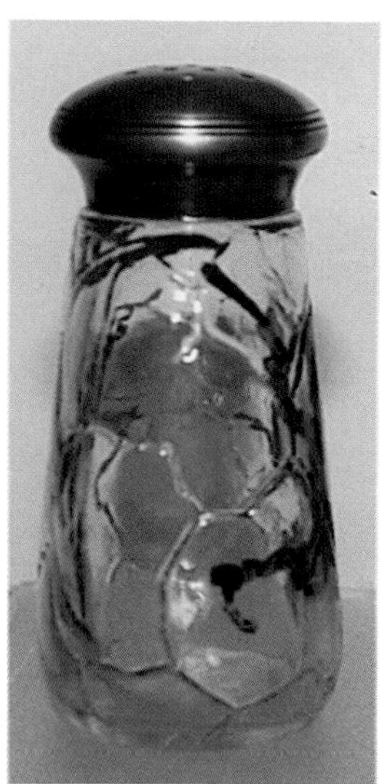

Puzzle, Intaglio (Napoli): Clear crystal glass, mold blown. This is a four-sided shaker with the outer surface containing intaglio designed segments that are analogous (reminiscent) of a jigsaw puzzle. This shaker pair (enhanced by white beads for a clear photograph) are "Napoli" art glass, which comprises a special type of HP decoration involving both the inside and outside glass surfaces. One shaker contains a HP Palmer Cox Brownie policeman that is running with a raised club in his right hand. The other shaker contains a Brownie elf that is dressed similar to a leprechaun with top hat and tails holding a musical instrument (perhaps some type of horn). The backside view (opposite the leprechaun) contains a HP black cat; the backside view (opposite the policeman) is decorated with a HP brown spotted running pig. All of the aforementioned comic characters are hand painted on the inside surface of each shaker in the Mt. Washington/Pairpoint "Napoli" style which was patented by Albert Steffin on May 22, 1984. The Steffin patent papers stipulate that the decoration is accomplished by first outlining the basic design form on one surface of a piece which will serve as a guide for producing the design details on the opposite surface. Thus, the initial outline that is formed upon one side will, by reason of the glass transparency, blend with the principal body of the decoration on the opposite side, thereby producing a novel and picturesque visual effect (almost like 3-D). The "Napoli" forms that are usually encountered, reveal that the outlining was first done on the exterior surface in gold or silver metallic paint; with the main body of the colored enamel decoration being applied to the inside surface of each hollow glass item. Such a laborious technique imparts a visual feeling of depth which could not be produced if the entire decoration had been applied to the outer surface only. As is the case with these shakers, most "Napoli" forms will have a gold (or silver) interconnecting network that is reminiscent of a jigsaw puzzle; although some see it as spider webbing. Circa 1894 – 1895. 2¾" tall. The tops are believed to be original. With tops removed, the shaker with the Brownie policeman weighed 1¾ oz.; the other shaker weighed 2 oz. These shakers are extremely rare! No retail pricing data base exists within current trade publications. **NPD.**

Krauss collection

Krauss collection

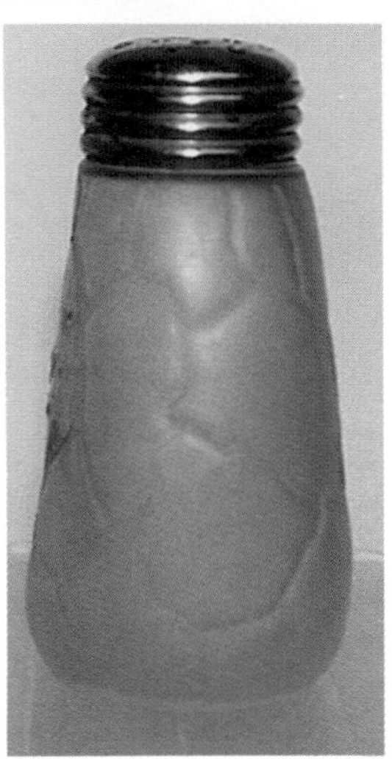

Puzzle, Intaglio (Verona): Frosted translucent "Verona" art glass, mold blown. This shaker pair is identical in shape and mold design to the "Napoli" shakers. The principal difference is that the frosted front surface (left) contains a gleaming pink and yellow pansy with a lengthy green stem. The backside (right) has a HP yellow/white floral sprig. Of significance is the fact that Pansy decorations were often used by Mt. Washington/Pairpoint on their various crystal and translucent frosted "Verona" decorated items. Circa 1894. 2¾" tall. The tops, while old, are not believed to be original. As was the case with the "Napoli" shakers, one weighed 1½ oz.; the other 2 oz. The weight difference no doubt was caused by the amount of glass (metal) gather used by the gaffer. Also, in consonance with the "Napoli" shakers, the glass threaded top rims have been ground-off smooth after their removal from the pontil rod.[4] Rare! **NPD.**

Authors' collection

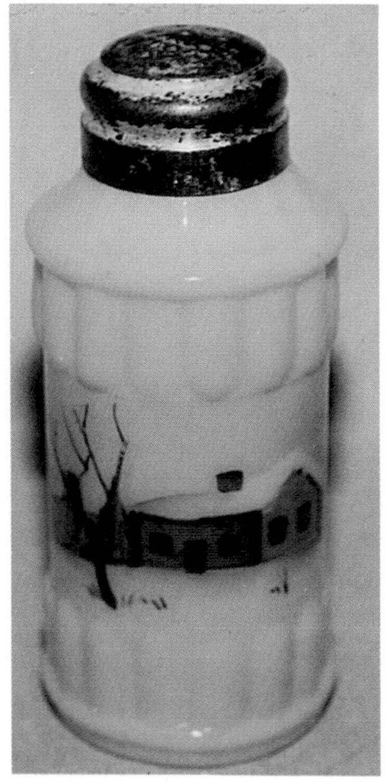

Rib, Narrow Double: Opaque white opalware, mold blown. This pattern is illustrated in our Vol. II, p. 249 by the pattern title "Rib, Double." We have added the word "narrow" to this title to clear up pattern name duplicity since a syrup jug is recorded as "Double Rib" in H-3, p. 49. The shaker pattern has a band of 15 short embossed ribs at the top and bottom. The smooth center contains an elaborate house and barren tree snow scene done by the Smith Bros. decorating department at Mt. Washington. Circa 1891 – 1895. 3⅞" tall. Very scarce. **$100.00 – 125.00.**

Harris collection

Saucer-Like: Clear cranberry glass, dual mold blown. Shaped like a saucer. The inside surface contains IVT. The smooth exterior surface edge is encircled with a floral band of white daisies and green/yellow leaves. Circa 1886 – 1890. 1⅝" tall. The base has a short round extension for use within a condiment holder. Rare! **$205.00 – 225.00.**

Ridgway collection

Sphere, Short Variant: Opaque white opalware, mold blown. The pattern amounts to a smooth surfaced sphere with an indented circular bottom. The pattern name describes the shaker's shape. The principal motif depicts a small sailboat on a body of water. The opposite side contains vertical green lily leaves with two HP red flowers. Circa 1892 – 1896. 2⅛" tall with a two-piece metal top. This is a basic shape[5] that was used by the factory to portray various HP scenes for an extended period of time. Very scarce! **$60.00 – 75.00.**

Krauss collection

Sphere, Small Honeycomb: Translucent homogeneous amber glass, dual mold blown. As the pattern name implies, this is a small round shaker with an inside series of honeycombs and a smooth exterior that contains HP red and white daisies and a dark blue bodied flying insect with green shaded wings. Essentially identical in size to the "Little Apple" shaker. Circa 1885 – 1891. 1⅞" tall with a two-piece metal top. Very scarce! **$65.00 – 85.00.**

Coalmer collection

Sphere, Stretched Inverted Thumbprint: Clear blue glass, dual mold blown. This is a small footed shaker with IVT on the inside surface. The outer surface contains an extended (elaborate) HP floral spray around the largest portion of the circumference. Designed for use within a companion metal condiment holder. The HP floral decoration is typical of that produced by the Mt. Washington/Pairpoint decorating department. 2½" tall with a two-piece metal top. Circa 1885 – 1889. Very scarce! **$80.00 – 90.00.**

Krauss collection

Swallow Song: Opaque blue cased glass, dual mold blown. This pattern was named by Peterson and he attributed it to the Pairpoint Mfg. Co.[6] The outer surface contains two HP flying swallows beneath a partial sheet of music entitled "When The Swallows Homeward Fly." 3⅝" tall with a two-piece metal top. Circa 1894 – 1897. Rare! **$200.00 – 225.00.**

Rathbun collection

Twins Variant: Opaque satinized opalware, mold blown with two-piece matching metal tops. Somewhat bellshaped with a flared out base having a small extension for fitting within a condiment set holder. 2⅝" tall. Circa 1886 – 1893. Similar to the shakers illustrated in our Vol. II, page 262, but not dual mold blown to produce an inside pattern. Very scarce! **$210.00 – 230.00** matched pair.

Rathbun collection

Harris collection

Krauss collection

Two Flower Sprig: Pink opaque homogenous glass, mold blown with two HP white flowers on a single branch containing dark green leaves. The shaker has a spheroid shape with outstanding satin glass smoothness that compares favorably to that found on "Mother-of-Pearl" art glass. First documented on the back cover of our 1976 book and later in our Vol. II, p. 152 in opaque blue with the aforesaid type of HP motif. All of these shakers were designed to utilize a two-piece metal top. Circa 1885 – 1890. In all our many years of shaker specialization, we have only observed one other of this type of shaker in pink opaque as described. 2¼" tall. In addition we are also illustrating this same shaker form in satinized opalware with a fired-on pink wash and no floral decoration. The slightly receding bottom is not painted and the white opalware is clearly visible. Both are rare shakers! "Two Flower Sprig," **$575.00 – 600.00.** Pink opalware, **$65.00 – 85.00.**

Urchin: Clear cranberry glass, mold blown. This shaker shape is identical in form to the "Bird Arbor" shaker produced by Mt. Washington/Pairpoint Glass Co., New Bedford, Massachusetts circa 1886 – 1891.[7] Aside from the basic cranberry colored glass, the exterior contains a HP small child reclining within a flowering tree branch.[8] The decoration detail and quality is outstanding. 3⅞" tall with a two-piece metal top. Very rare! **$250.00 – 280.00.**

Condiment/Cruet Sets

Harris collection

Barrel, Baby Thumbprint (condiment): Clear blue glass, dual mold blown. Refer to our Vol. II, p. 129 for essentially the same pattern. This pair is slightly shorter and contains a HP pink rose and green vine on the exterior surface; the inside surface contains baby IVT. Circa 1884 – 1889. 2⅜" tall with two-piece metal tops. The silverplated holder is marked Wilcox Silver Plate Co., Meridan, Connecticut. Rare as a complete set. **$250.00 – 290.00** set.

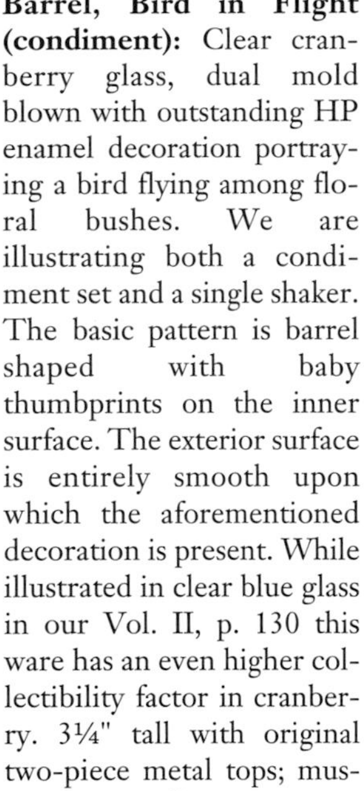

Krauss collection

Rathbun collection

Barrel, Bird in Flight (condiment): Clear cranberry glass, dual mold blown with outstanding HP enamel decoration portraying a bird flying among floral bushes. We are illustrating both a condiment set and a single shaker. The basic pattern is barrel shaped with baby thumbprints on the inner surface. The exterior surface is entirely smooth upon which the aforementioned decoration is present. While illustrated in clear blue glass in our Vol. II, p. 130 this ware has an even higher collectibility factor in cranberry. 3¼" tall with original two-piece metal tops; mustard, 2¾" tall. Circa 1883 – 1889. The silver-plated holder is marked "E.G. Wester & Bro. N.Y."; it is 7¼" tall to the top of the lifting handle. Very rare in this color! **$950.00 – 1,100.00** set; single shaker, **$250.00 – 290.00.**

Krauss collection

Krauss collection

Barrel, Ellipse Oval (condiment): Clear shaded Rubina glass, dual mold blown. Two views are shown to illustrate the mustard. The inside surface has continuous ellipse ovals in raised relief. The smooth outer surface contains HP sunflower floral sprays with shaded green to yellow leaves. The unusual leaf-shaped metal holder was made by Meriden Silver Plate Company, Meriden, Connecticut. This company was organized in 1869 by George Casper, who was president. This was one of the original group of companies that formed the International Silver Co. in 1898. Each shaker is 3" tall; the mustard is 1⅞" tall. Circa 1885 – 1890. Rare as a complete set. **$545.00 – 590.00** set.

Krauss collection

Barrel, Ellipse Oval Alternative (condiment): Clear Bluina glass, dual mold blown. This set has the same pattern as the Rubina "Ellipse Oval Barrel" set; also, the silver-plated holder is marked "Meriden Silver Plate Co." but is of a different design. Shakers, mustard dimensions, HP flowers, and retail value are also the same. Because of the overall glass quality, and consumer demand, various silver-plate houses procured such quality glass to add to their sales profits. Circa 1885 – 1890. **$545.00 – 590.00** set.

Harris collection

Barrel, Honeycomb Rigaree Flowered: We are illustrating a complete three-piece amber glass condiment set consisting of salt, pepper, and mustard within a metal holder manufactured by Reed & Barton. Also pictured is a single clear light blue shaker; this ware is dual mold blown. The inner surfaces of each piece have large honeycombs that diminish in size towards their base. The smooth outer exteriors contain a mixture of HP orange round berries interspersed with individually attached (fused-on) round red glass berries adhering to an intricate series of painted white stems and gold foliage. A very involved and unusual example of detailed quality decoration. Circa 1886 – 1892. Shakers, 3¼" tall with a two-piece metal top; mustard, 2⅞" tall. A pair of crystal spangles hang downward on each side of the condiment set's holding stand lifting handle. The complete set is 9½" tall to the top of the lifting handle. Rare! Amber condiment set, **$680.00 – 750.00**; blue shaker, **$285.00 – 310.00.**

Authors' collection

Krauss collection

Barrel, Ribbed "Blue Dot" (condiment): Opaque opalware glass, mold blown. This classic Mt. Washington/Pairpoint pattern is shown and described in our Vol. II, pages 130 and 131. This particular set consists of salt, pepper, and mustard. Each has HP leaves in autumn colors of shaded brown and yellow. The flowers are represented by HP blue dots that are interconnected by purple stems. As we have explained in our write-up of the "Pillar, Ribbed Blue Dot" condiment, current advanced collectors attempt to collect as many shapes and forms as possible of the "Blue Dot" type of decoration. This has resulted in a high collectibility factor for this type of art glass. Circa 1886 – 1892. Salt and pepper, 2¾" tall; mustard, 2⅝" tall; all have two-piece metal tops. The set is contained in an original Pairpoint silver-plated metal holder that has three metal loops above the base for retention of the three condiment dispensers. The holding stand is 6¼" tall to the top of the lifting handle. Rare as a complete set! **$840.00 – 875.00** set.

Bette Howard collection

Barrel, Ribbed Burmese (condiment): Illustrated is a very rare hand-decorated Burmese condiment set in an original Pairpoint silver-plated holder. Both shakers have been decorated in the so-called "Blue Dot" floral style that advanced collectors seek out in the various shapes/forms that Mt. Washington produced. This opaque homogeneous heat sensitive glass shades from salmon pink to a pale yellow and is barrel shaped with 24 small embossed vertical ribs. The glass is highly fluorescent under UV illumination. The shakers are 2¾" tall; the two-piece metal tops are original. The metal holder is 5" tall and 4½" in length. Circa 1886 – 1890. Very rare as a complete set! **$950.00 – 1,100.00** set.

Krauss collection

Brownies on a Tray (condiment): Opaque white satinized opalware, mold blown. The set consists of salt, pepper, toothpick, and holding tray. The shakers and toothpick contain Palmer Cox Brownies involved in various action scenes. All of the applied/painted Brownie elves were produced by use of a transfer technique. The companion tray may not be original, but we verified that it provides a practical form, fit, and function to the condiment set. The shakers do have the proper (original) metal tops for this type of egg-shaped shaker pair; the 1889 patented Flat End Egg two-piece domed tops will not fit on the illustrated Brownie decorated eggs which contain threaded glass top edges. Circa 1894 – 1901. The shaker and companion toothpick measure 2¼" tall. Very rare as a set! **NPD.**

Krauss collection

Burmese, Glossy (cruet set): Opaque glossy Burmese art glass shading from pink to a soft yellow, mold blown. All three-pieces have excellent color shading in a most difficult to acquire type of Burmese art glass.[9] As is true of all types of Burmese glass, the pieces have a striking fluorescence under black light exposure. The shaker's tops and the cruet's stopper are original. "Ribbed Pillar" shakers, 3⅝" tall; handled cruet, 5⅛" tall. The silver-plated metal holder is marked "Wm Rogers Mfg Co" and measures 7⅛" to the top of the lifting handle. Circa 1885 – 1887. Very rare! **$2,900.00 – 3,100.00** set.

Eldridge collection

Eldridge collection

Chick Head (condiment): Opaque blue and tan colored glass shakers, mold blown with HP floral sprays on the back and sides of the egg-shaped dispensers. The basic pattern is that of a chick emerging from an egg. The patented special molded metal tops contain spring loaded sawtoothed prongs that push into the egg opening. The special original and very rare unmarked metal condiment holder (also separately shown) has been specifically designed to accommodate a pair of Mt. Washington/Pairpoint "Chick Head" shakers. What remains a mystery is whether Mt. Washington had this custom holder made for them by an outside vendor, or, whether one of the many silver-plating houses, that existed during the period, independently purchased this shaker pattern ware for subsequent sales of "Chick Head" shakers to their own customers. This dilemma will remain unsolved unless a catalog from the specific silver manufacturer is discovered through diligent research. Each shaker is 1¾" tall; the holder measures 3⅝" between the most distant supporting feet (tip-to-tip); it is 1⅝" between the end supporting feet. Circa 1890. Extremely rare as a complete set! No monetary market value base line exists for this set since it is the only one of which we are aware. **NPD.**

Krauss collection

Bulging Base, Short (condiment): Clear blue glass, mold blown. Each shaker has a white HP floral sprig. As the pattern name implies, the physical shape amounts to a short bulging base with a narrow neck ring. The base has a small protruding extension for fitting into a condiment holder. The metal cupped holder is marked Wilcox Silver Plate Co. Each shaker is 2¼" tall with a two-piece metal top. Circa 1885 – 1891. Very scarce! **$325.00 – 350.00** set.

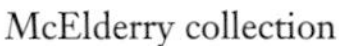

Krauss collection

McElderry collection

Creased Neck, Unfired Burmese (condiment): Opaque uranium satin glass, mold blown. The pattern name describes this pillar-shaped ware that contains HP floral motifs.[10] Some collectors and dealers mistakenly refer to this ware as custard glass; however, Mt. Washington/Pairpoint has never been formally listed or cataloged as a custard glass producer. When subjected to black light illumination, this ware gives off a striking fluorescence. Two condiment sets are illustrated; shaker, 3¾" tall; 1¾"wide. The twisted wire silver-plate metal holder is "Pairpoint" marked; the holder on the set is unmarked. Circa 1888 – 1890. Rare with gold tipped decoration, also HP butterflies. Single shaker, **$190.00 – 210.00**; each condiment set, **$525.00 – 540.00.**

Krauss collection

Cylinder, Tall Heavy (condiment): Clear cobalt blue thick glass, mold blown. The pattern name describes the physical shape. The outside surface contains hand-engraved fern-like leaves encircling the shaker center. Above and below the fern leaves is a cut-in series of bull's eyes surrounding the shakers.[11] Each shaker is 3⅞" tall with two-piece metal tops. The unique metal stand is designed for the insertion of a table napkin in between the shaker pair. The bottom is marked Simpson Hall Miller & Co." and is 6¼" tall to the top of the lifting handle. Very scarce! **$190.00 – 220.00** set.

Rathbun collection

Cylinder, Tall Inverted Thumbprint (condiment): Clear Rubina shaded glass, dual mold blown. As the pattern name indicates this set contains a pair of tall IVT shakers in classic Rubina coloring with extensive HP white flowers and shaded green leaves encircling the shaker circumference. The 6" tall silver-plated holder is marked "James Tufts – Boston." Circa 1889 – 1895. Shakers, 3⅝" tall with two-piece metal tops. Very scarce! **$315.00 – 325.00** set.

Krauss collection

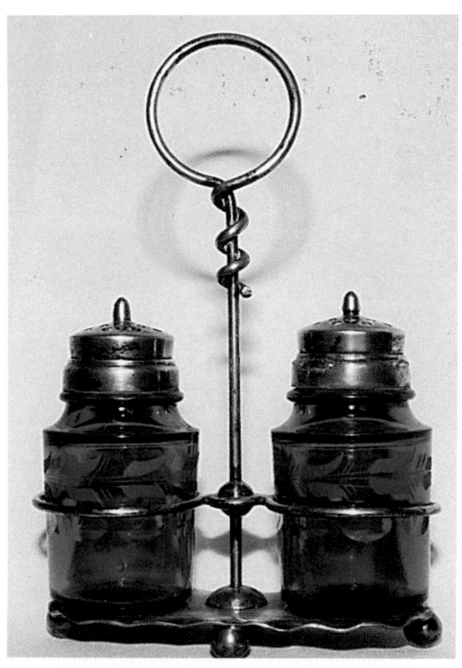

Cylinder, Wide (condiment): Cobalt blue glass, mold blown. This is a pair of short shakers having a fairly wide base diameter. Each shaker contains a prominate band of hand-engraved leaves encircling the outside perimeter. Below the engraved motif is a band of eight cut-in ellipses. This glass pattern is fully illustrated in an 1894 Pairpoint Manufacturing Co. catalog on pages 39, 40, and 41 within an assortment of "Dinner Casters." The illustrated silver-plated holder is marked with the "Diamond P" Pairpoint signature/trademark. Circa 1894. 3" tall x 1⅝" base diameter. Rare as a complete set in blue ! **$335.00 – 360.00** set.

Coalmer collection

Krauss collection

Egg, Flat End Variant (condiment): Opaque opalware with elaborate HP decoration, mold blown. These egg-shaped shakers contain the patented spring finger tops that insert into the top of each shaker.[12] One shaker has a pale pink painted background, the other a pale blue. 2⅜" tall. Circa 1891 – 1894. The metal holder is marked "Made & Guaranteed by Meriden Brittany" and it is 6½" tall to top of the metal lifting handle. Rare as a complete set! **$500.00 – 550.00** set.

Egg in Blossom (condiment): Opaque white satin glass with a large HP floral sprig, mold blown; has the original special metal tops. Pattern name by A.G. Peterson. While a single shaker is illustrated in our Vol. II, page 136, a full condiment set with companion holder is quite a rarity. Produced circa 1891. The shakers are 2" tall. The bulging base lobes are in raised relief. The elaborate silver-plated holding stand is marked on the bottom "Homan Silver Plate Co." which existed at Cincinnati, Ohio, from 1847 until 1896 after which the company was succeeded by Homan Mfg Co.; no existence for this latter company could be confirmed after 1942. Rare! **$600.00 – 650.00** set.

Neale collection

Fig (condiment): Translucent cranberry satin glass, mold blown. The exterior surface has HP flowers. The pattern name describes the physical shape which Peterson referred to as a "Fig" or "Onion."[13] There is a Mt. Washington catalog drawing of this shaker pattern that shows a thin curled metal stem attached to the pointed end of the spring fingered top; the shaker is labeled as a "Beet." However, in all our years of salt shaker viewing and handling, we have never seen one of the aforementioned tops. It is our belief that due to the fragility and impractical design of such a top, there were too many factory production problems associated with it and, it was never released to production. The actual patent drawing filed March 31, 1891, shows no curling stem associated with the shaker top.[14] The ornate silver-plated metal holding stand is marked "Aurora S.P. Mfg Co." This silver factory was organized in 1869 and located at Aurora, Illinois, where it operated until around 1915 when it was succeeded by "Mulholland Bros. Inc." It is obvious that the metal condiment holder was specifically designed to hold a "Fig" salt and pepper shaker. The shakers are 1¾" tall with HP floral decoration. Circa 1891 – 1895. Very rare as a complete set! **$925.00 – 975.00** set.

Roland collection

Coalmer collection

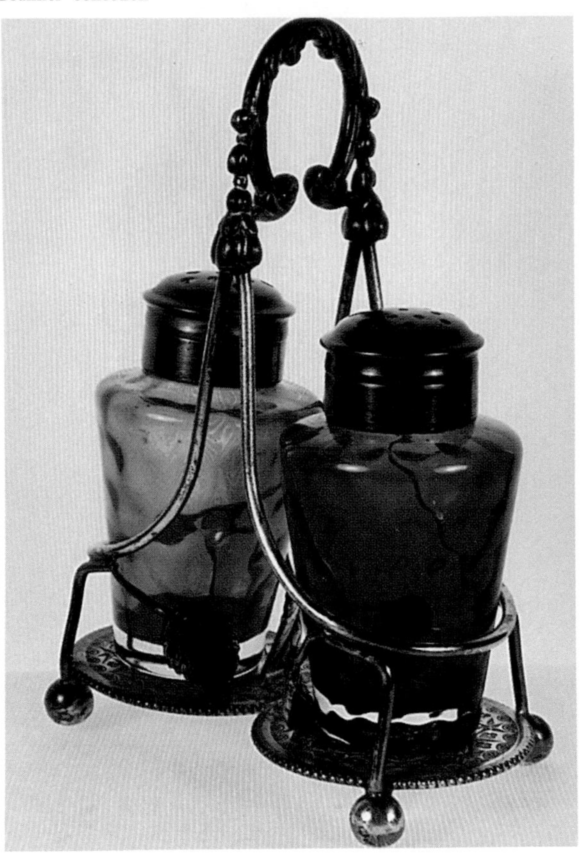

Inverted Thumbprint, Tapered Pegs (condiment): Clear cranberry glass, dual mold blown with an extended HP orange, white, and green stemmed floral garland encircling the exterior. The inside surface has small IVT. The visual geometric shape was achieved by a pattern design that has each side gradually tapering down toward the base. Each of the two illustrated ornate silver-plated holders are unmarked. Circa 1883 – 1887. The shakers are 2⅜" tall x 1½" wide; 1" base diameter. Rare! **$325.00 – 360.00** each set.

Harris collection

MOP Diamond Quilted (cruet set): Opaque satinized rose-to-white shaded cased glass containing a Diamond Quilted air trap pattern; mold blown. The shakers have a barrel shape. The 5" tall cruet (measured without stopper) has excellent deep rose-to-white coloring; the salt and pepper shakers likewise. There are several chipped-out air trap segments on the cruet base which has caused exposure of the inner white cased layer. The 3⅞" long clear glass stopper is not original.[15] The metal holding stand is stamped "Pelton Bros & Co." St. Louis, Missouri. It is 11⅞" in height to the top of the loop-shaped lifting handle. Circa 1885 – 1889. Rare as a complete set! Salt and pepper, **$850.00 – 900.00.** Cruet, due to damage and lack of original stopper very little monetary value!

Krauss collection

Mother of Pearl Herringbone (condiment): Opaque satinized shaded blue cased art glass with a herringbone air trap pattern, mold blown (see our Vol. II, p. 145 for a similar type shaker). Each shaker is 3¼" tall with matching two-piece metal tops. The ornate and unique quadruple plate metal holder is supported by four individual legs and is marked "Meriden B. Company." This silver house was established in 1879 and remained an independent firm until it merged with the International Silver Co. of Canada Ltd during 1912. Circa 1884 – 1888. Rare! **$900.00 – 950.00** set.

Herbert collection

Mother of Pearl Raindrop Barrel (condiment): Opaque blue and red to pink shaded art glass, dual mold air trap raindrop patterns on each condiment piece. The set consists of a salt, pepper, and mustard. The bulbous mustard shades from blue to a frosted translucent base. This shaker pattern is illustrated in our Vol. II, p. 147. The silver-plated holder is unmarked. Circa 1885 – 1890. Shakers, 3¼" tall; mustard, 3⅛" tall; all have two-piece metal tops. Rare set! **$1,000.00 – 1,100.00** set.

Pearl, Christmas (condiment): Opaque opalware glass, mold blown. In our Vol. II book we documented that significant quantities of the "Christmas Pearl" shakers were produced by Mt. Washington for Dana Alden and that they were subsequently fitted with the December 25, 1877, dated salt shaker tops containing his patented agitator.[16] The companion "Christmas Pearl" pepper tops, etc. are not dated. We are illustrating the fact that various HP and transfer-colored designs were applied to this ware primarily in the form of floral sprays. To complete the story of this ware we are, showing a trio of "Christmas Pearl" condiment dispensers in an original Alden castor set metal holder. These metal retaining holders can be found marked "Alden Griffith & Co. Boston, Mass" or "Alden Salt Castor Co. Dana K. Alden PAT'Ds Griffith, Boston, Mass." An example of each stand (which have the same form and shape) was loaned to us by Lesley and Dick Harris so that the aforementioned bottom markings could be verified by us. These sets were sold for a decade or so during the 1880s and early 1890s. From an aesthetic standpoint they lack eye appeal, perhaps this is a reason why a complete set is rarely seen in today's antique glass market place; the shakers do have collector appeal. Rare as a complete set! **$700.00 – 800.00** complete set.

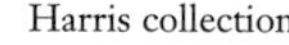

Harris collection

Rathbun collection

Krauss collection

Krauss collection

Pillar, Ribbed "Blue Dot" (condiments): Opaque opalware glass, mold blown. This ware is an outstanding example of the artistic capabilities of the Mt. Washington/Pairpoint decorating department. We are illustrating a matched shaker pair condiment containing HP reddish leaves with very thin stems and randomly applied round painted blue dots over a tan colored background. Also shown is a three-piece condiment set consisting of salt, pepper, and mustard having brown leaves and HP blue dots on a white background. Today's art glass collectors refer to this type of ware as "Mt. Washington Blue Dot Decoration." At various times the factory produced a wide variety of forms/shapes containing these small round blue dots. Various advanced Mt. Washington/Pairpoint collectors try to obtain as many examples of the "Blue Dot" pieces as possible; thus, giving this ware a very high collectibility factor. All the shakers and mustard are circa 1885 – 1894. Shakers, 3⅜" tall with the matched decorated pair having single screw-on metal tops; the shakers on the three-piece condiment set have two-piece metal tops. Mustard, 2⅝" tall. The matched shaker pair metal holder was made by F.B. Rogers Silver Co., Taunton, Massachusetts; the three-piece condiment holder was produced by Wilcox Silver Plate Co., Meriden, Connecticut. Rare! **$400.00 – 430.00** two-piece set; **$610.00 – 635.00** three-piece set.

Krauss collection

Pillar, Ribbed Burmese (three-piece condiment): Opaque satinized heat sensitive "Burmese" glass, mold blown with very good pink to yellow shading. This set consists of a salt, pepper, and mustard having yellow, lavender, and green floral sprays encircling each shaker; the mustard has blue, white, and green decoration. All of the aforesaid pieces are contained within an original wire-formed Pairpoint marked stand that is 7½" to the top of the lifting handle. The shakers, 3¾" tall; mustard, 2⅝" tall; all have two-piece metal tops. Circa 1885 – 1890. Rare as a complete decorated set! **$1,900.00 – 2,000.00** set.

Krauss collection

Pillar, Ribbed Burmese (four-piece condiment): Opaque undecorated satin "Burmese" glass, mold blown. The set consists of a salt, pepper, mustard, and oil bottle. The silver-plated holder is marked "F.B. Rogers Silver Co." Salt and pepper, 3¾" tall; oil bottle, 3⅞ tall with stopper removed; mustard, 3⅝" tall. The holding stand is 7¼" tall to the top of the lifting handle. Circa 1885 – 1891. Four-piece Burmese condiment sets are very rare! **$2,200.00 – 2,400.00** set.

Krauss collection

Pillar, Ribbed Garish (condiment): Opaque white opalware glass, mold blown. The term garish means too bright, glaring, showy, or gaudy. We will leave it up to the reader to pick an appropriate word that relates to this set. Each shaker contains HP dark green foliage that shades into orange and tan coloring at the base of each condiment dispenser. The two-cup silver-plated metal holder was made by Morgan Silver Co., Boston. This set is circa 1886 – 1894. Each shaker is 3⅝" tall with two-piece metal tops. Very scarce! **$170.00 – 200.00** set.

Herbert collection

Pillar, Ribbed Opalware (condiment): Opaque shiny opalware glass, mold blown. This is a seldom seen condiment set in basic milk glass. The set consists of salt, pepper, and mustard in an original Pairpoint marked metal holder. Shakers, 3⅝" tall; mustard, 2⅝" tall; all pieces have two-piece metal tops. Circa 1890 – 1894. Very scarce as a complete set. **$255.00 – 270.00** set.

Krauss collection

Krauss collection

Pillar, Ribbed Mt. Washington Peachblow (condiment): Opaque homogeneous satin glass shading from a pale grayish-blue to pink; mold blown in what we call the classic "Ribbed Pillar" pattern that was used by Mt. Washington on some of their other types of shakers. The coloration is achieved by the use of a heat sensitive glass containing a small amount of cobalt or copper oxide as a colorant.[17] The condiment set, containing a matching salt and pepper, is shown in an original "Pairpoint" silver-plated holder. The shakers are 3⅝" tall with original two-piece metal tops. Circa 1886. This is an extremely rare art glass produced for only a very short period of time. We are also separately illustrating two additional shakers; a satinized piece (left), and a glossy (not satinized) shaker (right). The glossy Peachblow pieces are the rarest and most difficult to collect. All of the shakers are in excellent condition. There is no established value baseline for the shakers we have illustrated. **NPD.**

Krauss collection

Krauss collection

Pillar, Ribbed "Signed" Burmese (condiment): Opaque satinized "Burmese" glass, mold blown. This popular factory pattern was used on various types of art glass. The unique and rare thing about this set is the presence of a Mt. Washington signed paper label with the words "MT.W.G.CO. Burmese PATD.DEC.15,1885" on the bottom of each shaker (see the illustration).[18] Consisting of a salt, pepper, and oil bottle, the glass shades from pink to yellow on each piece shown within their original Pairpoint metal holder. Salt and pepper, 3⅜" tall; oil bottle, 3¼" tall to the top of the opening. Circa 1885 – 1886. Extremely rare with signature labels! The glass lacks some depth of pink coloring. **NPD.**

Krauss collection

Krauss collection

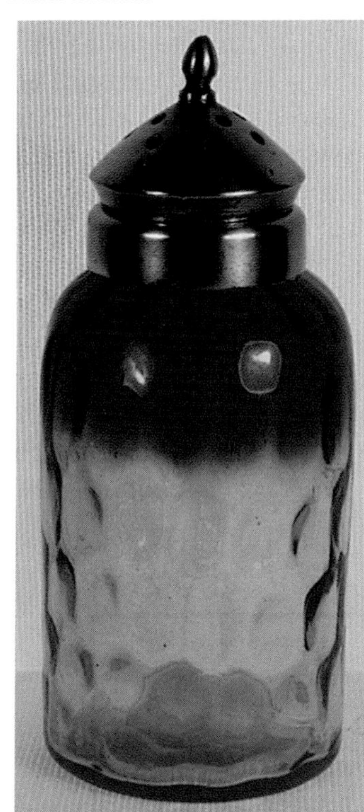

Coalmer collection

Rose Amber (two- and three-piece condiments): Clear deep ruby glass shading to a delicate amber color at the shaker base, dual mold blown. The pattern consists of IVT on the inside; the exterior surface is smooth and undecorated. For additional details, the reader is referred to our Vol. II, pages 150 and 156. This type of heat sensitive glass is generally referred to as "Amberina Art Glass" today despite the fact that Mt. Washington referred to it as "Rose Amber" to avoid patent and trademark litigation with the New England Glass Co., who had patent rights to the product name "Amberina." "Rose Amber" ware will be found in various silver-plated condiment holders, since salt and pepper shakers, etc. were often purchased from Mt. Washington by various silver companies and marketed to the public by use of their own in-house manufactured condiment holder configurations. Likewise, Mt. Washington purchased condiment holders from various outside silver-plate manufacturers in order to realize monetary savings by way of competitive bids. The pictured shakers are 3¼" tall with two-piece metal tops; the stoppered oil bottle in the three-piece set is 4¼" tall with stopper removed. Circa 1884 – 1888. Rare! Salt and pepper, **$775.00 – 800.00** set; three-piece set with oil bottle, **$1,300.00 – 1,400.00** set.

Krauss collection

Krauss collection

Twelve Optic Ribbed Barrel (condiment): Clear amber glass, dual mold blown. This is barrel-shaped ware containing 12 optic vertical ribs on their inside surface and enamel HP floral sprays on the smooth exterior surfaces. Circa 1884 – 1890. The set consists of salt, pepper, mustard, and oil cruet bottles. The silver-plated holder was made by Rogers Bros. The salt and pepper are 3¼" tall with two-piece metal tops; the mustard 3⅛" tall including metal top; the cruet is 3½" tall with glass stopper removed. Rare as a complete set! **$550.00 – 600.00** set.

NATIONAL GLASS COMPANY
19 Different Factories
(January 1900 – January 1904)

Various independent factories began signing up (selling out) to the National Glass combine during the fall of 1899. Official corporate business began on January 1, 1900. In an effort to survive, National Glass was operating as a holding company in 1904 by leasing their surviving factories to their managers. By 1908 the firm had been in bankruptcy and was forced into receivership. Ultimately, only the McKee, Cambridge, and Indiana, Pennsylvania, factories managed to pull out of National with their workers, reputations, and factories intact. During the aforementioned failure many molds were sold that turned up later being sold by a number of different factories to the consumer markets. Thus, absolute pattern attribution (by modern authors) of various National patterns can present various challenges.

Lockwood collection

National's #1004: Opaque white opalware glass, mold blown. This pattern was produced by National at the Lancaster Glass Works, Lancaster, Ohio.[1] A round-shaped shaker with a ring at the neck and tapering outward to a wider base. Has a horizontal band of 15 slanted concave panels near the bottom. Each panel is separated from the next one by a slightly zippered line. The bottom is rayed. Circa 1901. 2½" tall x 1¾" wide. Scarce! **$9.00 – 15.00.**

Lockwood collection

Radiant No. 512: Clear glass, mold blown and pressed. Clear sparkling glass in a cylindrical shape. Lower one-third bulges below a wide beveled horizontal line and above a scalloped foot. Each scallop holds an impressed daisy.[2] This pattern is also known as "Hobble Skirt." Produced at Riverside Glass Works while being operated by National Glass. Also produced in frosted crystal. Circa 1901. 3" tall x 1⅞" wide. Very scarce! **$25.00 – 35.00.**

Lockwood collection

Wellsburg (National's #681): Clear heavy glass, mold blown and pressed. The pattern amounts to six vertical panels with beaded borders and six convex ovals filling the panels that graduate in size from a panel's top to become larger at the bottom. These panels are separated by slightly wider concave vertical panels.[3] This pattern is known to have been produced in toothpick holders with gold or ruby stain. This National pattern was also produced at Dalzell, Gilmore & Leighton, Findlay, Ohio. Circa 1901. 2¾" tall x 2⅞" wide at the bottom. Scarce! **$19.00 – 26.00.**

NEW ENGLAND GLASS COMPANY
Cambridge, Massachusetts
(1818 – 1888)

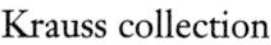

Krauss collection

Agata (three-piece cruet): Opaque shiny rose shading to off-white at the bottom, mold and free-blown finished. Distinct mottled Agata-stained splotches cover the majority of each of the three-pieces.[1] The set consists of two shakers and a handled cruet with the original stopper in place. The shakers are 3⅝" tall with original two-piece metal tops; the cruet, 4⅛" tall to the top of the pouring spout. It should be noted that the value of Agata art glass is dependent upon the quality of the mottled staining present on each piece. The illustrated cruet has outstanding color but has been broken and professionally repaired. The salt and pepper shakers are in excellent condition. Circa 1887. The metal condiment stand is 10" tall to the top of the lifting handle. Very rare! **$2,200.00 – 2,400.00** set.

Krauss collection

Agata (two-piece condiment): Opaque shiny rose glass shading to an off-white with Agata mottled stain. Mold and free-blown finished. The unmarked silver-plated stand is 5¼" tall to the top of the lifting handle. Circa 1887. Very rare! Excellent condition. **$2,400.00 – 2,550.00** set.

Krauss collection

Barrel, Inverted Honeycomb: Clear amber glass, dual mold blown. This barrel pattern tapers at both ends from a bulging center. The inside surface is completely covered with inverted honeycombs. The smooth exterior surface has a HP blue/white and pink floral spray that covers approximately two-thirds of the shaker. Circa 1884 – 1887. 3¼" tall with a two-piece metal top. Very scarce! **$135.00 – 155.00.**

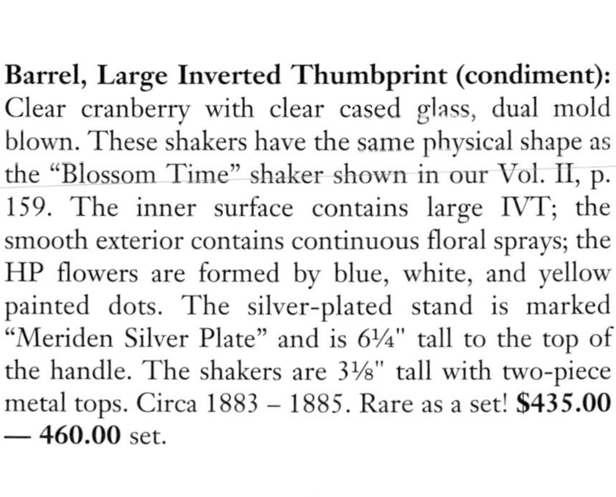

Barrel, Large Inverted Thumbprint (condiment): Clear cranberry with clear cased glass, dual mold blown. These shakers have the same physical shape as the "Blossom Time" shaker shown in our Vol. II, p. 159. The inner surface contains large IVT; the smooth exterior contains continuous floral sprays; the HP flowers are formed by blue, white, and yellow painted dots. The silver-plated stand is marked "Meriden Silver Plate" and is 6¼" tall to the top of the handle. The shakers are 3⅛" tall with two-piece metal tops. Circa 1883 – 1885. Rare as a set! **$435.00 — 460.00** set.

Krauss collection

Coalmer collection

Barrel, Tall Optic Rib: Clear amethyst glass, dual mold blown. The pattern amounts to a tall (stretched) barrel containing 10 optic ribs on the inside surface. The exterior surface contains a large HP blooming plant on the front and back of the shaker. Circa 1884 – 1887. 3⅝" tall with a two-piece metal top. Also produced in decorated Amberina. Rare! **$175.00 – 200.00.**

Krauss collection

Barrel, Varying Honeycomb (condiment): Clear electric blue glass, dual mold blown with the inner surface containing a raised honeycomb motif that varies in size when viewed from top to bottom. This is the same mold that was used by the New England Glass Co. to produce their "Blossom Time" shaker (see page 159 of our Vol. II). The smooth exterior surface of the mustard and shakers are decorated with what appears to be HP apple blossom(s) supported by an extended green vine encircling the circumference of each piece. The shakers are 3⅜" tall; the mustard is 2⅝" tall; all have two-piece metal tops. Circa 1884 – 1887. The silver-plated metal holder was made by E. G. Webster & Son, Brooklyn, New York, which was formed as an outgrowth from the E. G. Webster & Bro., in 1886. This firm remained in business until it was purchased by the International Silver Co. in 1928, and the factory was then moved to Meriden, Connecticut. Rare as a complete set! **$415.00 – 435.00** set.

Krauss collection

Blossom Time (condiment): Clear decorated Amberina art glass, dual mold blown. This pattern was named by A.G. Peterson and has a fuchsia-red color that extends approximately three-quarters of the distance downward and then shades into a soft amber. The shakers have elaborate hand-decorated floral sprays applied to the barrel shaped motif containing IVT on the inside surface of each shaker (see our Vol. II, p. 259). Circa 1883 – 1885. The shakers are each 3⅛" tall with two-piece metal tops. The silver-plated holder is stamped "Wilcox Silver Plate Co., Meriden, CT." Overall height of the holding stand is 7" to the top of the lifting handle. Rare! **$825.00 – 850.00** set.

Coalmer collection

Coalmer collection

Bull's Eye, Elaborate Amberina: We are illustrating a front and back view of a clear fuchsia-red color that extends approximately three-quarters of the distance downard and then blends into a soft amber to provide outstanding Amberina coloration. The dual mold blown shaker contains a small bull's eye inside surface pattern. The exterior surface contains delicate HP decoration of the type that is present on the "Small Amberina Bulb" shaker illustrated in our Vol. II, p. 158. The physical configuration is very similar to the "Blossom Time" piece shown in our Vol. II, p. 159. Circa 1883 – 1885. 3¼" tall with a two-piece metal top. This type of decorated Amberina art glass is very rare! **$750.00 – 775.00.**

Krauss collection

Curved Ribbing: *Clear* Amberina and *plated* Amberina glass, dual mold blown. This disclosure has taken a long time to verify! However, these illustrated shakers prove that this pattern mold was used to produce Amberina shakers and was later utilized for the production of an extremely rare plated Amberina shaker.[2] Over the years we have viewed several prominent Amberina collections and had never seen both Amberina glass types produced in this pattern; nor, had we ever heard of any known production from our contacts with prominent art glass collectors and dealers. Circa 1883 – 1886. 1⅞" tall with the original type two-piece metal tops. The Amberina shaker is very rare! Plated Amberina extremely rare! Amberina, **$900.00 – 1,000.00;** plated Amberina, **NPD.**

Krauss collection

Cylindrical Plated Amberina (condiment): Opaque golden yellow at the base shading to a deep fuchsia-red at the top, mold blown. Thin protruding ribs are present on the outer glass layer; the inside has a creamy colored opal lining. The silver-plated condiment holder is unmarked. The shakers are configured in a simple cylinder-shaped pattern with a small creased neck beneath a single glass ring. Each shaker is 3½" tall with original two-piece metal tops. Fuchsia coloration length is outstanding, adding considerably to the value of the set. Circa 1886. Extremely rare! **NPD.**

Coalmer collection

Honeycomb, Tapering Barrel: We are illustrating a pair of Bluina art glass shakers that are dual mold blown. These shakers have an inside honeycomb pattern with a smooth exterior surface. The pair have HP pink and white flowers supported by a green-to-yellow shaded leaf stem. Circa 1884 – 1887. 3⅜" tall with two-piece metal tops. Rare! **$360.00 – 375.00** pair.

Rathbun collection

Harris collection

Honeycomb, Tapering Barrel, Variant: Illustrated are two shaker rarities; on the left is a HP Rubina; on the right a HP Bluina. It is significant to note that the pair is well matched in terms of their HP floral decorations. Both are dual mold blown glass with a smooth outside surface, each inside interior has a small honeycomb pattern. Their physical shape amounts to a flat shouldered barrel having two-piece metal tops that are not original. In addition we are illustrating a pair of Amberina art glass shakers of a similar pattern mold configuration that have the correct type of two-piece tops. 3⅛" tall. Circa 1886 – 1890. Rare! Bluina and Rubina pair, **$310.00 – 330.00;** Amberina pair, **$700.00 – 750.00.**

Lockwood collection

New England Miniature Variant: Opaque cased art glass, dual mold blown. The inside layer has fired-on yellow-to-white shaded coloring. The smooth outer surface layer contains an elaborate white and blue floral sprig. This is the same shaker mold as shown in our Vol. II, page 161 in a New England Peachblow miniature condiment set. Circa 1885 – 1887. 2½" tall with a two-piece metal top; the shaker was probably part of a condiment set. Rare! **$450.00 – 500.00.**

Krauss collection

Opaque Green, New England's (cruet set): Opaque homogeneous pale green satin art glass, mold and free-blown finished. The shakers have a bulging base that forms a convex (tapering) surface toward the top that is narrowest within the lower neck area. The handled cruet, with an original stopper, has a large bulging base with the mottled blue staining on the narrow neck area. The process for producing this novel type of stained glassware was patented January 18, 1887, by Joseph Locke of the New England Glass Works at Cambridge, Massachusetts. His patented process also encompasses the Agata and Pomona stained art glass produced by this glasshouse. The staining methods employed are fully described in our Vol. II, p. 158 relative to Agata art glass. An excellent example of the applied blue metallic stain pattern is illustrated on page 54 of *Nineteenth Century Glass* by A.C. Revi; also see page 64 of *Art Glass Nouveau* by Grover. Obviously, the value of each opaque green piece is contingent upon the condition of the mottled blue metallic stain that is present on each article. Circa 1887. The shakers are 2⅝" tall; cruet, 4⅝" tall to the edge of the pouring spout. The elaborate silver-plated holder is marked "Aurora SP Co. quad. plate" and measured 11" tall to the top of the lifting handle. Very rare as a complete set! **$3,000.00 – 3,200.00** set; shakers, **$750.00 – 800.00** pair.

Coalmer collection

Coalmer collection

Pillar Optic Rib: Clear amethyst and blue glass, dual mold blown. The various HP flowers and leaves are applied at random to the exterior surface of both shakers. The floral colors are shaded blue, yellow-to-orange, pink, and white etc. on the amethyst shaker; HP white is prominent on the blue shaker which provides a three-dimensional pseudo-cameo look. The physical pattern is that of a nonsymmetrical pillar with a creased ring neck at the top. The inner surface has optic ribbing. This ware is a variation of the "Ten Rib Optic" shaker illustrated in blue in our Vol. II, p. 261. Circa 1883 – 1887. 4⅛" tall with two-piece metal tops. Rare! **$160.00 – 175.00** each.

Krauss collection

Krauss collection

Pomona, Blueberry and Leaf (condiment): Translucent frosted clear glass; mold and free-blown finished. We illustrated an identical shaker in our Vol. II, p. 162 indicating that it is first grind; instead, these shakers are second grind Pomona.[3] This ware was made by the New England Glass Co. for a very short period of time, circa 1886, and are therefore quite rare in shakers. Each shaker is 3⅝" tall with two-piece metal tops. The silver-plated holder is marked "Meriden B Company." **$850.00 – 900.00** set.

Ribbed, Dual Mold Amberina: Clear fuchsia-red that extends approximately one-half of the way downward before blending into a soft amber; dual mold blown. This is a cylindrical pattern with 12 inside optic ribs and a ring-shaped collar.[4] Circa 1883 – 1886. Shakers, 3¾" tall with two-piece metal tops. The metal holder is marked "Meriden B Co." and has a height of 6¾" to the top of the lifting handle. Rare as a complete set! **$475.00 – 525.00** set.

Authors' collection

Tapered Rib, Optic: Clear electric blue glass, dual mold blown. The pattern amounts to a small round shaker containing eight optic ribs inside. The outer surface is smooth and has a single HP pink-white pair of roses with shaded green leaves. The bottom has a short glass extension for condiment set retention. Circa 1884 – 1887. Also produced in Amberina. 2⅜" tall with a two-piece metal top. Rare! **$180.00 – 205.00.**

THE NEW MARTINSVILLE GLASS MFG. CO.
New Martinsville, West Virginia
(1900 – 1944)

Factory production began in early 1901. The factory made both commercial and art/pattern glass. While over the years there were ownership and corporate name changes, the factory managed to remain in continuous operation. Their art glass was no doubt produced due to early-on employment of Joseph Webb after he left the Phoenix Glass Co. Webb remained at New Martinsville until March, 1905. For additional detail refer to our Vol. II, page 163.

White collection

Palm Tendril: Opaque clambroth-like opalware glass, mold blown. This is a relatively plain shaker except for three embossed leaf patterns that are properly spaced around the body circumference. Because the embossed pattern was quite weak, the owner temporarily painted it so it would be visible when photographed. The general glass coloration leans in the direction of a clambroth appearance that was not to be picked up by the camera. Circa 1917 with production into the 1920s.[1] 2⅞" tall x 2⅜" wide; 2½" base diameter. Very scarce! **$25.00 – 33.00.**

Lockwood collection

Pleated Medallion: Clear (uncolored) glass, mold blown. Originally cataloged as the factory's No. 713 in 1910. This is a busy pattern having four vertical ellipses, each framed by bands of pleating. Each frame overlaps the adjacent one forming a diamond. Each "V" above and below between the frames has a fan-ray pattern. Centered in each oval is a depressed rayed formal daisy with a raised central bead.[2] The body of the shaker is tapered to a larger round bottom. Also produced in plain gold and ruby decoration. Circa 1910. 3⅜" tall; 2¼" wide. Scarce! **$23.00 – 30.00.**

Lockwood collection

Vining Rose: Opaque white opalware glass, mold blown. The upper round shape flares to a bulging lower half; the embossed branch with full-blown roses and leaves is repeated on the back side. The HP motif is done in pink and green. A 1904 New Martinsville catalog illustrates and lists this shaker as their No. 57. This ware was also produced in various shades of turquoise, salmon, and opal (some with gold paint).[3] Circa 1904. 3⅛" tall x 2¼" wide. Very scarce. **$40.00 – 50.00.**

THE NICKEL PLATE GLASS CO.
Fostoria, Ohio
(1888 – 1891)

The company was formed during March 1888, and began production during August of the same year. A.J. Smith was president and Charles Russell, manager. The company was named Nickel Plate because it was located adjacent to the Nickel Plate Railroad tracks within the Nickel Plate subdivision of Fostoria, Ohio. Such skilled glass men as A.J. Smith, formerly with the Elson Glass Co, and B.M. Hildreth, formerly from Hobbs Brockunier, were with the factory from the beginning. The factory made both crystal and opalescent ware and a new blown line of tableware and bar goods with key border known as "Grecian Key." The plant became Factory N of the U.S. Glass Co. during mid – 1891.

Rathbun collection

Greek Key, Double: Translucent vaseline opalescent glass; mold blown. As the pattern name implies, this rather bulbous-shaped shaker contains an opalescent Greek Key motif with a single neck ring and a small extended base for possible use within a condiment holder. Also, there is known production in white opalescent and crystal. 2⅝" tall. Circa 1892. Rare! **$75.00 – 90.00.**

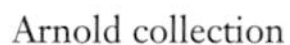

Arnold collection

Greek Key, Double (mustard): Translucent light blue opalescent glass; mold blown. We are illustrating this piece because it was originally offered for sale as a salt shaker. Over our many years of collecting we have seen this type of mistake occasionally occur because a seller has added a salt shaker top to a what was originally a mustard that had become separated from a three- or four-piece condiment set.[1] 3" tall; 2½" at widest point; 1⅝" diameter base. Circa 1892. Rare! **$100.00 – 115.00.**

HARRY NORTHWOOD GLASS PATTERNS
Various Factory Locations
(1887 – 1925)

As we pointed out in our previous two books, Harry Northwood's glass career from 1887 to 1920 involved him in at least eight glass factories (not to mention his involvement with National Glass Corporation beginning in 1899, or Phoenix Glass in 1883 to early 1884). The many designs and patterns that he either innovated or influenced are numerous. In our opinion, trying to tie down with *absolute certainty* exactly which pattern was made at which particular factory within a specific time frame by way of absolute attribution presents too many pitfalls and uncertainties. However, our hat is off to authors William Heacock and James Measell for their efforts and accomplishments relative to various Northwood factory pattern attributions.

We cited examples in our 1992 book (updated in 1996 and now labeled as Vol. II) as to why we believe it best to simply list and illustrate the various known Northwood patterns and leave it up to our readers to decide as to which factory each pattern was produced. The reader should remain cognizant of the National Glass Corporation's policy of moving various molds from factory to factory to meet the needs of their corporate business. In various instances, this type of manufacturing operation further obscures absolute Northwood attribution certainty.

To cite additional examples of where we are coming from, let's address the situation involving the Northwood/Dugan/Diamond factories who at different times each manufactured glass at the same Indiana, Pennsylvania, factory location, also Northwood's earlier years.

It has been definitely established that Harry Northwood introduced custard glass at his Indiana plant in 1897. Among the patterns innovated by him was "Inverted Fan & Feather." In the Dugan/Diamond book, authors Heacock, Measell, and Wiggins declared on pages 37 and 38 that the pink slag color of this pattern was developed by Harry Bastow after Northwood had left the Indiana plant and it was operating as part of National Glass. The final perfection of the pink slag formula is credited to Thomas E. A. Dugan, who made the pink slag pattern in Inverted Fan & Feather after the plant became Dugan Glass in early 1904. Dugan also produced this pattern in opalescent blue and emerald green. Our point relative to attribution is that the producing of the Inverted Fan & Feather pattern in other colors does not change the fact that the pattern design was first conceived and produced by Harry Northwood, therefore, it should be attributed to him. In antique glass literature, patterns are usually attributed first to a factory and then to the individual that created it if known. Subsequent added pattern colors by others are interesting but don't change who first conceived the pattern.

In our current Hobbs, Brockunier write-up of the pattern that Peterson named "Pillar, Sixteen" (which comes in two salt shaker sizes), Bill Heacock raises additional disputation relative to the attribution of this pattern.

In Volume 3, page 41 of his pattern research book series entitled *Collecting Glass* Heacock states that both "Pillar, Sixteen" and "Spatter Glass Pleat" mold designs are Northwood circa 1889. Heacock further states that his previous attribution of this ware to Hobbs (beginning with his Book 1 on toothpicks) was based upon the displays of these pattern(s) at the Oglebay Institute Mansion Museum at Wheeling, West Virginia, that attributed them to Hobbs. Additional negative comments are made about some of the museum's other attributions.

An attempt to further attribute the aforesaid patterns to Northwood was carried over into his book *Harry Northwood The Early Years* by way of the "Ribbed Pillar" pattern discussed on pages 26 and 27. However, in our opinion, precise Northwood attribution of "Pillar, Sixteen" is not established. If the reader wants a complete picture of the aforementioned facts and theory it will involve detailed reading of the Heacock books already mentioned plus H-9, page 57. We wish you luck!

Coalmer collection

Alaska: Cobalt blue homogeneous glass, dual mold blown. This is a bulging based shaker containing an external fine threaded neck. Usually the inside surface of this pattern contains 16 vertical ribs; however, due to the deep cobalt blue coloring the ribbing does not show up. This is a rare shaker in this color; we are very pleased to present and confirm its existence. 2⅜" tall. Rare! **$135.00 – 150.00.**

Rathbun collection

Bubble Lattice, Opalescent: Translucent yellow opalescent glass, dual mold blown. The pattern name (Lattice) refers to the crossing of slanted diagonal lines that produce a diamond-shaped design. This particular shaker was produced by use of a "Quilted Phlox" mold. Many of today's collectors refer to this ware as vaseline opalescent glass. However, here is another classic example of a Northwood pattern that was first made at the *Northwood Glass Works*, Martin's Ferry, Ohio; subsequently at *The Northwood Company*, Indiana, Pennsylvania; and by *National Glass* and possibly *Dugan Glass* after 1900.[1] The latter three factories, all located at the same Indiana, Pennsylvania, site, have this pattern attribution based upon glass shards unearthed there. As a result of the aforesaid, this ware is circa 1888 to 1904. This shaker produces a strong florescence under black light exposure. 3"tall. Rare in this color! **$225.00 – 250.00.**

Coalmer collection

Beaded Crosstie: Two shakers are illustrated; one in cased green, the other in homogeneous blue opaque glass, mold blown. Both shakers have an extended base to configure them for usage as part of a condiment set. The pattern name was innovated by Peterson. This ware has been attributed to Harry Northwood by authors Heacock, Measell, and Wiggins by way of color and motif similarity.[2] The shakers are illustrated in both the *Harry Northwood The Early Years* and The *Dugan/Diamond* books written by the aforementioned authors. 2¼" tall. Circa 1894 – 1900. Very scarce! **$90.00 – 110.00** pair.

Krauss collection

Krauss collection

Chrysanthemum Sprig "Pagoda" (cruet set): We are illustrating two complete cruet sets in this pattern; one in opaque blue and the other in opaque custard glass.[3] Both sets contain gilt decorated chrysanthemum floral sprigs and are very difficult sets to acquire in today's antique market.[4] Shakers, 3" tall; cruet, 5¼" tall with stopper removed; round holding tray, 6⅛" in diameter. The cruet stoppers are original. Circa 1898 – 1904. Rare in a complete set! Custard set, **$1,400.00 – 1,500.00;** opaque blue set, **$2,100.00 – 2,200.00.**

Flat Flower: Translucent/frosted Rubina glass, mold blown. This is a four-sided shaker having two large flat panels, each containing an embossed, large fully petaled flower in a unique pink-to-clear colored shading. This pattern is illustrated in our Vol. II, page 171, and it's a Harry Northwood item, circa 1894 – 1896. We are also illustrating another shaker in opaque white iridescent glass with an embossed petaled flower in yellow and dark red. Shakers, 4" tall; very rare in the frosted Rubina color! Rare in yellow and dark red! Rubina, **$325.00 – 350.00**; yellow and dark red, **$185.00 – 200.00**.

Krauss collection

Ridgway collection

Rathbun collection

Northwood's Jewel (Threaded Swirl): Clear Rubina, mold blown glass. The base and neck of each shaker contains raised threaded glass. First documented in our Vol. II on page 173, which shows one of these shakers in a cranberry opalescent motif. However, our illustrated pair is unique from the standpoint that it highlights that the base swirling of one shaker slants in a different direction from the other. AAGSSCS President Phil Rathbun raised questions relative to the left/right base swirling methodology involving this pattern. We telephoned Frank Fenton at the Fenton factory and discussed how the aforesaid directional swirling was accomplished. As a bottom line statement Frank said, "The internal ribs began vertical, but are twisted one way or the other by the blower while using the final shape mould. The movement directional pressure established the ribs inside location on the piece being made." During our discussion he indicated that he could think of no reason why a swirl in one direction would be any more rare or significant than one in the opposite direction. It has been established that these Northwood shakers original manufacturer's name (OMN) was "Jewel," and that they were produced circa 1890. 3" tall. Very scarce! **$275.00 – 300.00** pair.

Rathbun collection

MacAllister collection

Jeweled Heart (aka "Victor"): Clear green slightly opalescent glass, mold blown. The pattern name pretty well describes the shaker since the principal motif amounts to a grouping of large inverted heart shapes containing what might be interpreted as a type of jewel adornment. The shaker is bulbous in shape with a beaded neck just below the shaker top. While primarily produced and advertised after the factory operated as Dugan Glass, it is another one of those patterns that has not been clearly attribution separated from National Glass and possible earlier Northwood influence. 2⅝" tall with a base diameter of 1⅜". Circa 1902 – 1912. Very scarce! **$70.00 – 90.00** each.

Krauss collection

Jeweled Heart (cruet set): Clear blue gold decorated glass, mold blown and pressed. The cruet set consists of salt, pepper, toothpick (concealed behind shakers), cruet, and tray.[5] Salt and pepper, 2⅝" tall; toothpick, 2⅜"; cruet, 5⅝" to top of the pouring spout; stopper is original; gold beaded glass tray, 6⅜" in diameter. Circa 1903 – 1908. Rare as a set! **$900.00 – 950.00** set.

Authors' collection

Authors' collection

Nestor: Clear amethyst glass, mold blown. The principal motif of this shaker consists of eight vertical oval panels; every other panel is hand decorated with complex thin white enameled lace work. The round footed base was designed so the shakers could be used as part of a condiment set with a cruet and glass tray.[6] Also produced in decorated and undecorated blue and light green.[7] Circa 1902 – 1906. 3⅛" tall. Due to a high collectibility factor, the decorated shakers are very difficult to obtain. The complete cruet set is rare! Single shaker, **$80.00 – 95.00;** complete cruet set, **$950.00 – 1,100.00.**

Tutelo collection

Opal, Venetian: Opaque opalware, mold blown. This is a bulbous-shaped shaker with an extended bottom for use in a condiment set. The smooth exterior surface contains a HP pink and green floral motif. These opal salts and peppers somewhat resemble C.F. Monroe floral designs, but a considerable opal tableware line was produced at the Indiana factory.[8] Circa 1897 – 1907. 2⅝" tall x 2¼" wide; 1½" base diameter. Very scarce! **$75.00– 90.00.**

Paneled Holly: Translucent white opalescent glass, dual mold blown. This pattern consists of a large oval concave thumbprint that is enclosed within a diamond-shaped panel below stippled holly leaves and berries in raised relief. The pattern appears three times around the shaker circumference. The aforesaid motifs have HP gold decoration. This pattern was also made in blue opalescent, green, crystal, and carnival.[9] Circa 1907 – 1908.[10] 3" tall x 2⅜" wide. Very scarce! **$170.00 – 190.00.**

Lockwood collection

Coalmer collection

Parian Swirl: We are illustrating a pair of opaque satinized blue and cranberry mold-blown glass shakers. The pattern consists of eight lightly embossed swirling ribs. There is considerable analysis of attribution by similarity that resulted in this ware being firmly attributed to Harry Northwood.[11] Due to questionable data, positive attribution was withheld in our Vol. II where we listed it under the Peterson published pattern name "Parian Ruby."[12] This ware is circa 1894 – 1896. 2¾" tall. Very scarce! **$220.00 – 240.00** pair.

Krauss collection

Quilted Phlox: Translucent lavender glass, mold blown. This pattern has two rows of bulging diamonds; each diamond is separated by an embossed flower. While this shaker is discussed in our Vol. II, p. 173, we are illustrating a color that we did not know existed in salt shakers. 3" tall. Rare in this color! **$165.00 – 180.00.**

Rathbun collection

Regent (aka "Leaf Medallion"): Translucent cobalt blue glass, mold blown. An inward curved paneled shaker. The name "Leaf Medallion" seems to pretty well describe this pattern since it amounts to a gold decorated oval shaped motif (in raised relief) that appears to resemble a leaf. "Regent" is the OMN.[13] Circa 1904. 3⅛" tall. Very difficult to obtain in shakers. Also produced in green and amethyst. Rare! **$410.00 – 435.00** pair.

Rathbun collection

Lockwood collection

Venetian, Northwood's: Clear green glass, dual mold blown. The early pattern name by Heacock was "Utopia Optic." The principal exterior motif is an elaborate HP white floral sprig over inside vertical optic ribbing. This optic effect was created by the dual mold process. The physical shape consists of a narrow ringed neck that expands outward into a bulging body. Early trade ads indicate the "Venetian" line was introduced circa 1899 by Northwood. 3" tall x 2⅛" wide. This ware was also produced with an added short extended circular bottom piece for condiment set usage which changes the shaker dimensions to 3¼" tall x 2¼" wide.[14] Other known colors are clear ruby and blue. Rare! **$250.00 – 300.00** pair.

Armstrong collection

Wild Bouquet: Translucent light blue glass with slight opalescence, mold blown. Apparently first produced in custard (Ivory) glass, circa 1898 – 1899. The pattern name is by Metz. The custard pieces contain HP decoration with the raised panel beads outlined in gold.[15] Our illustrated shaker has no decoration. Also produced in light green and opalescent green; some will have HP decoration. Based upon a Butler Bros. catalog[16] this pattern was apparently produced as late as 1903. 3⅜" tall. Rare! **$235.00 – 250.00.**

Zippered Corners condiment (aka "Royal Silver" [OMN]): Pink cased spangled glass, dual mold blown with a clear pressed glass holder utilizing four twisted metal straps to retain the four condiment set pieces. The holder is supported by four large scalloped feet. This pressed glass holder may not be a factory original. Overall stand height is 8½" to the top of the glass lifting handle. Pattern name is by Peterson.[17] The salt and pepper are 3⅜" tall; mustard, 3¾" tall; oil/vinegar bottle, 4½" tall. One of these shakers is pictured in our Vol. II, page 175. These pieces are Harry Northwood's "Royal Silver" pattern, circa 1889 – 1891. However, a *Crockery & Glass Journal* dated June 25, 1891, states Harry Northwood "added lustre to the brilliant lines that they were preparing for the fall season; the latest is sprinkled with gold or silver"[18]...So! from our point of view, the factory name of "Royal Silver" is a bit of a misnomer. Rare as a complete set! **$750.00 – 850.00** set.

Krauss collection

NOVELTY GLASS COMPANY
Fostoria, Ohio
(1891 – 1893)

The plant opened during February 1891, having been built on the site of the burned down Butler Art Glass factory. Henry Crimmel was appointed manager having been a former manager at the Blemont Glass Co., Bellaire, Ohio. A direct quote from a Bellaire, Ohio, newspaper stated that he had purchased some of the moulds from the Belmont Glass Co. The Novelty Glass Co. became part of the U.S. Glass Co. during mid-1892 as Factory T. Unfortunately, the factory was completely destroyed by fire on April 2, 1893, leaving several hundred unemployed.

Krauss collection

Krauss collection

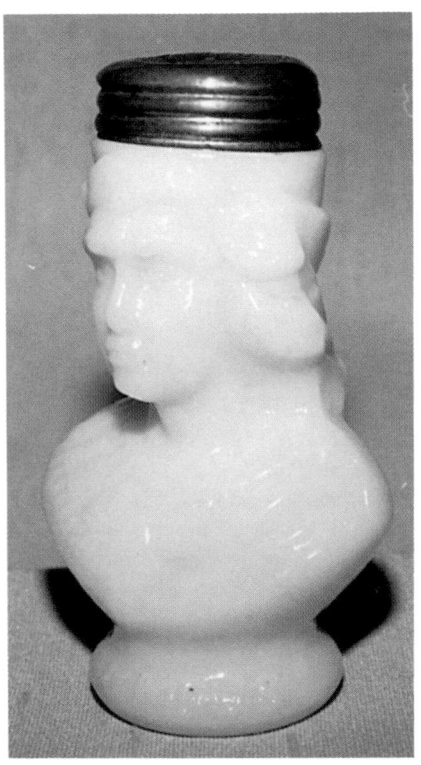

Columbus: Opaque white opalware, mold blown. This is a non-bearded figurine bust of Christopher Columbus that contains a perforated metal top for dispensing condiments such as salt and pepper. The base of the shaker is embossed with the word "Columbus." Today, this ware is sought after by both figurine bottle collectors and antique salt and pepper shaker collectors. An almost identical Columbus shaker is illustrated in our Vol. II, p. 213; the principal difference being that a so-named "Columbus, Bearded" comprises the principal pattern, and the glass color is opaque Nile green. Author Melvin Murray of Fostoria, Ohio, attributes this ware to the Novelty Glass Co. at Fostoria, Ohio, circa 1892 – 1893.[1] 3⅝" tall. Rare! **$850.00 – 900.00** pair.

Krauss collection

Krauss collection

Krauss collection

Columbus, Bearded: Opaque white opalware and clear glass, mold blown and pressed. Two items are illustrated. One of our photographs has the reader looking at a very rare embossed clear pressed glass punch cup containing a gilt painted bust of Columbus. Beneath him is the embossed inscription "1492 COLUMBUS 1892." Obviously if there is a punch cup, somewhere there is a punch bowl. The curators at the Fostoria Glass Museum at Fostoria, Ohio, are still trying to locate one. If any of our readers can help, please let us know. Also illustrated herein is an authentic "Bearded Columbus" shaker in opalware as it was originally produced by Novelty Glass, circa 1892. Within the Imitation Glass section of this book we expose the existence of a fake Bearded Columbus shaker with appropriate explanatory details. The opalware shaker is 3½" tall. This ware was also produced in homogeneous Nile green. Opalware shaker, **$650.00 – 700.00;** punch cup, **NPD.**

Pettijohn collection

Isabella: Opaque green glass, mold blown and pressed. This pair of shakers provides a detailed front and back view of the companion to the "Bearded Columbus" shaker.[2] It is our opinion that the main reason for the collection rarity associated with Isabella is due to the short time frame of existence the factory had before it was destroyed by fire. 3⅝" tall. Circa 1891 – 1892. Very rare! **$1,500.00 – 1,700.00** pair.

OHIO FLINT GLASS COMPANY

Dunkirk, Indiana
(1893 – 1899)
Lancaster, Ohio
(1899 – 1908)

The factory began at Bowling Green, Ohio, using a leased factory while their new one was being constructed at Dunkirk. Unfortunately the Indiana factory was destroyed by fire, so they built another new factory at Lancaster and shortly thereafter became part of the National Glass conglomerate who expanded their production capabilities. After National Glass was pretty much dissolved and became a holding corporation in 1904, the factory was operated independently by their manager(s). The factory finally closed in 1908. One of their rare patterns (today) is "ADA".[1] In late 1908 this factory was reopened as a new tableware glasshouse called the Lancaster Glass Company. Lancaster was absorbed by the Hocking Glass Corporation in 1937.

White collection

Synora Lace: Opaque opalware glass, mold blown. Originally cataloged as pattern #1002; the intricate embossed scrolled motif pattern is repeated four times around this shaker body perimeter. There is a good possibility that this piece was at one time decorated since it has been seen with orange decoration on the raised design motif. Circa 1901 while the factory was part of National Glass. 3¼" tall x 2¾" wide; 2⅜" base diameter. Scarce! **$15.00 – 22.00.**

THE PADEN CITY GLASS MFG. COMPANY

Paden City, West Virginia
(1916 – 1951)

Began operations on November 15, 1916. The factory was created by Mr. David Fisher, and became its first president and CEO. The factory produced quality, handmade, glassware, both pressed and mold blown which was primarily in color. The factory closed on September 21, 1951. Of the 35 years that this glasshouse existed, at least two-thirds involved production during the history-recorded Depression Era in America. In a similar manner to other glass factories, few of their patterns were assigned names but instead were assigned numbers and were so listed in their catalogs to outside jobbers and wholesalers.

Authors' collection

Cone, Thin Footed: Clear dark red pressed glass. This round, plain shaker has no pattern motif other than a tall thin footed cone shape; hence the pattern name it has been given. Red was a common factory produced color, and pieces can sometimes be found that have not received a uniform heating (striking) which caused the red to taper to a yellow colored edging. Some folks have tried to refer to this as an Amberina which is incorrect. Paden City did not produce Amberina glassware. The shakers contain a special weighted metal top that exposes internal star-shaped condiment perforations so that salt or pepper will be able to flow when a shaker is tipped downward. When replaced in the normal upright position the weighted top drops back in place thus protecting its contents from damp air exposure. Circa 1928 – 1936. 3½" tall. Rare! **$115.00 – 130.00** pair.

Tutelo collection

Tree (OMN): Clear glass, mold blown. A plain top portion with a neck ring. The principal pattern has a series of vertical fish-bone rows equally spaced around the body. Arched flutes are established between the vertical fish-bone rows. The shaker has a rayed bottom.[1] Circa 1915 – 1920. 2¾" tall. Very scarce! **$20.00 – 25.00.**

Authors' collection

Ribbed Cone, Footed: Clear red glass, mold blown and pressed. A cone-shaped shaker containing 20 narrow vertical ribs in raised relief on a smooth circular foot. Circa 1924 – 1935. 3⅜" tall with a top that is believed to be original. We have had this shaker in our collection for over 30 years. Very scarce! **$40.00 – 50.00.**

Authors' collection

Thumbprint, Concave Footed: Translucent ruby red glass, dual mold blown. The exterior surface is completely smooth; the inside contains IVT. We described and illustrated this shaker in our 1976 book on page 110. The top edge of this piece shades to a yellow color due to non-uniform heating during production. Circa 1925 – 1936. 3⅜" tall. Rare! **$75.00 –85.00.**

Coalmer collection

Tube, Ringed Base: Clear red glass, mold blown. The shaker pattern consists of a small glass circular tube with an expanded ring at the base. Excellent quality glass. Circa 1927 – 1937. 2⅛" tall with solid silver screw-on tops. Very scarce! **$95.00 – 120.00** pair.

PHOENIX GLASS COMPANY
Monaca, Pennsylvania
(1880 – 1987
...closed as part of Anchor Hocking)

Art glass forms were produced at Phoenix starting in late 1883, and continued on into 1893, when the factory began production of cut glass. An 1885 trade ad advertised Phoenix as the "sole manufacturers of Webb Art Glass." Production of art glass was made possible by the employment of Joseph Webb in 1883 as factory superintendent. To add to the influence of Phoenix colored blown ware was the fact that Harry Northwood was also employed by Phoenix during 1885 until early 1886. Northwood joined Phoenix from the LaBelle Glass Works who had been forced out of business as the result of a flood disaster. Mr Webb was a nephew of Thomas Webb of English art glass renown. While at Phoenix, Webb was awarded several patents relative to the production of art glass among which were rose-pink heat sensitive glass formulas. There is no doubt that Webb plus Northwood influenced the production of both art and opalescent glassware. Trade journal ads confirm that Phoenix produced crackled ware, water sets, ice cream sets, salt and pepper sets; glassware that shades within one and the same article; articles having a body of one color that are plated or cased inside with another color, etc.[1] Webb remained at Phoenix for 10 years. He left in 1893 to accept a position at Libbey Glass in Toledo, Ohio.

Herbert collection

Peachbloom (condiment): Opaque heat sensitive cased glass shading from a deep rose to a delicate pink, mold and free blown finished. This ware has a white inner lining with an exterior heat sensitive color changing layer that has been clear glass covered on the exterior.[2] In an unmarked silver-plated holder the set consists of salt, pepper, and mustard; all have two-piece metal tops. Circa 1884 – 1888. Shakers, 3¼" tall; mustard, 3⅛" tall. Rare! **$1,400.00 – 1,500.00** set.

Ridgway collection

Ridgway collection

Peachbloom, Miniature (condiment): Opaque rose shaded cased art glass, dual mold and free-blown finished. We are illustrating one of the shakers by itself and a separate photo of the complete set and holder. A smooth undecorated satin barrel shaped shaker with heat sensitive glass and a white layered interior. The outer glass layer shades from a light pink at the base to a deep rich red at the top. This type of glass can be found with many richness-of-color variations based upon the time of refiring exposure and gaffer skill at the glory hole. This art glass has been produced in both a glossy and satin finish. These shakers fluoresce yellow under black light exposure because the heat sensitive glass batch apparently contains some oxide of uranium as part of the total batch mixture. Circa 1885 – 1887. 2½" tall with matching two-piece metal tops. The orange silver-plated holder is marked "Wilcox Silver Plate, Meriden, CT." and may not be original. Very rare! **NPD.**

Rathbun collection

Barrel, Deer Optic: Clear amber glass, dual mold blown. Despite our photographic camera angle, this is the same basic shape as the "Elk" shaker illustrated in our Vol. II book on page 177. Our illustrated shaker reveals the inside vertical optic ribbing; the smooth outer surface has a HP brown colored buck and doe grazing in a grassy field area. Another reason for the slight difference in appearance is the lack of a two-piece metal top. Circa 1885 – 1890. 3" tall. Rare! **$100.00 – 125.00.**

Authors' collection

Coin Dot, Phoenix: Clear apricot opalescent glass, dual mold blown. One of the many wide waisted tapering shaker forms that decreases gradually toward its base. The inside surface is completely covered with raised opalescent coin dots that diminish in size in the downward direction. The exterior surface is a smooth apricot color. Circa 1884 – 1887. 2¾" tall with a two-piece metal finial top believed to be original. Rare in apricot! **$175.00 – 200.00.**

H. M. RIO COMPANY
Philadelphia, Pennsylvania

H. M. Rio Co. was a decorative glasshouse that sold decorated glass novelties made from opalware (milk glass) blanks purchased from various glass factories. They produced ladies' vanity powder and pin boxes, salt and pepper shakers, sugar shakers, etc. Their principal line was called "Keystone Ware" which was marketed during the late nineteenth and early twentieth centuries.[1]

Rathbun collection

Keystone Ware: Opaque opalware glass, mold blown. We are illustrating a salt and pepper pair and a salt and sugar shaker. The salt and pepper base exteriors contain four embossed large leaves. The sugar shaker has a similar pattern with three large HP flowers in pink, yellow, and blue; each salt and pepper contains HP flowers in white, orange, and yellow. The aforesaid floral decorations encircle the middle of each shaker. The overall exterior surface has a heavily painted wash in shades of brown. Each piece is bottom signed "R.M.R & Co PHILA KEYSTONE WARE" (see illustrated photo). The salt and pepper are 3" tall; the sugar shaker is 4½" tall; all have two-piece metal tops. Circa 1898 – 1906. Rare! Salt, **$150.00 – 175.00;** sugar shaker, **$375.00 – 400.00;** salt and pepper, **$295.00 – 320.00**

Krauss collection

Rathbun collection

RIVERSIDE GLASS WORKS
Wellsburg, West Virginia
(1880 – 1908)

This factory was established by an experienced group of talented glass craftsman that had left Hobbs, Brockunier, and the Buckeye Glass Co. The Riverside factory specialized in ruby stained and emerald green glass patterns. The firm joined the National Glass Co. in 1899, and lost control of many of their pattern molds as a result of production moves within the conglomerate. After the close-out of National Glass, the factory went into receivership during 1908.

Authors' collection

Box-in-Box (aka Riverside's #420 pattern): Clear ruby stained glass, mold blown. The pattern amounts to a band of six rosettes in high raised relief that completely encircle the lower part of this bulbous shaker. The center of each hex-shaped rosette is ruby stained. The staining of the various #420 pattern forms was done by The Mueller Glass Staining Co.[1] Also produced in crystal, green, and gold.[2] Circa 1894. 2⅞" tall. Very scarce! **$55.00 – 70.00.**

Harris collection

Brilliant, Riverside's: Clear ruby stained glass, mold blown and pressed. The pattern amounts to a series of rounded vertical panels; every other panel contains a petaled medallion; the other smooth surfaced panels are ruby stained. Also produced in amber stained and clear. Circa 1895.[3] 2⅞" tall. Very scarce! **$48.00 – 65.00.**

Authors' collection

Circle and Fan: Clear green glass, mold blown and pressed. Pattern name by Peterson which describes the principal raised motif that is present on these shakers. This is a reversed variation of Riverside's No. 449 pattern line that was used on some of their oil lamps. Circa 1895 – 1897. The shakers are 2⅝" tall; the glass holder is 4⅜" tall. Rare set in this color! **$250.00 – 290.00** set.

White collection

Duchess: Clear emerald green glass, mold blown and pressed. The pattern consists of six gold-trimmed vertical panels and a 12 multi-toed base. Very similar in appearance to the "Empress" shakers.[4] This pattern was also produced in crystal, blue, crystal with frosted panels, canary yellow, and white opalescent.[5] Circa 1900. 3" tall. Very scarce! **$65.00 – 85.00.**

MacAllister collection

Florentine (aka "Single Rose"): Clear dark green glass, mold blown. This is a bulbous based shaker with the principal motif amounting to an embossed single rose below drooping leaves. A detailed view of the pattern can be seen in *Glass Salt Shakers* by Peterson on page 38-B. Dale MacAllister submitted our photo illustration and brought this pattern to our attention. Additional pattern information is available.[6] Circa 1906. 2¾" tall. Rare in this color! **$60.00 – 75.00.**

Authors' collection

Ransom (aka Gold Band): Clear canary (vaseline) glass, mold blown and pressed. This is a polygonal-shaped shaker with a plain horizontal band encircling near the center providing a rich, stylish appearance. Radiates high florescence under black light illumination. Also produced in clear, green, and gold. Circa 1899.[7] 3⅛" tall. Very scarce in canary! **$65.00 – 80.00.**

Krauss collection

Empress (set): Clear green glass with gold decoration, mold blown and pressed (see our Vol. II, p. 179). The group consists of a salt, pepper, cruet, and spoon tray. It should be noted that we have not designated the configuration as a cruet, set because Riverside Glass did not produce a cruet set in this pattern configuration.[8] However, our hands-on physical analysis showed that when the salt and pepper and cruet are emplaced upon the spoon tray they are very practical (accessible) in terms of form, fit, and function. We have little reservation in postulating that the spoon tray was used to form a condiment set grouping by many a Victorian housewife. The group height dimensions are salt and pepper, 3¼"; cruet, 8" to top of the pouring spout; the tray, 9½" long x 6" wide. Circa 1898 – 1899. Rare as a set! **$675.00 – 725.00** set.

Lockwood collection

Winsome: Clear heavy gold decorated pressed glass. The pattern has six vertical wide panels with beaded curved lower borders and topped by wide protruding arches. The panels and arches are divided by deep vertical grooves. The base contains scroll work. The gold decoration is badly worn from the ravages of time. Circa 1903.[9] 3⅛" tall x 2½" at the widest point. Rare! **$10.00 – 15.00** due to wear.

THE ROYAL GLASS CO.
Marietta, Ohio
(1898 – 1903)

The first glass was produced by this factory during October 1898. Martin F. Noll was president, Addison Thompson was general manager and Thomas Charleton factory manager. The factory was destroyed by fire on November 26, 1903, and it was never rebuilt by National Glass.

Fenton Museum collection

Harris collection

Rathbun collection

Bulbous Ribbed: Opaque chocolate and clear glass, mold blown and pressed. Both types are being illustrated. We had always been certain that this ware was created by one of the National Glass factories. During November 1994, we made a scheduled trip to the Fenton Art Glass Factory at Williamstown, West Virginia, to meet with Frank Fenton relative to some Fenton glassware identification. During our visit with Mr. Fenton, we were pleasantly surprised to find this pattern on display in the Fenton factory museum along with positive documented attribution to the Royal Glass Company, Marietta, Ohio. The Royal factory was sold to the National Glass Corp. during August 1899, and Jacob Rosenthal was installed as the new general manager having been transferred in from another National Glass factory. Thus, Royal became National Glass Factory No. 18 and lost its identity as an independent glasshouse. This shaker pattern contains 18 protruding vertical ribs and is 3" tall. With the courtesy of Frank Fenton, we were permitted to photograph a complete clear (uncolored) salt and pepper condiment set with companion glass tray that was on display in the Fenton museum. Thanks to Lesley and Dick Harris we are also illustrating this set in chocolate glass made by Royal. Rare as a complete clear set! Very rare in chocolate glass! Single chocolate shaker, **$375.00 – 425.00**; complete clear castor set, **$295.00 – 325.00**; complete chocolate castor set, **$1,600.00 – 1,800.00.**

STEUBEN GLASS WORKS
Corning, New York
(1903 – Present)

The Steuben Glass Works began on March 2, 1904. Founders were Thomas G. Hawkes, Townsend deM Hawkes, and Frederick Carder. The Works was productive and profitable while under Mr. Carder's leadership. He remained with the Works until 1934, after which time he continued to actively work with his colored art glass as an independent, using floor space inside the factory.

In 1933, A.A. Houghton Jr. became head of the Steuben factory. His control and management resulted in the production of a high quality crystal clear glass which has been continuously made up to the present time. The bottom of the crystal salt shakers (and other ware) are signed by a craftsman using a diamond point, and writing the word "Steuben." It is a definitive signature and not a trademark. The crystal shaker we are illustrating was signed in the aforementioned manner.

Authors' collection

Steuben Variant, Crystal: Clear high quality crystal glass, free blown and signed with the written word "Steuben" by use of a diamond point. From a visual optic stand point, the shaker has the appearance of a somewhat tapered cone with a thick heavy flanged base that provides good stability when the shaker is placed upright on a table. A variation of this shaker is illustrated in our Vol. II, page 183. This item is circa 1935 – 1940. 3⅝" tall with a sterling silver two-piece metal top. Very scarce! **$120.00 – 135.00.**

Lockwood collection

Iverene: These art glass shakers comprise a translucent off-white glass with an iridescent surface, mold blown with copious hand finishing. Iverene glass is considered to be the closest that Fredrick Carder ever came to producing a milk-white glass. The Iverene glass batch contained feldspar and cryolite; the iridescent surface was created by the use of stannous chloride spray that was applied at the fire. It is well established that most Carder Steuben glassware is free blown. Where it was deemed necessary to employ a mold technique, after annealing, such items were subjected to multiple actions including hand polishing, mat or satin finishing, removal of rough edges, etc. In the case of our illustrated shaker pair, they were subjected to hand cut/etched floral designs on each paneled surface. The pair was obviously made to special order, since the initials of the owner was hand inscribed on one of the six vertical panels in a difficult to read English-type script lettering. Author Paul V. Gardner (who worked with Carder for years) stated that "So few Carder Steuben pieces were molded that some items are rarer than the free blown pieces." These shakers are circa 1918 – 1925. 2⅞" tall with sterling silver mother-of-pearl tops. Very Rare! **NPD.**

STEVENS AND WILLIAMS GLASS WORKS
Brierly Hill Staffordshire
England
(1847 – Present)

This famous old English glass factory has always produced glassware to the highest quality standards; periodically they have supplied glassware to the Royal Family. Their Victorian era art glass has always been among the best that could be obtained. This factory continues to operate today producing a very high quality crystal.

Krauss collection

Plain Bulbous: Opaque shiny variegated (peach/white streaked) art glass. Mold and free-blown finished. This is a plain, smooth surfaced shaker that is bulbous at the top and tapers downward into a ring supported base. Circa 1885 – 1890. 2⅝" tall with a two-piece press-fit pressure finial top. Believed to be part of a condiment set. Rare! **$280.00 – 310.00.**

Krauss collection

Barrel, Twenty-One Rib Rainbow: Brilliant cranberry glass displaying a continous turquoise-green flashed irregular spiraling stripe. This is a beautiful art glass shaker representing quality innovative craftsmanship. The overall motif comprises 21 vertical ribs, each individual rib contains a series of stippled bumps. When viewed from the bottom, the shaker portrays a pinwheel-shaped collage of cranberry, turquoise green, and crystal colors. The shaker has a two-piece press fit metal top that is often found on various English condiment dispensers from the Art Nouveau era. It has been established that this ware was also produced in a three-piece condiment set in the form of a pepper, open salt, and mustard retained in an English marked silver-plate metal holder. Circa 1884 – 1892. 2⅝" tall. Very rare! **$650.00 – 700.00** single shaker.

Ridgway collection

Bulb, Pinched-In: Opaque unfinished/undeveloped Burmese glass, mold and free-blown finished. The pattern amounts to a small bulb that is pinched in thus creating a four-sided shaker. This identical shape in Peachblow is illustrated and described in our Vol. II, p. 183. The smooth satinized exterior is hand painted in a very artistic pink and green floral spray that encircles the upper half of the shaker. The green leaves have been outlined in gold. The shaker displays a striking florescence when exposed to UV black light radiation. 2⅝" tall with a two-piece metal top. Circa 1885 – 1890. Very rare! **$800.00 – 850.00.**

TARENTUM GLASS COMPANY
Tarentum, Pennsylvania
(1894 – 1918)

The Tarentum Glass Company appeared in early 1894, as an outgrowth from Richards & Hartley Flint Glass Co., Factory E of the U.S. Glass Co. H. M. Brekenridge was president and L.R. Hartley, secretary.

The factory produced a considerable amount of pressed crystal glass tableware; much of which was ruby stained. Around 1903, Tarentum was into cut crystal glass, opalware, and custard glass which some of the trade journals at that time referred to as "Tarentum's Pea Green Glass."

This glasshouse continued to produce tableware until around 1916 when the trade ads began to show that Tarentum was producing light fixtures. The factory was completely destroyed by fire in 1918, and was never rebuilt.

Rathbun collection

Beaded Square: Translucent, dark amethyst glass with four beaded large panels. Each panel contains a HP leaf and flower that is reminiscent of a lily. The shaker bottom contains a beaded circle. This type of shaker is fully described in our Vol. II, page 184 where it is shown in HP opalware. Circa 1898 – 1904. 2¼" tall. Rare in this color! **$50.00 – 60.00.**

Lockwood collection

Columbia, Tarentum's: Clear uncolored glass, mold blown and pressed. While this pattern was long known as Tarentum's Harvard, a trade ad clearly shows that our illustrated shaker is their Columbia pattern.[1] Circa 1898 – 1899. 2⅝" tall. Scarce! **$9.00 – 17.00.**

Harris collection

Portland, Tarentum's: (aka "Cradled Buttons & Notches"): Clear ruby stained glass, mold blown and pressed. Smooth concave paneled for application of decoration; in this case ruby stain. The aka pattern name describes the general motif. Also produced in clear glass. Circa 1907.[2] 3" tall. Very scarce! **$55.00 – 70.00.**

Lockwood collection

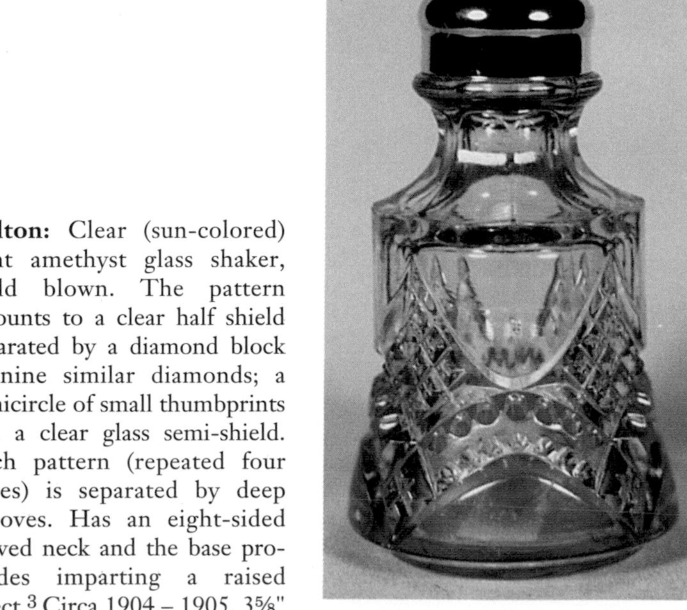

Dalton: Clear (sun-colored) light amethyst glass shaker, mold blown. The pattern amounts to a clear half shield separated by a diamond block of nine similar diamonds; a semicircle of small thumbprints and a clear glass semi-shield. Each pattern (repeated four times) is separated by deep grooves. Has an eight-sided curved neck and the base protrudes imparting a raised effect.[3] Circa 1904 – 1905. 3⅝" tall x 1¾" wide at the waist; 2⅛" base diameter. **$18.00 – 23.00.**

TIFFIN GLASS COMPANY
(Factory R, U.S.G.C.)
Tiffin, Ohio
(1914 – 1962)
TIFFIN ART GLASS COMPANY
Tiffin, Ohio
(1962 – 1985)

After functioning primarily as a producer of pressed tumblers and bar ware, on September 8, 1914, the U.S. Glass Co. decided to have the Tiffin factory change to the production of lightweight hand and mold-blown glass on a trial basis. The decision proved to be successful. Tiffin Glass produced a new manufacturing look and began to concentrate on the production of quality ware which proved to be a sustaining factor in the plant's longevity. From 1927 through the Depression years the factory remained profitable and in business. With the demise of U.S. Glass, the factory became the Tiffin Art Glass Company in 1962. The plant was completely dismantled during 1985.

Coalmer collection

Maxfield collection

Tear, Tiffin (Parakeet): Clear blue and frosted blue glass, mold blown. Both glass types are illustrated. The pattern is a footed, teardrop-shaped shaker with pleasing lines. The frosted pair with the bird decoration was advertised in 1926 as "The Parakeet Twin," No. 6207.[1] Also produced in green and vaseline. 2¾" tall by 1¼" at widest point. Very scarce! **$70.00 – 85.00** pair; single clear blue, **$30.00 – 40.00.**

THE THOMPSON GLASS COMPANY
Uniontown, Pennsylvania
(1889 – 1895)

Julius Proeger joined this factory in 1890. This talented designer is credited with establishing the company's early successful production. The factory had early troubles with fuel/gas and lost considerable time establishing their initial glass production. This firm didn't remain in business very long after Mr. Proeger left to join Greensburg Glass in late 1891.

Krauss collection

Thompson's No. 77 (aka Truncated Cube): Clear ruby stained glass, mold blown and pressed. The shaker's upper half is a smooth ruby stained cylinder; the lower half consists of two rows of eight rounded cubes in high raised relief.[1] Circa 1894. 2⅞" tall. Very scarce! **$55.00 – 70.00.**

THE UNITED STATES GLASS COMPANY
Pittsburgh, Pennsylvania

U. S. Glass was formed July 1, 1891. It represented the merging of 18 independent glasshouses. Thc corporate president was Daniel C. Ripley. By 1904 the number factories that made up the corporation had dropped to six. After the initial merger, all independent factories lost their original identities and were simply referred to as factories A through T. Later two additional factories were built and became known as U and GP.

Rathbun collection

Acorn Pattern Group: Illustrated in a group are Peterson's "Acorn, Little," 2⅜" tall with a pebbly brass top (left); "Acorn," 2¾" tall (center) by Hobbs, Brockunier; "Acorn, Little Variant," 2¾" tall (right) by U.S. Glass, Factory C, opaque blue glass, mold blown. This shaker is illustrated in our Vol. II on page 188 as "Acorn, Little." In an attempt to achieve pattern name clarification for our readers, we are renaming it with the added word "Variant" since the shaker that Peterson lists in his salt shaker book on page 153-C has a larger opening and requires a pebbly type brass top. It appears that our 2¾" tall shaker variant is a circa 1891 U.S. Glass, Factory C version of the earlier "Acorn" shaker produced by Hobbs. We went into considerable extra dimensional detail in Vol. II hoping this would alleviate pattern confusion but failed to take into account that we had recorded two slightly different shakers with the same pattern name. Scarce! **$30.00 – 35.00.**

Krauss collection

Bohemian (aka Florador): Illustrated are two shakers; one is clear rose-flashed glass; the other is clear green glass. The shakers are each supported by four glass feet. Their motifs are quite complex; consisting of a background of ornate embossed fruit, foliage, and a scroll design over a stippled background. Also, liberal applications of gold coloring are present on various parts of the aforementioned motifs. This pattern was originally listed as U. S. Glass no. 12063, circa 1899 – 1901.[1] 3½" tall with large screw-on metal tops. Rare! **$335.00 – 350.00** pair.

Lockwood collection

Feather Band (OMN Wreath): Clear glass, mold blown. This is a tall shaker bulging above and below the horizontal feather band around the middle. The feathers are incised. The bottom is comprised of a shallow supporting ring.[2] Circa 1910. 3½" tall x 2⅜" wide. Scarce! **$15.00 – 20.00.**

Coalmer collection

Hexagon Block: Clear pressed glass with partial amber staining below the metal top. The pattern consists of a series of small intaglio blocks that begin in the middle and continue downward into the supporting foot. An etched floral band is present within the amber stained top area. First produced at Hobbs circa 1889 with continued production at U.S. Glass, Factory H after 1891.[3] See our Vol. II, page 191. 3⅛" tall. Rare! **$75.00 – 90.00.**

Rathbun collection

Kansas (aka "Dew with Dewdrop"): Clear transparent glass, mold blown. The pattern has eight vertical panels; four plain and four stippled that have three jewels in raised relief. Part of the U.S. Glass "States Pattern Series." This shakers was produced by Factory K, circa 1901.[4] Very scarce! **$25.00 – 35.00.**

Lockwood collection

Louisiana: Clear pressed glass. The pattern consists of a row of diamonds around the top, each broken up into nine smaller faceted diamonds. Fitting into the spaces between the diamonds is a row of long sharp pointed ovals encircling the shaker. Another row of diamonds, similar to the ones at the top, are distributed around the base. This is another "States Pattern," circa 1898. Produced at Factory B. Apparently not made in color. 2⅝" tall x 1¾" base diameter. Very scarce ! **$28.00 – 37.00.**

Harris collection

Maryland (aka "Inverted Loops & Fans"): Clear ruby stained glass, mold blown and pressed. A small footed shaker containing ruby stained inverted loops and clear embossed diamonds and fans from center to top of the supporting foot. Introduced circa 1897.[5] Part of the U.S. Glass "States Patterns"; their no. 15049. Also produced in clear glass. 2½" tall. Very scarce in ruby stained! **$65.00 – 80.00.**

Krauss collection

O'Hara Diamond: Clear ruby stained glass, mold blown and pressed. This is U.S. Glass pattern no. 15001 in the U. S. Glass catalogs after O'Hara became Factory L during 1891. Ruth Webb Lee named it "Sawtooth and Star" which represents a concise description of this pattern. The plain upper half of the shaker is ruby stained; the lower half is clear glass and forms a heavy based six-pointed star. Circa 1891 – 1900. 1⅞" tall. Very scarce! The lower portion of our illustrated shaker has some minor chipping. **$25.00 – 30.00.**

Harris collection

Ruffles: Clear ruby stained glass, mold blown. The pattern amounts to a smooth front and back flat circular panel. The narrow sides are completely encircled with small sharp protruding ribs. Produced at Factory G (formerly Gillinder at Greensburg) circa 1892. Designated as U.S. Glass pattern no. 15008.[6] 2⅛" tall. Also produced in clear glass. Rare in ruby stained! **$75.00 – 90.00.**

Authors' collection

Pattee Cross: Clear partial amber stained glass, mold blown and pressed. U.S. Glass pattern no. 15112.[7] The stained shaker neck has six plain flutes top and bottom. The shaker body contains three large double beveled circles with a large diamond that is filled with small diamonds. This design interlocks with three four-petaled crosses. Also produced in clear and green without any neck stain. Circa 1909 – 1910. 3⅜" tall x 2¼" at widest point; 1⅞" base diameter. Scarce! **$14.00 – 22.00.**

Harris collection

Stippled Bar: Clear ruby stained glass, mold blown and pressed. This pattern has wide slanting embossed stippled bars that flow downward from the top of the shaker. Each clear (unstained) vertical panel has thin serrated vertical ruby stained bands applied to each edge. This is U.S. Glass pattern No. 15044 set. Circa 1895.[8] Also produced in clear glass. 3" tall. Rare in stain! **$85.00 – 100.00.**

Lockwood collection

Sunbeam (OMN): Clear glass, mold blown and pressed. The pattern consists of two long pointed ellipses filled with diamond point; joined at the bottom and spreading to an arch at the top with a concave button between that is topped by a row of vertical fanned rays. This motif appears three times around the shaker. Between each is a lower triangle formed by the pointed ellipses and filled with hexagonal buttons in cane work. Kamm named this pattern "Twin Snowshoes" (referring to the two long pointed ellipses).[9] Circa 1908. 3¼" tall x 1⅞" wide. Scarce! **$12.00 – 18.00.**

Lockwood collection

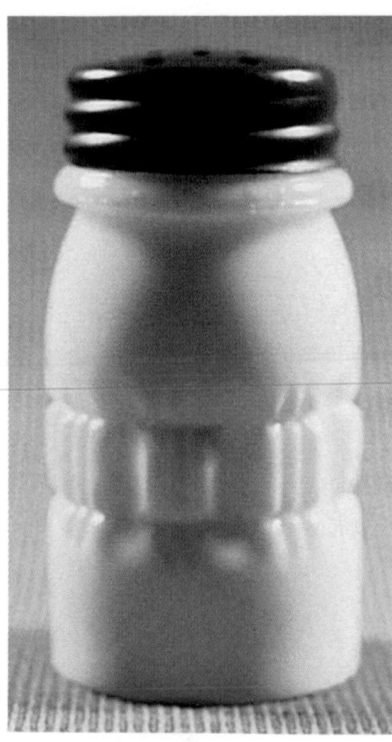

U.S. Glass #160: Opaque opalware glass, mold blown. A ring-necked cylinder with a pattern of two deeply indented lines encircling the middle. Intersecting these lines are eight concave long ovals separated by sharply embossed lines. The shaker bottom is smooth. Produced at Factory B, circa 1891.[10] 3" tall x 1⅝" wide. Scarce! **$12.00 – 16.00.**

Harris collection

Washington (aka "Beaded Base"): Clear heavy glass, mold blown and pressed. One of the U.S. Glass "States" patterns, circa 1901. Our illustrated shaker contains somewhat worn ruby stain within an encircling band above two round rows of clear beads. Catalog listed as U.S. Glass pattern #15074.[11] 3¾" tall. Very scarce! **$18.00 – 25.00** due to decoration wear.

THOMAS WEBB & SONS
Stourbridge, England

Coalmer collection

Coalmer collection

Herbert collection

Bulb, Webb Peachblow: Rose to pink, heat sensitive cased Peachblow glass, mold and free blown finished with HP off-white flowers on pink colored stems. In the single pictured shaker there is also large, gold colored, foliage in the area between the off-white flowers. As the pattern name implies, the physical shape is reminiscent of an extended bulb. This is a rare art glass that was produced circa 1885 – 1888. The inside glass casing is an off-white color. 3⅝" tall with a two-piece metal tops; mustard, 2¾" tall. Very rare! Single, **$800.00 – 900.00;** pair, **$1,800.00 – 2,000.00** pair; complete set with shakers, mustard, and metal holder, **$4,000.00 – 4,500.00.**

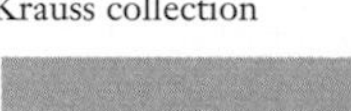

Buck collection

Burmese, Webb Decorated: Opaque homogeneous non-refired Burmese art glass, mold blown. This is a short, round cylinder-shaped shaker with an extended glass base indicating that it was part of a Webb condiment set. Because Mt. Washington had secured a patent for their Burmese ware in England on June 16, 1886, Thomas Webb & Sons purchased a license to produce Burmese glass at their factory in England. The shaker has HP quality old floral decoration of a type that Webb used on various types of their art glass. Circa 1886 – 1888. 2¼" tall with a two-piece pressure fitted finial metal top. Rare! **$400.00 – 425.00.**

Krauss collection

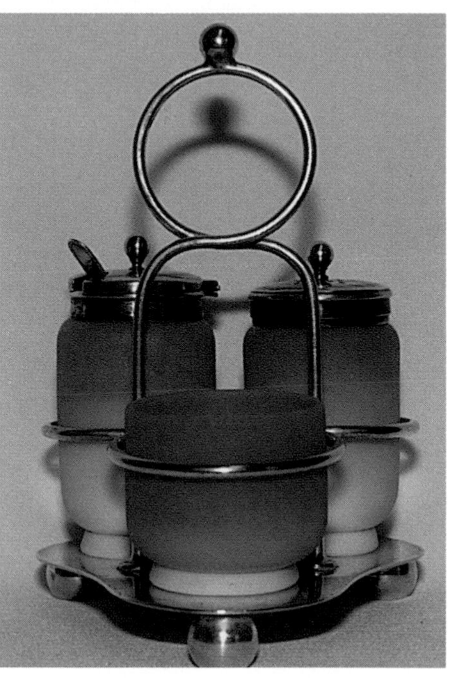

Burmese, Webb Undecorated (condiment): Opaque homogeneous Burmese satin art glass, mold and free-blown finished. The set consists of a pepper, open salt, and mustard. The pepper has an English type two-piece, press fit finial top. The Burmese pieces are held in an original English electro-plated nickel silver holder marked "Sam Birdsall, 34 High St. Skipton — No. 3032." The metal mustard top is marked E.P.N.S. The outstanding refired pink coloring extends to a one-half or better distance downward before shading into the yellow glass base. The open salt is 1⅝" tall x 1¾" wide; pepper, 2⅝" tall x 1¾" wide; mustard, 2⅝" tall x 1¾" wide. Each condiment piece has an extended glass base support measuring 1⅜" diameter x 3/16" length. It is interesting to note that Stevens & Williams experimented extensively to produce a ware similar to Burmese without infringing on the Mt. Washington patent. Their results never got beyond the research/experimental stages; thus they were never able to compete in the Burmese commercial art glass market.[1] However, they did produce an off-white colored glass that reacts the same as Burmese under black light illumination. There is no known U.S.A. established monetary market for this complete Webb set; **NPD.**

Ridgway collection

Cylinder, Peachblow: Opaque red to pink shaded glossy Peachblow art glass, mold and free-blown finished. This shaker is a relatively uniform shaped cylinder with a rounded shoulder and a short added bottom extension for retention within a condiment holder. As produced by Thomas Webb & Sons in England, this is a two layered ware, the outer layer consists of the heat sensitive glass; the inner layer is an off-colored cream with a slightly greenish hue.[2] The outer surface contains outstanding HP gold floral decoration. Circa 1885 – 1889. 2⅛" tall with a two-piece pressure fit type top. Rare! **$750.00 – 800.00.**

Harris collection

Four Lobe, Webb: Clear Rubina art glass, dual mold blown. This same mold was used by this factory to produce Webb Peachblow shakers.[3] The inside surface contains small IVT. The exterior contains HP green and white shaded leaves on each corner edge. Circa 1884 – 1886. 2⅜" tall with original two-piece metal tops. Rare! **$400.00 – 450.00.**

Krauss collection

Krauss collection

Plain Barrel: Translucent satinized Rubina glass, mold blown. This shaker pair shades from a deep rose at the top to a frosted crystal at the base. The exterior surface has HP white floral sprays that are supported by yellow/orange colored stems and leaves. The bottom of each condiment dispenser has a short glass extension to accommodate insertion into some type of condiment holder. Circa 1887 – 1892. 2¾" tall with two-piece metal tops. Rare! **$180.00 – 205.00.**

Hexagon Panel, Webb: Opaque triple cased "Webb Peachblow"[4] art glass shading from a deep rose at the top to a pale pink at the base. The physical shape consists of a hexagon containing six vertical panels; the panels are decorated with small lavender HP floral sprigs in raised relief. The clear glass bottom (part of the outer layer) has been fire polished. A small intaglio circle is present in the center of the shaker bottom. This is the same type of Peachblow art glass illustrated in our Vol. II, p. 20. Circa 1882 – 1886. 2" tall with a two-piece metal top. Very rare! **$1,275.00 – 1,300.00.**

Rathbun collection

Rathbun collection

Lobed Sprig: Two opaque triple cased, dual mold blown Webb art glass shakers are illustrated. The pink shaded shaker is Webb Peachblow; the other shaker contains a heat sensitive middle layered blue shaded glass. Both shakers have the same six lobe pattern and every other lobe is embossed with HP cream colored flowers and leaves; the remaining three lobes contain embossed random spaced dots with the same HP cream coloring. Manufacture of the blue shaded glass was accomplished by the substitution of cobalt or copper colorant to a heat sensitive metal that could be developed into different colors and shades by reheating certain portions of the article at the furnace. Also, a variant six-lobed clear homogeneous cranberry shaker is pictured that has similar floral and dot features that has been accomplished by HP enamel decoration. All three shakers are 2½" tall and have two-piece metal tops. Circa 1882 – 1888. The opaque Peachblow and blue shakers are very rare! The clear cranberry shaker is rare! Peachblow, **$1,000.00 – 1,100.00;** shaded blue, **$550.00 – 600.00;** clear cranberry, **$225.00 – 250.00.**

WESTMORELAND SPECIALITY COMPANY
(1890 – 1924)
WESTMORELAND GLASS COMPANY
(1924 – 1984)
Grapeville, Pennsylvania
(Westmoreland County)

If the reader desires detailed historical information about this glass factory refer to our Vol. II, page 196.

Lung collection

Westmoreland #1775: Clear pressed glass with a glass top that is held in place by a metal spring wire. A classical column shape having six panels with an arch at the top and a flared support base. The neck contains a round protruding ring to assure the special glass top adherence. The base is marked "Pat May 24, 1910."[1] Circa 1910. 3" tall with 1⅜" base diameter. Scarce! **$20.00 – 28.00.**

Harris collection

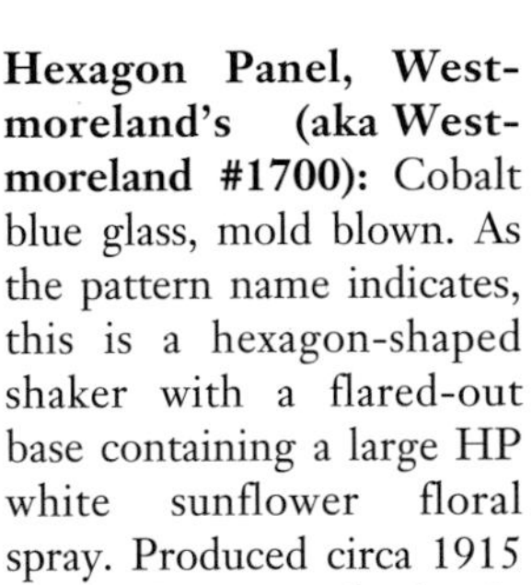

Hexagon Panel, Westmoreland's (aka Westmoreland #1700): Cobalt blue glass, mold blown. As the pattern name indicates, this is a hexagon-shaped shaker with a flared-out base containing a large HP white sunflower floral spray. Produced circa 1915 in what Westmoreland referred to as "Belgium blue." This basic pattern shape also saw production in clear glass with gold decoration and silver filigree design up into the 1930s. 3¼" tall. Very scarce in this color! **$40.00 – 55.00.**

Authors' collection

Wellington (aka "Staple"): Clear ruby stained glass, mold blown and pressed. This pattern is part of Westmoreland's 400 line.[2] A short heavy glass shaker containing three encircling upper bands of very small shaped diamonds. The main motif is a series of six ruby stained intaglio ellipses that are separated by three raised vertical ribs. These are heavy condiments considering their small size. Circa 1903 – 1912. 2⅜" tall. Rare in ruby stain! **$125.00 – 150.00** pair.

THE WEST VIRGINIA GLASS COMPANY
Martins Ferry, Ohio
(1894 – 1899)

As an independent factory this glasshouse didn't last too long. It produced pressed and mold blown glassware and also bar goods. After becoming part of the National Glass Co. during 1899, it disappeared in terms of glass advertisements.

Coalmer collection

Scroll with Cane Band: Clear crystal and amber stained glass, mold blown and pressed. The motif consists of a large, well-rounded continuous scroll in raised relief that is intersected through the middle by a horizontal band of cane. Pattern name by Kamm.[1] Originally called this factory's #213. Also made in ruby stained and emerald green. Circa 1895 – 1898. 2½" tall. Very scarce! **$55.00 – 70.00.**

Authors' collection

Gathered Top: Opaque homogeneous buff colored glass, mold blown. Made from the same mold as illustrated in our Vol. II, page 198. However, because of the opaque glass an optic effect is not visible. Gives a pink colored reaction when exposed to UV black light radiation. Circa 1896 – 1899. 2⅜" tall x 2¼" wide; 2" diameter base. Very scarce! **$30.00 – 40.00.**

POTPOURRI

As was the case in our two previous books, this section contains a miscellany of glass salt shakers that can be collected/found by today's collectors and dealers. We continue to receive many reader inquiries relative to unknown patterns that antique glass salt and pepper shakers were produced in by the various glasshouses that existed during the Victorian era. This variety of ware is a tribute to the innovative craftsmanship of the various factory designers and gaffers who created such a myriad of beautiful shapes for such a practical table application; viz: "dispensing condiments at the dining table."

A NECESSARY EXPLANATION

The AAGSSCS has spent more than a decade encouraging its members to submit data and a photo of unlisted shaker patterns for publication in the club's quarterly newsletter known as *The Pioneer*. Prior to publication, each member's submittal is studied and screened by a group of advanced club collectors and experts, called the ID committee, to determine if each piece is indeed an unknown and unlisted pattern that should be disseminated to all members by way of *The Pioneer*. Over the years more than 700 such patterns have been accumulated.

To their credit, the club's founders have tried to form a group of member volunteers to write a book that encompassed all of the unlisted shaker patterns that have been collected. They wanted such a book to be published in the AAGSSCS name; much along the lines that the National Toothpick Society had done in their 1992 toothpick publication. The bottom line is *no one wanted to take on such a task!*

Since the initial publication of our Vol. II 1992 book, we have been engaged in writing this Vol. III salt shaker book. As charter members of the AAGSSCS, we wrote a letter to the society's president offering to include the aforementioned unknown patterns in our book so that all of the many years of membership effort could be recognized (not wasted) and widely promulgated to the pattern glass collectors and dealers arena. Our offer was accepted by the AAGSSCS board of directors despite heavy opposition by the club's founders who decided to boycott the club's decision. Unfortunately, as a result, there will be some member patterns that we have been unable to publish.

The aforesaid scenario has been written so that the AAGSSCS membership will understand what has transpired relative to some of the club's unknown patterns that were originally ID committee accepted and published in *The Pioneer*.

Despite continuing research by ourselves and various members of the AAGSSCS, recorded hereinafter are numerous patterns that cannot be positively attributed to a specific glasshouse or manufacturer. However, the reader will find that in addition to permanently recording the existence of this ware, the following additional helpful criteria is presented to current and future collectors:

1. Distinct pattern detail by use of close-up photography.
2. Establishment of an individual pattern name listing.
3. Known production colors that were originally manufactured.
4. Approximate dates of first manufacture (circa).
5. Existence of imitations if known.
6. Relative height measurements of each shaker to within plus or minus ⅛ of an inch.
7. Current retail market value guidance.

In some instances we may offer an opinion as to who made a pattern based upon our years of experience, cautious analysis, museum attributions, and/or knowledgeable authorities. However, please understand that the opinion given should not be taken to represent absolute!

We would like to further emphasize that many of the assigned pattern names were created by a consensus of AAGSSCS members present at the various annual salt shaker conventions sponsored by the society.

The reader should also understand that the Victorian era American factories/glasshouses were highly competitive with each other. As a result, they copied each other's popular patterns; traded and sold molds; were absorbed into larger corporations that reissued patterns at other corporate factories or at later dates; and often pirated away and employed skilled glass designers, gaffers and workers from other competitive glasshouses. It is obvious that these types of actions (at times) make attribution extremely difficult and in some instances virtually impossible. We welcome reader input that can result in positive attribution of any of the various shakers we have presented.

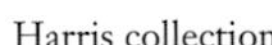

Harris collection

Acanthus Scroll: Clear pressed heavy pattern glass. Each corner column has a slightly raised acanthus leaf pattern and curves inward to form a scroll foot. The center of the shaker has a fused-on metal band with a handle on each side; at one time it contained gold-colored paint which has pretty well worn off. Peterson considered this a rare shaker pattern.[1] We could not find any history of color production. Circa 1881 – 1891. 3" tall. **$15.00 – 20.00** due to minor chipping.

Rathbun collection

Acanthus, Stippled: Translucent mold blown glass containing six acanthus flowers in raised relief over a stippled background surface. Pattern name by A.G. Peterson. The entire shaker surface has a sort of greenish hue. 2⅝" tall. Circa 1891 – 1899. Rare. **$75.00 – 90.00.**

Harris collection

Arch, Fancy: Clear green pressed glass. The pattern amounts to a pair of raised stippled bands with gold paint applied to their downward sloping top edges. A gold colored sunburst array radiates upward from the point where the stippled bands converge to form a diamond containing an intaglio rosette. Pattern name is by Peterson.[2] Also produced in clear glass. Circa 1891 – 1903. Scarce in green! **$22.00 – 30.00.**

Maxfield collection

Arched Pioneer: Clear pattern glass, mold blown. The pattern's geometric design amounts to the lower one-third being ribbed vertically while the upper portion has an arched pattern that is repeated six times around the total circumference. As is the case with all the variations of this type shaker, it contains a C.P. Crossman wooden agitator. Just above the ribbed part of the glass pattern is embossed "PAT'D SEPT 15, 1863." Apparently, the various agitators used inside this ware varied in their basic material content from solid hard wood to wood containing lead, etc. to give the agitator more weight. The shaker being illustrated has a corked bottom inside and is 4" tall x 1⅞" base diameter. Due to the obvious age of the various Pioneer shakers, some will be found with no evidence of having had a corked bottom, since cork will disintegrate over time, it's hard to firmly state that all these shakers originally had a corked bottom. Perhaps the addition of the heavier type (solid lead) agitators resulted in the addition of bottom corking at a later date. A.G. Peterson has stated that C.P. Crossman should be given credit for the Pioneer shakers.[3] Circa 1863 – 1870. Rare with agitator! **$70.00 – 85.00.**

Lockwood collection

Arched Plumes: Opaque white opalware glass, mold blown. This is a flared-out base shaker with a top neck ring. The principal motif consists of embossed gold colored curving scrolls of varying sizes grouped together just below the neck ring. The lower part of the shaker contains a HP pink floral sprig with green leaves. Circa 1899 – 1905. 3¼" tall x 2⅜" wide; 1½" base diameter. **$15.00 – 21.00** due to worn decoration.

White collection

Arrowhead Belt: Clear quality glass, mold blown and ground on its threaded top edge. The principal pattern consists of a band of arrowheads around the center. The top and lower portions have 12 ribs. Circa 1905 – 1913. 2⅜" tall x 1⅞" wide. **$8.00 – 14.00.**

Krauss collection

Baby Optic Rib: Clear crystal glass, dual mold blown. The physical shape is spheroidal. The outer surface is smooth and contains orange and yellow flowers with interconnecting vines that encircle the circumference of the shaker. The inside has 12 vertical optic ribs. Circa 1893 – 1897. 2" tall x 1¾" wide. Scarce! **$80.00 – 95.00.**

Rathbun collection

Ball, Footed: Bright blue opaque glass, mold blown. This is a round, footed shaker with hand-enameled decorations of flowers and leaves with a two-piece metal top. The decoration quality is excellent and very much like that frequently used by Mt. Washington/Pairpoint decorators. This shaker was first recorded by C.W. Brown on page 107 of his book *Salt Dishes, Supplement.* 2¼" tall; 2⅛" wide; 1¾" base diameter. Circa 1889 – 1897. Very scarce. **$95.00 – 120.00.**

Lockwood collection

Ball, Venetian Diamond: Clear cranberry glass, mold blown. This shaker has a flattened ball shape. The exterior surface has an allover diamond design; embossed lines form the diamonds which are graduated from small at the top to larger below. A HP enamel motif of green leaves and white dot flowers is applied over the diamond pattern. Circa 1886 – 1891. 2¼" tall x 2" wide with a two-piece metal top that appears to not fit properly. Very scarce! **$100.00 – 125.00.**

Banded Diamond & Sunburst: Cobalt blue and clear cased glass, mold blown. Progresses from a narrow tubular shape into a large expanded base. Of European origin, containing extensive hand wheel cutting to form an embossed series of diamond shaped bands. Each of the large formed diamonds has eight blue colored raised dots. This motif is repeated three times around the center perimeter of the shaker. The bottom contains an intaglio 16-point rayed star. Circa 1892 – 1901 with a two-piece brass top. 3½" tall. Rare! **$130.00 – 150.00.**

Harris collection

Lockwood collection

Barrel, Alluring: Homogeneous lusterless white smooth satin glass, mold blown. The HP heavy enameled motif consists of pink on the flower petals and bud with a butterscotch yellow flower center, leaves, and vine. 3⅜" tall x 2" wide with a two-piece metal top. Circa 1881 – 1889. Rare! **$210.00 – 230.00.**

Hess collection

Barrel, Avery: Opaque blue glass, mold blown. This shaker pattern amounts to a medium size shaped barrel with heavy enamel HP lavender and white floral sprigs. Circa 1888 – 1895. 2¾" tall x 1½" wide with a two-piece metal top. Very scarce! **$140.00 – 160.00.**

Armstrong collection

Armstrong collection

Barrel, Amberina Ribbed Optic: Clear Amberina glass, dual mold blown. The pattern name describes the physical configuration of this unlisted Amberina pattern. One of our photos shows the single threaded dark (charcoal colored) metal top that was originally wedged on it at the time of purchase. Our other photo shows this same condiment dispenser containing an appropriate (but not necessarily the correct) type of two-piece top that should be used on it due to the fact that there is no glass threading at the top edge of the piece. It is an absolute fact that the top that was originally used by the factory of origin contained a metal collar/bezel that was attached to the glass top edge by plaster of Paris adhesive so that the other portion of the top could be attached. While the seller represented to the present owner that this condiment piece is a very rare Mt. Washington/Pairpoint "Rose Amber" Amberina salt shaker, our detailed hands-on inspection, and many years of specialization, resulted in our opinion that this items is an Amberina mustard that was produced by the New England Glass Co., Cambridge, Massachusetts, circa 1884 – 1887 as part of a condiment/castor set. We sent a photo of this item to two experienced Amberina collectors; a subsequent reply was received that one of them has a complete condiment set in the pattern and that the item in question is indeed a mustard. Both Amberina collectors were certain that production (creation) of various inside surface optic ribbed swirl patterns was often used by the New England Glass Co. on some of their Amberina ware. The illustrated piece is 2⅜" tall x 1¾" wide with a 1¼" top opening diameter. Magnified visual analysis of the glass revealed excessive surface scratches, very small chipping, and random glass bubbles that are not found on "Rose Amber" art glass pieces. Extensive research has not revealed this pattern in Mt. Washington/Pairpoint Victorian era catalogs and factory issued ads. Also, no privately authored books written about the aforesaid factories disclosed this to be a known Mt. Washington/Pairpoint pattern. It is also important that the reader understand that the market collectibility value of Amberina glassware is determined by the amount of fuchsia-red coloring that is present on a piece; and, the measurement in length/distance of this type of coloration. The Amberina coloring length on this particular item amounts to less than one-fourth of the piece's total surface. Therefore, based upon the aforementioned facts, the current retail value is **$225.00**

Lockwood collection

Barrel, Blushing: Opaque heat sensitive art glass, dual mold blown with weak coloration that shades from pink at the base to off-white at the top; and it fluoresces under black light exposure. This appears to be the same mold as the "Peachbloom" shaker illustrated in our Vol. II, p. 244. Circa 1884 – 1888. 3¼" tall x 2" wide with a two-piece metal top that is not original and causes the shaker to look out of proportion. It is our opinion that this shaker was produced by Phoenix Glass Co. Rare! **$135.00 – 150.00** due to wear.

Krauss collection

Barrel, Bull's Eye: Translucent, flashed marigold colored glass, dual mold blown. A barrel shaped shaker containing six horizontal rows of bull's eyes on the inside surface; the outer surface has a series of orange and white HP dots in between an upper and lower white and red dotted band that encircles the center of the shaker. 3¼" tall with a two-piece metal top. Circa 1887 – 1891. Rare. **$175.00 – 190.00.**

Krauss collection

Barrel, Celestial: Opaque black homogeneous glass, mold blown. A tapered barrel containing random silver colored decoration with HP blue dots throughout the exterior surface. Believed to be a Stevens & Williams piece. 2¾" tall x 2" wide with a two-piece press fit metal top. Circa 1885 – 1891. Rare! **$210.00 – 230.00.**

Krauss collection

Barrel, Coralene: Basic white satinized opalware onto which a subtle pseudo-Peachblow (fired-on) paint is present that covers approximately one-fourth of the upper part of the two shakers which are mold blown and 2⅝" tall with two-piece metal tops. Tiny yellow glass beads have been spread around and attached to the exterior surface of each shaker so that a pattern resembling "Sheaf of Wheat" has been formed. This type of decorating technique is called Coralene. On July 7, 1883, a patent for the aforesaid process was issued to Arthur Schiefholz of Plauen, Thuringa (part of the German Empire). By way of summary, the process involves the application of designs with enamel of a syrupy consistency, either colored or transparent, and strewing thereon small glass beads. After the glass is subsequently subjected to heat sufficient to melt the enamel, the beads become cemented to the glass. While history credits this type of decoration to have had its beginning in Europe (no doubt due to the aforesaid patent), Coralene decorated Mt. Washington Burmese, and other art glass began appearing in America during the mid-1880s. Coralene beading is a unique type of surface decoration that has been applied to many types of art glass by many foreign and American glass factories. The subject shakers that we have evaluated are in above average condition and are believed to be of European origin. Circa 1884 – 1887. Rare! **$490.00 – 525.00** pair.

Authors' collection

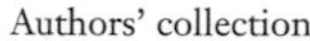

Barrel, Dignified (condiment): Opaque yellow painted opalware glass, mold blown. The smooth surfaced shakers and mustard are in the form of an enlarged barrel; each condiment dispenser has a flowing curved neck ring. The separately illustrated large glass oval-shaped bottom extension has been added to each piece to assure proper retention within the silver-plated condiment holder, which is marked "Wilcox Silver Plate Co., Meriden, Conn." This is the original metal holder that was designed for this particular condiment set. The shakers and mustard contain HP red tulip-shaped floral sprays with green leaves. Each flower is outlined in gold. Believed to be imported Thomas Webb Glass for subsequent marketing by Wilcox. Shakers, 3¼" tall with two-piece metal tops; mustard, 2⅞" tall with hinged lid open. While the glass has a custard glass color appearance, it does not react when exposed to black light illumination. Circa 1887 – 1892. Rare as a complete set! **$550.00 – 600.00** set.

Lockwood collection

Barrel, Elegant: Clear blue glass, dual mold blown. Barrel-shaped with a protruding top neck ring and flared supporting foot. The inside surface contains wide optic vertical panels. The smooth exterior has HP fine white enamel floral sprays. Circa 1885 – 1891. 3¾" tall x 1⅞" wide with a two-piece metal top. Very scarce! **$105.00 – 125.00.**

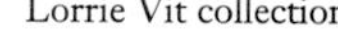

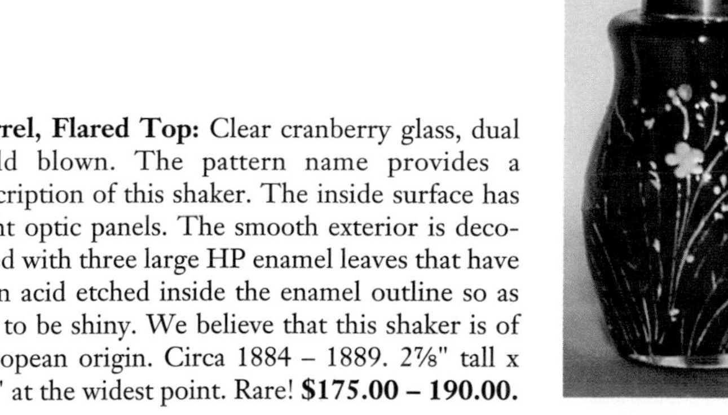

Barrel, Flared Top: Clear cranberry glass, dual mold blown. The pattern name provides a description of this shaker. The inside surface has eight optic panels. The smooth exterior is decorated with three large HP enamel leaves that have been acid etched inside the enamel outline so as not to be shiny. We believe that this shaker is of European origin. Circa 1884 – 1889. 2⅞" tall x 1¼" at the widest point. Rare! **$175.00 – 190.00.**

White collection

Krauss collection

Barrel, English Bristol (castor): Opaque homogeneous greenish Bristol glass, mold blown. We are illustrating two complete versions of this set which amounts to an open salt dish with a metal lip band, a pepper, and a mustard. Each piece has a HP enameled pink, white, and green floral spray that is encircled by HP lily-like vertical green leaves. Each of the three-part silverplated condiment holders have English silver marks on them. The pepper and mustard dispensers are 2⅝" tall. The pepper has a two-piece metal top (of typical English design) and is composed of a perforated lid with a separate cemented-on bezel that is designed for the pressure fit top. The mustard has a bezel with a hinged top attached that matches the design of the pepper top. The mustard lid has a slot to take a spoon. The open glass salt is 1½" tall. These sets were produced by one of the finer English glasshouses, circa 1888 – 1894. The set containing the lids with the pointed finial are believed to be original. Very scarce as a complete set. **$350.00 – 375.00** each set.

Coalmer collection

Barrel, Honeycomb Expanded Base: Satinized translucent Rubina glass that shades from a dark rose red at the top to crystal; dual mold blown with small raised honeycombs on the inner surface. The exterior contains a large HP orange and yellow floral spray with green and brown leaves. The pattern name is intended to describe the physical shape of this shaker which is slightly concave toward the expanded base. 2½" tall with a two-piece metal top. Circa 1884 – 1890. Very scarce! **$180.00 – 200.00.**

Krauss collection

Barrel, Inside Wide Rib (condiment): Clear green glass, dual mold blown. Barrel shaped with 10 wide inside optic ribs; the exterior surface has a tall, large, white, pink, and yellow flowered floral spray with lily-like green leaves. Circa 1885 – 1890. 3⅛" tall with a two-piece metal top. The silver-plated holder is 6" tall to the top of the lifting handle and is marked "Rogers Smith & Co., Meriden, CT." Very scarce! One of the shakers has a crack so current retail value is **$125.00 – 135.00** set.

Arnold collection

Barrel, Inverted Thumbprint Charmer: Clear Rubina glassware, dual mold blown. As the pattern name indicates, the shaker's inside surface has IVT and the smooth exterior contains a large HP white, orange, and green floral spray. Also produced in a light blue. Circa 1885 – 1890. 3½" tall x 2½" wide. Very scarce! **$185.00 – 205.00.**

Barrel, Lunar: Opaque creamy ivory-tinted glass, mold blown. A barrel-shaped shaker that appears the same as the "Coloratura" molded type shaker illustrated in our Vol. II, p. 177. The smooth surface contains HP butterscotch colored floral sprays. We believe that this shaker is a patented Joseph Webb (Phoenix Glass Co.) ivory finished item, 1887 patent #17,664. Circa 1887 – 1890. 3⅛" tall x 1¾" wide with a two-piece metal top. Very scarce! **$250.00 – 300.00.**

Lockwood collection

Authors' collection

Barrel, Mouse: Clear homogeneous cranberry glass, dual mold blown. Has the form of a small shaped barrel. The inside surface is covered with varying sized honeycombs; the smooth exterior surface contains a crowded together white/yellow and green-leafed floral bouquet. Circa 1887 – 1893. 2⅛" tall with a two-piece metal top. Rare! **$135.00 – 155.00**

Krauss collection

Barrel, Miniature Inverted Thumbprint (condiment): Clear amber glass, dual mold blown with tiny inside surface IVT. The smooth exterior surface is encircled with a continuous HP white and yellow floral spray that is attached to very thin lavender colored stems. The silver-plated, two segment, single handled condiment holder was produced by "Meriden B Co., Hamilton, Canada." This firm was established in 1879 for the production of 1847 Rogers Bros. silverplate, sterling silver flatware, silver-plated nickel silver, and white metal hollow ware. The company merged with the International Silver Co. of Canada Ltd. about 1912. The salt and pepper shakers are 2½" tall with two-piece metal tops that are believed to be original. It is our opinion that the glass shakers were purchased from the New England Glass Co., Cambridge, Massachusetts, by the aforesaid silver plate firm. Circa 1885 – 1887. Very scarce! **$280.00 – 320.00** set.

Maxfield collection

Maxfield collection

Barrel, Oblong Stretched: Translucent blue satinized art glass, mold blown. The pattern name pretty much describes this shaker. The principal motif consists of HP white floral and leaf decoration on the front and back. Both views are illustrated. The paint coloration thickness configures this piece to portray a pseudo-cameo effect. Circa 1890 – 1898. 3⅜" tall with an original two-piece top. Believed to be of European origin. Rare! **$215.00 – 235.00.**

Coalmer collection

Barrel, Optic Honeycomb: Clear cranberry glass, dual mold blown. The inner surface contains (reflects) a honeycomb motif. The smooth outer surface has a large HP floral spray that covers the shaker from top to bottom. The flowers are colored pink-to-white and rise upright from small green leaves at the shaker bottom. The shaker is narrower at the center and expanded at the base. Believed to be of European origin. Circa 1884 – 1889. 3⅛" tall with a two-piece metal top. Rare! **$135.00 – 145.00.**

Maxfield collection

Barrel, Ringed Base: Cranberry translucent glass, mold blown. As the pattern name implies, this is a bulging barrel with a base support ring. The smooth surface contains a pink and white HP flower that is extensively outlined in rounded geometric gold bands. Believed to be of European origin. Circa 1888 – 1894. 3" tall x 1½" base diameter. Very scarce! **$75.00 – 90.00.**

Lockwood collection

Barrel, Shaded Illusion: Opaque homogeneous satin finished glass, mold blown. Barrel shaped with medium "Peachbloom" shaker.[4] Decorated by a HP spray of blossoms in enameled rusty red-green leaves on a brown branch. Circa 1884 – 1888. 3¼" tall x 1¾" wide with a two-piece metal top. Very scarce! **$275.00 – 310.00.**

Krauss collection

Barrel, Short Neck: Clear cranberry and blue glass, dual mold blown. Each inside surface contains IVT. The exterior of each shaker has a large HP floral spray; the cranberry has white and yellow flowers; the blue has pink and white flowers. Each shaker also has a protruding base ring; an indication for possible use in a condiment set holder. 2⅛" tall; 1⅝" wide; 1" wide neck. Circa 1886 – 1891. Rare! **$225.00 – 250.00** pair.

Krauss collection

Barrel, Shimmering (condiment): Clear amber homogeneous glass, mold blown. The glass pieces are thin walled, light weight condiments with inside surface IVT. The exterior surfaces are undecorated. The 3¾" tall shaker tops screws onto threaded glass. Mustard, 3" tall. The metal holder is marked "Wilcox Silver Plate Co." and is 7½" tall to the top of the lifting handle. Circa 1891 – 1897. Very scarce! **$230.00 – 250.00** set.

Krauss collection

Barrel, Short Pseudo-Cameo: Translucent satinized cranberry glass, dual mold blown with HP white leaves and flowers. The thickly applied white enamel paint produces the visual appearance of cut cameo glass due to a so-called three-dimensional effect. Similar type decoration is illustrated in our Vol. II, p. 211 and in this book. The physical pattern shape of the shaker consists of a short smooth surfaced barrel. Circa 1894 – 1900. 2⅜" tall with a two-piece metal top. Very scarce. **$110.00 – 125.00.**

Lockwood collection

Lockwood collection

Barrel, Slender Inverted Thumbprint: Clear cranberry stained glass, dual mold blown. The inside stained surface contains IVT; the smooth outer surface has HP cherries on one side with leaves on the other. The cherries and leaves have a matte finish highlighted with white enamel. The shaker is tapered slightly smaller at the top and bottom. Believe to be of European origin. Circa 1887 – 1893. 2½" tall x 1¼" wide with a two-piece metal top. Scarce! **$130.00 – 145.00.**

Coalmer collection

Barrel, Small Bull's Eye: Clear orange homogeneous glass, dual mold blown. The inside of the shaker contains a series of small bull's eyes that produce a magnified prism-effect to the viewer. The exterior surface is smooth and undecorated. Produced by one of the finer New England glass manufacturers. Circa 1886 – 1888. 3¼" tall with a two-piece metal top. Rare in this color. **$150.00 – 175.00.**

Lorrie Vit collection

Barrel, Spattered Jewel: Translucent spatter glass, mold blown with an unusual shape that has a sharp bulging center. The spatter effect is present on the inside of the shaker. This shape is similar to the "Bulging Baby Thumbprint" shown in our Vol. II, p. 291. The exterior surface has an elaborate floral crystal decoration that appears to contain molten glass (most unusual). Believed to be a Hobbs product. Circa 1885 – 1887. 2⅝" tall; 1¾" wide with a two-piece metal top. **$215.00 – 225.00.**

Lockwood collection

Barrel, Straight Neck: Opaque white opalware glass, mold blown. A barrel-shaped shaker with a straight neck. The motif decoration amounts to a faded pink flower and bud with green and brown leaves. Circa 1904 – 1912. 2½" tall x 1¾" wide with a unique top that fits by friction inside the neck of the shaker; the glass top contains no threads. **$10.00 – 16.00.**

Krauss collection

Barrel, Twelve Optic Ribbed: Clear cranberry art glass over which a thin crystal cased exterior glass coating has been applied and is clearly visible at the shaker base. This is a dual mold blown piece that radiates 12 vertical optic ribs that are present on the inside surface. As the pattern name implies, the shape is reminiscent of a small barrel. This is quality art glass; the shaker bottom has been fire polished. The exterior surface contains a meticulously HP doe and buck grazing in a forest. It is our opinion that this is a Phoenix Glass Co. (Joseph Webb) shaker. 3" tall with a two-piece metal top that is not original. Rare! **$375.00 – 400.00.**

Krauss collection

Barrel, Tiny Flat Top (condiment): Clear cased cranberry glass, dual mold blown. The shakers have a very small flat shoulder with large HP five petaled white-shaded flowers covering the entire outside circumference. We believe this is glassware produced by the New England Glass Co. Circa 1884 – 1887. The silver-plated metal supporting stand is marked "Toronto Silver Plate Co." The shakers, 2⅜" tall; metal stand, 5⅜" tall to the top of the lifting handle. Very scarce! **$185.00 – 210.00** set.

Sine collection

Barrel, V-Belt: Clear bright blue glass, mold blown and pressed. A barrel shaped shaker having 12 vertical panels separated by elongated "V's" and a belted "V" approximately one-third from the ringed bottom. Circa 1891 – 1900. 2⅝" tall x 1⅞" wide base diameter. Scarce! **$30.00 – 40.00.**

Rathbun collection

Beaded Base & Top: Opaque white opalware, mold blown. This is a six sided, urn shaped, ring neck, and footed shaker with a circle of beads at the neck and foot. Each scalloped panel has a three leaf tassel where each panel joins. The illustrated shaker is suffering somewhat from worn gilt paint at the top of each panel and the neck rim and base foot. Circa 1900 – 1910. Scarce! **$12.00 – 16.00.**

Lockwood collection

Beaded Belt: Opaque white opalware, mold blown. Has a belt of 20 beads at the waist from which small arches rise to the collar descend to the base. Circa 1899 – 1907. 2¼" tall x 1¾" wide at the waist; 2¼" base diameter. Top is not original as the shaker top edge has only one thread. Very scarce! **$28.00 – 37.00.**

Lockwood collection

Beaded Embroidery: Opaque white opalware glass, mold blown. A slightly curved neck shaker with a bulging lower half that has a pattern of eight squared-off ovals. Each oval is bordered with embossed beads and shares a common border with the next oval. Inside each oval is an embossed bead and scroll design. Each oval has alternating green and yellow coloring around the shaker perimeter. Circa 1898 – 1906. 3" tall x 2¼" wide. Scarce! **$28.00 – 37.00.**

Krauss collection

Beads & Scroll: Clear green glass, mold blown. A long narrow necked shaker with a flared bottom. The vertical rows of embossed beads flow downward to an elaborate scrolling (in raised relief) that encircles the base. The bottom contains an intaglio six-point rayed star. Circa 1899 – 1908. 3" tall. Scarce! **$33.00 – $45.00.**

White collection

Beaded Top & Bottom Variant: Opaque white opalware glass, mold blown. This shaker has four embossed scroll patterns; very similar to the shaker in our Vol. II, p. 118 except that the Wave Crest Monroe shaker is shorter and contains only two embossed scrolls; the other two sides are smooth for application of an appropriate colored decoration. Circa 1900 – 1905. 2¾" tall. Very scarce! **$25.00 – 35.00.**

McElderry collection

Krauss collection

Bead Work Cruet & Condiment Sets: Both sets have identical opaque red triple cased glass salt and pepper shakers that are dual mold blown. Each shaker contains three elaborate HP beaded medallions that are somewhat reminiscent of an arabesque type pattern. Believed to be of European origin; probably English. The shaker physical motif is configured in the form of a tapered barrel; however, this pattern name was created by A. G. Peterson and is shown within the colored art glass plate of his book *Glass Salt Shaker: 1,000 Patterns* published in 1970. The shakers, 3¼" tall with two-piece metal tops. The two-piece silver-plated condiment holder was made by the "Wilcox Silver Plate Co.," Meriden, Connecticut, that existed under the aforesaid company name from 1869 until it became a part of the International Silver Co. in 1898. The blue satinized cased glass cruet (part of the elaborate three-piece set) has similar HP decoration accentuated by striking, vivid off-white floral sprays. It has an amber handle and blown topped stopper that is attached to a fiery opalescent plug. The cruet is 5¾" tall to the top of the pouring spout. What makes the cruet set so beautiful is the special designed (quality) silver-plated holding stand that stands 12" tall and is marked "Aurora MFG SP Warranted" "Quadruple Plate." Many of the Victorian era silver-plate manufacturers purchased art and pattern glass from both domestic and foreign sources to fit into their various condiment frames for subsequent selling to the Victorian consumer. Circa 1884 – 1889. Very rare! two-piece condiment set, **$950.00 – 1,000.00;** three-piece cruet set, **NPD.**

Harris collection

Bell, Centennial: Clear heavy pressed glass. Another Liberty Bell-type shaker containing a special metal top. The shaker metal top condiment perforations form the words "Centennial U.S."; the center of the metal top has a square protruding metal tab that is embossed with the number "76." Circa 1876. 1⅞" tall. Rare! **$150.00 – 175.00** with special top.

Krauss collection

Bell, Inverted Thumbprint: Clear dark blue glass, dual mold blown. The IVT pattern is present on the inside surface. The smooth outer surface contains an elaborate HP leaf and floral sprig that is painted in green, white, and brown. The physical shape of this shaker is reminiscent of a bell. Circa 1884 – 1889. 3" tall with a two-piece metal top. Very scarce! **$140.00 – 170.00.**

Krauss collection

Bell, Metal Encased: Clear cranberry glass, mold blown. Illustrated are a pair of removable bell-shaped glass shakers with threaded tops that are retained within an arabesque type patterned sterling silver holder. Metal encased glass shakers were first illustrated and discussed by A.G. Peterson.[5] Examples are also displayed in our 1976 salt shaker book.[6] The various types of metal covered ware are fully discussed by A.C. Revi.[7] Research has revealed that metal encased condiment dispensers were produced in both Europe and the United States in both art and pattern glass. In their basic glass form these cranberry shakers are 1⅞" tall x 1½" at widest point with a 1⅛" base diameter. Circa 1887 – 1894. Rare! **$290.00 – 325.00** pair.

Bette Howard collection

Belladonna Variant: Clear cranberry glass, dual mold blown. The inside surface contains IVT. The exterior contains an elaborate HP floral spray having white, blue, and reddish petals. Believed to be a Mt. Washington/Pairpoint shaker. Circa 1887 – 1891. 3¼" tall with a two-piece metal top. Rare! **$185.00 – 205.00.**

Bell, Ring Necked: Transparent cranberry satin glass, mold blown. This is a bell-shaped shaker with a prominent neck ring. The smooth exterior surface has been hand painted with white flowers and leaves to provide a pseudo-cameo effect. Also produced in blue satin with a similar HP flower/leaf motif. Circa 1890s. 3" tall; 2¼" wide; 1¼" base diameter. Very scarce! **$80.00 – 100.00.**

Arnold collection

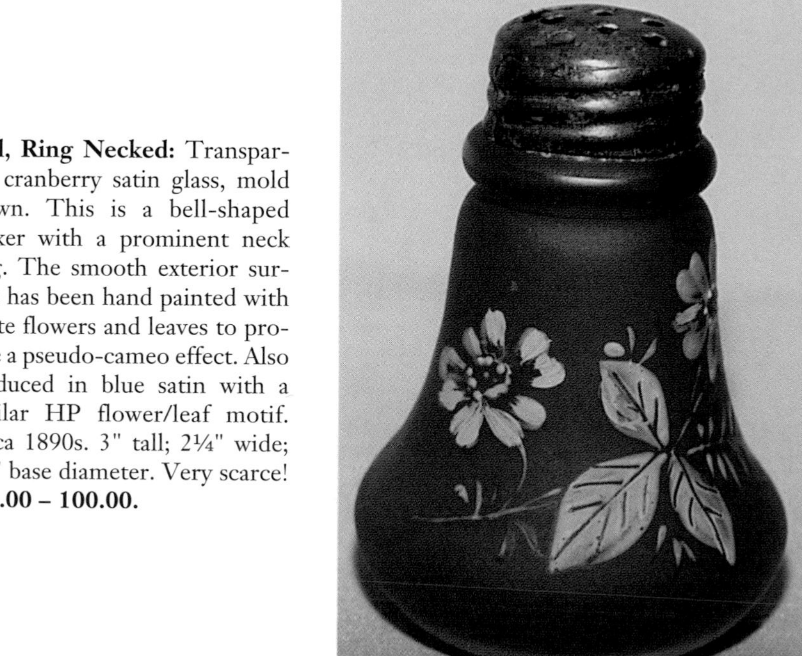

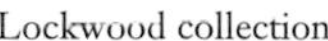

Lockwood collection

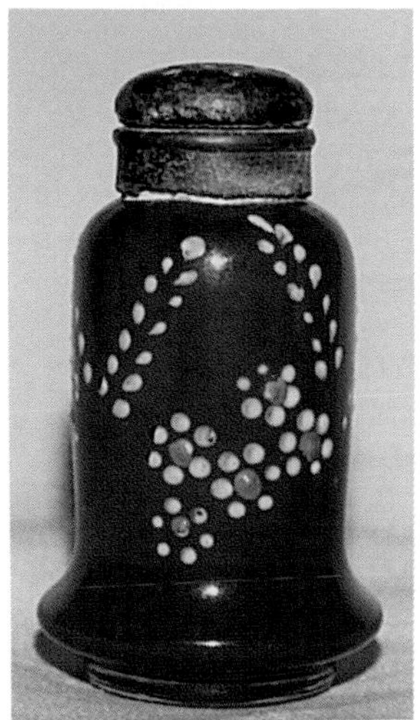

Bell, Tall: Clear cranberry glass, dual mold blown. This is the same shaker shown in our Vol. II, p. 262. The only variation is that this shaker has inside optic ribs and a different HP floral decoration. All of the aforementioned shakers have extended bottoms for use within a condiment set. Believed to have been produced by Mt. Washington/Pairpoint circa 1886 – 1892. 2⅞" tall x 2⅛" wide with a two-piece metal top. Very scarce! **$95.00 – 110.00.**

Lockwood collection

Berry, Inverted Thumbprint: Clear cranberry glass, dual mold blown. We are including this shaker under this AAGSSCS pattern name but, it appears to be the same pattern named "IVT Dainty" illustrated in our Vol. II, p. 235; of course the HP decoration and color are different. Circa 1885 – 1891. 2⅜" tall x 1¾" wide with a two-piece metal top. Very scarce! **$125.00 – 140.00.**

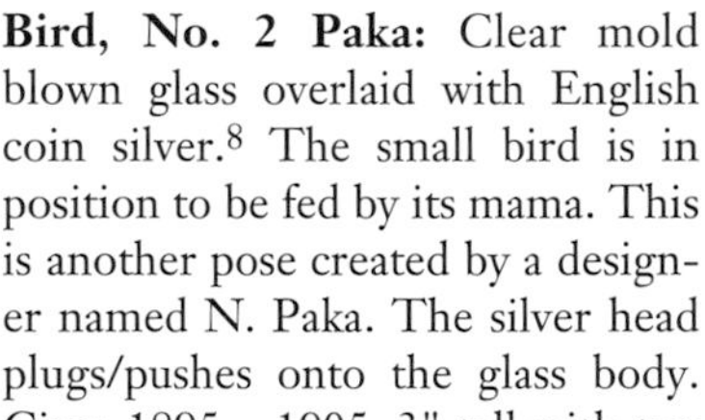

Authors' collection

Bird, No. 2 Paka: Clear mold blown glass overlaid with English coin silver.[8] The small bird is in position to be fed by its mama. This is another pose created by a designer named N. Paka. The silver head plugs/pushes onto the glass body. Circa 1895 – 1905. 3" tall with top in place. Rare! **$170.00 – 200.00.**

Rathbun collection

Binoculars: Clear glass, mold blown and pressed. This is an unusual version of a pair of salt and pepper shakers in an all glass holder with a center metal lifting handle. Each shaker is 2⅛" tall. The tops are believed to be original. The set is 7¾" tall to the top of the lifting handle. Rare as a complete condiment set. **$300.00 – 350.00** set.

Krauss collection

Bordeaux: Opaque pottery ware, mold formed. We have made a detailed (magnified) examination and comparison of these shakers against several "Longwy" condiment dispensers and have concluded that the "Bordeaux" shakers lack both quality and craftsmanship. In our opinion they are not Longwy Faience Co., pottery. Both lion/dragon (take your choice) and the black background arabesque lined scrolling were each created separately on some type of parchment paper and then adhesively attached to the basic pottery and covered with a thick clear glaze. The neck area has been hand painted in blue enamel over a crude, non-symmetrical, black leaf-like motif. Each at the two principal oval-shaped animal motifs have their edges encircled with a thin yellow painted raised border that simulates a picture frame and at the same time obscures any paper edging irregularity. We have been unable to determine if "Bordeaux" shakers emanate from another French factory called Bordeaux or if this word is simply a tradename. American glass potters copied each other's designs; why should the French pottery trade operate any different? These shakers are circa 1880 – 1890. 3¼" tall with two-piece metal tops. **$60.00 – 75.00** pair due to chipping damage.

Rathbun collection

Broadside Floral: Opaque white opalware glass, mold blown. Rectangular in form with narrow sides. The principal front and back panels contain an embossed stylized flower surrounded by scrolls. Each of the narrower side panels has an embossed four petal flower surrounded by a chain of oval beads. The base is footed. Contemporary glass. 2⅝" tall; 2" at the widest point; 1⅝" base diameter. Scarce! **$18.00 – 26.00.**

Harris collection

Bulb, Pseudo-Cameo: Translucent canary satinized art glass, mold blown. As our title indicates, the pattern shape is reminiscent of a light bulb. The exterior surface contains a large HP pseudo-cameo floral spray. The craftsmanship and glass quality are excellent. When exposed to UV (black light) the shaker radiates a striking florescence. Believed to be of English origin. Circa 1887 – 1892. 3¼" tall with a special silver plug-in type top. Rare! **$275.00 – 310.00.**

Harris collection

Bulb, Skinny: Clear dark blue glass, mold blown. Has an extended top neck ring that expands into a somewhat narrow bulb-shaped base. The glass below the base ring is threaded to accept a metal screw-on bottom. Circa 1905 – 1915. 3¾" tall with the metal bottom in place. Very scarce! **$35.00 – 50.00.**

Harris collection

Bulb, Stretched: Clear dark blue glass, dual mold blown. As the pattern name indicates this has the appearance of a stretched out bulb with a prominent neck ring. The inside surface contains IVT. The HP floral decoration consists of leaves and rose buds. Circa 1887 – 1894. 3¼" tall x 1⅞" wide with a two-piece metal top. Believed to be of European origin. The base appears to be configured for use in a condiment holder. Very scarce! **$180.00 – 200.00.**

Tutelo collection

Bulge, Four: Clear glass, mold blown. Having a column shape, this shaker has four vertical bulging panels separated by rows of white beads and flat panels. The bulged out panels have HP multicolored red, blue, and white floral sprays. Believed to be of European origin. Circa 1886 – 1891. 2¾" tall x 1¼" wide. Rare! **$110.00 – 125.00.**

Neale collection

Bulbous Base, Optic: Clear glass with selective amber stain, dual mold blown. This is a bulbous shaker containing six inside raised optic vertical ribs that are amber stained. Believed to be a Hobbs shaker. Circa 1887 – 1891. 2¾" tall; 1½" wide. Very scarce. **$45.00 – 60.00.**

Lockwood collection

Bulging, Baroque: Clear thin homogeneous cranberry glass, mold blown. The pattern amounts to a shaker with a wide range neck that tapers outward to a bulging bottom over a slanted ring base. The word "baroque" means irregular in shape. The main outer surface has an enamel HP row of white beads from which hang three gold washed triangular shapes; each containing bluish-white dot flowers. Thin-lined white scroll work is included on the lower portion. We believe this shaker was produced in Europe; probably England. Circa 1884 – 1890. 3⅛" tall x 2⅜" wide with a special metal top having closable perforated holes. Rare! **$195.00 – 225.00.**

Krauss collection

Lockwood collection

Bulging Lobes, Footed: Opaque heavy opalware glass, mold blown and pressed. The pattern comprises a ring neck over six wide lobes with a tapered scrolled foot. The pink and green floral decorated lobes have essentially disappeared due to washing wear and tear. The supporting foot has retained most of the goofus-type gilt paint. Circa 1900 – 1910. 3⅞" tall x 2⅞" wide. Scarce! **$8.00 – 15.00** due to wear.

Bulging Base, Miniature: Clear cranberry cased glass, dual mold blown; a thin cased crystal exterior glass coating has been applied that is clearly visible at the base of the shaker. The pattern name describes the shaker's physical configuration. The outer surface is decorated with HP intricate floral sprigs that are interspersed with small ruby colored scrolls with their edges outlined in gold. The pattern shape of this piece is identical to the A.G. Peterson named "Mary Gregory" shaker illustrated on page 20 of our Vol. II. Circa 1880 – 1885. 3¼" tall with a two-piece metal top; believed to be of European origin and probably Thomas Webb. Rare! **$300.00 – 350.00.**

Harris collection

Krauss collection

Butterfly & Tassel: Opaque blue glass, mold blown. Has a spheroid shape with four embossed butterflies connecting to four tassels. Also produced in opaque white opalware with painted decoration. Circa 1894 – 1900. 3" tall; 2½" wide; 1⅜" base diameter. Scarce! **$35.00 – 45.00.**

Butterfly, Large: Opaque blue glass, mold blown. The front and back of this shaker contains a large butterfly in high raised relief. Each narrow side contains eight protruding horizontal ribs, heavy glass for the 2⅞" tall size of the shaker. Circa 1894 – 1903. Rare! **$90.00 – 100.00.**

Rathbun collection

Caramel Slag Castor Set: Caramel and white opaque glass, mold blown. This is a small cased glass set consisting of open salt, pepper, and mustard in a silver-plated metal holder having English hallmarks. The inside layer of each piece is white; each outside surface consists of variegated caramel colored streaking. The pepper and mustard contain two-piece press fit metal tops with a center knob finial. Open salt, 1½" tall; pepper, 2½" tall; mustard, 2½" tall; metal holder, 5¾" to the top of the lifting handle. Believed to have been produced by Thomas Webb of Stourbridge, England. Circa 1910 – 1920. Very scarce. **$120.00 – 135.00.**

Krauss collection

Cathedral Square: Opaque homogeneous opalware glass, mold blown. Has eight curved-in neck scallops and four large petals pointing upward. Circa 1899 – 1908. 3⅛" tall x 1¾" wide. Scarce! **$14.00 – 20.00.**

Bruce collection

Centennial Christmas Salt: Opaque opalware glass, mold blown. Here is a small barrel-shaped shaker with a washed gray painted coloring over which a HP thin brown band has been added. It is unique because of its agitator and patent date. The agitator is a blade that crushes the salt when the extension protruding from the top is pushed. Salt is sealed by a gasket when the top is not depressed. The metal top contains a patent date of June 13, 1876.[9] Circa 1876. 2⅛" tall x 1½" wide. Rare! **$55.00 – 70.00.**

Lockwood collection

Chubby, Big: Opaque thin opalware glass, mold blown. A two-step ringed neck that expands into a well rounded body with a narrower base to accommodate a shallow ringed foot. The crude decoration amounts to three bands; one has pink and one has blue wash. Completely topped-off with gold paint in a random stippled pattern as if done with a sponge. Circa 1908 – 1915. 2⅞" tall x 2¾" wide. Scarce! **$13.00 – 17.00.**

Coalmer collection

Chrysanthemum Leaf: Clear mold blown glass. Pattern name by Ruth Webb Lee. A bulbous shaker containing exaggerated curved leaves with HP gilt raised buttons that diminish in size toward the base. Since this shaker saw limited chocolate glass production, the consensus of opinion is that it was produced at one of the National Glass factories, circa 1900 – 1903. McKee is a good prospect, but unverified! 2½" tall. A rare pair! **$105.00 – 125.00** pair.

Harris collection

Clemmer: Clear silver deposit glass, mold blown. This is one of the many types of mechanical shakers patented during the Victorian era that was configured to hold both salt and pepper condiment (within a single vessel) with a capability for individual dispensatory control. The elaborate silver deposit glass makes this a unique item. The inside of the shaker has a fixed glass divider; one side for salt, the other for pepper. The silver top has a handle, shaft and levers to close either of the two adjacent compartments.[10] The aforesaid mechanical design was patented by George Clemmer of Trenton, New Jersey, on May 3, 1910. 3" tall. Rare in silver deposit glass! **$130.00 – 150.00.**

White collection

Clock Tower: Opaque opalware glass, two-piece mold blown. Each center panel has what appears to portray the hands of a clock; hence the pattern name given. This is a tall shaker and believed to be of English origin. Perhaps intended for use as a pepper. The bottom contains an embossed Ro??7331; the first two numbers are not legible. Circa 1910 – 1920. 4¾" tall x 1¾" at widest point. **$20.00 – 25.00.**

Authors' collection

Coinspot, Spherical: Clear homogeneous opalescent green glass, dual mold blown. A small globe-shaped form with three horizontal rows of opalescent coinspots. Close magnified examination reveals normal random wear marks consistent with old glassware. The coinspot motif was made by numerous Victorian glass factories both in America and Europe. Chemical testing conducted for us by a chemical engineering friend verified that no residue(s) consistent with perfumes or colognes was present on the inside surface. He did find NaCl (salt) residue. Circa 1895 – 1905. 2½" tall with a two-piece metal top. Very scarce! **$65.00 – 85.00.**

Krauss collection

Krauss collection

Krauss collection

Clover and Timothy (condiment): Opaque yellow-shaded cased art glass, dual mold blown. The shakers are in the form of a narrow rectangle containing elaborate HP floral sprigs in blue and white with black leaves and petals which are painted in groups of three that form a trefoil. Pattern name by Peterson. It is our opinion that this ware is of European origin and probably Webb. The yellow shaded glass contains a white inner lining layer. 2⅞" tall; 1⁷⁄₁₆" wide; and 1¹⁄₁₆" thick. The shaker bottoms have been fire polished. The two-piece metal tops appear to be original. The silver-plated holder is marked "Meriden Co." A rare set! **$475.00 – 525.00** set.

Krauss collection

Collard Bulge: Clear cranberry homogeneous glass, mold blown. A bulging shaker with sparse distribution of white enamel flowers (five) on each side. Circa 1888 – 1897. 2¾" tall x 2" wide at the base. Very scarce! **$60.00 – 75.00.**

White collection

Collared Ribs: Opaque homogeneous blue glass, mold blown. The pattern consists of a round cylinder with 16 embossed vertical ribs that start at the base but stops about ¼" from the top of the shaker due to the presence of a prominent collar. Circa 1893 – 1901. 2⅞" tall x 1½" base diameter. Scarce! **$25.00 – 35.00.**

Cohen collection

Column, Concave: Opaque custard glass, mold blown. The pattern name describes this shaker configuration. The bottom edges of the shakers are rolled and smooth. The HP roses and leaves decoration and color of the custard glass are similar to Heisey's "Ring Band" and other known Heisey pieces. Circa 1903 – 1906. 3¼" tall x 1⅞" base diameter. Very scarce! **$210.00 – 225.00** pair.

Sine collection

Harris collection

Column, Cross-Base: Cobalt blue cased spangled art glass, dual mold blown. The pattern amounts to a geometric design with four preponderate vertical concave surfaces from shoulder to base containing silver-colored mica particles.[11] As a result of the cobalt blue color, the shaker is a thing of beauty and quite a rarity. Believed to be of European origin, circa 1878 – 1884, via production under one of the several English spangled glass patents that prevailed during the aforesaid dated years. The illustrated top is not the right type for this piece. 3⅛" tall. We are also illustrating this pattern in a mold blown clear pale blue shaker containing European style HP decoration. Rare in spangled glass! Blue spangled glass, **$600.00 – 700.00;** pale blue, **$75.00 – 100.00.**

Krauss collection

Column, Tall and Wide: Opaque pink cased glass, dual mold blown. As the pattern name indicates, this shaker is shaped like a tall column. The solid pink inner layer is cased with a clear glass outer layer that has an outstanding HP brown bird with a white breast perched among a white flowered green leafed bush. Believed to be of European origin; probably English. 3⅝" tall x 2⅛" wide with an unusual type of two-piece metal top. Circa 1885 – 1891. Rare! **$210.00 – 225.00.**

Lorrie Vit collection

Column, Enlarged Base: Opaque custard glass, mold blown. The pattern amounts to a cylindrical shape with an enlarged base. The smooth surface contains HP enameled pink and blue flowers placed diagonally along an extended gold stem. The shaker displayed high florescence under black light illumination. Believed to be part of a condiment set. Circa 1900 – 1905. 2¾" tall x 1½" wide with a two-piece metal top. Very scarce! **$40.00 – 55.00.**

Krauss collection

Column, Twelve Paneled Small: Clear ornate dark blue quality cut glass, mold blown. This is an almost translucent shaker due to its prism-like appearance as a result of 12 dense cut vertical panels. The outer surface is decorated with three HP marsh-like plants over which a butterfly/dragonfly is on the wing. It is our opinion that this shaker is of European origin. Circa 1895 – 1905. 2⅝" tall with a two-piece metal top. Rare! **$160.00 – 185.00.**

Rathbun collection

Concave Honeycomb: Translucent frosted Rubina glass, dual mold blown. This is a small curved-body shaker with a faint honeycomb pattern in the lower one-third of the body. The mold is almost identical to the "Twins" shaker(s) illustrated in our Vol. II, page 262. The smooth exterior contains a busy floral spray with the leaves slightly edged in gold. We believe this is a Mt. Washington/Pairpoint shaker. Circa 1886 – 1892. 2½" tall x 1½" wide. Very scarce! **$200.00 – 230.00.**

Harris collection

Cone, Inverted Tapered: Opaque frosted glass, mold blown. A smooth surfaced inverted cone pattern undoubtedly produced for souvenir-type decoration. The illustrated pair contains two different transfer applied colored scenes appropriately labeled relative to the Gettysburg, Pennsylvania, area. Circa 1910 – 1920. 3" tall. Scarce! **$35.00 – 50.00** pair.

Harris collection

Cone, Large Inverted: Translucent varicolored art glass, mold and free-blown finished. From a basic amber glass batch, this shaker has a variety of different inside stained reddish-orange color streaks. Believed to be of European origin. Circa 1906 – 1915. 3⅜" tall with a two-piece silver top of the plug-in pressure fitting type. Rare! **NPD.**

Krauss collection

Coralene On Bristol (condiment): Blue opaque glass, mold blown. Pattern name by Peterson. The set consists of a pepper, mustard, and open salt dish. Each piece contains HP floral decoration composed of various colored small beads that have been attached by the Coralene Process.[12] Shaker and mustard, 2½" tall with two-piece metal tops; the open salt, 1¼" tall. Probably English produced. Circa 1889 – 1895. The metal holding stand is marked "4596" and measured 5⅝" to the top of the lifting handle. Rare as a set. **$335.00 – 350.00** set.

Rathbun collection

Corn with Husk, Footed: Clear crystal glass, mold blown and pressed the pattern motif consists of a footed shaker containing embossed kernels of corn with husks in raised relief. The pattern name was established by A. G. Peterson and is illustrated on page 25-R of his 1970 salt shaker book *Glass Salt Shakers: 1000 Patterns*. Produced circa 1890 – 1900. 3¼" tall. Very scarce. **$40.00 – 50.00.**

Coalmer collection

Coalmer collection

Cord and Pleat: A clear cobalt blue and a cranberry colored shaker is shown in two sizes. The pattern depicts a tied cord below each shaker's neck along with random vertical pleats on the body. Pattern name by Peterson who illustrates this pattern on page 157-L of his 1970 salt shaker book. Cranberry shaker, 3¼" tall; the one in cobalt blue, 2½" tall. Believed to have been produced by The West Virginia Glass Co., Martins Ferry, Ohio. Circa 1896 – 1899. Other known colors produced are clear, green, and amethyst. Very scarce. Cobalt blue, **$60.00 – 75.00;** cranberry, **$85.00 – 95.00.**

Nebel collection

Corset, Elongated: Opaque opalware glass, mold blown. The pattern consists of a corset waisted shaker with HP daisies over a wash of white, green, and yellow paint. Circa 1905 – 1912. 3⅛" tall with a 2" circular base diameter. Scarce! **$8.00 – 12.00.**

Lockwood collection

Cotton Candy, Short: Translucent frosted thin glass, mold blown. This is the same shaker that is illustrated in our Vol. II, p. 216 with slightly different color shading. The height measurement is within our + or - ⅛" tolerance factor. Circa 1887 – 1894. Believed to be of European origin. 2¾" tall x 1¾" wide. Very scarce! **$125.00 – 150.00.**

Lockwood collection

Craquelle, Barrel: Clear gold iridescent crackle glass, mold blown. A corpulent-shaped barrel, smaller at the bottom. Circa 1887 – 1895. 2½" tall x 2" wide with a two-piece metal top. **$75.00 – 90.00.**

Bruce collection

Craquelle, Tapered: Translucent Rubina colored glass, mold blown. This is a tall tapered tubular shaker with a neck ring and flared bottom that has been produced by a craquelle treatment process.[13] The shaker appears to be a European piece. Circa 1884 – 1893. 3⅝" tall x 1¾" base diameter. Rare! **$85.00 – 100.00.**

Krauss collection

Creased Neck, Clouded (condiment): White opalware satin glass, mold blown. These are very unique decorated shakers. The floral motif was created by a masking technique. The white flowers and clouds have been formed against a surrounding pink and white background and are outlined by HP gold. Due to the smooth HP decorative surface this pattern design offers, several Victorian glass factories produced a basic "Creased Neck" form. Thus, absolute attribution could not be established. 3⅝" tall with two-piece metal tops. Circa 1890 – 1897. The intricately designed metal holder, containing an eagle on globe, is marked "Meriden B. Co" and measured 2⅝" tall to the highest point of the eagle's wings. Rare as a set! **$210.00 – 225.00** set.

Nebel collection

Creased Neck, Craquelle (condiment): Translucent amber crackled glass, mold blown. A tall cylinder shaped shaker that has a small creased neck. The basic technique for creating crackled glass involved plunging the red hot piece into cold water and then reheating and reblowing it. Such a process provided an unusual ice or frosting appearance. We believe that the shakers are of European origin. The bird handled condiment holder was apparently unmarked. Circa 1886 – 1893. Shakers, 3⅝" tall x 1⅝" wide with two-piece metal tops. Rare ! **$135.00 – 150.00** set.

Harris collection

Creased Neck, Dutch Windmill: Opaque opalware glass, mold blown. One of the many "Creased Neck" patterns used by Mt. Washington/Pairpoint to depict various painted scenes. No doubt produced during the same time period that the so-called "Pairpoint Delft" decoration took place. Circa 1896 – 1901. 3½" tall; top in not original. Scarce! **$30.00 – 43.00.**

Krauss collection

Creased Neck, Giant: Opaque white opalware, mold blown. This shaker is in the shape of a tall pillar containing a large HP pink and green vertical floral spray. Probably marketed for use as a saloon condiment dispenser. Circa 1894 – 1905. 5⅜" tall. Rare! **$110.00 – 125.00.**

Creased Neck, Frosted: Translucent frosted glass, mold blown. This is a uniform tubular-shaped shaker containing a creased neck pattern. This uncomplicated pattern type was used by many glass factories during the 1880s and 1890s because the smooth exterior surface was readily adaptable to a wide variety of HP decorative motifs. The shaker contains outstanding HP floral decoration in purple flowers with green, orange, and gold veined leaves. Believed to be a very scarce frosted example that was produced by the New England Glass Co. Circa 1884 – 1887. 3¾" tall with a two-piece metal top. **$95.00 – 115.00.**

Krauss collection

Krauss collection

Creased Neck, Rounded (condiment): Opaque white opalware, mold blown. Pillar shaped with a creased neck collar on rounded shoulders. The smooth exterior surface has a HP matched blue and green floral spray. Circa 1898 – 1906. 3½" tall. The metal holder is marked "Simpson, Hall, Miller & Co" and is 7" tall to the top of the lifting handle. Scarce as a matched set! **$80.00 – 100.00** set.

Lockwood collection

Creased Neck, Short Variant: Opaque opalware glass, mold blown. A small column shaker tapering at the shoulder to a smaller circular neck. The shaker bottom has a circular indent about dime size. The shakers have the same HP floral-shaped decoration; one has a pink; the other a pale blue stained background. Circa 1894 – 1900. 2⅝" tall x 1¼" wide with two-piece metal tops. Scarce as a matched pair. **$60.00 – 75.00** pair.

Creased Side Panel: Translucent satinized Rubina glass, mold blown with HP orange and yellow floral sprigs vertically emplaced (one above the other) on the exterior surface of each of the shaker's four sides. The front and back panels are 1⅜" wide; the narrower sides measured ⅞" wide and contain a vertical intaglio crease. Believed to be of European manufacture. Circa 1883 – 1887. The two-piece metal top appears to be original. Rare! **$160.00 – 175.00.**

Coalmer collection

Cube, Tapered Shoulder (condiment): Opaque opalware glass, mold blown. These are four-sided cube-shaped shakers with vertically placed HP pink and green floral sprigs on the front and back panels. The other sides contain smaller individual pink floral decor. Believed to be of European origin. Circa 1898 – 1906. 3½" tall with two-piece metal tops. The metal holder is stamped "Rogers and Bros. Triple plate." Very scarce! **$150.00 – 175.00** set.

Harris collection

Harris collection

Harris collection

Harris collection

Crown (condiment): Clear royal ruby glass, mold blown. The pattern name is based upon the fact that this set's physical appearance (form) is reminiscent of a royal crown. However, when the complete set was initially purchased it contained a mustard that is an exact color match to the Northwood Rose Du Barry "Leaf Umbrella" pattern. Also, the glass stopper in the "oil bottle" is the same as that used in the "Leaf Umbrella" cruets. To add still further to our data scenario is the fact that the set's red coloration appears to be the same as Northwood's ruby color in which his various "Leaf Umbrella" forms were produced. Initially, we tried to stear our attribution research in the direction of the Consolidated Lamp & Glass Co. but the aforementioned criteria contradicted such logic. In comparing this pattern to Harry Northwood's No. 263 ("Leaf Umbrella") design sketches[14] there is considerable format similarity between the two designs. Unfortunately, we have no factory antique catalog, trade journals, etc. to substantiate that this "Crown" pattern is Harry Northwood glassware. At least the reader has been given the aforesaid thoughts and logic that we employed relative to researching this ware. Circa 1889 – 1891. Salt and pepper, 2¼" tall; oil bottle, 3⅛" with stopper removed; Rose Du Barry colored mustard, 2¼" tall; matching Ruby glass base, 3" tall with a bottom diameter of 4¾". Overall set height to top of the metal lifting handle 10" tall. Very rare! **NPD.**

Bette Howard collection

Cue Ball: Dark ruby stained souvenir glass, mold blown. A short ball-shaped shaker purchased from the 1901 Pan American Exposition by the Davidsons whose name and the aforesaid information are stylus engraved on the surface of the piece. Circa 1901. 2⅜" tall with original metal tops. Very scarce! **$65.00 – 80.00** pair.

White collection

Curved Body, Big: Opaque heavy opalware glass, mold blown. The basic shape is that of a pillar that expands outward toward the bottom and ends up in the form of a bell. The smooth surface is decorated with HP blue dot flowers and green leaves. It is our opinion that this shaker was produced by the New Martinsville Glass Mfg. Company. Circa 1905 – 1910. 3¼" tall x 2⅜" base diameter. Very scarce! **$28.00 – 35.00.**

Authors' collection

Cylinder, Classic: Opaque variegated glass, mold blown. As far as form is concerned this piece has the characteristics of a tall smooth surfaced cylinder. It contains a series of varying lavender and purple streaks that encircle the shaker from top to bottom. Very similar to the color mixtures featured by Challinor, Taylor. Circa 1888 – 1891. 3⅜" tall. Rare! **$145.00 – 165.00.**

Krauss collection

Cylinder Creased Neck (condiment): Clear rose to crystal Rubina mold blown glass. The exterior floral motifs were created by a glass cutting wheel; although, to view this ware from a short distance one might think that the glass had been acid etched. The set consists of salt, pepper, and cruet within a silver-plated holder produced by Rogers & Brothers Co., Waterbury, Connecticut, which was established by Asa, Jr. & Simeon Rogers in 1858. This was one of the original companies to become part of the International Silver Co., in 1898. Circa 1888 – 1894. The salt and pepper shakers are 3⅝" tall; the cruet is 4⅛" tall with stopper removed. Rare! **$460.00 – 490.00** set.

Rathbun collection

Cylinder, Creased Neck Variant (condiment): Clear Rubina mold blown glass. The exterior floral motifs were created by a glass cutting wheel; although, to view this ware from a short distance, one might think that the glass motif had been acid etched. The sets consists of salt, pepper, and mustard within a silver-plated holder that has stamped within two circles "Meriden B. Co. Quadruple plated 057." The glass condiments are believed to be of European origin. Circa 1888 – 1894. The salt and pepper shakers are 3⅝" tall; the mustard is 2¾" tall. Rare! **$430.00 – 460.00** set.

Authors' collection

Cylinder, Large: Clear electric blue glass, mold blown. This is a large diameter shaker (1⅞") with three HP white petaled flowers front and back. Between the floral motifs are random painted white dots. 3¼" tall. Circa 1897 – 1906. Very scarce! **$60.00 – 70.00.**

Coalmer collection

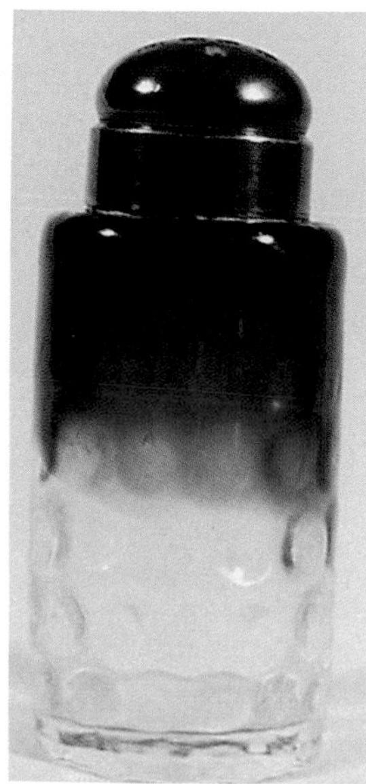

Cylinder, Optic Honeycomb: Clear Bluina glass, dual mold blown. A squared-off shoulder cylinder that is smooth outside with an inside honeycomb motif. A good example of inside blue staining with a very pointed color cut off. This type of Victorian pattern with slight variations was produced by several glasshouses. Circa 1886 – 1895. Also produced in Rubina and clear colorless shakers. 2¾" tall x 1½" wide. Very scarce! **$145.00 – 160.00.**

Krauss collection

Cylinder, Long Neck: Clear cranberry glass, dual mold blown. This is a very short bulging cylinder with a 1" slender neck. The outer surface has a HP blue/white forget-me-not floral spray with gold leaves encircling the shaker body; the top of the cylinder shoulder contains 19 HP white dots. The inside surface has small IVT. 2¾" tall with a two-piece metal top. Circa 1884 – 1889. Rare! **$100.00 – 120.00.**

Krauss collection

Cylinder, Round Shouldered Ceramic: Opaque ceramic ware, mold formed. This same pattern form was extensively used by various glasshouses during the Victorian era; there are various examples illustrated in both our salt shaker books. We felt that this matched shaker pair, in an unmarked silver-plated holder, deserved to be recorded because over the years we have observed an identical shaker in glass. Each shaker is decorated the same with a HP bird eyeing a flying insect (possibly a bee). Circa 1900 – 1910. 3⅜" tall. Very scarce! **$160.00 – 180.00** set.

Krauss collection

Cylinder, Round Shoulder (condiment): Molded glazed ivory ceramic. The pattern name describes the condiment shakers physical form. The salt and pepper has HP pink and green floral sprigs and a blue winged mayfly. The mustard has quite a large circumference and contains a HP orange floral spray encircling it. Salt and pepper, 3¾" tall; mustard, 3½" tall. All the condiment dispensers have two-piece metal tops. Believed to have been produced in Europe. Circa 1889 – 1900. Metal holder is unmarked. Very scarce! **$150.00 – 175.00** set.

Lockwood collection

Cylinder, Short: Opaque white opalware glass, mold blown. Has a short cylindrical body and a narrow, flat shoulder. The smooth surface is decorated by a red/orange with yellow center floral spray. Circa 1890 – 1896. 2½" tall x 1½" wide with a two-piece metal top. **$35.00 – 48.00.**

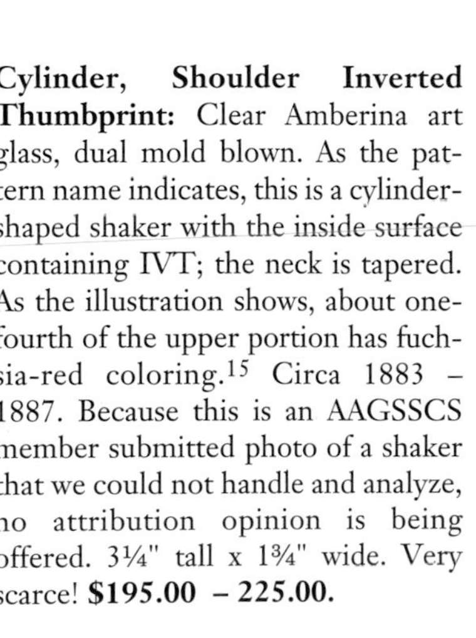

Cylinder, Shoulder Inverted Thumbprint: Clear Amberina art glass, dual mold blown. As the pattern name indicates, this is a cylinder-shaped shaker with the inside surface containing IVT; the neck is tapered. As the illustration shows, about one-fourth of the upper portion has fuchsia-red coloring.[15] Circa 1883 – 1887. Because this is an AAGSSCS member submitted photo of a shaker that we could not handle and analyze, no attribution opinion is being offered. 3¼" tall x 1¾" wide. Very scarce! **$195.00 – 225.00.**

Lockwood collection

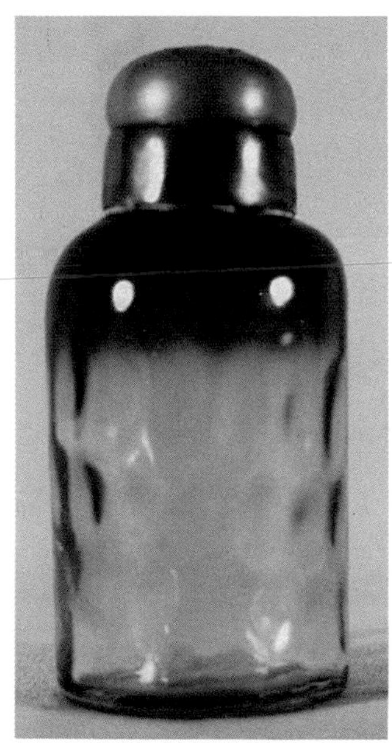

Lockwood collection

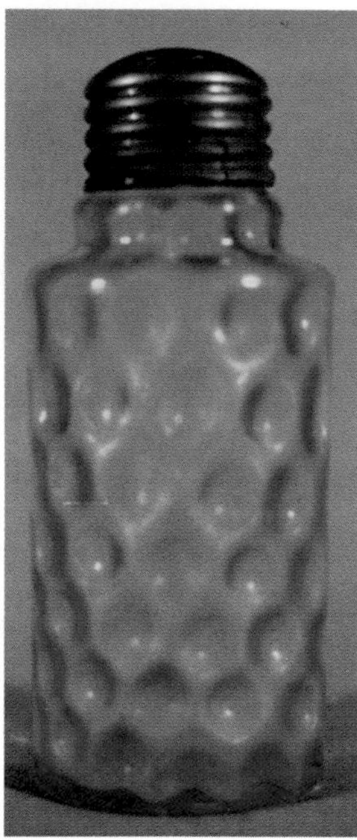

Cylinder, Small Neck: Clear apple green glass, dual mold blown. The cylindrical shape contains inside IVT with a small neck ring. Circa 1894 – 1905. 3½" tall x 1⅝" wide. Scarce! **$40.00 – 50.00.**

Lockwood collection

Dagger: Clear blue homogeneous pressed glass. The name assigned by Peterson for this shaker describes the pattern very well. The visual appearance is reminiscent of series of daggers in raised relief. Circa 1886 – 1891. 3⅛" tall. Very scarce! **$40.00 – 50.00.**

Tutelo collection

Daisy & Button, Curved Feet: Translucent amber glass, mold blown and pressed. Translucence is caused by the continuous daisy and button design covering the shaker. This type of pattern was made by numerous glass factories and has been imitated continuously throughout the years. The shaker is supported by six scallops that form the feet. Circa 1885 – 1900. 4¼" tall x 1½" wide. Scarce! **$20.00 – 25.00.**

Authors' collection

Daisy & Button, Footed: Translucent vaseline mold blown and pressed glass. A small bulging Daisy & Button pattern shaker with a large neck ring and a footed base containing a peg hole for insertion into a special matching glass condiment holder. Pattern name by Peterson. Circa 1878 – 1885. Has high illumination when subjected to UV black light radiation. The threaded glass edging has fine chipping from being broken off from a pontil rod. 2⅞" tall. Very scarce in vaseline glass! **$25.00 – 30.00.**

Authors' collection

Daisy & Button, Oval: Clear blue homogeneous glass, mold blown. Named by Peterson; an oval shaped form that is narrow at the top and bottom. Contains two encircling rows of daisies at the center and base with gaps in between. Believed to have been produced by either Bryce or Duncan. Circa 1890 – 1900. 3⅛" tall. Scarce ! **$15.00 – 20.00.**

Authors' collection

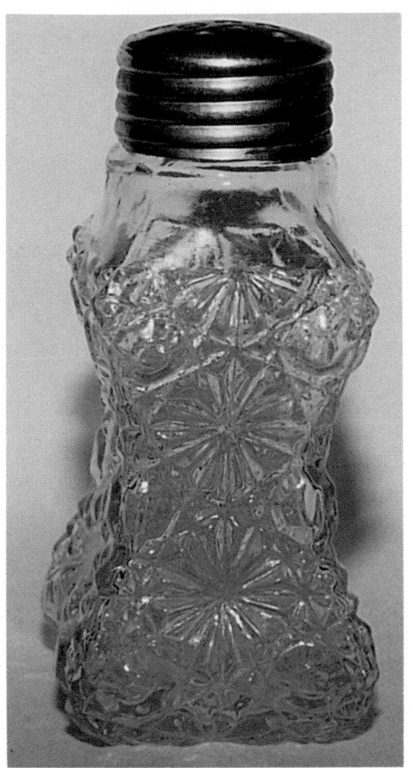

Daisy & Button, Plain: Clear homogeneous vaseline glass, mold blown. The pattern amounts to three large daisy and buttons on each of the four sides. Being illustrated to verify that these shakers were produced in vaseline. Displays very high fluorescence when exposed to black light. Circa 1878 – 1885. 3⅛" tall. Very scarce in vaseline! **$60.00 – 75.00.**

Randall collection

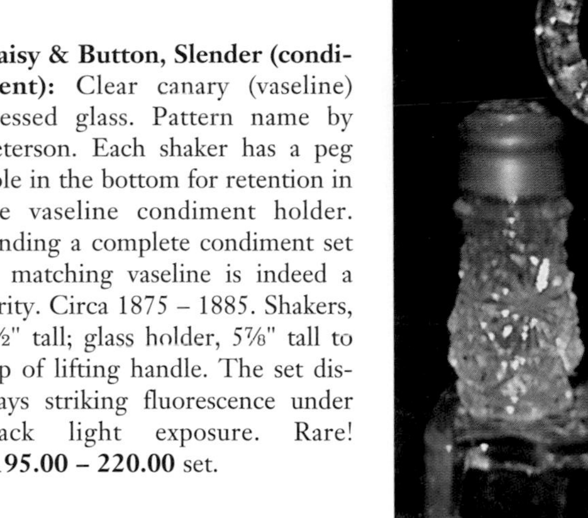

Daisy & Button, Slender (condiment): Clear canary (vaseline) pressed glass. Pattern name by Peterson. Each shaker has a peg hole in the bottom for retention in the vaseline condiment holder. Finding a complete condiment set in matching vaseline is indeed a rarity. Circa 1875 – 1885. Shakers, 2½" tall; glass holder, 5⅞" tall to top of lifting handle. The set displays striking fluorescence under black light exposure. Rare! **$195.00 – 220.00** set.

Krauss collection

Daisy & Lattice: Opaque white opalware, mold blown. Has an embossed petaled banded top, a short narrow neck with a bulging base. The principal motif consists of a lattice panel containing a HP designed daisy flower in raised relief. Circa 1898 – 1908. 3" tall x 1⅞" wide; 2⅜" base diameter. Scarce! **$27.00 – 35.00.**

Harris collection

Desert Storm: Clear green glass, mold blown. So the reader will understand the pattern title, this shaker was unearthed and brought back from the Saudi Arabian Desert by a U.S. military person as a souvenir of the Desert Storm War. The glass quality would not get a high mark due to random sized air bubbles throughout the shaker. The pattern is a complete unknown to us and (for all we know) may have been produced by a Middle East glass blower. However, we doubt that it is a one-of-a-kind pattern. It certainly is unique because of the way it was obtained. 3⅛" tall. A souvenir rarity. **NPD.**

MacAllister collection

Diamond Base: Clear emerald green glass, mold blown. The pattern amounts to a bulging based shaker with approximately one-third of the shaker base having continuous bands of diamonds around the perimeter. The orange HP floral spray is located at the half-way point. Also produced in decorated amber and opalware.[16] Circa 1901 – 1907. 3¼" tall. Very scarce in this color. **$45.00 – 60.00.**

Lockwood collection

Diamond & Double Fan: Opaque white opalware glass, mold blown. Each large diamond is filled with raised dots connected by raised lines reminiscent of a fishnet design. Bordered by zippered strips meeting at a plain diamond at each corner. Pattern by E. G. Warman.[17] Circa 1895 – 1905. 2½" tall x 2¼" wide. Scarce! **$25.00 – 35.00.**

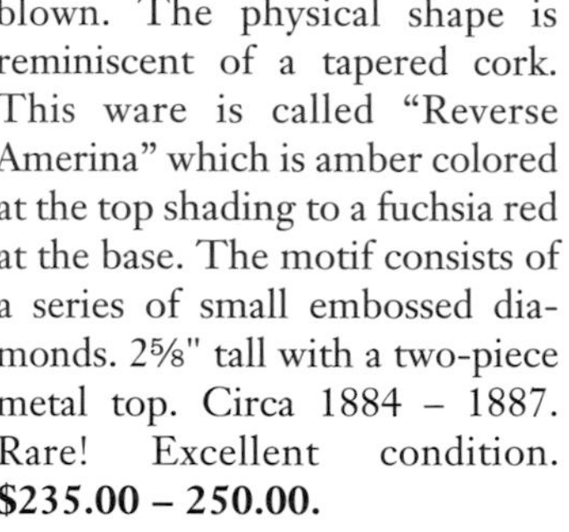

Diamond Cork: Clear reverse Amberina glass, dual mold blown. The physical shape is reminiscent of a tapered cork. This ware is called "Reverse Amerina" which is amber colored at the top shading to a fuchsia red at the base. The motif consists of a series of small embossed diamonds. 2⅝" tall with a two-piece metal top. Circa 1884 – 1887. Rare! Excellent condition. **$235.00 – 250.00.**

Krauss collection

Arnold collection

Diamond, Fine: Cranberry to clear Rubina glass, dual mold blown. The interior surface contains a continuous small diamond pattern; the outside surface is undecorated. The Rubina stain has a sharp cut-off point within the top portion of the shaker. Circa 1888 – 1891. 2¾" tall; 2" at widest point; 1¼" base diameter. Very scarce! **$70.00 – 85.00.**

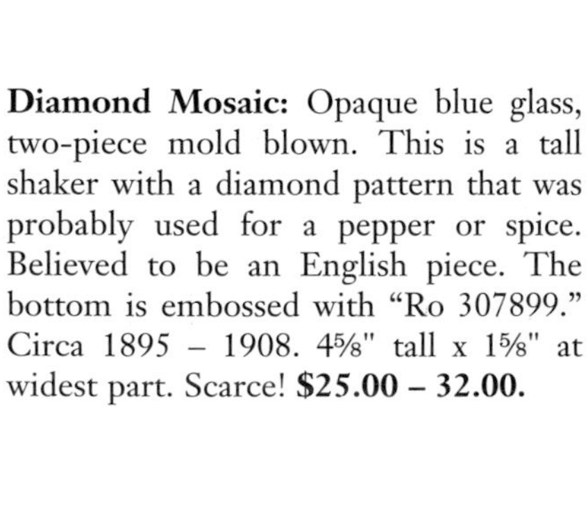

Diamond Mosaic: Opaque blue glass, two-piece mold blown. This is a tall shaker with a diamond pattern that was probably used for a pepper or spice. Believed to be an English piece. The bottom is embossed with "Ro 307899." Circa 1895 – 1908. 4⅝" tall x 1⅝" at widest part. Scarce! **$25.00 – 32.00.**

White collection

Lockwood collection

Diamond, Petaled: Translucent frosted blue glass, mold blown. This pattern has eight plain flat panels in the upper portion. The lower half is covered with beveled diamonds. Each diamond contains an embossed flower with many petals. Each panel holds five impressed, fan-shaped rays about the diamonds. Circa 1898 – 1906. 3⅜" tall x 1⅝" wide. Scarce! **$35.00 – 45.00.**

Krauss collection

Diamond Surface (condiment): Clear (uncolored) pressed glass. The pattern name describes the motif very well. The shakers and mustard have an intaglio ray star on their base. Circa 1897 – 1910. The glass holder matches the shaker and mustard pattern and has a center attached metal lifting handle. Shakers, 2¾" tall; mustard, 2¾" tall. The holding stand is 5" tall to the top of the lifting handle. Scarce! **$105.00 – 115.00** set.

Arnold collection

Wasson collection

Diamond Point, Tapered (condiment): Translucent amber glass, mold blown and pressed. The shakers contain a fine sawtooth motif that tapers downward to fit into a smooth glass holder having small securing projections. The circular lifting ring may have been designed to hold a small napkin. Despite the thoughts of some collectors, there is nothing in antique glass literature to verify that this set was produced by Sandwich. Also produced in blue. We are also illustrating a similar "Bird" salt and pepper set in clear glass that sometimes gets promoted by some sellers as possible Sandwich (which it isn't!). Circa 1878 – 1884 (both sets). Amber set shakers, 2¼" tall x 1¼" at widest point; 1¼" base diameter. Very scarce! Amber set, **$100.000 – 120.00;** Clear set, **$80.00 – 90.00.**

Rathbun collection

Diapered Flower: Opaque opalware glass, mold blown. The shape outline is that of a bulging inverted cone. The pattern consists of a series of raised diamonds with flat raised bars forming dividing lines. At the points where the lines cross there is a small forget-me-not HP green flower that has a small center bead. An initial look at this pattern made us think of its similarity to the Northwood "Quilted Phlox" pattern. Kamm indicated that it may be a Westmoreland Glass Co. pattern out of the 1890 time frame.[18] Peterson does not list or illustrate this pattern in his salt shaker book. Circa 1896 – 1904. 3⅜" tall; 2⅜" at widest point. Very scarce! **$25.00 – 35.00.**

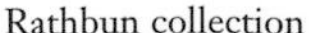

Rathbun collection

Dome, Inverted Thumbprint, Variant: Clear cranberry stained glass, dual mold blown. The inside surface is completely covered with small IVT. The smooth outer surface is decorated with HP gold and blue flowers. Circa 1885 – 1890. Believed to be of European origin. 2½" tall x 1¾" wide with a two-piece metal top. Rare! **$175.00 – 200.00.**

Lockwood collection

Dome, Little: Opaque white opalware glass, mold blown. As the pattern name indicates, this is a short, dome-shaped shaker. The HP motif amounts to a pink five-petaled flower with green leaves. Circa 1900 – 1906. 2" tall x 1¾" wide. **$22.00 – 30.00.**

Krauss collection

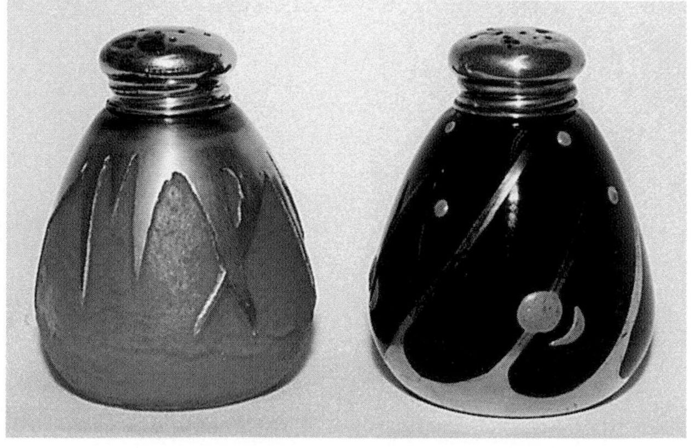

Authors' collection

Dome & Icicles: Three shakers are shown, black, green, and orange. All are opaque glass, mold blown. They are dome shaped and two are acid cut-back glass with the black having HP orange and yellow decoration; the green shaker contains a gold painted motif; the shiny orange shaker is lined in black. The pattern name (assigned by an AAGSSCS group) was created because they viewed the shakers as being reminiscent of icicles of varying length. This is European glass that was probably English produced. Circa 1900 – 1910. 2⅜" tall; 1⅞" wide; 1½" diameter with two-piece sterling tops. Very scarce! **$125.00 – 140.00** pair; orange single, **$60.00 – 70.00.**

Lockwood collection

Dome, Small Inverted Thumbprint: Clear cranberry glass, dual mold blown. A very short dome-shaped shaker with IVT on the inner surface. The outside is smooth and has HP shaded white-blue flowers with greenish yellow leaves. Circa 1885 – 1891. 2" tall x 1¾" wide. Very scarce! **$85.00 – 100.00.**

Door Knob: Opaque opalware, mold blown. This is a large expanded bulbous shaker containing a HP brown leafy branch below an embossed ring neck. 2" tall; 2½" wide. Circa 1905 – 1910. Scarce. **$18.00 – 23.00.**

Rathbun collection

Krauss collection

Egg on Pedestal: Clear blue and cranberry contemporary art glass, mold and free-blown finished. The pattern amounts to a mold-blown tapered egg fused on to a glass base that is intended to give each shaker configuration proper weight and balance. Each shaker contains a HP white colored female in Victorian style clothing; the raised right arm is holding what appears to be a fan or glass. On top of each glass base is a series of white painted dots that form a complete circle. The top of each shaker has round perforations for condiment dispensing. The appropriate salt or pepper condiment is loaded from the bottom and secured in place by a cork. The glass is of excellent quality and believed to be of European origin. Circa 1960 – 1970. Very scarce. **$375.00 – 400.00** pair.

Arnold collection

Double Bubble Inverted Thumbprint: Clear amber glass, dual mold blown. This shaker consists of two spheroid shaped expanded bulbs separated by a thin center waistline. The inside surfaces have a complete IVT spread. The exterior contains random spaced HP white/pink flowers. We believe this is a European shaker. Circa 1885 – 1890. 3¼" tall x 2½" wide. The threaded glass top surface has been ground smooth. Very scarce! **$175.00 – 190.00.**

Lockwood collection

Elephant, Tall: Translucent clear, lightweight glass, mold blown. The pattern name describes this unusual shaker. The translucent effect is caused by the busy pattern which depicts a standing elephant fully clothed in coat tails with hands in pockets standing on a platform. This appears to be one of those early candy containers that was configured for dual usage; candy first, and later as a salt or pepper condiment dispenser. First pictured in the Peterson book on p. 160-D. Circa 1925 – 1935. 4⅞" tall. Rare. **$225.00 – 250.00.**

Coalmer collection

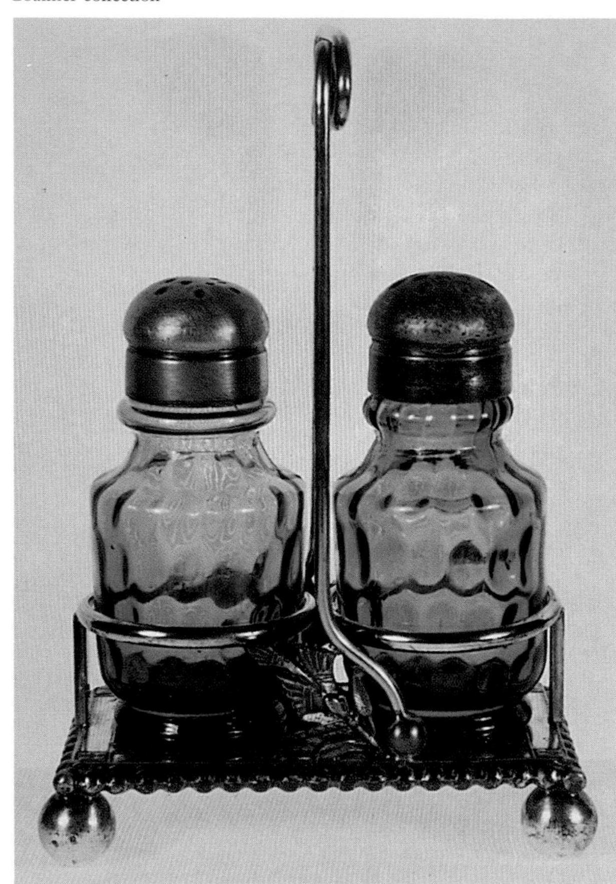

Ellipse, Footed (condiment): Clear electric blue glass, dual mold blown. The two shakers are undecorated. They each have a large protruding ring, just below their two-piece metal tops, that is part of a somewhat elongated neck that blends into a barrel-shaped body. The inside surface pattern consists of a series of embossed ellipse shapes; the exterior surface is smooth with an attached footed base. The silver-plated holder was made by the Meriden B. Company of Meriden, Connecticut, which existed from 1852 until their merger into the International Silver co. in 1898. It is believed that this glassware was obtained by the Meriden B. Co. from one of the finer New England glasshouses that existed circa 1894 – 1898. This set, along with other glass types, was frequently marketed by various silver plating companies during the 1880s and 1890s. 3⅛" tall. Rare as a set! **$230.00 – 260.00** set.

McElderry collection

Ellipse, Vertical: Clear amber glass, dual mold blown. A tapered bulb-shaped shaker with the inside surface containing vertical ellipses. The outer surface has a single HP green and white floral spray covering approximately three-fourths of the exterior. Circa 1885 – 1892. 2⅝" tall with a two-piece metal top. Very scarce! **$85.00 – 100.00.**

Krauss collection

Elongated Spheroidal Bulb (condiment): Clear cranberry art glass, dual mold blown with interior IVT and random opalescent splotches. The exterior surface is smooth and not decorated. This two-piece condiment set contains a salt and pepper held within a fancy, unmarked, silver-plated holder that is supported by four Queen Ann style ball feet. Believed to have been produced by either the Phoenix Glass Co. or Hobbs, Brockunier & Co. Circa 1884 – 1888. 3⅛" tall with two-piece metal tops. Rare as a set! **$320.00 – 340.00** set.

Authors' collection

Elvira's Butterfly Variant: Clear Rubina stained glass, dual mold blown. The inner surface contains tiny IVT; the smooth exterior contains a heavy enamel HP yellow and blue tipped butterfly of exactly the same artistic shape and detail as the shaker illustrated in our Vol. II, page 225. The shaker form is a wide shaped shoulder that gradually decreases in size toward the base. We believe this to be an English Stevens & Williams piece. Circa 1886 – 1891. 2½" tall with a special two-piece metal top having a flared-out metal collared bezel and finial top. Rare! **$210.00 – 225.00.**

Rathbun collection

Faint Feather: Opaque opalware glass, mold blown. A bulging shaker that narrows toward the base. Has a series of limited length embossed irregular veins that are distributed in a random fashion starting at the top of the shaker. The majority of the outer surface is smooth and contains a HP pansy-like floral spray below yellow staining. 3⅛" tall. Circa 1894 – 1902. Scarce. **$30.00 – 42.00.**

Fancy Heart: Opaque green glass, mold blown. The pattern amounts to a beaded heart that is repeated three times around the shaker. Physical upright support amounts to a round step foot. Circa 1895 – 1903. 2⅞" tall x 1¾" wide; 1⅝" diameter base. Very scarce! **$90.00 – 115.00.**

Rathbun collection

Rathbun collection

Feather, Fine: Translucent cobalt blue, mold blown. The pattern consists of three large vertical feather-like panels in raised relief that are equally spaced around the shaker body. This shaker form is illustrated on page 28-P of the Peterson book, *Glass Salt Shakers*. Circa 1897 – 1904. 3⅛" tall. Rare in this color. **$50.00 – 60.00.**

Krauss collection

Fence: Clear blue homogeneous glass, mold blown. The pattern consists of three encircling bands, each containing 18 vertical ribs. 2⅞" tall. Circa 1891 – 1901. **$18.00 – 20.00.**

Krauss collection

Fine Cut & Block: Clear ruby stained mold blown and pressed glass. The pattern amounts to a tall cylinder with three rows of ruby stained diamonds in raised relief. Between each diamond pair is a clear fan. The bottom of the shaker has 12 ruby stained diamonds. This shaker is illustrated in Peterson 160-S. Additional details are also delineated in Kamm 1 – 42. 3¾" tall. Circa 1890 – 1900. Rare shaker! **$30.00 – 40.00.**

Krauss collection

Flared Panel: Clear amber glassware, dual mold blown with eight wide vertical optic ribs inside. The outside surface is smooth and reflects a HP posterior view of a Victorian child fully clothed in a long collared dress wearing a hat and black and white footwear. Believed to have been produced in Europe. Circa 1889 – 1895. 3½" tall with a two-piece metal top. Very scarce! **$150.00 – 175.00.**

Nebel collection

Fleur-de-Lis, Beaded: Aquamarine translucent glass, mold blown. This small bulged-out base shaker contains three vertical fleurs-de-lis separated by three beaded vertical lines. Circa 1894 – 1898. 1¾" tall x 2" base. Very scarce! **$33.00 – 45.00.**

Ridgway collection

Tutelo collection

Fleur-de-Lis, Petite: Opaque opalware, mold blown. A small plain tubular shaped shaker containing an embossed fleur-de-lis band around the shoulder; no doubt part of a condiment set. The color on the motif was applied to make the pattern stand out for photography. Circa 1898 – 1904. 2⅛" tall x 1½" wide. Scarce! **$12.00 – 18.00.**

Fleur-de-Lis & Flower: Clear blue glass, mold blown. This is a bulging based shaker; narrowing toward the top. The pattern consists of an embossed fleur-de-lis and flower motif with a leafy scroll around the bottom. Circa 1890 – 1900. 3⅛" tall; 2½" bottom diameter. Very scarce! **$38.00 – 50.00.**

McElderry collection

White collection

Fleur-de-Lis Spike: Translucent aqua blue spatter glass, mold blown. A narrow necked shaker with six panels containing fleurs-de-lis in raised relief. Barbara White has expressed doubts as to whether this is a shaker or a bottle. However, it was accepted by the AAGSS-CS ID Committee as a shaker and assigned the aforesaid pattern name. We are also illustrating another collector's shaker displaying a myriad of spatter coloration with a two-piece metal top. 4" tall x 2⅜" wide; 1¾" base diameter. Very scarce! **$55.00 – 70.00.**

Krauss collection

White collection

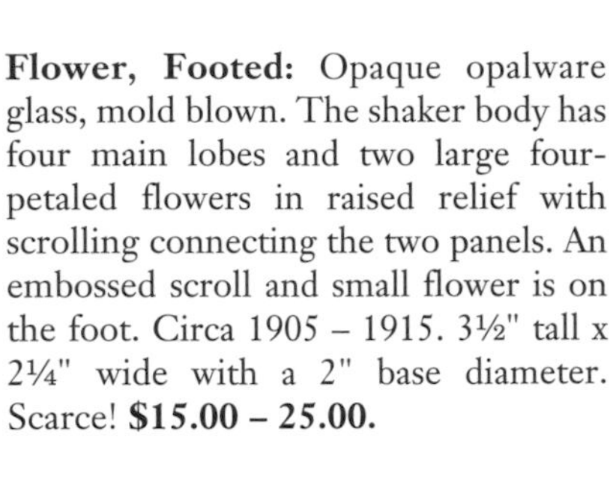

Flower, Footed: Opaque opalware glass, mold blown. The shaker body has four main lobes and two large four-petaled flowers in raised relief with scrolling connecting the two panels. An embossed scroll and small flower is on the foot. Circa 1905 – 1915. 3½" tall x 2¼" wide with a 2" base diameter. Scarce! **$15.00 – 25.00.**

Floral Band, Footed: Opaque white opalware glass, mold blown. A footed bulging shaker embossed with flowers front and back. The two bands of flowers on the shoulder are possibly mums. Circa 1904 – 1912. 2½" tall; 2¾" wide; 1¾" base diameter. Scarce! **$16.00 – 22.00.**

Tutelo collection

Flower in Circle: Clear electric blue glass, mold blown. The pattern title reveals the principal design which consists of a large circle with a rayed flower that is repeated three times. Between the flowered circles are bunches of fagoting held together at the middle by a diamond shaped feature. Circa 1888 – 1898. 3½" tall x 2" wide. Also produced in clear glass. Very scarce! **$25.00 – 30.00.**

Tutelo collection

Flower in Teardrop: Opaque opalware glass, mold blown. Here is an expanded based shaker with a relatively intricate embossed motif. The expanded neck is encircled with a scroll flower band that tapers down to the bulbous base. The entire base has scrolls that enclosed a raised floral design. There is no doubt that at one time this shaker contained some type of cold painted decoration that has since worn off. Circa 1901 – 1912. 3⅛" tall x 2¼" wide; 1¾" base diameter. Scarce! **$7.00 – 12.00.**

Lockwood collection

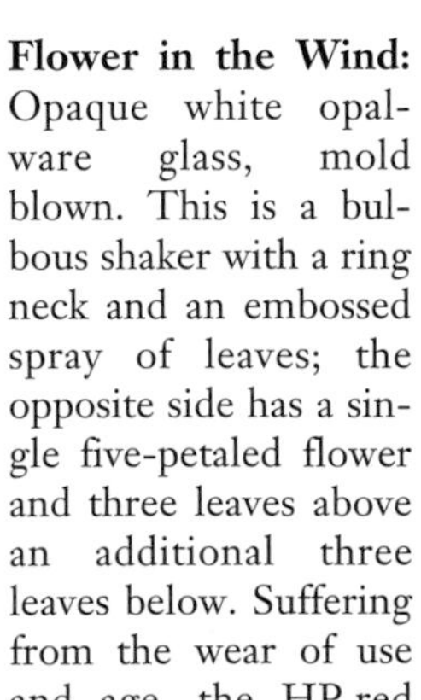

Flower in the Wind: Opaque white opalware glass, mold blown. This is a bulbous shaker with a ring neck and an embossed spray of leaves; the opposite side has a single five-petaled flower and three leaves above an additional three leaves below. Suffering from the wear of use and age, the HP red and green goofus coloring is about half missing. Circa 1900 – 1908. 1¾" tall x 2⅞" wide with a 2" base diameter. **$8.00 – 10.00.**

Lockwood collection

Flower Swirl: Opaque white opalware glass, mold blown. The pattern amounts to a shaker with a bulging bottom curving to a smaller round top with a ring neck. The left-to-right swirls are widest at the bottom and graduate in size toward the top. The swirls are interrupted front and back by an intaglio seven-petaled flower and leaves with a top bud. Pattern name is by Warman.[19] Circa 1900 – 1910. Scarce! **$18.00 – 22.00.**

Lockwood collection

Footed, Eighteen Panel: Opaque homogeneous pale bluish glass, mold blown. A bulging shaker with 18 smooth curved vertical panels tapering to a narrow ring and then flaring into a round two-tiered foot. Circa 1900 – 1909. 2½" tall x 2½" wide with a metal flange top having a perforated celluloid insert. Scarce! **$20.00 – 28.00.**

Tutelo collection

Footed Six Pea: Opaque opalware glass, mold blown. Here is a busy pattern along with an ungainly shape. Just below the neck ring are six large beads (peas) on the shoulder; six panels taper down to a narrow form before spreading out to make a scrolled foot. Circa 1904 – 1914. 3⅞" tall x 2½" at widest point. Scarce! **$8.00 – 15.00.**

Four Band: Blue translucent cased glass containing a variegated dark and light blue inner layer beneath a crystal clear outer glass layer, mold blown. The exterior surface has a HP white floral design encircling the shaker between the top and bottom protruding ring bands. This is a tall shaker with a total of four ring bands in high raised relief. The design reflects probable usage as part of a condiment set. The overall motif is reminiscent of the "Flower and Rain Variant" shaker shown in our Vol. II, p. 55. 4⅜" tall with a two-piece metal top. Circa 1887 – 1895. Rare. **$175.00 – 200.00** .

Krauss collection

Lockwood collection

Four Ring: Opaque opalware glass, mold blown. This round bulging shaker tapers upward and has four large expanded rings that decrease in circumference to form the upper half. The smooth lower half contains a HP orange, white, and gray bird perched upon the branch of a bush. Circa 1899 – 1905. 3" tall x 2" wide. Very scarce with this decoration! **$50.00 – 65.00.**

Krauss collection

Four Ring, Tubular: Clear amethyst mold blown glass. Has a tubular shape with four large horizontal rings that encircle the lower portion of the shaker. The upper part is smooth and contains a HP skirted Victorian child attempting to catch a butterfly. The bottom has a dark amethyst base ring. 3⅝" tall with a two-piece metal top. Believed to be of European origin. Circa 1887 – 1896. Very scarce. **$160.00 – 180.00.**

Lockwood collection

Frosted Medallion: Clear translucent glass, mold blown and pressed. Almost an overshot surface containing a circular rosette medallion. Pattern name by Millard.[20] Circa 1881 – 1891. 2⅞" tall. Very scarce! **$14.00 – 20.00.**

Lorrie Vit collection

Franklin Panel: Opaque opalware glass, mold blown. This is a large plain footed shaker with six raised vertical ribs. When it was new, each rib was outlined in gold. Pattern name by Warman. Circa 1900 – 1910. 4" tall x 2¼" wide with 2¼" base diameter. Scarce! **$12.00 – 17.00.**

White collection

Garland of Roses: Clear crystal glass, mold blown and pressed. The main body of this shaker is on a pedestal of three stumps (stippled) rising out the rose covered foot. The body portion has cabbage rose style roses with embossed lines on petals to look like a buttonhole thread stitch. According to Heacock,[21] this pattern was also produced in vaseline and perhaps some examples in chocolate. Circa 1900.[22] 3¼" tall x 1⅞" wide. Very scarce! **$35.00 – 45.00.**

Krauss collection

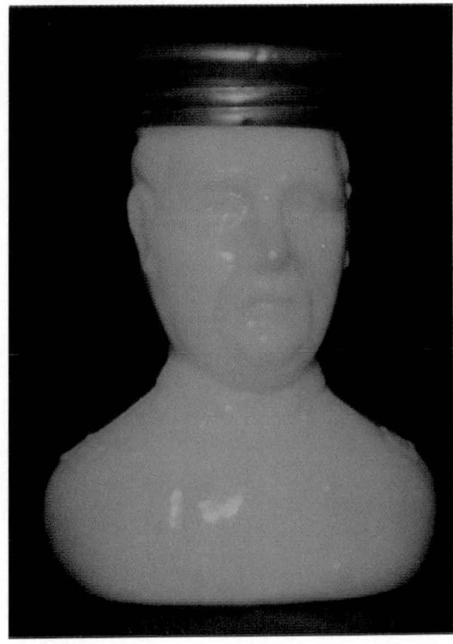

Krauss collection

General Shafter: We are illustrating two shakers: One is opaque white opalware and the other is translucent frosted glass, both are mold blown. These shakers are a bust of Spanish American War Major General William Rufus Shafter that displays his head, shoulders, and upper chest.[23] He was born on October 16, 1835, in Galesburg, Michigan. He died November 12, 1906, on his ranch (after retirement) near Bakersfield, California. General Shafter began his military career as a first lieutenant in the 7th Michigan Infantry in August 1861 during the Civil War. He distinguished himself in both wars and was promoted periodically as the result of such continuous recognition.[24] 3¼" tall x 1½" diameter. The frosted metal top is not original; the opalware shaker top is original. Circa 1900 – 1905. Very rare! **NPD.**

Maxfield collection

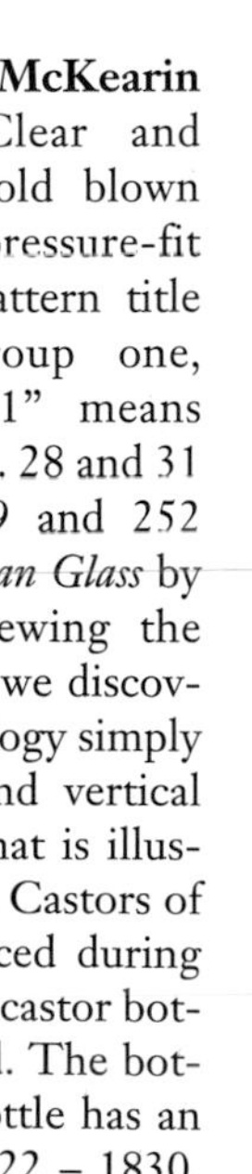

Harris collection

G1-28, & GII-31 McKearin Castor Bottles: Clear and cobalt blue three-mold blown glass castors with pressure-fit friction tops. The pattern title "G1-28" means group one, sketch #28; "GII-31" means group two, sketch #31. 28 and 31 appear on pages 249 and 252 respectively of *American Glass* by McKearin. Upon viewing the referenced sketch 28, we discovered that the terminology simply refers to the flute and vertical ribbed type pattern that is illustrated (left) on p. 249. Castors of this type were produced during the 1820s before glass castor bottles were top threaded. The bottom of each castor bottle has an open pontil. Circa 1822 – 1830. Our illustrated clear castor bottle (left) is 4" tall x 1⅝" base diameter; the cobalt blue bottle is 3⅞" tall. On page 266 McKearin states, "Any colored castor bottle is extremely Rare." **NPD.**

Maxfield collection

Maxfield collection

Globe, Columbian: Opaque white opalware glass, mold blown and pressed. Actually, this is a globe shaped two-part condiment set. The upper half of the globe consists of a fully enclosed shaker with a metal perforated top. When lifted off, the remaining lower portion becomes an open salt dish. The upper part is embossed with an 1492 date; the bottom piece has a 1892 date. Obviously, this unique condiment set design was created to recognize the 400th anniversary of the discovery of America by Christopher Columbus. For purposes of pattern clarity we temporarily colored the dates in red and outlined the banner ribbons in blue. Circa 1892 – 1893. 2" tall x 2¼" wide. Very rare! **NPD.**

Rathbun collection

Green Slag Castor Set: Green and white opaque variegated glass, mold blown. This cased glass set consists of an open salt, pepper, and mustard in a 4" tall metal holder that is marked E P N S (meaning, Electro Plated Nickel Silver). Each condiment piece has a white inside glass layer; the external surface has green/white variegated streaking. The press fit mustard and pepper two-piece tops have a small center knob finial. Open salt, 1⅜" tall; pepper, 1¾" tall; mustard, 1⅞" tall. Believed to be a product of Thomas Webb of Stourbridge, England. Circa 1915 – 1925. Very scarce! **$90.00 – 110.00.**

White collection

Harris collection

Haines, Short: Clear cobalt blue-green and cobalt blue glass, mold blown. The physical configuration of this shaker type is fully described in our Vol. II book.[25] When we discussed and illustrated this shaker in our previous book we stated that this ware was made only in clear glass. As the reader can see, it was also produced in the aforementioned colors. Circa 1878. 2⅝" tall x 1½" base diameter. The illustrated tops may not be original. Very rare in these colors and size! If anyone has this shaker in another color, we would appreciate a photograph of it. **NPD.**

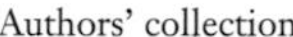

Authors' collection

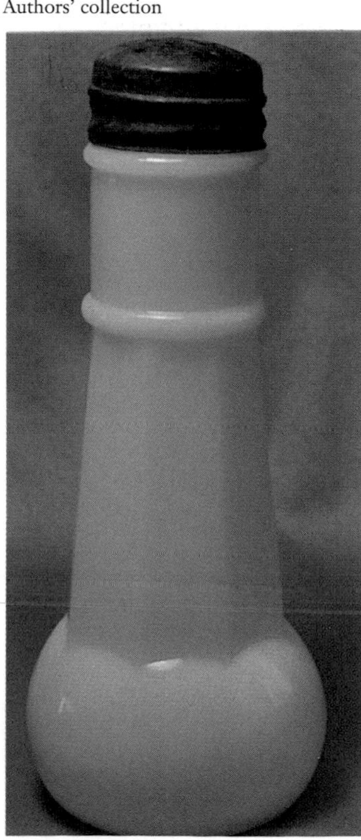

Harbor Light: Opaque glossy opalware glass, mold blown. This is an unusually tall shaker that was given the aforesaid pattern name because it appears to be reminiscent of an ocean marker buoy. The pattern consists of eight embossed vertical panels just below two protruding upper rings. Stabilized support is provided by a round bulging base. Circa 1930 – 1940. 5½" tall. Very scarce! **$28.00 – 35.00.**

Coalmer collection

Heavy Rib: Clear marigold carnival glass, mold blown and pressed. These are thick, heavy shakers due to the massive vertical ribbing on the exterior. This is excellent quality, brilliant glass in a very simple pattern. Each rib is well convexed and reaches from top to bottom. Circa 1913 – 1923. 2¾" tall; the tops are not believed to be original. Very scarce in this type of glass! **$68.00 – 90.00** pair.

Lockwood collection

Hero (OMN): Clear glassware, mold blown. This is a cylindrical-shaped shaker with a plain top; the base has a band of raised pointed pillows in beveled circles that touch but do not overlap eight of the circles. Circa 1892 – 1895. Aka "Pillow, Encircled" (Kamm 2-129). Heacock attributes this pattern to the Elson Glass Co. and the West Virginia Glass Co.[26] Also produced in ruby stained glass. 2¾" tall x 1½" wide; 1½" base diameter. Scarce! **$16.00 – 25.00.**

Lockwood collection

Hex-Curves: Opaque intense-white opalware glass, mold blown. A barrel-shaped shaker with six vertical flat panels that widen and then become narrow to conform to the bulging shape. Circa 1899 – 1910. 2¾" tall x 2" wide. **$22.00 – 30.00.**

Rathbun collection

Hexagon Leaf: Opaque opalware, mold blown. A six-paneled body containing an embossed serrated leaf at each bottom point; a circle of leaves droops from the top edge of the shaker neck. Decorated with HP floral sprigs over a light brown stained background. Believed to have been made by the Fostoria Glass Co. Circa 1900 – 1908. 3" tall. Scarce! **$25.00 – 30.00.**

Harris collection

Hippopotamus: Clear mold blown glass with a large, detailed metal hippopotamus head containing top perforations for condiment dispensing. No doubt an original candy container configured for use at the table as a shaker once the candy had been consumed. Circa 1925 – 1935. 2⅜" tall to the top of the hippo's ears. Very scarce! **$60.00 – 75.00.**

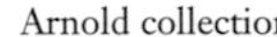

Bruce collection

Hobnail, Rib Base: Translucent amber glass, mold blown and pressed. This pattern has smooth hobs that are clearly separated. The base has 16 ribs that encircle the lower part of the main body. The translucence is the result of the hobnails that completely cover the shaker's exterior. Circa 1885 – 1896. 3¼" tall with a two-piece metal top; 2" base diameter. Scarce! **$25.00 – 30.00.**

Arnold collection

Honeycomb, Inverted Large: Clear blue glass, dual mold blown. As the pattern name implies, the inside surface of this cylinder-shaped shaker has large inverted honeycombs; the outside surface contains a HP orange, yellow, and white floral spray with white stems and green-to-white shaded leaves. It is our opinion that this ware was produced by the New England Glass Co., Cambridge, Massachusetts. Circa 1885 – 1887. 3½" tall; 1⅝" base diameter; has a two-piece metal top. Very scarce! **$85.00 – 105.00.**

Arnold collection

Honeycomb, Collared: Clear amber glass, dual mold blown. This is a short bulbous shaker with a prominent collar beneath the top. Known production in blue and cranberry. Circa 1890 – 1896. 2½" tall x 1¼" base diameter. Scarce! **$55.00 – 65.00.**

Lockwood collection

Lockwood collection

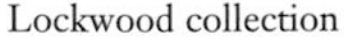

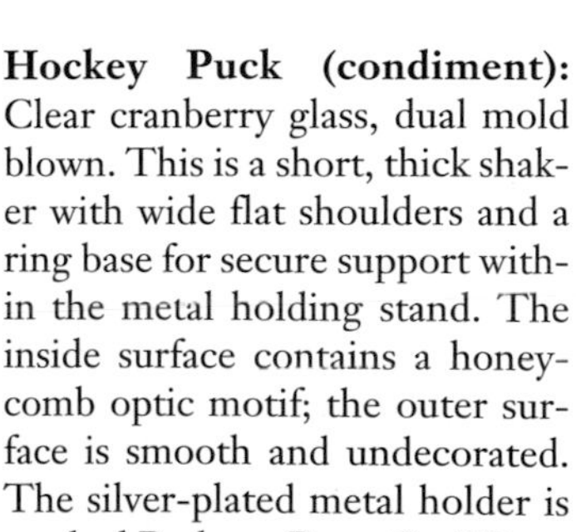

Hockey Puck (condiment): Clear cranberry glass, dual mold blown. This is a short, thick shaker with wide flat shoulders and a ring base for secure support within the metal holding stand. The inside surface contains a honeycomb optic motif; the outer surface is smooth and undecorated. The silver-plated metal holder is marked Barbour Bros. Co. We are showing two illustrations; a single shaker for clear pattern identification and a photo of the complete set. Circa 1885 – 1891. 2" tall x 2¼" wide; 1⅞" base diameter with two-piece metal tops. Rare as a complete set! **$375.00 – 425.00** set.

Coalmer collection

Honeycomb, Large: Two shakers: clear amethyst and cranberry glass, dual mold blown. Quality fire-polished glass with the inside of each shaker containing a large honeycomb motif. The outer surface is smooth and has a ringed neck. No exterior HP decoration is present. Believed to be of European origin. This ware uses unusually large diameter two-piece metal tops. Circa 1889 – 1896. 3⅛" tall. Rare! Pair, **$185.00 – 200.00;** single, **$80.00 – 95.00.**

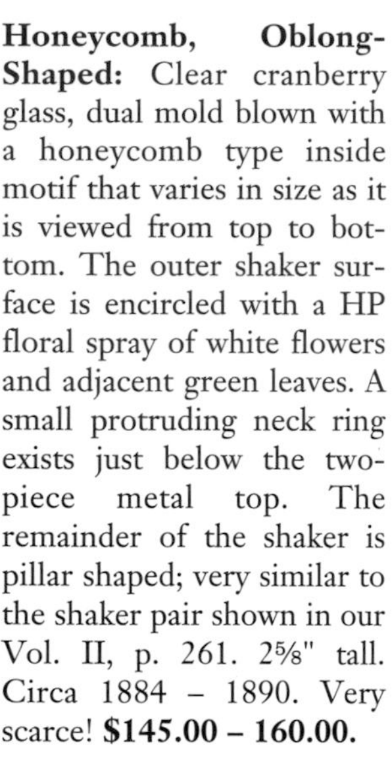

Honeycomb, Oblong-Shaped: Clear cranberry glass, dual mold blown with a honeycomb type inside motif that varies in size as it is viewed from top to bottom. The outer shaker surface is encircled with a HP floral spray of white flowers and adjacent green leaves. A small protruding neck ring exists just below the two-piece metal top. The remainder of the shaker is pillar shaped; very similar to the shaker pair shown in our Vol. II, p. 261. 2⅝" tall. Circa 1884 – 1890. Very scarce! **$145.00 – 160.00.**

Coalmer collection

Arnold collection

Honeycomb, Royal Clear blue glass, dual mold blown. The inside surface contains a series of varying sized honeycombs. The smooth exterior has a HP pink/white floral spray and a butterfly flying downward into the flowers. Just below the two-piece metal top is a small expanded neck ring. This is typical Mt. Washington/Pairpoint decoration. It is our opinion that it was made by the aforesaid glass factory. Circa 1886 – 1890. 2⅞" tall; 1¾" at widest point; has a two-piece metal top. Rare! **$115.00 – 125.00.**

Authors' collection

Honeycomb Sphere, Short: Clear homogeneous cranberry glass, dual mold blown. In the form of a short spherical section with a ringed bottom. The inside surface is covered with varying sized honeycombs; the outer surface is smooth and undecorated. Circa 1889 – 1894. 2½" tall with a two-piece metal top. Very scarce! **$58.00 – 75.00.**

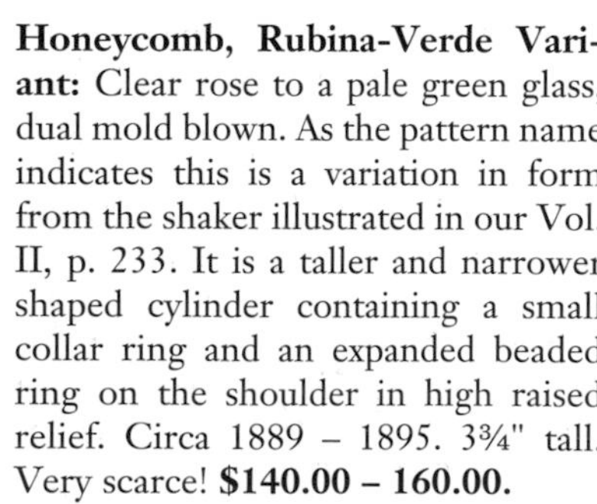

Honeycomb, Rubina-Verde Variant: Clear rose to a pale green glass, dual mold blown. As the pattern name indicates this is a variation in form from the shaker illustrated in our Vol. II, p. 233. It is a taller and narrower shaped cylinder containing a small collar ring and an expanded beaded ring on the shoulder in high raised relief. Circa 1889 – 1895. 3¾" tall. Very scarce! **$140.00 – 160.00.**

Krauss collection

Maxfield collection

Hybrid, Ornate: Cobalt blue glass, mold blown. This is an excellent example of metal encased" glassware;[27] consisting of a cylindrical shaped shaker with bulging multi-ribbed top supported within a metal case. In our opinion, this is an English condiment shaker. Circa 1904 – 1915. 2⅝" tall x 1½" base diameter. Very scarce! **$35.00 – 45.00.**

Bruce collection

Ice Cube: Opaque opalware glass, mold blown. The pattern name pretty well describes this shaker which has been pinched inward on each side. The smooth surface has been washed in a tan color painted background. The principal decoration consists of a HP lavender flower. Circa 1896 – 1904. 2⅛" tall x 1⅞" wide. Very scarce! **$35.00 – 45.00.**

Krauss collection

Inverted Bulb, Small Ring Base: Clear cobalt blue, mold blown. The upper portion has a bulbous shape that tapers into an expanded base ring. The exterior surface contains a large HP tri-leaf outlined in gold with three small daisies on each side. 2⅞" tall with a two-piece metal top. Circa 1890 – 1897. Very scarce! **$80.00 – 100.00.**

Krauss collection

Inverted Honeycomb Bulb: Clear vaseline glass, dual mold blown. The inner surface contains varying sized honeycombs; the smooth exterior surface has an elaborate HP floral spray consisting of white and green flowers with interconnecting orange stems. Radiates bright florescence when exposed to long wave black light. Circa 1890 – 1896. Very scarce! **$80.00– 95.00.**

Arnold collection

Inverted Thumbprint, Bell Based: Clear electric blue glass, dual mold blown. A bell-shaped pattern that has inside IVT and a smooth exterior surface with HP pink/white flowers with the leaves and stems outlined in gold. Circa 1886 – 1891. 3⅛" tall x 2¼" at widest point; 1½" base ring. Very scarce! **$60.00 – 70.00.**

Ridgway collection

Inverted Thumbprint, Bulging: Clear cranberry glass, dual mold blown. As the pattern name indicates, this is small bulging shaker with inside IVT throughout, including the shoulders. The outside surface has continuous HP white, orange, and brown floral spray groups that encircle the complete shaker. Circa 1887 – 1890. 2⅛" tall x 2⅛" wide; 1½" base diameter. Very scarce! **$165.00 – 180.00.**

Bacon collection

Inverted Thumbprint, Bulbous Short: Translucent cranberry opalescent glass, dual mold blown. A short bulbous shaker containing IVT on the inside surface and a smooth undecorated exterior. A good example of opalescent color control by the factory of production. Circa 1885 – 1890. 2⅜" tall with two-piece metal tops. Rare in this color! **$245.00 – 260.00** pair.

Lockwood collection

Inverted Thumbprint, Footed Brandy: Clear glass with an amber foot, dual mold blown. This is a small shaker with a globe-shaped body containing faint IVT to which a flared amber glass foot has been attached. Circa 1890 – 1898. 1⅞" tall x 1⅝" wide with a two-piece metal top. Scarce! **$20.00 – 26.00.**

Krauss collection

Inverted Thumbprint, Bulging (condiment): Clear cranberry glass, dual mold blown. This is a bulging shaker with inverted thumbprints on the inside including the shoulders area. The smooth exterior surface contains six small HP interconnected flowers in pink, white, blue, and orange. The unmarked silver-plated condiment holder has a center napkin ring. Circa 1885 – 1889. Each shaker is 2⅛" tall x 2⅛" wide; 1½" base diameter; each dispenser has a two-piece metal top. Rare as a set! **$235.00 – 260.00** set.

Lockwood collection

Inverted Thumbprint, Long Neck Barrel: Clear tall cranberry glassware, mold and free-blown finished. A barrel-shaped shaker with an extended long neck. The inside surface contains IVT, the outer surface is smooth and undecorated. Believed to have been produced by the New England Glass Co., Canmbridge, Massachusetts. Circa 1884 – 1887. 4¼" tall x 2" wide. Rare. **$180.00 – 200.00.**

Lockwood collection

Inverted Thumbprint, Pretty Woman: Clear Rubina glassware, dual mold blown. A short round shaker with inside surface IVT. The exterior surface contains HP enamel buds and leaves completely encircling the piece. The attached two-piece metal top makes this shaker aesthetically unsightly. We have trouble believing the top is original. Circa 1885 – 1890. Rare! **$125.00 – 150.00.**

Rathbun collection

Inverted Thumbprint, Rectangular: Clear cranberry glass, dual mold blown with inside IVT and smooth on the exterior surface. This is an unusual rectangular shape that contains elaborate HP floral sprigs on each panel. Due to the busy inside IVT pattern, the shaker is somewhat translucent. 2⅞" tall with two-piece metal tops. We believe this ware is a product of Mt. Washington/Pairpoint. Circa 1885 – 1890. Rare! **$195.00 – 220.00** pair.

Authors' collection

Krauss collection

Inverted Thumbprint, Saucer-Like (condiment): Blue translucent satin glass, dual mold blown. The interior surface contains tiny IVT. The smooth exterior is decorated with HP white foliage that radiates a pseudo-cameo appearance. Also illustrated is a single shaker in red satinized glass which was also part of a condiment set. Believed to be Phoenix Glass Co. shakers. The special original holding stand is marked "Barbour Bros. Co." Circa 1886 – 1891. 2" tall with two-piece metal tops. Rare as a set! **$210.00 – 225.00** set; single shaker, **$60.00 – 75.00.**

Authors' collection

Inverted Thumbprint, Small: Clear dark blue homogeneous glass, dual mold blown. A very small shaker containing inside IVT with a smooth undecorated outer surface. We think this shaker was part of a condiment set. Circa 1881 – 1889. 2⅝" tall with a two-piece metal top. Very scarce! **$38.00 – 47.00.**

Coalmer collection

Inverted Thumbprint, Spheroidal Footed Base: Clear cranberry glass, dual mold blown with a HP pink, yellow, and white floral spray on the smooth exterior surface. The shaker interior has small IVT in raised relief. Configured to be used within a condiment set. The footed bottom has been fire polished. Believed to be a product of Mt. Washington/Pairpoint. Circa 1884 – 1890. 2½" tall with a two-piece metal top. Rare! **$90.00 – 110.00.**

Arnold collection

Ivy Scroll, Jefferson: Clear blue glass, mold blown. This is a short bulged out base shaker containing 30 vertical ribs in raised relief that coincide with a flared bottom. The leaves contain gold paint. Author Bill Heacock indicated that this may be a Jefferson Glass Co. pattern.[28] Circa 1900 – 1905. 2¾" tall x 1½" wide base ring. Very scare! **$130.00 – 150.00.**

Coalmer collection

Janice Inverted Thumbprint (condiment): Clear cranberry glass, dual mold blown. The inside pattern amounts to small IVT; the exterior smooth surface contains a single, large floral spray of green and white flowers and leaves that are reminiscent of a marsh flower lily. This appears to be a product of one of the finer New England glass factories. Circa 1884 – 1889. Unable to determine if the silver-plated metal holder is original; but, it is of an unusual design. Shakers, 2⅝" tall. A rare set! **$230.00 – 250.00** set.

White collection

Lantern, Candy: Clear light blue glass, two-piece mold blown. A bulbous shaped shaker that has two dimples near the top to accommodate a wire handle. Probably was a lantern type candy container that could subsequently be used as a salt/pepper condiment dispenser. Circa 1915 – 1925. 2⅞" tall x 2⅛" wide. Scarce! **$15.00 – 25.00.**

Krauss collection

Ladder, Little (condiment): Clear blue and amber glass, mold blown and pressed. A single shaker is illustrated in our Vol. II, p. 236. Pattern name by Peterson. This is a three-piece set consisting of clear crystal holder with a unique attached toothpick holder as part of the lifting handle; has amber and blue salt and pepper shakers. Each shaker is retained in the holder by a protruding glass peg that inserts into the shakers. The shakers are 2¾" tall. The set is 6⅛" tall to the top of the lifting handle. Circa 1880 – 1890. Very scarce! **$85.00 – 100.00** set.

Tognetti collection

Tognetti collection

Last Rose of Summer: Opaque white opalware, mold blown. This shaker is obviously one of the many versions of the "Creased Neck" pattern. Ordinarily, we use pattern names that impart the physical description of a form, but this shaker is so unique, due to the comic scene painted upon it, that we believe it deserves the title that is printed below the male action comic scene. Dr. Peterson made similar pattern name decisions when he felt a shaker form warranted it. We believe this is a Mt. Washington/Pairpoint shaker due to the type of form used and because this factory (at times) made extensive use of the Palmer Cox Brownie comic scenes. It was necessary to take two photos due to the amount of surface drawing space involved with the characterizations. Circa 1894 – 1900. 3½" tall. Rare! **NPD.**

Lockwood collection

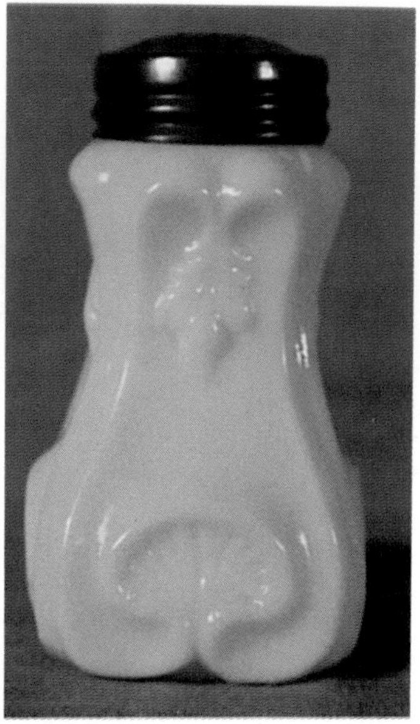

Rathbun collection

Leaf, Four Panel: Opaque white opalware, mold blown glass. The pattern comprises four pairs of raised opposing ribs that run from neck to base. The shaker is divided into four plain wide panels each containing an acanthus-like pendulant leaf drooping downward from the neck. The overall form displays a graceful taper from base to neck. Circa 1898 – 1906. 2⅞" tall; 2¼" wide at the bulge. Scarce! **$25.00 – 35.00.**

Leaf & Mushroom: Opaque white opalware glass, mold blown. This is a shaker that is square shaped with beveled corners. Each side has a leaf hanging between two scallops at the top. Rising up from the bottom is an ephemeral growth that flattens outward at the end to resemble a mushroom. Circa 1900 – 1910. 3¼" tall x 2¼" wide. **$28.00 – 34.00.**

Leafy Corners: Opaque pink variegated glass, mold blown. Sort of a triangular shaped shaker containing a square flaring at the bottom. The corners contain embossed ancanthus leaves. Believed to be a Dithridge & Co. shaker. Also made in opaque blue and custard. Circa 1894 – 1900. 2½" tall. Very scarce in this color! **$48.00 – 56.00.**

Rathbun collection

Lockwood collection

Leafy Scrolls: Clear thin yellow enamel painted glass, mold blown. The shaker has a ringed neck with a body containing an embossed leafy scrolled motif that is repeated three times around the perimeter. Circa 1900 – 1910. 2⅝" tall x 2" wide. **$20.00 – 29.00.**

Harris collection

Lesley's Quacker: Opaque white opalware glass, mold blown and pressed. A unique duck due to the overall design and varied orange, blue, and yellow HP colors. The body surfaces reflect embossed feathers. The threaded glass top opening leans in the direction of the duck's bill. The perforated metal flanged top, which may not be original, provides a sailor hat appearance. 3¼" tall. Rare! **$130.00 – 150.00.**

Lockwood collection

Lily Pond: Clear embossed glassware, mold blown. The overall surface of this ring-necked shaker contains six heavily embossed water lilies; the three that encircle the center contain HP pink enamel decoration. The remaining three are located within the lower one-fourth of the shaker near the base and are not decorated.[29] Circa 1899 – 1910. 2¼" tall x 3" wide. Scarce! **$25.00 – 30.00.**

Ridgway collection

Lemon, Large: Translucent yellow glass, mold blown. This is a larger lemon dispenser than the lemon salt illustrated in our Vol. II, p. 237. It may have seen use as a sugar shaker or store pepper. The yellow color has been painted and fired on to clear glass. The dimensions are 1½" tall; 4" long between each round pointed tip; 1⅜" top opening diameter. Circa 1895 – 1905. Rare! **$95.00 – 115.00.**

White collection

Light Bulb: Opaque white opalware glass, mold blown. The general shape seems to fit the pattern title. A bulbous-based shaker containing HP ferns with red berries. Possibly part of a condiment set. Circa 1897 – 1906. 3" tall x 2¼" at widest point; 1½" base diameter. Scarce! **$25.00 – 34.00.**

Lockwood collection

Little Apple, Variant: Opaque rose-pink variegated art glass, mold blown. A small sphere-shaped shaker that appears to be a slight variation of the Mt. Washington/Pairpoint "Little Apple" shakers. This type ware was also produced in Amberina and HP satinized opalware.[30] All of these types of condiment dispensers contain slightly recessive circular bottoms for purpose of dining table stability. Circa 1886 – 1900. 2" tall x 2" wide. Rare! **$200.00 – 225.00.**

Ridgway collection

Little Columns: Opaque white opalware, mold blown. The physical make-up amounts to eight vertical ribs in raised relief. The shaker body contains a large HP floral sprig. This pattern is shown in Heacock 4, p. 55; item 430 (named by him). 2" tall x 1⅜" wide. Circa 1904 – 1910. Very scarce! **$50.00 – 60.00.**

White collection

Little Columns, Tall: Opaque blue glass, mold blown. Very similar to the "Little Columns" shaker except that this piece has nine ribs and is taller. Both this and the aforementioned shaker pattern are believed to have been produced by the same glasshouse which we think was the Jefferson Glass Company. Circa 1904 – 1910. 2½" tall x 1⅜" wide. Very scarce! **$55.00 – 70.00.**

Maxfield collection

Lobed Elegance: Pink-to-white (selectively inside stained) opalescent shaded glass, mold blown. The shaker contains six lobes with random placed HP white and gold floral sprays encircling the upper half. The shape appears to be the same as the "Gillinder Mellon" shaker except slightly taller.[31] Close inspection revealed that the glass quality is average with a few random glass bubbles visible along with some partially worn off hand-applied decoration. Two of the vertical lobes have been stylus-engraved with the words "BESSIE" "WORLDS FAIR 1893" making this a Chicago 1893 World's Fair souvenir. Unfortunately the engraving is badly worn. It took 10 power magnification to enable us to read the engraving. Circa 1893. 3⅛" tall with a two-piece metal top that is not believed to be original Rare! **$90.00 – 110.00** due to overall condition.

Lockwood collection

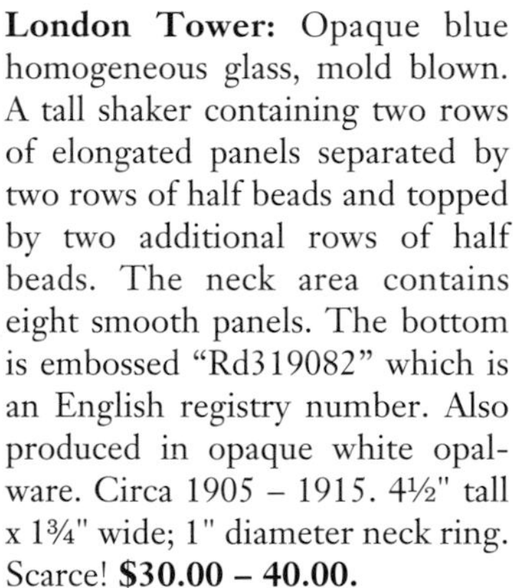

London Tower: Opaque blue homogeneous glass, mold blown. A tall shaker containing two rows of elongated panels separated by two rows of half beads and topped by two additional rows of half beads. The neck area contains eight smooth panels. The bottom is embossed "Rd319082" which is an English registry number. Also produced in opaque white opalware. Circa 1905 – 1915. 4½" tall x 1¾" wide; 1" diameter neck ring. Scarce! **$30.00 – 40.00.**

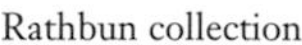

Rathbun collection

Locket: Translucent green homogeneous glass, mold blown and pressed glass. The translucence is created by the pattern density. This pattern was named by Peterson.[32] He described the pattern by stating it to be "A conglomeration of motifs." The center contains small embossed diamonds within larger diamonds. The base has a series of six sharp peaked scallops. Circa 1893 – 1902. Very scarce! **$28.00 – 35.00.**

White collection

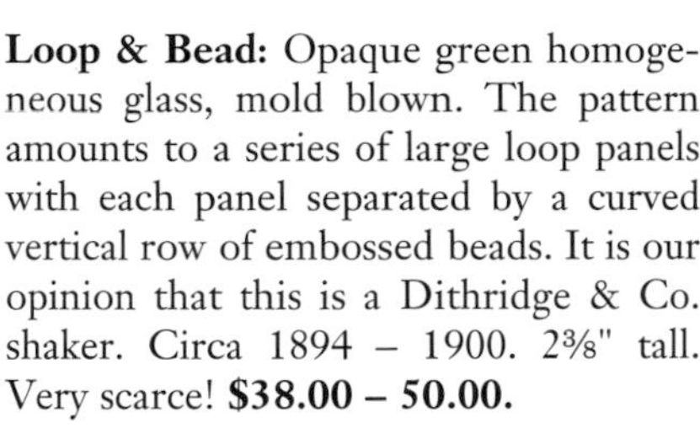

Loop & Bead: Opaque green homogeneous glass, mold blown. The pattern amounts to a series of large loop panels with each panel separated by a curved vertical row of embossed beads. It is our opinion that this is a Dithridge & Co. shaker. Circa 1894 – 1900. 2⅜" tall. Very scarce! **$38.00 – 50.00.**

Rathbun collection

Rathbun collection

Majestic: Iridescent multicolored free-blown art glass. These shakers are quite bulbous and when placed side-by-side it is immediately apparent their shapes are not identical since no mold-shaping guidance was used. Generally speaking iridescent glassware is created by a fine-ridged metallic film that separates ordinary daylight into its color elements and causes the light to be bent or refracted. Lobmeyer (of Zlatno, Hungary) is credited with displaying the first commercial production of iridescent wares at a Paris exhibition in 1878. Similar iridescent wares were also displayed there by Thomas Webb & Sons. Obviously, the creation of iridescence by surface treatment was a closely guarded secret by the various factories involved; primarily to limit competition. One of the early methods of producing iridescence artificially was accomplished by submitting hot glass to the action of water containing 15% hydrochloric acid which dissolved the alkaline silicates and left the glass surface finely ridged or corrugated causing it to refract the light with prismatic or rainbow colors. It is a fact that there are several ways to iridize surfaces; each methodology required a specific combination of certain elements dictated by the constituents of the material to be acted upon. We spent considerable time in studying this shaker pair and are satisfied that they were produced during the Art Nouveau era (1890 – 1910) by a producer that we are unable to specifically identify. These shakers were represented to be Loetz when sold to the current owners. However, the power magnification analysis revealed the basic glass quality is far below the standards produced by this Austrian factory. Despite this, the exterior HP floral and butterfly decoration is excellent; making these shakers a collectible rarity. Each shaker is 2⅞" tall and requires two-piece press-fit metal tops. The illustrated shaker tops are not believed original. Because this ware is free blown, one top opening is 1⅛" in diameter; the other is 1¼" in diameter. The shaker containing the three HP butterflies weighed 5½ oz; the floral shaker weight 3 oz. Not surprising since the pieces are free-blown created. Very rare! **NPD.**

Rathbun collection

Man On Horse: Cobalt blue mold blown and pressed glass condiment set. A most unusual configuration consisting of a heavy pressed glass base containing a man-like figure mounted upon a horse. In front of the horse are two deep recessed wells containing a pair of removable cobalt blue salt and pepper shakers. Research has been unable to verify whether or not the shakers are original pieces. However, they match the cobalt coloring of the rest of the set which is 5¼" tall to the top of the rider's hat; the shakers are 2¾" tall. Circa 1880 – 1884. Rare! **$415.00 – 435.00** set.

Krauss collection

Meaker: Clear uncolored glass, mold blown. The reader is looking at a dual condiment dispenser that is rare because engineering analysis indicates that it lacks producibility and practicality. The inventor was J. W. Meaker of Detroit, Michigan. The aluminum metal screw-on base contains stamped instructions as follows: 1. Fill to mark, then screw point into salt; (the mark encircles the glass holder ¾" up from the bottom). 2. For pepper add whole rice. The glass top contains five perforation holes for condiment dispensing. This shaker may have not gotten past the model and patent process. 3" tall. **NPD.**

Krauss collection

Mary Ann: Clear cobalt blue glass, mold blown. The exterior surface contains an elaborate HP flower and scroll scene with Cupid holding a bow and arrow. Believed to have been produced in Europe at one of the finer glasshouses. Circa 1897 – 1905. 2½" tall with a screw-on sterling silver threaded top. Very scarce! **$75.00 – 90.00.**

Eldridge collection

Melonette, Eighteen Rib: Opaque pink satin glass, mold blown. As the pattern name indicates, this is a small melon-like shaker containing 18 ribs in raised relief. The piece has no exterior surface HP decoration. The threaded neck is rough from having been snapped off from the pontil rod. Circa 1888 – 1895. 2¼" tall x 2½" wide. Rare! **$130.00 – 150.00.**

White collection

Melon, Scrolled: Opaque white opalware glass, mold blown. This pattern has the same lobed shape as the "Gillinder Melon."[33] As the pattern name indicates the exterior surface contains an added embossed shell and scroll motif. We believe this to be a Gillinder shaker. We have added temporary coloring so that the top scrolling can be seen. The surface contains a HP purple aster with green leaves. Circa 1891 – 1897. Scarce! **$30.00 – 35.00.**

Krauss collection

Middle Bulge: Opaque opalware glass, mold blown. As the pattern name indicates this shaker bulges in the middle and narrows at each end. Quite heavy glass for its size. The circle shaped motif consists of HP brown vines with traces of gold. The center contains a pink shaded mum. Circa 1889 – 1894. 2⅛" tall x 1¾"wide and a 1" base diameter with a two-piece metal top. Scarce! **$28.00 – 35.00.**

Coalmer collection

Melon, Six Lobe (condiment): Opaque opalware glass, mold blown with six protruding lobes containing a light tan background over which dark brown colored vertical floral sprigs have been HP on each lobe. A similar physical shape is shown in our Vol. II, page 145. It is our opinion that this ware was acquired by the Toronto Silver Plate house that produced the illustrated unique metal holder for marketing to their various consumers. 2⅝" tall with matching two-piece metal tops. Circa 1894 – 1900. Very scarce! **$95.00 – 110.00** set.

Krauss collection

Harris collection

Bruce collection

Meridan Peeler (condiment): Clear amber glass; also clear amethyst glass, mold blown. This is a cube-shaped shaker containing a HP divided circle that has four distinct colored segments of white, blue, orange, and yellow/lavender. Random applied leaves and daisy flowers are dispersed outside the segmented circle decorations. Also illustrated is an amethyst shaker in blue, white, and green. Only one panel of each shaker is decorated in the aforesaid manner.[34] This is believed to be European glassware. The amber set metal holder is marked Rogers Smith & Co., Meriden, Connecticut; the amethyst set Meriden B. Co. who no doubt imported this ware for insertion into their metal condiment holders. The shakers are 3⅝" tall with two-piece metal tops. Circa 1877 – 1883. Rare! Each set, **$400.00 – 425.00;** amethyst shaker, **$180.00 – 200.00.**

White collection

Necklace Bulbous, Variant: Opaque "Wave Crest" opalware glass, mold blown. With the exception of two elaborate embossed scrolls on the sides away from the orange and brown bouquet transfer decoration, this shaker is identical to the shaker illustrated in our Vol. II, p. 122. We believe it is a C. F. Monroe item. However, since we have not personally examined the piece for complete analysis, we cannot be 100% certain since Monroe had to acquire this basic glass blank from an outside glass factory. Circa 1903 – 1907. 2⅝" tall x 2¼" wide. Very scarce! **$70.00 – 85.00.**

Krauss collection

Mother of Pearl Bulbous Diamond Quilted: Opaque satinized blue cased glass containing a large varying sized diamond air trapped pattern, mold and free-blown finished. This shaker is essentially the same shape as the "Rainbow, Bulbous" shakers and has an identical two-piece metal top. This type of ware was produced around Murano, Italy. Italian-produced MOP forms were imported into the United States and distributed by various gift and antique reproduction wholesalers. MOP in general consists of three glass layers; i.e., a clear outer layer, middle colored layer, and an inside casing that is usually white. The old Victorian MOP pieces are relatively thin and seldom much more than 1⁄16 of an inch thick on items up to 10" to 12" tall. In comparison, contemporary Italian MOP usually has very thick looking edges that are ⅛" to ¼" thick. Generally speaking, the shorter the piece, the thicker the glass. One of the reasons the new MOP rims are thicker is due to the inner white casing. On the other hand, Victorian MOP pieces will usually have their inside casing the same thickness as the other layers. Our illustrated shaker is circa 1963 – 1970. 3⅛" tall. Rare! **NPD.**

White collection

Newel Post: Opaque white opalware glass, mold blown. The shaker contains a relatively long neck which blends into six downward curving undecorated panels. When bottom viewed the shaker is shaped like a hexagon. Circa 1898 – 1908. 3" tall x 2⅜" wide; 1⅜" base diameter. Scarce! **$18.00 – 25.00.**

Lockwood collection

Octagon, Paneled: Opaque white opalware glass, mold blown. The pattern amounts to eight flat panels slightly arched at the top that taper downward to a larger bottom. The bottom is smooth with a slightly concave center. The motif decoration consists of HP pink daisies with green leaves. Circa 1903 – 1910. 2¾" tall x 1⅝" wide. **$30.00 – 40.00.**

White collection

White collection

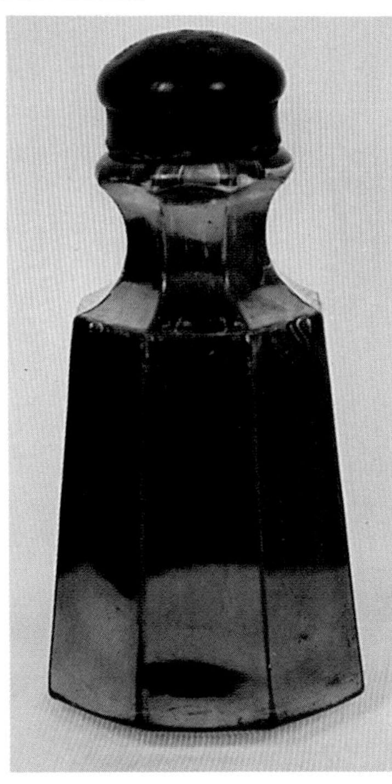

Octagon Beauty: Gold luster finish glass, mold blown. This is a tall heavy shaker with a plain vertical paneled neck and body. With the exception of the glass threads, the entire shaker has a gold luster stain. Circa 1909 – 1916. 4" tall x 2⅛" base. Scarce! **$25.00 – 38.00.**

Octagon, Saloon: Opaque blue satin glass, mold blown. This is a tall column-shaped shaker containing eight flat vertical panels that expand downward from a circular neck ring. An obvious utilitarian type shaker; hence, the assigned pattern name. Circa 1900 – 1908. 4¼" tall x 2⅛" wide. Scarce! **$40.00 – 55.00.**

Lockwood collection

McElderry collection

Olympic Variant: Clear amber glass, mold blown and pressed. This is a self-contained combination salt and pepper. We first illustrated this type of shaker in our 1976 book on page 96. The dispensing configuration consists of an internal metal divider (one side for salt and the other side for pepper) with a two-section top having perforations over each condiment vault. All perforations are in a normal closed condition. To obtain either salt or pepper, one must push in on a spring loaded metal tab which will open the appropriate holes for dispensing the desired condiment. There is no embossed lettering on the clear exterior glass surface. Circa 1920 – 1935. 3" tall with top removed. Rare in color! **$75.00 – 90.00**

Harris collection

Octagon, Skirt: Translucent frosted glass, mold blown. The pattern consists of eight vertical panels that form a geometric octagon. Each panel contains HP green vegetation with every other panel having white painted dots above the greenery. Circa 1908 – 1918. Very scarce! **$25.00 – 35.00.**

Rathbun collection

Opal Spot, Ribbed: Clear cranberry glass with opalescent coin spots, mold blown. This item is a variation of the Coinspot shaker shown on page 28 of our Vol. II. The principal motif differs by the fact that the base contains 22 vertical raised ribs.[35] While research has not resulted in a positive attribution, it is our opinion that this shaker was produced by either the Beaumont Glass Co. or Hobbs, Brockunier & Co. Circa 1890 – 1900. 3⅝" tall. Very scarce! **$95.00 – 115.00.**

Krauss collection

Optic Eight Panel, Bulbous: Clear blue homogeneous glass, mold blown. A rather plain shaker containing eight optic ribs inside with a smooth undecorated exterior. Similar to "The Central Glass" shaker shown in our Vol. II, page 35. Circa 1886 – 1891. 3⅛" tall x 2⅛" wide. Scarce! **$23.00 – 30.00.**

Bacon collection

Optic Paneling: Clear blue glass, dual mold blown. As the pattern name implies, the inside surface contains a complete encircling set of vertical optic panels that are completely visible from top to bottom. The smooth exterior surface has random spaced pink and white HP flowers with scattered white leaves. Circa 1892 – 1898. 2⅞" tall. Rare! **$145.00 – 160.00.**

Krauss collection

Coalmer collection

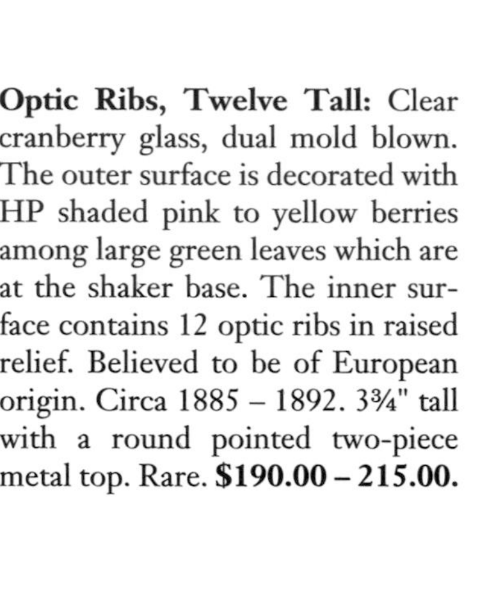

Optic Ribs, Twelve Tall: Clear cranberry glass, dual mold blown. The outer surface is decorated with HP shaded pink to yellow berries among large green leaves which are at the shaker base. The inner surface contains 12 optic ribs in raised relief. Believed to be of European origin. Circa 1885 – 1892. 3¾" tall with a round pointed two-piece metal top. Rare. **$190.00 – 215.00.**

Optic Rib, Handled: Clear amber homogeneous quality glass, dual mold blown. This is a 4" tall salt or pepper shaker containing eight interior vertical optic ribs. The exterior surface has an elaborate detailed HP blue May bird perched upon a pink and white flowered bush. In the several decades that we have specialized in antique glass salt shakers, we have never seen (or heard of) a Victorian era produced shaker with an applied, free-blown, fused-on attached handle. Detailed analysis has satisfied us that this is not a fake; it was probably produced experimentally in an effort to determine practical factory production cost analysis in conjunction with consumer sales appeal. Circa 1886 – 1894. Extremely rare! **NPD.**

Krauss collection

Arnold collection

Optic Treasure: Clear amber glass, dual mold blown. This is a tall ring-necked shaker. The inside surface has a vertical optic ribbed pattern. The optic effect flows downward into the ring-shaped foot. The principal outer surface HP decoration consists of pink/white flowers with leaves; the backside contains white colored weeds. Circa 1887 – 1891. 3⅞" tall x 2⅛," wide; 1½" base ring. Very scarce! **$75.00 – 90.00.**

Optic Wave with Rigaree: Clear blue glass, dual mold blown. This is a rather tall shaker containing 12 optic ribs on the inside surface. The exterior contains three large applied glass leaves in high raised relief generally known as rigaree. HP floral sprig decoration is present in between the aforesaid applied glass leaves. It is our opinion that this ware is a European product and probably Venetian. Circa 1895 – 1905. 4" tall with a two-piece metal top. Very scarce! **$80.00 – 90.00.**

Sine collection

Oval Loop, Beaded: Partially clear glass, mold blown. The pattern consists of a series of embossed beaded oval loops with a ringed top and base. The rather bland decoration appears in the lower portion and consists of goofus gold paint tinted with red. Circa 1900 – 1910. 3" tall; 1⅝" wide; 1¹⁄₁₆" base diameter. Scarce! **$16.00 – 20.00.**

Rathbun collection

Ovals, Six: Translucent opalescent vaseline, dual mold blown. This shaker has both wide and narrow opalescent striping that has been created by a dual mold process. Bulbous in shape, the motif consists of six raised panels around the shaker body. The bottom is slightly extended which is an indication that this ware was probably part of a condiment set. Circa 1887 – 1894. 2¾" tall; 1¼" wide. The shaker displays a striking fluorescence when exposed to UV black light. Very scarce. **$95.00 – 110.00.**

Ridgway collection

Oval with Roses: Clear cranberry glass, mold blown. The pattern name generally describes the shaker's motif. As the story goes, Cy Wright got the idea for this pattern while he was shaving in front of an old mirror that he liked. Since L. G. Wright Glass Company never manufactured glass, he had the pattern designed and made for him by one of the several glasshouses that did private mold work. In our opinion, the design, shape and color is very reminiscent of Paden City Glass Co. shaker production. The story behind the aforesaid pattern's creation was told to Maralyn Ridgway by Dorothy Stephan, now owner of L.G. Wright Co. This footed shaker is circa 1950. 3⅛" tall. Very scarce! **$45.00 – 60.00.**

Rathbun collection

Oval with Flower: Opaque white opalware glass, mold blown. When viewed from the bottom this shaker has an extended ellipse shape with the bottom having a ⅞" diameter recessed center circle. The pattern consists of two oval shaped panels (one on each side); each panel has a single embossed five-petal flower with various embossed leaves and flowers surrounding the outer perimeter. 3" tall. Circa 1895 – 1905. Scarce! **$22.00 – 30.00.**

White collection

Panel Christmas, Variant: Clear teal blue glass, mold blown. Contains 10 vertical glass panels; the glass is of good quality. It has been suggested this may possibly be a Sandwich piece by the owner, who has also indicated that this item was used as a bitters bottle. As the photo shows, the shaker takes the same type of top used on both the Christmas Barrel and Christmas Pearl shakers.[36] However, according to Sandwich authors Barlow and Kaiser, the types produced at Sandwich have a star bottom with a horizontal ring at the bottom and two above the convex wall.[37] The illustrated shaker does not meet this criteria! Also there is the fact that according to an April 26, 1888, issue of a *Crockery & Glass Journal* the Alden salts were gradually being introduced in Australia, France, Germany, Spain, and the British Isles. This is further added proof that not all Alden salts were made at Sandwich. Our pictured item was also produced in clear, blue, amber, and cranberry. 3" tall x 1½" wide. Circa 1877 – 1890. Very scarce. No trade value baseline exists! **NPD.**

Rathbun collection

Panels, Four Tapered: Clear dark blue homogeneous glass, mold blown. A very plain square-shaped shaker containing four tapered rectangular panels and a narrow rounded neck. There are a few glass blemishes present as a result of factory mold removal. Circa 1891 – 1900. 4" tall with a two-piece metal top. Very scarce! **$28.00 – 35.00.**

Lockwood collection

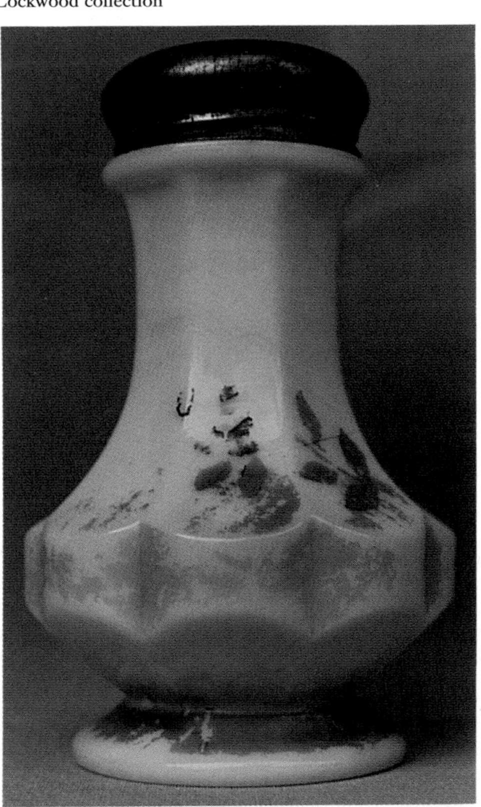

Panels, Footed Scalloped: Opaque white opalware glass, mold blown. A very large shaker with eight flat panels from the top neck ring down to scallops at the bulge which continue through the horizontal flaring that is scalloped top and bottom and tapers inward to the circular foot. The external HP yellow/brown floral motif is severely worn. There is certainly a possibility that this shaker was intended to be a saloon pepper or perhaps a sugar dispenser. Circa 1902 – 1912. 4¼" tall x 2¾" wide. **$10.00 – 15.00.**

Krauss collection

Krauss collection

Paneled Hexagon (condiment): Clear cranberry glass, mold blown. These are large six-paneled shakers containing two HP daisy segments in blue, green, and white that cover two of the six panels. Similar type decoration appears on a shaker named "Black Cube" see our Vol. II, p. 218. 4⅛" tall with unique, original two-piece metal tops. This is quality glassware. The shaker bottoms have been fire polished. Believed to have been produced in Europe. Circa 1894 – 1906. The silver-plated metal holder has two Cherubs holding up the center lifting handle. This very ornate stand is marked Meriden B. Co. and is 7" tall to the top of the lifting handle. We are also illustrating a single clear blue shaker for the purpose of pattern decoration clarity. Rare! Set, **$400.00 – 450.00;** blue shaker, **$55.00 – 65.00.**

Lockwood collection

Paneled Prism: Clear blue white-speckled glass, mold blown. The shaker has nine flat panels arched at the top and widening slightly down to the widest point of the shaker. Each panel border ends at a flat diamond shape which abuts the next diamond. There is another row of flat diamonds around the bottom. Circa 1887 – 1890. 2¾" tall x 1½" wide. Very scarce! **$150.00 – 175.00.**

White collection

Paneled Salt and Pepper: Opaque opalware glass, mold blown. This shaker has a hexagon-shaped base and consists of eight panels; four are blank and the other four panels are embossed "S A L T." The shaker opening has been ground to obtain a top fit. Circa 1910 – 1920. 2⅝" tall x 1½" base. **$12.00 – 17.00.**

Paneled Urn: Opaque white opalware glass, mold blown. This shaker has an urn-form pedestal with a slight dome shaped base with scrolls encircling it. The main portion of the body contains a raised large bulge with eight tassels hanging from a beaded rim. Some shakers will be found to contain goofus gilt coloring that forms four V's. 3½" tall x 2¼" at the bulge with a 1⅝" base diameter. Circa 1899 – 1908. Scarce. **$18.00 – 25.00.**

Rathbun collection

McElderry collection

McElderry collection

Pear, Dainty (condiment): Translucent pink-to-shaded pink cased art glass, dual mold blown. The design has a shape resembling a pear with a thin added bottom extension for condiment holder retention. Portrays an overall pearly-like appearance. Each shaker contains HP orange and white floral sprays. The silver-plated holder is marked "Roger Bros. Triple Plate." We are illustrating two views: the shaker pair, and the complete condiment set with shakers in place. Circa 1885 – 1890. Shakers, 2¾" tall x 1⅞" wide with original two-piece metal tops. Rare! **$430.00 – 455.00** set.

Lockwood collection

Pear, Footed: Clear thin glass, mold blown with applied pressed glass feet. A pear-shaped shaker with a two-piece pressure fit sterling-silver top. Has the letter "S" engraved on the bottom. Believed to be of European origin. 2⅜" tall x 1¾" wide. Scarce! **$18.00 – 25.00.**

Rathbun collection

Pearly Variant: Translucent custard glass, mold blown. Very similar to the shaker illustrated in our Vol. II p. 244 but it is somewhat more bulbous. The smooth exterior surface is decorated with lily of the valley type floral sprays and radiates a high level of florescence when exposed to black light illumination. 2⅝" tall. Believed to have been produced in Europe. Circa 1899 – 1905. Very scarce. **$55.00 – 60.00.**

Rathbun collection

Krauss collection

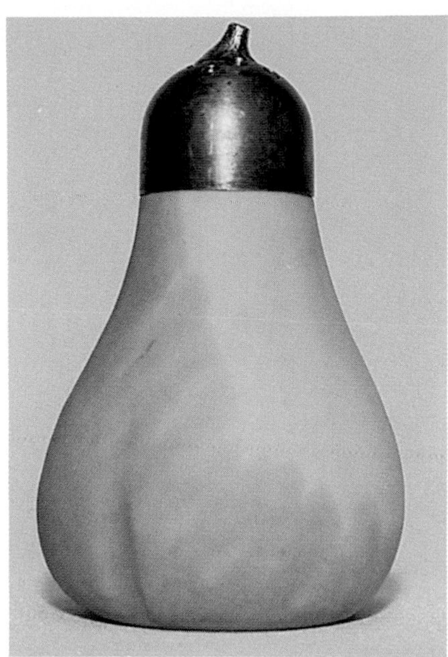

Neale collection

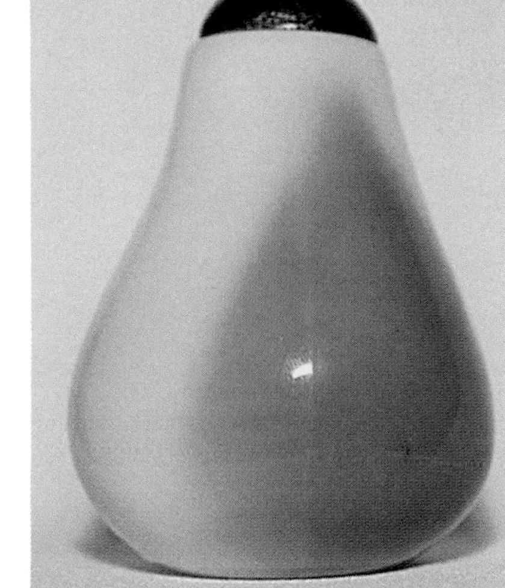

Pear, Paneled: Two types of glass are illustrated: Opaque pink and white variegated, and a decorated white opalware pair; both types are mold blown glass. The physical pattern configuration is reminiscent of a pear-shaped form that is established by the presence of the stemmed metal tops. The bulging glass shaker base contains short vertical intaglio ribs equally spaced on each side of its circumference. The views of the variegated pink shakers are an excellent example of the color control problems that sometimes happened during factory production. Two HP floral sprigs are present on the opaque white shakers. In addition we are revealing a pink shaded sugar shaker that has no base ribbing. It is interesting to note that it uses the same type top as a Mt. Washington "Egg, Flat Side." The pattern name was established by E. G. Warm's book *Milk Glass Addenda* plate 125. Shakers, 2¾" tall; sugar shaker, 3½" tall x 2¾" wide. Circa 1897 – 1903. It is our opinion that these shakers were produced by Mt. Washington/Pairpoint. The salt shakers are very scarce; the sugar shaker rare! Opalware pair, **$170.00 – 185.00;** pink variegated shaker pair, **$270.00 – 290.00;** sugar shaker, **$500.00 – 550.00.**

McElderry collection

Bette Howard collection

Pedestal Vasa: Clear blue glass, dual mold blown. This is a bulging, round shaker that tapers until it is narrowest at the point where it attaches to a round fire-polished supporting foot. The inside surface has eight internal vertical optic panels. The smooth exterior surface contains an encircling white and pink HP floral sprays. Believed to have been produced by the New England Glass Co. Circa 1884 – 1887. Very scarce! **$145.00 – 160.00.**

Ridgway collection

Pedestal Vasa, Variant: Clear cranberry glass, dual mold blown. This is a bulging, round shaker that tapers until it is narrowest at the point where it attaches to a round fire-polished supporting foot. The inside surface has continuous internal optic swirls. The smooth exterior surface contains an encircling white and brown leafed HP floral spray. Believed to have been produced by the New England Glass Co. Circa 1884 – 1887. Very scarce! **$175.00 – 190.00.**

Coalmer collection

Peg Leg, Round: Opaque homogeneous blue glass, mold blown. Pattern name by Peterson.[38] A short bulbous shaker containing four flowers in high raised relief and supported by four round knobby feet. This pattern has all the characteristics of Dithridge design, but we have been unable to verify who produced it. It has never been an easy shaker pattern to acquire. Circa 1894 – 1901. Also produced in opaque green, white, and pink. 2¼" tall. Very scarce! **$48.00 – 60.00.**

Rathbun collection

Nebel collection

Peterson's Plume: Translucent green glass, mold blown. The principal pattern consists of embossed feathered scrolling that extends completely around the outer perimeter; the neck contains a grouping of vertical plumed panels. The short extended base indicates that the shaker was configured for use in a condiment set. 2⅝" tall. Circa 1899 – 1906. Also produced in opaque white opalware. Very scarce. **$33.00 – 40.00.**

Krauss collection

Phoenix Pseudo-Cameo: Translucent satin glass, mold blown. These two barrel-shaped shakers (one in blue and the other in amber homogenous glass) each contain HP white colored flowers and foliage motifs that produce a pseudo-cameo appearance due to a 3-D visual effect. Each shaker is of a physical configuration type that William Heacock named "Coloratura" and ultimately attributed to the Phoenix Glass Co., Monaca, Pennsylvania. Circa 1886 – 1892 while this glasshouse was under the influence and design guidance of Joseph Webb (see our Vol. II, page 177). Each condiment dispenser is 3" tall and requires a proper two-piece metal top. The tops that were present when these shakers were photographed were to be removed and replaced, since they detract from the beauty of these art glass pieces. However, the glass and exterior decoration were found to be in excellent condition. Rare! **$475.00 – 525.00** pair.

Harris collection

Pillar, Arabesque: Opaque black molded glass. A smooth surfaced cylinder shaped shaker over which a gold and black colored complex design of intertwined foliage has been formed by what appears to be a masking technique in harmony with gold paint application. Such a technique allows the black glass to form the resultant principal design motif. It is our opinion that this shaker is of European origin. Circa 1905 – 1920. 3½" tall; the two-piece top is not believed to be original. Rare! **$160.00 – 175.00** due to decoration wear.

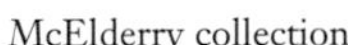

Pillar, Bulging-Based: Clear blue glass, dual mold blown. As the pattern name indicates, this is a small round pillar-shaped shaker with a bulging base containing HP pink and white floral sprays. A short added glass extension comprises the bottom section so that the shaker can be secured within a properly designed condiment holding stand. Circa 1885 – 1891. 2⅛" tall with a two-piece metal top. Also produced in decorated cranberry and amber. Very scarce! **$120.00 – 145.00.**

McElderry collection

Krauss collection

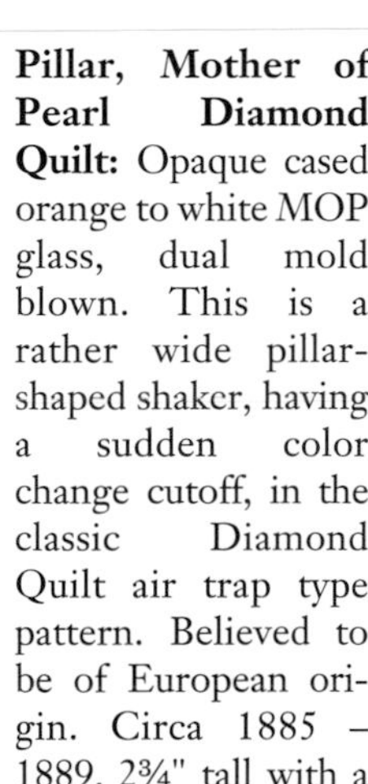

Pillar, Mother of Pearl Diamond Quilt: Opaque cased orange to white MOP glass, dual mold blown. This is a rather wide pillar-shaped shaker, having a sudden color change cutoff, in the classic Diamond Quilt air trap type pattern. Believed to be of European origin. Circa 1885 – 1889. 2¾" tall with a two-piece metal top. Rare! **$290.00 – 325.00.**

Krauss collection

Pillar, Rectangular: Clear dark blue glass, mold blown. As the pattern name implies, this shaker pair each contains four flat vertical panels. The front panel of each condiment dispenser has a HP white colored small child standing among foliage. The other three remaining panels contain a HP floral sprig created by fired-on white enamel paint. Believed to be of European origin. Circa 1893 – 1904. 3¾" tall with two-piece metal tops. Our illustrated pair is in fair condition due to numerous grinding (reworks) of the glass to remove exterior chipping. Rare! **$50.00 – 60.00** pair.

McElderry collection

Pillar, Short Bulging: Clear flashed amethyst glass, mold blown. The pattern name provides a physical shape description. The primary motif consists of an encircling band of HP orange, white, blue, and yellow colored floral sprays that vary in size. The overall glass radiates a pearly luster. Circa 1887 – 1893. 2¼" tall with a two-piece metal top. Very scarce! **$90.00 – 110.00.**

Krauss collection

Pillar, Short Inverted Thumbprint: Clear cranberry and amber glass, dual mold blown. Each shaker has small IVT on the inside; the exterior surface is smooth. The shakers are 2⅝" tall with two-piece metal tops. The silver-plated holder is marked "Meriden Silver Plate Co." and measured 5" tall to the top of the lifting handle. Circa 1888 – 1894. Very scarce! **$140.00 – 160.00** set.

Krauss collection

Pillar, Skinny (condiment): Opaque white opalware, mold blown. The pattern amounts to a short, narrow round pillar with a HP yellow/purple and white/red floral spray. The shakers are 2⅜" tall. Circa 1896 – 1905. The silver-plated holding stand is marked "Meriden Silver Plate Co." and is 5" tall to the top of the lifting handle. Very scarce! **$160.00 – 175.00** set.

Krauss collection

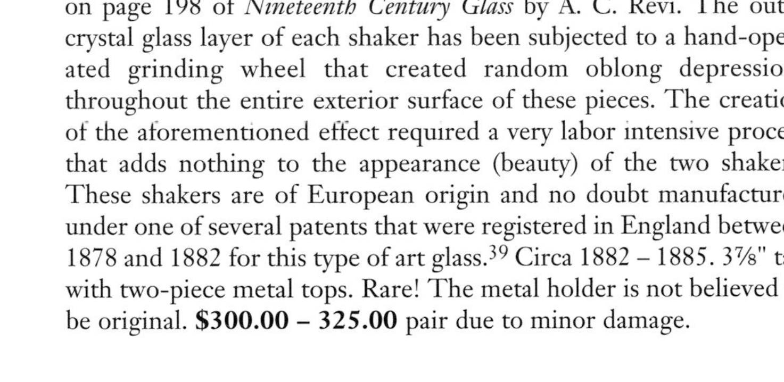

Pillar, Spangled Glass (condiment): A translucent pair of tall red and green cased spangled glass shakers, mold blown. As the pattern name suggest, these are pillar-shaped items that are similar to the "Creased Neck" patterns illustrated on page 119 of our Vol. II book. Each shaker contains embedded gold and silver mica flakes; the manufacturing process involved to create this type of art glass is described on page 198 of *Nineteenth Century Glass* by A. C. Revi. The outer crystal glass layer of each shaker has been subjected to a hand-operated grinding wheel that created random oblong depressions throughout the entire exterior surface of these pieces. The creation of the aforementioned effect required a very labor intensive process that adds nothing to the appearance (beauty) of the two shakers. These shakers are of European origin and no doubt manufactured under one of several patents that were registered in England between 1878 and 1882 for this type of art glass.[39] Circa 1882 – 1885. 3⅞" tall with two-piece metal tops. Rare! The metal holder is not believed to be original. **$300.00 – 325.00** pair due to minor damage.

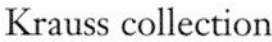

Krauss collection

Pillar, Swirled (condiment): Clear reverse Rubina colored glass, dual mold blown. The inside surface of the condiment dispensers contains continuous inner-spiral swirling ribs. The outer surface is smooth and is decorated by hand painting individual blue, red, and white floral sprays. The shakers are a cylindrical shape. Circa 1888 – 1895. 3¼" tall with two-piece metal tops. The silver-plated condiment holder was produced by the Meriden B. Company, Meriden, Connecticut. The metal lifting handle is quite ornate and unusual. Rare as a complete set! **$360.00 – 380.00** set.

Harris collection

Pillar, Tall Rounded: Opaque variegated green glass, mold blown. We have a pair of these in our collection and despite continuing research we have been unable to establish what factory produced them. To us, the glass appears to be identical to the Fenton produced Mongolian green that was manufactured circa 1934 – 1935.[40] During 1994 we hand carried our shakers to Frank Fenton only to have him state that while the glass make-up was very similar to their Mongolian green, there were no records to verify Fenton shaker production. During 1967, Lesley & Dick Harris provided a partial answer to our perplexity. We are illustrating their shaker/dispenser with the original brass top. As the reader can see, the top is designed with a protruding metal tab that has to be pushed inward to dispense a powder or condiment. It has perforated top holes so it can be used for either purpose. If any of our readers can shed further insight relative to this ware we will appreciate hearing from you. 4¾" tall. Very scarce! **$75.00 – 100.00.**

White collection

Plain Joe: Opaque opalware glass, mold blown. The basic shape is almost identical to "Opal Ribbon, Short" shown in our Vol. II, p. 98. The smooth glossy surface contains an extended HP floral spray of blue flowers and brown leaves. The base has a very short glass extension which is an indication it may have been part of a condiment set. Circa 1897 – 1903. 2⅝" tall x 2" wide. Scarce! **$28.00 – 36.00.**

Bruce collection

Plain, Totem: Clear ruby stained glass, mold blown. This is a plain cone-shaped shaker that has a souvenir type transfer in white. Circa 1905 – 1915. 3" tall; 1⅝" base diameter. Scarce! **$30.00 – 40.00.**

Krauss collection

Pseudo Pomona: Translucent frosted glass, mold blown. The inside surface has 12 vertical optic ribs; the exterior contains three embossed gold colored swimming fish. Two fish are swimming downward and the other is swimming upward. Also, there are three embossed plants that are clear (not frosted). Pattern name is by Heacock. The shaker is 2⅝" tall x 2" wide. Our careful analysis did not reveal any Pomona-like decorating technique certainly nothing coinciding with the Pomona process patented by Joseph Locke of New England Glass. Circa 1889 – 1891. Very scarce! **$75.00 – 90.00.**

Harris collection

Polka Dot: Translucent blue cased glass, dual mold blown. A short, round stubby shaker. The motif amounts to a series of central blue spots displayed throughout the casing. This type of pattern was produced by The West Virginia Glass Co., Hobbs Brockunier, Harry Northwood, and Beaumont, just to name a few.[41] The most popular color for this type design seems to have been in cranberry opalescent. Circa 1888 – 1896. 2⅛" tall with a large two-piece metal top. Rare in this shape and color! **$250.00 – 300.00.**

Sine collection

Putnam's Salt Bottle: Clear uncolored glass, mold blown. A Waspish waist shaker that is dominated by an unusual metal top marked "G.W. PUTNAM, PAT'D NOV 6, 1867." The top has only six holes; must have been quite a chore getting coagulated salt to come out. Circa 1867. 2⅞" tall x 2½" at widest point. Rare! **$30.00 – 40.00.**

Rathbun collection

Pyramid S4: Opaque white opalware with a greenish cast, mold blown. This is an eight-sided pyramid-shaped shaker having a single over-emphasized embossed letter S on alternating panels. Each of the remaining sides has a single HP floral sprig. The shaker is 2¾" tall x 2½" wide; 2¾" base diameter. Circa 1898 – 1905. **$30.00 – 38.00.**

Herron collection

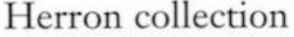

Pyramid, Studded: Opaque opalware glass, mold blown. The pattern pretty well identifies this shaker's shape with the pegged borders. The gaudy cold painted colors hardly make it desirable (at least to us). The borders are decorated with goofus type gilt paint. The bottom has four small feet with a 1" circular depression. Circa 1907 – 1915. 2¾" tall x 2⅝" at widest point. Scarce! **$15.00 – 22.00.**

Lockwood collection

Rectangle, Pinched-In: Clear glass, mold and free-blown finished. A rectangular-shaped shaker with tiny white flowers encircled by HP yellow dots; each dot has a pinpoint size red center. Similar type flower and dot decoration can be seen in Heacock's *1,000 Toothpick*, p. 48, fig. 142. Circa 1888 – 1895. 2¾" tall with a two-piece metal top. Very scarce! **$95.00 – 120.00.**

Harris collection

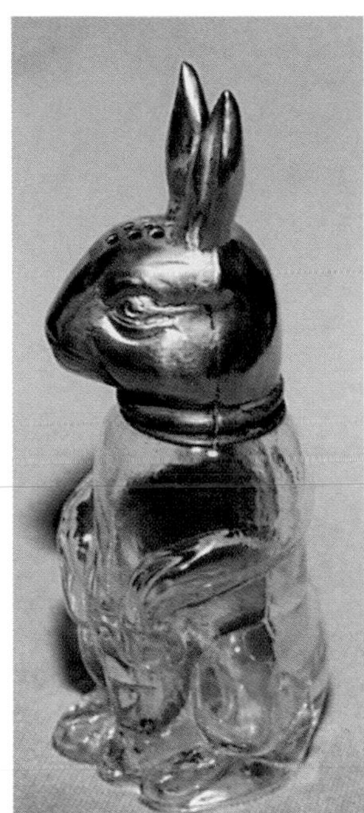

Rabbit: Clear thin glass, mold blown. This is one of the many forms of candy containers that was configured so that it could subsequently be used as a salt /pepper condiment dispenser once the candy had been consumed. Marked "made in Germany." Circa 1930 – 1940. 2" tall. Scarce! **$28.00 – 40.00.**

White collection

Rib, Band: Opaque opalware glass, mold blown. A bulging cylinder-shaped shaker with a smooth upper half; the lower half contains 20 vertical ribs in raised relief. There is also a very short extended glass base which configures it for use in a condiment set holder. 3¼" tall x 2⅛" wide and a 1¾" base diameter. Circa 1890 – 1900. Scarce! **$15.00 – 25.00.**

Harris collection

Authors' collection

Krauss collection

Krauss collection

Krauss collection

Regal: Illustrated are four cobalt blue and white cut overlay layered glass shakers having various shaped oblong elliptical panels. While each shaker has its own cut-in type of design, they are all similar. Each example reflects outstanding artistic and quality workmanship. These shakers are all of European origin, circa 1897 – 1907. 4⅜" tall. Each used a specific special type of metal two-piece pressure-fit silver top to dispense its condiment. One photo shows the unique mechanical top make-up. Rare! Excellent condition. **$325.00 – 350.00** each shaker.

Ridgway collection

Rib, Bulbous Optic: Clear cranberry glass, dual mold blown. As the pattern name indicates this is a small bulbous-shaped shaker containing continuous inside wide optic ribs. The smooth external surface contains what appears to be small, individual HP white daisies covering the shaker's entire circumference. Circa 1889 – 1894. 2¼" tall x 1⅜" base diameter with a two-piece metal top. Very scarce! **$75.00 – 90.00.**

Ridgway collection

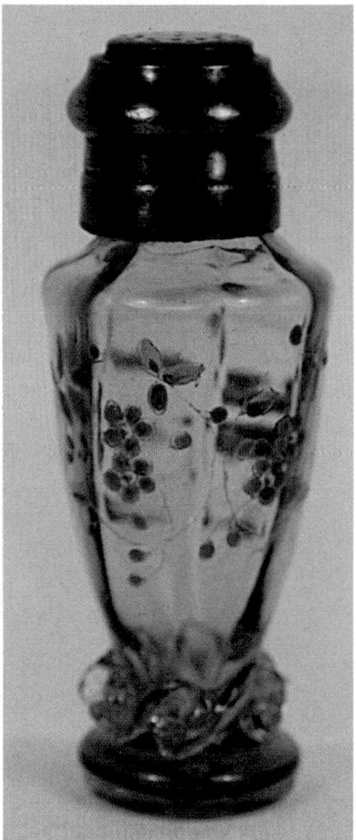

Rib, Optic Eight: Clear olive amber glass, dual mold blown. The pattern name describes the principal configuration of this shaker which contains eight prominent inside vertical optic ribs. The smooth exterior has HP blue and green floral decoration. The footed ring base is encircled with hand-applied rigaree in the form of twisted glass ruffling. We believe this ware is of European origin. Circa 1887 – 1892. 3⅝" tall with a two-piece metal top that appears to be oversized (not original). Rare! **$210.00 – 225.00.**

Rathbun collection

Rib, Thirty-Two Basc: Clear blue homogeneous glass, mold blown. As the pattern name states, this shaker has 32 small base ribs on top of the base; the lower portion of the shaker body has a sharp external ring. Circa 1885 – 1893. 3" tall. Very scarce! **$34.00 – 46.00.**

Harris collection

Rib, Wide Optic: Translucent blue cased glass, dual mold blown. A bulbous shaker containing eight light blue internal vertical panels separated by narrow panels of clear glass creating an optic rib effect. The base is encircled with clear, fused-on rigaree scrolls just above the flared out supporting bottom. Believed to be of European origin. Circa 1885 – 1893. 3½" tall x 2⅛" at widest point. Rare! **$310.00 – 345.00.**

Harris collection

Ribbed, Concentric: Clear green glass, mold blown. This is a raised pattern of ribbed concentric circles expanding outward from a common center. Circa 1915 – 1925. 2½" tall. The inside surface has a large bubble flaw covering three encircled ribs. Very scarce! **$13.00 – 18.00.**

Krauss collection

Neale collection

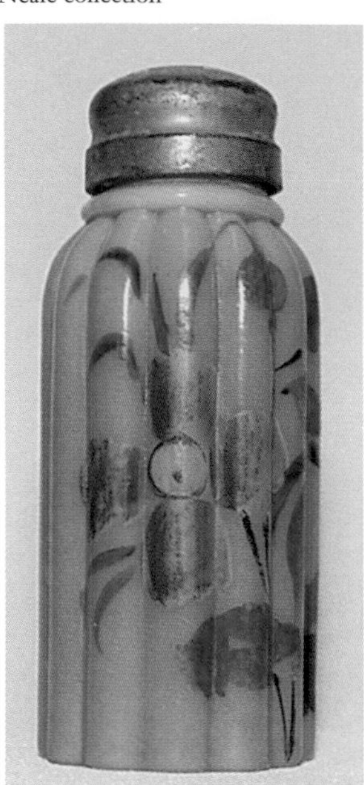

Ribbed Cylinder: Opaque opalware glass, mold blown. A tall cylindrical-shaped shaker containing 12 uniform ribs that taper inward at the shoulder to a circular collar. The HP motif on one of the shakers consists of a large orange four-petaled flower and associated dark green leaves that have been painted over a light green background. The other shaker has a similar pink four-petaled floral spray against the unpainted natural white opalware. The shaker bottom has an indent the size of a quarter. Circa 1896 – 1904. Each shaker is 3¾" tall x 1⅝" wide. Very scarce! **$45.00 – 60.00** each.

Lockwood collection

Ribbed Shorty: Clear blue glass, mold blown. A small shaker with a shallow ring neck and foot. There are 18 vertical convex ribs. Circa 1900 – 1907. 1¾" tall x 1¾" wide. Scarce! **$30.00 – 40.00.**

Rathbun collection

Ribbed Opalescent Spots: Translucent cranberry glass, dual mold blown, with opalescent coin spots interspersed among 20 vertical ribs in raised relief. The glass translucence is the result of the opalescent coin spot distribution among the vertical ribbing. Unverified, but believed to have been produced by Hobbs, Brockunier Co., Wheeling, West Virginia. Circa 1887 – 1891. The pattern names were established by A. G. Peterson. 2¾" tall. Rare! **$150.00 – 165.00.**

Rathbun collection

Ribbed Shoulder: Opaque white opalware, mold blown. A cylinder-shaped shaker with a creased neck having 22 pleats on the shoulder below. The smooth outer surface contains a HP pink and green floral spray. 3⅝" tall with 1½" diameter base. Circa 1898 – 1906. Scarce! **$25.00 – 30.00.**

Authors' collection

Ribbed Triangle & Sawtooth: Green stained to clear shaded pressed glass. This is a short bulbous shaker containing 10 adjacent pairs of cut-in triangular-stepped vertical ribs that tie into 10 large upper and lower dual sawtooth bands encircling the shaker perimeter. Circa 1900 – 1910. 2⅛" tall. Very scarce in this shaded color! **$38.00 – 45.00.**

Arnold collection

Ribs, Eighteen: Clear uncolored glass, mold blown. The shaker pattern amounts to 18 raised vertical ribs over the total exterior circumference. Circa 1890s. No other known colors. 3¼" tall; 1¾" wide at widest portion; 1½" base diameter. Scarce! **$20.00 – 30.00.**

Neale collection

Krauss collection

Ribs, Skinny: Opaque opaline glass, mold blown. This pattern is very much like the Mt. Washington/Pairpoint "Pillar, Ribbed" shaker[42] except that it is taller and has 24 vertical ribs. The exterior contains a random orange and black paint application that doesn't portray an identifiable motif. 3¼" tall; 1⅝" wide. Circa 1896 – 1900. Also produced in opaque green and clear amber. Very scarce. **$25.00 – 35.00.**

Rathbun collection

Ridge Swirl: Clear cobalt blue glass, mold blown. The pattern was created in a three-piece mold and contains continuous protruding swirls throughout the shaker's surface. Pattern name by Ardelle Taylor. Described and pictured in H-3, page 38 in a sugar shaker. Circa 1900. Also produced in clear and amber. 3" tall x 1⅝" wide. Very scarce! **$34.00 – 43.00.**

Krauss collection

Rigaree, Tall (condiment): Clear blue glass, dual mold blown. Each shaker contains hand-applied clear rigaree glass runners hanging downward from the top. The shakers are shaped similar to an elongated bulb and contain vertical optic ribs; the exterior surface has HP white and red floral sprays. The glass is believed to be of European origin. Circa 1883 – 1887. The shakers are 4¼" tall with two-piece metal tops. The ornate silver-plated metal holder is marked "Meriden B. Co. quadruple plate." Rare! Unfortunately, the illustrated shakers are in poor condition and have little (if any) monetary value due to glass damage.

Rathbun collection

Ring Neck Twist: Greenish-white opalescent glass, mold blown. This is a simple swirl pattern containing 13 swirls derived from a three-part mold. Circa 1888 – 1894. 2¾" tall x 2⅛" wide. Very scarce! **$48.00 – 65.00.**

Krauss collection

Ring Necked Orb: Translucent inside surface frosted glass, mold blown. A circular form with a ring neck. The exterior surface contains a HP yellow/red and white floral spray. Circa 1896 – 1905. 3" tall x 2½" wide; 1½" base diameter. Also produced in clear. Scarce! **$32.00 – 45.00** pair.

Lockwood collection

Ring Salt: Opaque homogeneous green glass, mold blown. This is a round shaker that is tapered from the middle to a smaller top and bottom. The protruding plain rings encircle the body and have stippling between them. Circa 1896 – 1905. 1⅞" tall x 1⅝" wide. Pattern name by Warman.[43] Scarce! **$22.00 – 30.00.**

Krauss collection

Ringed Bulb: Clear blue glass, dual mold blown. As the pattern name indicates, this shaker is shaped like a bulb with IVT on the inside and a HP yellow/white floral spray with large green shaded leaves on the exterior. 3⅝" tall with an unusually long threaded top. Circa 1890 – 1895. Very scarce! **$75.00 – 90.00.**

Maxfield collection

Rogers, Smith & Co. No. 50: Clear mold blown glass. A tall cylinder-shaped shaker with a HP white, red, and green floral sprig. Introduced by Peterson in *Glass Salt Shakers* as part of a Rogers, Smith & Co. 1882 catalog listing on page 178. 3⅝" tall x 1⅜" base diameter; the two-piece metal top is original. Rare! **$75.00 – 95.00.**

White collection

Rose Necklace: Opaque white opalware glass, mold blown. The pattern name was selected because of the embossed neck motif. The rest of the shaker consists of eight plain downward curved panels. The shaker has been seen with a brown stained shoulder and a HP rose spray decoration on the panel(s). Circa 1896 – 1906. 2¾" tall x 2⅝" wide; 1⅝" base diameter. Scarce! **$18.00 – 28.00.**

Lockwood collection

Round Yo-Yo: Clear dark amethyst glass, mold blown. A very short, squatty, heavy shaker with a ring neck and shallow extended foot for securing within a condiment set. Circa 1890 – 1897. Believed to be of European origin. 1¾" tall x 1⅞" with a two-piece metal top. Very scarce! **$45.00 – 60.00.**

Authors' collection

Round Shoulder Cube: Opaque white opalware glass, mold blown. The pattern name describes the appearance of this shaker. The decoration amounts to symmetrical spaced dark blue daisy blooms on each side. Circa 1898 – 1906. 2¾" tall with a special single threaded metal top. Very scarce! **$25.00 – 30.00.**

Harris collection

S and P: Opaque white opalware glass, mold blown and pressed. As the reader looks at the illustration of these shakers, it should be readily apparent why the pattern name was assigned. The letter on each shaker is in high raised relief and is hand painted in dark blue with red and green floral decoration. Certainly a unique designed pair. Circa 1896 – 1908. Believed to be of foreign origin. 3½" tall with MOP center tops. Rare! **$110.00 – 130.00** pair.

Harris collection

Salt, Sure Grip: Clear dark green glass, mold blown. As the pattern name implies, this is a small bulging shaker with a fused-on clear glass handle that appears to be of English origin. A Victorian era salt or pepper containing a glass handle is indeed an unusual design. Circa 1890 – 1900. 2⅛" tall with a silver two-piece pressure fitting top. The possibility that this may have been part of a child's toy set exists; we have no documentation that verifies our theory. Rare! **NPD.**

Lockwood collection

Scroll, Arched: Opaque homogeneous opalware glass, mold blown. Here is a shaker with a gracefully bulging top that curves to the bottom where it is supported by four shallow rolled feet. The front and back have the largest expanse. The sides are narrower with flattened corners between. All four sides have embossed scroll borders. The decoration consists of HP budded sprig; the front has a full-blown red floral spray and green leaves. The thin neck and flattened corners have a pink colored wash. Circa 1898 – 1905. 2⅝" tall x 2" wide side to side; 1¾" wide front to back. Scarce! **$45.00 – 55.00.**

Lockwood collection

Scallops & Beads: Opaque white homogeneous opalware glass, mold blown. This is a curved, smooth-neck shaker that flares outward from the mid-point to the bottom. There is a horizontal indented scalloped line over each of the beaded four lobed base portions. Circa 1900 – 1908. **$13.00 – 19.00.**

White collection

Scallop Shell & Seaweed: Translucent opalescent glass, mold blown. We are illustrating three shakers to show that two are stained with marigold luster or brown coloring; also, two AAGSSCS collectors have reported a shaker with complete exterior carnival staining. All of these various stains will wear off over time; no doubt due to kitchen wash and wear. Circa 1892 – 1900. 3⅜" tall x 2" wide; 1⅜" base diameter. Scarce! **$30.00 – 100.00** depending upon condition.

Beale collection

Beale collection

Tutelo collection

Scrolls, Climbing: Opaque opalware glass, mold blown. This shaker has a narrow upper section that expands outward into a flared out base with a short glass bottom extension for use within a condiment holder. The upper two-thirds contain embossed HP reddish floral sprays. We believe this shaker was produced by Eagle Glass & Mfg Co. Circa 1898 – 1904. 4⅔" tall x 2⅝" wide. Scarce! **$13.00 – 18.00.**

Coalmer collection

Scroll, Low: Opaque blue glass, mold blown. The shaker has six identical scrolled panels that rise from a hexagon-shaped base. This pattern is attributed to Consolidated Lamp & Glass Co. by author Mel Murray but we have been unable to verify it. We did not report a blue color in our 1976 book. These shakers were also produced in opaque white, pink, and green. Circa 1894 – 1902. 2½" tall. Very scarce! **$40.00 – 50.00.**

Krauss collection

Scroll, Narrow Base, Variant (aka Canadian #7): Opaque blue glass, mold. The shaker has eight sides, four large and four small. The narrow base is plain; the large scrolls face left. Circa 1894 – 1900. 3½" tall x 1⅞" wide. Scarce! **$30.00 – 42.00.**

White collection

Shrimp Base: Clear glass, four-piece mold blown. A bulged out base containing 21 ribs. The glass opening has been snapped off from the pontil rod. Circa 1890 – 1900. 3" tall x 2¾" at the widest part. Scarce! **$8.00 – 12.00.**

Rathbun collection

Rathbun collection

Sequoia, Variant: Clear canary yellow (vaseline) glass, mold blown and pressed. This is considered a variation of the "Sequoia" pattern documented in Paterson 172-G. The portion of each shaker base that fits into the condiment holder has 24 small vertical ribs. The shaker body, containing a fine cut design, tapers slightly from the shoulder to the ribbed base so that it extends over the rib band. 2¾" tall. Circa 1878 – 1885. Also produced in clear and amber. Very scarce. **$160.00 – 175.00** set.

Krauss collection

Skirt: Translucent lavender Bristol glass, mold blown. The physical shape is similar to a circular skirt with the exterior surface containing a single HP floral wreath with a pair of bell-shaped white flowers. The bottom has a small extended glass flange for insertion into some type of condiment holder. Produced by one of the English glasshouses. Circa 1895 – 1900. 2¼" tall with a two-piece metal top. Has some decoration wear. Very scarce! **$30.00 – 40.00.**

Coalmer collection

Skirt, Wide Pleat: Opaque glossy white, mold formed, quality porcelain with embossed swirled vertical ribbing reminiscent of a pleated skirt. We have also observed identical opalware shakers in this same pattern. The exterior decoration is unique; containing small HP, random-placed red floral sprays interspersed with large round blue dots. Circa 1890 – 1897. 2¾" tall with two-piece metal tops. Rare! **$160.00 – 180.00** pair.

Krauss collection

Small Inverted Thumbprint Bell: Clear cranberry glass, dual mold blown. The inside surface contains small IVT; the outer surface is smooth and contains an elaborate, central located, white, yellow, and orange floral spray with small green leaves. The physical shape is similar to the "Bell-shaped IVT" shaker shown on page 206 of our Vol. II book. Circa 1886 – 1892. 2⅜" tall with a two-piece metal top. Very scarce! **$155.00 – 170.00.**

Roland collection

Snow, Ball (aka Ball, Snow): Opaque opalware glass, mold blown. This is a smooth spheroid pattern containing cold painted, somewhat faded-brown leaf decoration. The shaker has been embossed like the "Jackson" pattern with the bottom having a number "3." Circa 1904 – 1914. 2½" tall; 2½" wide; 1½" diameter base. Scarce! **$15.00 – 22.00.**

Krauss collection

Sphere, Honeycomb Opalescent: Clear amber colored glass with opalescent polka dots, dual mold blown. The physical make-up is a small sphere with the inside surface having an embossed honeycomb pattern, and the external surface is smooth. Circa 1888 – 1894. 2¼" tall with a two-piece metal top. Very scarce! **$75.00 – 90.00.**

White collection

Spool Neck (aka Madoline):[44] Opaque opalware glass, mold blown. A spheroid-shaped shaker containing worn transfer decoration of birds and branches applied over a faded pink stain background. Circa 1901 – 1908. 2¾" tall x 2½" wide. The Lockwoods have floral decorated and "Francesware" decorated shaker(s), but we have no photo of them. **$7.00 – 15.00** for the shaker illustrated.

Coalmer collection

Spangled, Pseudo: Opaque homogeneous molded. Essentially a copy of a Creased Neck shaker except the basic material is a dark brown pottery clay. However, due to artistic talent it looks like gold micro flakes within a red basic batch. So unusual we had to include it. Circa 1885 – 1893. 3⅞" tall with a two-piece metal top. Rare! **$35.00 – 40.00.**

Krauss collection

Square Block, Cut-in: Clear thick ruby-red homogeneous glass, mold blown. The pattern amounts to six vertical rows of blocks in raised relief; each encircling row contains 10 individual blocks. The shaker bottom has a large 18 point intaglio star. 3⅞" tall with a two-piece metal top. Circa 1895 – 1904. Very scarce. **$145.00 – 165.00** pair.

Krauss collection

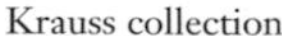

Arnold collection

Square, Royal (condiment): Clear amber glass, mold blown. A tall cube-shaped shaker with slightly rounded shoulders. The glass is heavy and of an excellent quality that has been achieved by hand-fire polishing. The principal decoration has been hand painted in white and portrays a young Victorian child holding her dress with the left hand while standing in a meadow picking flowers. It is completely incorrect to use the terminology Mary Gregory for this type of decoration since it has been thoroughly substantiated that Mary Gregory never painted this type of decoration.[45] The other three shaker sides contain white HP floral sprigs. This ware is of European origin. Circa 1888 – 1893 with silvered pagoda-shaped tops. 4⅜" tall; 1½" wide; 1½" base diameter. The ornate silver-plated condiment holder is marked "Meriden B. Co." Rare as a complete set! Single shaker, **$250.00 – 275.00;** set, **$1,200.00 – 1,300.00.**

Lockwood collection

Squat Bottom: Opaque homogeneous opalware glass, mold blown. The pattern amounts to series of roses with scrolls on the narrow neck and around the top. The shaker was no doubt decorated at one time; but, time and the Victorian era dish pan have removed any external coloring. We agree with Marilyn Lockwood that this is no doubt a Fostoria Glass shaker. Circa 1900. 2⅝" tall x 2¼" wide. Pattern name by Warman. Scarce! **$15.00 – 20.00** (due to wear).

Lockwood collection

Square, Tapered: Translucent, satinized Rubina glass; also, a cranberry shaker, mold blown. The Rubina have random spaced HP white flowers and pale orange leaves that are outlined in black. The cranberry shaker has a green and white floral sprig. The vertical edge of some of the shaker's sides contain a series of HP pink dots. The tapered shape is very similar to the "Triangle, Pinched-In" shaker shown in our Vol. II, p. 262. Believed to be of European origin. Circa 1883 – 1887. 2⅞" tall with a two-piece metal top. Also produced in custard, Rare! **$115.00 – 125.00.**

Coalmer collection

Staggered Beads: Clear amber glass, mold blown and pressed. A pillar-shaped shaker containing continuous raised beads that are alternately arranged throughout the exterior surface. Circa 1903 – 1914. Believed to be of English origin with original tops. The bottom contains an intaglio rayed star. 2⅝" tall x 1⅝" diameter at the base. Pattern name by Coalmer. Very scarce! **$48.00 – 62.00** pair.

Krauss collection

Startled Rabbit: Clear and amber glass, mold blown. As the pattern name implies, this is a rabbit sitting upright on his haunches reflecting an alert facial expression. The head is amber and the body clear glass. Circa 1930 – 1940. No doubt a candy container configured for use as a salt/pepper once the candy was consumed. 2⅜" tall. Very scarce! **$75.00 – 85.00** pair.

Authors' collection

Star & Rib: Clear vaseline pressed glass. The upper half of this shaker contains three large eight-pointed stars in raised relief. The center has two encircling rows of small intaglio ellipsoids. The lower portion consists of 22 curved vertical ribs. The bottom is recessed and contains a full-size rayed star. Pattern name by Peterson.[46] Exposure to ultraviolet black light results in a strong yellow illumination. Circa 1885 – 1891. 3" tall. Very scarce in vaseline glass! **$65.00 – 80.00.**

Maxfield collection

Strawberry Delight: Opaque homogeneous blue glass, mold blown. This an intricately involved, fine detailed, pattern that consists of leaves around the lower bulge and strawberries on long stems in high raised relief on the upper cylindrical-shaped portion. Encircling rows of embossed beads are on the neck of the shaker. We concur with the owner and believe this shaker was produced by Dithridge & Co. Circa 1894 – 1900. 3" tall x 2¾" wide. Very scarce! **$55.00 – 70.00.**

Lockwood collection

Strawberry, Footed, Inverted Thumbprint: Clear inside-flashed cranberry glass, dual mold blown. With a strawberry shape, the inner surface contains IVT, the outside surface is smooth and undecorated. The bottom has a concave ringed center with the outer circumference containing 14 buttons upon which the shaker sits. Circa 1885 – 1891. 2⅜" tall x 1⅝" wide. Scarce! **$25.00 – 30.00** due to wear.

Rathbun collection

Swag, Ruffle: Green opaque satin glass, mold blown. The pattern consists of three embossed, individual ruffle-like, elongated scrolls that encircle the base of the shaker body. It is our opinion that this shaker is a product of the Consolidated Lamp and Glass Co., Pittsburgh, Pennsylvania, circa 1894 – 1900; however, no catalogs or trade ads have been found to verify this opinion. 2¾" tall. Very scarce! **$80.00 – 95.00.**

Lockwood collection

Swirl, Dainty: Translucent reverse Rubina glass, mold blown. A cylinder-shaped shaker containing exterior surface fine swirls that flow from the upper left to lower right thus causing a translucent effect. Looks European to us! Circa 1889 – 1894. 3⅜" tall x 1½" wide with a two-piece metal top. Very scarce! **$130.00 – 150.00.**

Coalmer collection

Swirl, "Petal Swirl" (aka Swirl, Wide): Clear ultramarine colored glass, mold blown. This pattern is illustrated in *The Collector's Encyclopedia of Depression Glass* by Gene Florence, 3rd Edition, page 192. Peterson illustrates it in his salt shaker book on page 41-M and named it "Swirl, Wide." This ware was produced by the Jeannette Glass Co. Circa 1937 – 1938. The pattern was produced in pink, ultra-marine, and delphite. According to Florence, the pink shakers are rare! 3¼" tall. Very scarce! **$75.00 – 90.00** pair.

Krauss collection

Swirled Rib, Peloton: The basic glass batch is clear blue, mold blown. A somewhat spheroidal shape containing 10 large swirled ribs to which has been randomly applied various colored glass filament-type decoration. Such a technique is recognized by the trade as Peloton art glass. This general technique was first patented on October 25, 1880, by Wilhelm Kralik of Neuwelt, Bohemia. The methodology, as described in his patent, is fully documented on pages 115 and 116 by A. C. Revi in his book *Nineteenth Century Glass.* We could find no documented proof that this type of art glass can be accredited to American glass factory production. Circa 1881 – 1886. 2⅞" tall with a two-piece metal top. Extremely rare in shakers! **NPD.**

Coalmer collection

Swirl, Spiral: Clear cranberry colored glass, mold blown. The pattern amounts to a symmetrical-shaped column containing a series of close spaced diagonal swirls in high raised relief. The glass quality is excellent. Circa 1888 – 1894. 3" tall. Rare! **$80.00 – 95.00.**

McElderry collection

Tank, Inverted Thumbprint: Clear amber glass, dual mold blown. Here is a shaker with a shape that is reminiscent of a round glass tank. The inside surface contains IVT; the smooth exterior has a HP blue, white, and green vertical floral spray. Circa 1887 – 1894. 3⅛" tall with a two-piece metal top. Very scarce! **$150.00 – 175.00.**

Neale collection

Tapered Bulge: Opaque green glass, two-piece mold blown. The pattern name applies to the pattern shape which has a thin flanged base. The glass is reminiscent of New England opaque green art glass that was created by adding the proper amount of copper oxide to an opal glass batch. However, there is no known documented proof or previous publications of such a plain undecorated pattern having ever been produced by this glasshouse. Authentic opaque green forms are all very plain but contain a relatively simple mottled blue mineral stain decoration.[47] In the case of our illustrated pair, one shaker has a glossy surface finish, the other has a satin exterior. Circa 1887 – 1893. 2½" tall; 1⅞" wide at the shoulder; 1¾" base. Rare! **$360.00 – 390.00** pair.

Lockwood collection

Tapered Bulge Bottom: Clear medium blue glass, mold blown. Has a ring neck, tapering to a bulge bottom over a ring supporting foot. There are three evenly spaced vertical lines extending from the ring neck to ring foot. Good quality glass with fire polished mold marks. Circa 1896 – 1900. 2⅞" tall x 2⅞" wide with a two-piece metal top. Scarce! **$45.00 – 55.00.**

Bruce collection

Tapered Shoulder, Variant: Translucent dark amethyst glass, mold blown. The pattern is a cylindrical shape with a slightly rounded shoulder having excellent quality HP white enamel floral decoration. An identical pattern shaped shaker is illustrated in our Vol. II, p. 260 except that shaker is shorter. Circa 1885 – 1887. 4⅛" tall with a two-piece metal top;1¾" wide. Rare! **$90.00 – 110.00.**

Krauss collection

Tapered Speckle: Translucent amber glass, mold blown. This is an inverted cone-shaped shaker containing hand-applied white paint flecks in simulation of the classic spatter effect. 3⅛" tall; 1⅞" base diameter. Circa 1898 – 1910. Also produced in blue. Scarce! **$37.00 – 45.00.**

Coalmer collection

Thousand Eye, Contemporary: Clear vasoline to ruby stained glass, mold blown. While this ware has the visual appearance of Reverse Amberina, it is vaseline glass with the lower portion having inside surface ruby stain. The so-called Thousand Eye pattern makes these shakers somewhat translucent. When exposed to UV black light radiation it emits a strong fluorescence. Circa 1965 – 1975. 2⅝" tall with tops that are believed to be original. Scarce! **$38.00 – 50.00** pair.

Authors' collection

Thousand Eye, Ringed Center: Clear canary (vaseline) glass, mold blown and pressed. The pattern name describes the physical form of this shaker. Circa 1878 – 1888. 3⅛" tall. Also produced in clear, blue, amber, and green. Peterson has declared this a rare pattern.[48] **$65.00 – 80.00.**

Arnold collection

Threaded Swirl, Bulbous: Clear blue glass, dual mold blown. This is a medium-sized bulbous shaker that has swirled grooves slanting downward from top to bottom. The ribbed exterior contains HP pink and white floral sprigs with random interconnecting stems. The base has a short extended bottom that indicates probable usage as part of a condiment set. 2¾" tall x 2" wide; 1¼" base diameter with a two-piece metal top. Circa 1888 – 1893. Very scarce. **$135.00 – 150.00.**

Krauss collection

Thumbprint, Four: Opaque homogeneous opalware, mold blown. As indicated, this is a ring-neck pillar that has four large intaglio thumbprints distributed equally around the middle. A HP floral sprig has been applied across the top edges of the thumbprints. Circa 1898 – 1907. 3⅜" tall x 1¾" wide; 1½" base diameter. Scarce! **$22.00 – 30.00.**

Thumbprint, Flared Base (cruet set): Clear Bluina glass, dual mold blown. The pattern shape reflects a flared-outward shaped bell with an extended base for fitting securely within the condiment holder. The lower half of the glass pieces contain a row of inside surface thumbprints.[49] The smooth exterior HP floral decoration is in orange, yellow, and white. The metal stand is marked "Aurora SP MFG Co" and stands 11" tall to the top of the lifting handle. Salt and pepper, 3⅛" tall; cruet, 5½" tall to the top of the pouring spout. Believed to have been produced by the Mt. Washington/Pairpoint Glass Co. Circa 1886 – 1890. Rare in a complete set! **$875.00 – 1,000.00** set.

Krauss collection

Coalmer collection

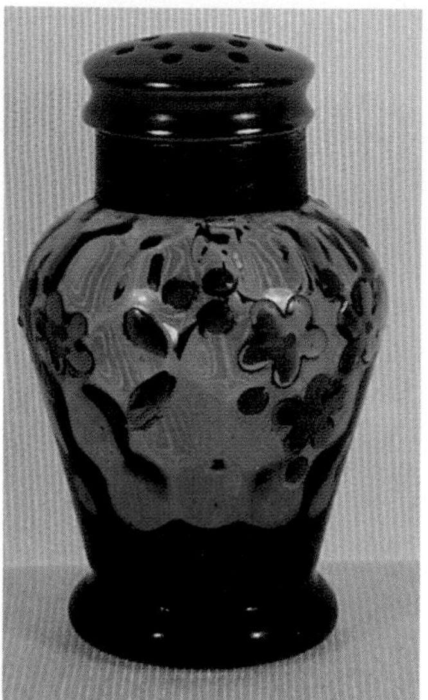

Thumbprint, Irregular: A small clear electric blue shaker, dual mold blown. The inside contains a series of small, irregular thumbprints. The exterior surface is decorated with HP pink, white, and gold flowers and associated random placed foliage. The bottom has an extended round base; an indication that this shaker could have been used in a condiment holder. 2⅜" tall with a two-piece metal top. Circa 1888 – 1894. Rare! **$85.00 – 100.00.**

Krauss collection

Thumbprint, Oval (condiment): Clear Rubina glass, dual mold blown. The glass pieces are of a cylindrical shape with varying sizes of oval thumbprints embossed within their inner surface. The smooth exteriors contain four vertical HP floral sprigs equally spaced around each glass item; all basic colors are present. The condiment set consists of two 3½" salt and pepper dispensers and a 3⅞" tall oil bottle with clear glass stopper removed. The metal holding frame is heart shaped with a metal honeycomb surface design that was produced by James W. Tufts, Boston. This silver plate manufacturer was incorporated in 1881 and went out of business around 1915. The aforesaid glass pieces are circa 1881 – 1889. Rare as a complete set!

Coalmer collection

Thumbprint on Spearhead: Clear ruby glass, mold blown. The pattern name, created by A. G. Peterson, provides a very good description of the shaker's principal motif.[50] This ware has excellent glass quality. Millard called this pattern "Cats Eye" in his book *Goblets II.* Circa 1924 – 1931. Rare! **$140.00 – 160.00** pair.

Lockwood collection

Tiered: Opaque opalware glass, mold blown. This pattern name was undoubtedly assigned because the shaker is arranged in tiers with worn gilt colored paint on the top tier. The bulging base contains short embossed vertical ribs that vary in length. This pattern is listed in Peterson but not illustrated.[51] Circa 1896 – 1905. 2¾" tall x 2¼" wide. Scarce! **$12.00 – 17.00.**

Rathbun collection

McElderry collection

Tortoise Shell Bulb Variant: Translucent splotches of multicolored glass primarily involving shades of white and brown over which HP floral sprigs have been applied; mold blown and freehand finished. This shaker is a variation of the one illustrated in our Vol. II, p. 262; the main difference being the presence of exterior HP decoration. The overall physical shape consists of an elongated bulb that is 3¼" tall with a two-piece metal top. A rare decorated art glass shaker, circa 1881 – 1887. **$350.00 – 375.00.**

Lockwood collection

Tree of Life: Clear (uncolored) translucent pressed glass. A. G. Peterson designates the "Tree of Life" shakers as rare.[52] However, this pattern type was produced by various Victorian glasshouses for various reasons. A primary reason involved overshot ware that was used during the 1870 – 1880 period as a method to hide defects that resulted from a poor glass batch.[53] The overshot process was employed to cover-up speck defects, cloudiness, unmelted sand, etc. and as a result has often been erroneously referred to as a "Tree of Life" pattern by both collectors and dealers. To be brief, overshot consists of the application of ground glass particles to the exterior surface of a piece that resulted in a so-called "Tree of Life" pattern affect. If the reader desires additional detail we suggest you study Kamm 3, pages 120 and 121, which involves several glass factories of possible attribution that results in contradictory conclusions along with failing to address the overshot aspect of this type of ware. As a bottom line, A.C. Revi discusses this pattern in connection with several glass factories.[54] In our opinion, this shaker pattern has been placed in our book where it belongs; among the unknown aspects of positive attribution. Circa 1874 – 1885. 2⅞" tall. **$35.00 – 45.00.**

Krauss collection

Triangle, Blunt (condiment): Clear amber glass, dual mold blown with HP blue, green, and white floral sprigs. Similar in shape to the "Pinched-In Triangle shown in our Vol. II, p. 262. The inside surface contains small IVT. 2¼" tall with two-piece metal tops. The metal holder is marked "Rogers Smith & Co. Meriden, CT." The holder is 5⅜" tall to the top of the lifting handle. Circa 1885 – 1890. Very scarce. One shaker contains a large crack; the other one is in very good condition. **$75.00 – 90.00** set.

McElderry collection

Triangle, Inverted (condiment): Clear amber and blue pressed glass. Each shaker's surface has a prominate inverted triangle design that is present all the way down to where the rounded foot is attached. Their general shape also resembles an inverted triangle with a slightly rounded shoulder. The shaker foot design is configured to fit upon a protruding glass retention peg that is present on the clear vaseline pressed glass holding stand. Circa 1883 – 1890. Shakers, 2¾" tall; holding stand, 5⅞" tall to the top of the lifting handle. Very scarce as a complete set! **$105.00 – 125.00** set.

Lockwood collection

Triplets: Opaque white opalware glass, mold blown. This pattern name was created by Heacock; undoubtedly due to fact that there are multiple lines of molded threading around the top, middle, and bottom.[55] The two smooth areas of the shaker contain HP yellow floral blobs with red dot centers attached to lavender branches. It is our opinion that this shaker was produced by the Co-operative Flint Glass Company. Circa 1901 – 1905. 3⅛" tall x 2¼" wide. Very scarce! **$33.00 – 45.00.**

Tutelo collection

Tripod with Diamond Band: Clear canary yellow vaseline glass, mold blown and pressed. As the pattern name indicates this shaker contains a center located band of squashed diamonds and it stands on three legs.[56] Also produced in clear glass. Circa 1904 – 1910. 3½" tall x 1⅞" wide. Very scarce! **$55.00 – 75.00.**

Tulip Spray: Opaque homogeneous glass, mold blown. This shaker has a bulging lower body that curves to an expanded neck ring that is "zippered" all around with upright concave lines. The principal motif portrays embossed tulips, stems, and leaves on one side. Circa 1899 – 1910. 3⅛" tall x 2½" wide. Also produced in blue milk glass. **$15.00 – 21.00.**

Lockwood collection

Lockwood collection

Twenty Stripe, Opalescent: Translucent blue opalescent glass, mold blown. A round cylindrical shaped shaker containing 20 vertical opalescent stripes that blend together at the shaker bottom. Similar to the shaker shown in our Vol. II, page 99, but with a larger top opening and more opalescent striping. Circa 1887 – 1891. 3¼" tall. Rare! **$170.00 – 190.00.**

Rathbun collection

Twisted Cane: Opaque blue glass, mold blown. The pattern consists of 12 twisted ribs in raised relief. Also produced in opaque pink with a cased white inner glass layer. 2⅝" tall x 1¼" wide as measured at the base. Circa 1895 – 1905. Very scarce! **$48.00 – 60.00.**

Harris collection

Rathbun collection

Twist Pillar (aka "Yarn"): Illustrated is a mold blown Reverse Amberina art glass condiment set and a translucent multicolored cased spatter glass shaker that is dual mold blown. This is a cylindrical twisted shaker pattern with a flat shoulder. The swirled ribbing runs from left to right. This pattern was also produced in cranberry frosted spatter, cased clear, red white and blue spatter, and no doubt in other color combinations. With the appearance of an Amberina set having threaded glass top edges, there is a possibility that this ware was produced by Hobbs, Brockunier. So far, no one has reported any of this ware having HP decoration. 3" tall x 1⅝" wide. Circa 1889 – 1891. Metal holding stand is marked "Barbour Bros. Co." Quad. plate; 7½" tall to top of lifting handle. Very scarce! Shaker, **$120.00 – 140.00;** Amberina set, **$350.00 – 410.00.**

Lockwood collection

Urn, Bristol: Opaque white Bristol glass, mold blown. This is a tall round narrow shaker containing two separate neck rings over a sloping shoulder. The body tapers downward to another protruding ring which is located just above a flared out foot. The decoration motif consists of HP deep red rings and flowers with green and blue leaves encircling the body. Believed to be of European origin. Circa 1898 – 1909. 4" tall x 1¾" wide with a 1¼" base diameter. Scarce! **$28.00 – 35.00.**

Lockwood collection

Vine, Entwined: Opaque homogeneous opalware glass, mold blown. The shaker has straight symmetrical sides and shoulder. The principal pattern design is an embossed elongated diamond starting at the base with the top extending upward into the shoulder area. This design is repeated three times around the shaker perimeter. On either side of the diamond are leaves and tendril-like scrolls and other leaves that tie it to the next adjacent design. Circa 1899 – 1909. 2⅝" tall x 2" wide at the waist. Also produced in sapphire blue and clear. Opalware, **$14.00 – 22.00;** sapphire blue, **$30.00 – 35.00.**

Lockwood collection

Violet Ovals: Opaque pink homogeneous glass, mold blown. The pattern consists of four shield-like panels with each panel containing two violet flowers, one bud and one leaf all in raised relief. Circa 1894 – 1900. Also produced in opaque light blue. 3" tall x 2⅜" at widest point; 1⅝" base diameter. Believed to be a Gillender shaker. Scarce! **$38.00 – 50.00.**

Lockwood collection

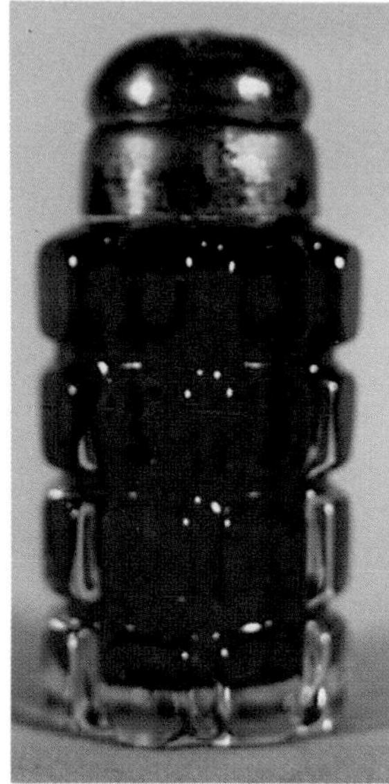

Waffle Columns: Clear inside ruby stained pressed glass. The pattern amounts to an eight sided, four vertical row block motif. The shaker has a very slight downward taper. Circa 1891 – 1898. Also produced in clear glass. 3" tall x 1½" widest at the top; 1¾" base diameter with a two-piece metal top. The bottom is smooth. Very scarce! **$65.00 – 75.00.**

Harris collection

Waisted Spirals: Clear green glass, mold blown. A narrow waisted pattern with four raised ridges that slope from right to left. Circa 1897 – 1906. 2⅞" tall x 1¾" wide. Scarce! **$20.00 – 30.00.**

Lockwood collection

Wee Puff Ball: Opaque homogeneous opalware glass, mold blown. A tiny sphere-shaped shaker with a slightly concave bottom. Each illustrated shaker contains either HP enamel blue or red flowers with green leaves and brown stems. Circa 1890 – 1900. 1½" tall x 1⅝" wide with two-piece metal tops. Scarce! **$48.00 – 60.00** pair.

Coalmer collection

Waffle with Starbursts: Opaque deep blue homogeneous glass, mold blown. The pattern is a waffle design with an eight-pointed starburst on alternating panels. The upper neck area contains 12 curved vertical ribs. Believed to be of European origin; possibly English. Circa 1900 – 1915. The bottom is embossed "Ro 238856." 4⅞" tall; very scarce! **$70.00 – 80.00** pair.

Harris collection

Zippered Borders: Clear ruby stained thin glass, mold blown. This is a square shaker with gently curving sides and zippered corners. While Bill Heacock speculated the pattern is possibly Northwood, we could not find any substantiating literature to verify his theory. The ruby staining was created for marketing to the various circus, carnivals, fairs, etc. so that various individual attendees could purchase on-the-spot personalized souvenir etched engraving. Circa 1898 – 1903. 3½" tall x 1⅝" wide; 2" wide from corner to corner. Also produced in cranberry. Very scarce! **$65.00 – 80.00.**

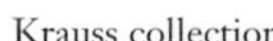

Krauss collection

Wheel, Hub: Clear blue glass, mold blown. The pattern name is based upon its shape. The shaker appears to be similar to the mold used on "Baby Thumbprint, Bulging" (our Vol. II, p. 201) but, this shaker has no thumbprints; it has a smooth surface inside and out. The exterior contains eight dotted arrows divided by vertical painted lines. Circa 1894 – 1900. Very scarce! **$65.00 – 80.00.**

Krauss collection

Wolf Hound: Clear uncolored glass, mold blown. The pattern name describes this shaker pretty well. We are not knowledgeable of all the various dog breeds, but, it is our understanding that this well defined metal head is reminiscent of a wolf hound dog. The head screws onto the glass body and does not have the typical glass eyes found on the Farber-type animal and bird shakers which were imported by Farber from Czechoslovakia. 2¼" tall. Circa 1928 – 1939. Very scarce! **$105.00 – 120.00.**

Rathbun collection

Wide & Narrow Striped Barrel: Clear cranberry opalescent glass, dual mold blown. Identical barrel shaped shakers; one containing wide vertical opalescent stripes and the other narrow ones. Circa 1887 – 1891. 3" tall with two-piece metal tops. Very scarce! **$210.00 – 225.00** each.

Zippered Corner, Ring Necked: Translucent ruby stained souvenir glass, mold blown. As the pattern name indicates, the shaker is square shaped with zippered corners and a protruding neck ring. From our perspective this seems to have been a very marketable pattern since several glass factories produced similar versions; no doubt because the plain square stained panels provided ease of individual engraving at the various fairs, circuses, etc. Heacock stated that this shaker pattern was probably produced at National's Cambridge from a Northwood mold.[57] Circa 1900 – 1905. 3" tall x 1⅞" wide. Scarce! **$40.00 – 50.00.**

Lockwood collection

Reproductions, Look Alikes, Reissues, and Fakes

By formal dictionary definition, the word "imitation" encompasses all of the aforesaid word titles of this section of our book; each of these individual titles stipulates items that, in one way or another, represent a produced product that imitates a genuine original piece. Unless specifics are intended, we will use the word "imitation" to represent produced items that are not old original and authentic throughout this book.

Nevertheless, in the antique trade it seems that many like to use the word "reproduction" to cover all of the aforementioned categories. Then, as an individual discussion progresses, the precise subject possibly becomes refined into more specific detail; i.e., "reproduction," "look alike," "reissue," etc. Be that as it may, it all too often means that somebody has purchased something (usually for too much money) because it was thought or represented to be an old, genuine, authentic antique.

In our opinion, one of the principal reasons for the existence of very few published books relative to imitation "antiques and collectibles" guidance is based upon the fact that it takes years of specialization, ability, and experience to be able to discern what comprises an individual fake, look alike, reissue, or reproduction from an original (genuine) manufactured item.

The collector often hears that most imitations are recognizable and can be readily detected by the individual who knows what to look for; such as the item being priced way below market value; pattern variations involving design details, size, weight; absence of visual indications of natural wear; and the presence of colors or decorations that were never used on the authentic originals (more particulars on this later). Sounds Relatively easy! Doesn't it?

However, the truth of the matter is that none of the aforementioned evaluations can be made without *experience and knowledge!*

Experience: Activity that includes training, observation of practice, and personal participation.
Knowledge: Acquaintance with facts; range of information, awareness, or understanding. All that has been perceived or grasped by the mind; learning; enlightenment.

How Can The Collector Attain This?

Begin by specialized collecting after the decision has been made as to what type of antiques appeal the most to you and will provide the most collecting enjoyment. Specialization along with experience and knowledge makes a happy collector.

Next, spend as much of your available time as you can obtaining and reading books written by experts that address your category. Many such books are available through your local library. If you are a beginner, the bibliography at the back of this book will be of considerable help in furthering your collecting perception and knowledge. Books that are listed as being out of print can usually be obtained by your local library processing a request for a book loan (on your behalf) from their state library.

Go to as many of the antique shops and malls as possible; engage in conversations with dealers that seem to feature the type of items that you collect. Attend antique shows to further your knowledge of what is currently being sold and the latest prices associated with your area of interest.

Because of the personal interaction involved, auctions can be entertaining; but until you are an advanced collector, monetary participation can be risky. If you wish to go for the learning experience, get there early so that you can carefully scrutinize any merchandise within your category of interest that will be offered for sale; take special note of the physical condition of each item. Be aware that just because a piece is sold in conjunction with many old things, this does not necessarily mean that it too is old or authentic.

Remember that few, if any, auctioneer's statements relative to a piece being presented on the auction block are binding on the auction house involved. The name of the auction game is "caveat emptor" (let the buyer beware)! Go to the auction house office and obtain a copy of the rules that govern how the auction of interest will be conducted. After reading them, you may decide (as we sometimes have) to leave before the auction commences.

Through the learning and buying experience, many collectors try to develop the identity of well recognized dealers that have established a reputation for honesty and reliability and will stand behind what they offer for sale. It may cost a bit more to obtain this type of purchasing security, but should a piece turn out to be something other than what was represented, return of the item will usually result in a monetary refund. It has been our personal experience that reputable dealers do not knowingly handle imitations.

Today's collector, whether beginner or advanced, will be well advised to join one of the national organizations (clubs or societies) that exist and specialize in your collection category of interest. They comprise discrete groups of advanced collectors and experts; and each club publishes some type of periodical newsletter containing information of general interest to its membership. The revelation and tracking of reproductions is one of the subjects covered within many club periodicals.

Whenever a purchase is made, a sales slip (from the seller) should be obtained. Each receipt should list the seller's name, address, phone number, and a concise description of each item and the amount paid for it by the buyer. If the purchase was made on an "as is" basis, this should also be noted. This is not only a good business practice, but can go a long way toward settling customer disputes should any arise at a later time.

Now Let's Specifically Discuss Antique Glassware Imitations

Speaking from an overall perspective, today's glassware field is mined with reproductions, reissues, look alikes, fakes, and forged marks (sometimes called "signatures") that have plagued glass collectors for many years. The total subject encompasses an almost infinite amount of material and information. The aforesaid categories of imitation glassware are defined as follows:

Reproductions: Copies of originals produced from new molds.
Reissues: Glassware produced from old original molds.
Look alikes: A glass form that imitates the original pattern motif but was never part of the pattern's original production.
Fake: Changing an item from its original form for the purpose of obtaining increased market selling value.

Speaking of forged marks/signatures: Many collectors and dealers erroneously believe that signed or trademarked glassware is safe to purchase. Since signed pieces usually command a higher price than an unsigned piece, the unscrupulous are only too happy to supply the antique market with scarce/rare pieces containing forged signatures and trademarks.

By way of examples, we have seen glass items that were manufactured by Sinclair marked "Frederick Carder" or "Steuben." The similarity of items produced by these two glasshouses can be very confusing to the uninitiated. A forger will always go for a Carder/Steuben signature because it will bring the highest selling price.

In the case of Tiffany glassware, the antique universe is full of phony signatures. Unfortunately, many collectors and dealers don't realize this; often because they want to believe! So...play it safe!

Never purchase an expensive piece of glass based upon a seller represented signature or trademark alone.

Do not shop/buy by announcing that you are looking for signed or trademarked items.

If an unknown seller offers you a signed piece, ask if the signature/trademark is genuine and if it has been authenticated? You may find the answer to be most interesting. Remember, signed pieces are attached to a high price tag, so ascertain if the seller is willing to stand behind it in writing. A knowledgeable seller will agree.

There is a lot of personal satisfaction in finding, buying, and owning a fine piece of glass that has been produced by gifted glassware designers and gaffers. With careful analysis and study you will learn to recognize the craftsmanship and style of different companies. Each glass factory had its own designs, colors, and controls. Once such knowledge is attained, you won't ask if the piece has been signed. You will know through your own knowledge and analysis if a potential purchase is genuine or not.

Use of a Longwave Black Light for Glassware Examination

Use of a black light involves the employment of ultraviolet radiation (UV) which is a type of light that is not visible to the human eye. When a selected surface is scrutinized by black light illumination exposure, it is subjected to dense, invisible particle radiation that may result in various eye visible colors of reactive fluorescence.

As a consequence, black light is often useful in the examination of glassware due to the fact that the matter contained in the various material types being inspected, reacts to release a visible light variance that the eye can detect. For example, an old authentic item will many times contain certain chemicals that have not been used in a newer contemporary imitation piece. As a result, the old original unit will usually procure a different detectable color fluorescence from its imitation counterpart.

There are several detection advantages that are useful to the collector and dealer relative to long wave black light examination of antique glassware. Proper usage will often provide detection of surface blemishes, chipping/cracks, decoration discontinuities, added material repairs such as polymers or clear plastic resins, and the presence of basic chemical constituents that cause each glass type to radiate a specific color fluorescence illumination. Due to the fact that black light techniques require detailed guidance, we have provided a reference bibliography if more individual detailed instruction is desired.

The Imitation Glassware Problem Accelerates

Prior to 1960, many glass manufacturers avoided becoming involved in making imitations. However, various economical impacts eventually forced various American factories to join in this lucrative business to help keep their business in operation.

Most American manufacturers that produced a reproduction or imitation glass object represented it as such. Some companies did this by marking each item with their name or trademark. However, many of the identification markings were (and still are) in the form of a paper stick-on label. Once purchased, the paper labels could be easily removed or lost and the pieces could then be represented as originals. Such ware can be very confusing to the new or uninitiated collector; many of whom depend to a great extent upon the integrity of dealers when they make a purchase from them.

Reproductions, copies, and reissues from the 1960s and early 1970s are having the most serious impact upon today's antique glass collectors and dealers; particularly those folks that have entered the glassware field within the last decade or so.

By way of a prominent example: For many years a wide variety of Victorian glass patterns have been reissued and reproduced by the L. G. Wright Glass Company of New Martinsville, West Virginia.

Beginning in the late 1930s, Wright became a serious purchaser of old glass molds from departed early American glass factories. Wright contracted with such outstanding glass factories as Fenton, Imperial, Fostoria, and Westmoreland to reissue glass using old original molds, and the resultant wares were sold by Wright to various dealers, jobbers, and wholesale outlets.

As one might expect, many of these glass patterns ultimately found their way into various antique shows, shops, and malls throughout America. Any markings (if such originally existed) by paper label had long since disappeared and this ware could be represented as old pieces. Now that 20 to 40 years have passed, many of these pieces have acquired some visual wear, which adds still further to the difficulty of identifying them from the authentic original Victorian patterns.

Over the years, the importance of the L. G. Wright account at Fenton was considerable. As the years passed by, the many contracts amounted to hundreds of thousands of dollars involving what Fenton called "private mold work."

According to Fenton factory records beginning in 1959, a six year period involved almost $600,000 of glassware that was delivered to L. G. Wright from Mr. Wright's personally owned molds. In 1965 Fenton produced 125 pressed glass and 140 blown forms for Wright. The pressed ware consists of at least 25 Daisy & Button patterns, a large quantity of covered animal dishes, and assorted goblets and compotes.

The blown ware involved lamp fonts and lamp shades in both ruby overlay and various opalescent colors, large pitchers, tobacco jars, barber bottles, cruets, sugar shakers, toothpicks, tumblers, and salt and pepper shakers. Wright died in 1969, but the business has been continued by members of his family. Periodically, additional reorders involving some of the better selling reproductions and reissues were placed by the Wright factory throughout the 1970s and 1980s.

It is true that few glassware imitations can pass as authentic if placed side-by-side with an original piece. However, it is also obvious that few collectors have the luxury of being able to do so, since individual possession of both the authentic and imitation item would be required.

Details and Aspects of the Imitation Glassware Issue

From our many years of collecting and studying the antique glass market place, it has become readily evident that certain types of antique and collectible glass categories are subject to a larger production volume of imitation items than others. Production costs associated with ease of manufacture, often decided which categories would be imitated. The following discussions will highlight some of the more prominent imitation glass categories that plague current collectors and dealers.

Tumblers

Synonymous with cruets, toothpicks, salt and pepper, and sugar shakers, this ware was made in all shapes and patterns and encompasses the entire Victorian glassware universe.

In terms of reproductions and reissues, we believe that tumblers currently rank in the second position behind toothpicks due to their relationship to lower factory production and labor costs. As a result, today's retail market is loaded with imitations.

This highly collectible glass category consists of three genus classifications; viz. art glass, pattern glass and carnival glass. While many tumbler patterns were sold as part of a water set with a companion pitcher, they were also sold boxed in groups of four, six, eight, etc. by themselves. The various art, pattern, and carnival glass types are often collected on a singular basis and are displayed by collectors within their home in this manner.

Examples of art glass tumbler imitations include Amberina, Plated Amberina (primarily from Europe), Burmese, Maize, Coralene, Holly Amber, Mother of

Pearl Satin Glass, and New England, Mt. Washington, and Wheeling Peachblow just to name a prominate few.

Examples in pressed and mold blown pattern glass include Cranberry (both hand decorated and plain), Cranberry Opalescent (particularly in Coin Spot, Thumbprint, and Inverted Thumbprint, and Stars and Stripes), Hobnail (all colors) and Hobnail opalescent, Daisy and Button (all colors including Pressed Amberina), Cactus (in Chocolate and many non-original colors), Ruby Thumbprint, Spanish Lace (in Cranberry opalescent and Vaseline), and Carnival glass patterns etc.

Over the years we became involved in collecting individual tumblers with our daughter Ellen. It wasn't very long before we ran into a glaring example of existing collector confusion involving various imitation tumblers being sold that had been produced by L. G. Wright's creation of the Northwood "N in a circle" signature appearing on the bottom exterior surface of some of their reproduction patterns that had never been made by Northwood. Fortunately, we were able to communicate with other advanced collectors and determined that authentic Northwood tumblers were all signed with the aforesaid trademark/signature on the inside bottom.

A primary collector general defense against tumbler imitations is the "random wear test" by use of ten power magnification. Old authentic original tumblers should portray random wear marks on top rims and on the bottom. Consider any uniform pattern wear marks to have been artificially created for purposes of deception. Carefully check pattern detail and quality. If the piece has been hand painted/decorated, some paint wear should be noticeable. An old authentic Victorian table tumbler was generally put to use within the dining area and did not escape the many washings associated with its use.

Imitation Glass Salt Shakers

Despite the fact that antique Victorian glass salt and pepper shakers have not (as a whole genus) been given a top priority by the various firms that participate in creating imitation and fake glassware; the point is rapidly approaching where this type of glassware is more frequently appearing as part of today's confusing collecting scene.

To compensate for the growing shortage of quality shakers, a more concerted effort is being expended to assure a more vigorous turnover and profit within this sphere of glassware collecting.

Inasmuch as antique glass salt shakers comprise our speciality, we have made it a point to track imitation shakers for many years. In fact, the aforesaid is the primary reason why we decided to include a special section in Vol. III that will update our readers as to where things stand in today's salt shaker retail market place. The unscrupulous are very much out there!

Since the initial publishing of our 1992 (now Vol. II) antique art and pattern glass salt shaker book, we had acquired some additional unlisted shakers that displayed certain glass characteristics that caused us to think that they might have been produced by the Fenton Art Glass Co. of Williamstown, West Virginia. The quantity of shakers in question amounted to more than a dozen different patterns; so a trip to the Fenton factory to meet with Frank Fenton was arranged during the late fall of 1994.

During the course of our several hours of discussion with Frank, and excluding the past Fenton private mold work contracted for by L. G. Wright, we inquired as to why the Fenton glasshouse had not produced a larger quantity of salt and pepper patterns over the many decades that they have been in business?

We were particularly curious as to why no shakers had been made in the beautiful Fenton Burmese glass that the factory has periodically manufactured since the 1960s?

Frank's reply was very straightforward. "Over time, the factory marketing experience had revealed that salt shakers cost too much money to manufacture versus the monetary profit that would be realized. Also, they did not sell (as an individual entity) in sufficient quantity to the general public."

To us, his answer provided additional conclusive verification of our observations as to why antique glass salt shakers (as a category) have enjoyed much less imitation production distribution than some of the other imitation glass categories that we have presented.

Personal experience has confirmed the aforesaid to be particularly true relative to the various types of Victorian art glass shakers originally made by such outstanding glass factories as Mt. Washington/Pairpoint, New England Glass Co., Hobbs Brockunier, Moser, Webb, Tiffany, Steuben, etc. To state it another way: Why should modern day glass producers and distributors bother imitating salt shakers in recognized art glass patterns when there is more profit to be realized from reproducing such ware in the form of a toothpick, tumbler, vase, or cruet?

Of course, the aforesaid is not true where mold blown and pressed pattern glass salt shakers are involved. The private mold work contracted out to the previously mentioned large American glass factories by L. G. Wright accounted for a large portion of the imitation salt and pepper shakers that have been distributed over time; particularly during the 1960s and 1970s.

Of course, smaller factories such as St. Claire, Summit Art Glass, Boyd's Crystal Art Glass, L. E. Smith Glass Co., Fostoria Glass Co., Pilgrim Glass Co., etc. produced such ware to a lesser degree in the form of reproductions, look alikes, and reissues.

Since this book primarily addresses antique glass salt shakers, known imitations are exposed throughout it on a pattern by pattern basis. Unfortunately, things have reached the point where a special color book could now be produced on the subject instead of just simply revealing to the reader that a shaker has been imitated.

We will begin our imitation glass salt shaker revelations with the details of a special study that we conducted involving the reproduction of the Mt. Washington/Pairpoint Tomato pattern form:

Mt. Washington Tomato Salt & Pepper Reproductions (Collectors' Alert)

The original patent for the Mt. Washington Tomato salt and pepper shaker was issued to Albert Steffin on December 31, 1889, via patent No. 19,539. Within the original patent verbiage it mentions that the shaker is shaped in the form of a tomato; hence, the pattern name that has been assigned to this ware.

The information we are presenting is the result of several years of personal research, investigation, and verification. None of our data is based upon hearsay!

Both beginners and advanced collectors have been fooled (or at least confused) by the Tomato salt shaker reproductions that we are illustrating.

We wish to thank Stan and Shirley McElderry who made it possible for us to make direct side-by-side visual comparisons between the reproduction and authentic Mt. Washington Tomato shakers. Barbara White also contributed her knowledge to some of the comparative data gathering and analysis.

How It All Began

During our attendance at a 1993 antique glassware convention, many collectors (including us) became fascinated by an individual display of an extraordinary looking pair of cased glass Tomato salt and pepper shakers. One was color shaded rose to white, the other blue to white. Neither shaker contained any exterior HP decoration (see illustrations).

Close visual inspection disclosed that each one of these shaded cased glass colorations had been created by the classic gaffer technique of reheating the appropriate heat sensitive glass layer at the glory hole during the manufacturing process. Production of this ware required the use of a dual mold process.[1]

With the owner's permission, the shakers were photographed and again carefully scrutinized by Mildred and I along with another highly experienced art glass dealer friend (Victor Buck).

Subsequent discussion resulted in our mutual agreement that these shakers were contemporary reproductions; definitely not authentic Mt. Washington/Pairpoint ware.

Bacon collection

Reproduction Tomato forms of 1993 convention

Bacon collection

Bottom view of cased glass reproduction Tomato shakers: A few random darker blue glass bubbles are present on the blue-to-white shaded lobes. The camera was unable to pick up any random bubbles within the bottom white lobed area of the pink-to-white shaker. However, our top view photo does show at least one of the white random bubbles that is present in the darker pink area of one of the glass lobes.

Bacon collection

Top view of cased glass reproduction Tomato shakers

Additional Investigative Facts

Since the aforesaid 1993 encounter, an additional three years of subsequent investigation has taken place relative to the aforementioned Tomato reproduction matter. The following additional data has been acquired for dissemination to our readers:

1. The authentic Mt. Washington Tomato form was produced from homogeneous in-the-mix ingredients. Consequently, a dual mold production process was not required.

2. No original factory catalogs, trade journals, ads, or previously authored antique publications have been located that stipulate there was ever any production of authentic Mt. Washington Tomato shakers in cased glass.

3. Mt. Washington/Pairpoint did produce some of their Tomato shakers in their classic Burmese and Mt. Washington Peachblow art glass processes which required specific formulated homogeneous heat sensitive metal (glass) batches.

4. Two additional cased glass Tomato shaped items have been located that are configured as a perfume with an attached metal atomizer. We have personally confirmed that it is possible to attach an authentic two-piece Tomato salt shaker top in place of an atomizer; thus, allowing the creation of a fake salt or pepper shaker.

5. A well known Midwest auction house advertised and auctioned off a cased glass Tomato form containing a cemented-on non-perforated top. Their preauction catalog advertised the piece as "Mt. Washington Peachblow," despite the fact that the item's coloration amounted to a pink shaded type colored glass. Despite such an obvious advertising error, the piece was sold-off at a final bid of more than $500.00.

Authentic Mt. Washington Peachblow Glass

By way of further clarification and understanding, let's refresh our memories as to what comprises authentic Mt. Washington Peachblow:

The tradename papers of Peachblow – Peach Skin glassware were filed by Frederick S. Shirley on July 20, 1886. The ware consists of a homogeneous, single layered, heat sensitive glass that shades from pink at the top down to a pale blue. If a piece has been subjected to an outer surface satinized treatment (as many pieces were) the pale blue portion tends to portray a slightly gray coloration.

Actually, the Peachblow glass formula is a variation of the patented Mt. Washington Burmese formula. Peachblow was created by the addition of cobalt or copper as a colorant in place of the oxide of uranium used to produce Burmese glassware.

When the initial glass batch emerges from the furnace it is colored blue; the portion of the piece that is subsequently subjected to refiring at the glory hole causes the blue to change to a pink color. Because this is a single layered homogeneous glass, the color shading will be visible on both the inner and outer surfaces.

The majority of this art glass was produced satinized (acid treated or grit blasted). Both free and mold blown items were made, and exterior hand-decorated pieces are considered to be choice and very rare. Due to poor Victorian consumer sales, historical records show that this type of Peachblow glass was produced for less than one year by Mt. Washington.

However, the Mt. Washington Tomato form (by itself) was a popular Victorian consumer pattern. In addition to Burmese and Mt. Washington Peachblow salt and pepper shakers, this form was also produced in sugar shakers. Both forms of Tomato shakers will be more frequently found to consist of opalware glass (plain and satinized) with various HP floral designs that are usually applied over a contrasting painted background.

During our many years of specialization, we have seen and handled at least several hundred authentic Tomato shakers. None comprised cased glass! Other than an occasional plain white homogeneous opalware piece, all were found to have been meticulously hand decorated; some by the Smith brothers.

McElderry collection

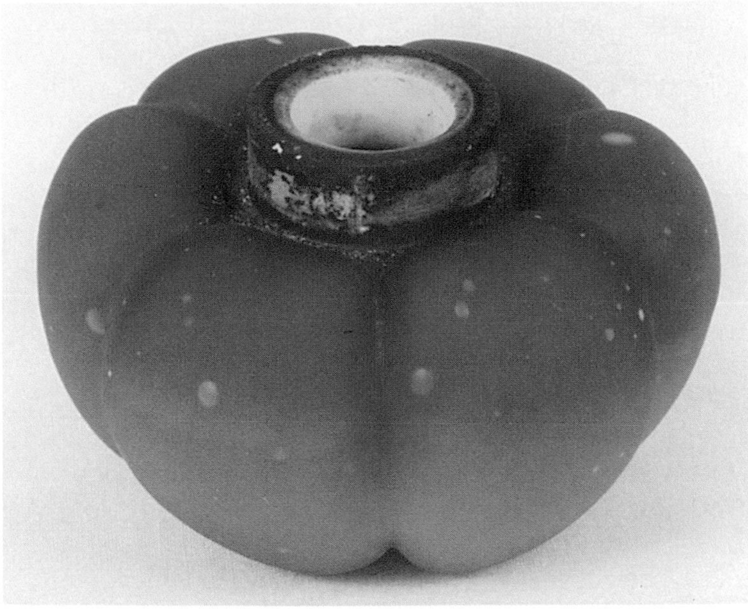

Reproduction triple cased Tomato form sold by a Midwest auction house and advertised as Mt. Washington Peachblow. Note random glass surface bubbles and ground down top opening.

McElderry collection

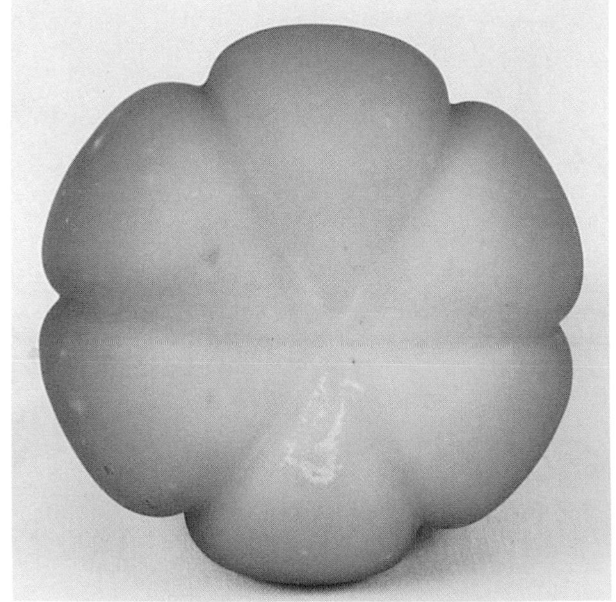

Bottom view of auction house Tomato form

Authentic vs Reproduction Side-by-side Comparison

A side-by-side comparison of the previously discussed auction sold, pink shaded cased glass Tomato reproduction versus an authentic homogeneous, non-decorated opalware Tomato shaker disclosed several obvious differences between the two (see our various illustrations).

1. The triple cased pink Peachblow reproduction contained a frosted glass outer layer. The middle layer consisted of a refired heat sensitive pink colored Peachblow-like glass that shades from deep rose at the top to a delicate pale pink at the base. The innermost layer is striking white opalware (milk glass).

2. The frosted outer layer contains obvious random air bubble distribution; an indication of questionable quality control. Mt. Washington did not produce poor quality glass Tomato shakers having haphazard surface bubbles (at least we've never seen any).

3. The cemented on metal collar, to which the screw-on metal perforated top had been attached, would not seat properly due to insufficient existing space between the repro shaker's bulging lobes and the shaker top opening. This condition was caused by the presence of the triple cased/layered glass.

4. Each of the repros six bulging lobes that formed the Tomato motif are different in appearance (shape) than the authentic Mt. Washington Tomato. This noticeable physical variation is caused by the presence of the additional outer layer of frosted glass on the reproduction shaker.

5. At the top opening, all three cased glass layers have all been ground down smooth and even. On the authentic Mt. Washington homogeneous glass Tomato that we used for comparison, the opening had been snapped off from the pontil rod and contained some irregular chipping.

6. Our visual comparison also disclosed that the repro Tomato's protruding glass top opening stood taller than the opening on the comparative Tomato shaker; this variant caused the metal collar to fit improperly and would necessitate the use of a larger amount of plaster of Paris filler compound in order to level-off the metal collar and provide a reasonably symmetrical appearance of the reproduction shaker's perforated top.

McElderry collection

Top view of authentic opalware shaker (left) vs/pink cased reproduction (right): Difference in lobe shape and size is clearly distinguishable. Also, the ground-down top opening of the cased glass layers is readily apparent.

McElderry collection

Side view with threaded metal part of two-piece top in place: Note the difference in height of the top opening between the reproduction and authentic shakers. The extra height on the reproduction has a deleterious affect on top emplacement and symmetry.

It is significant to note that in the case of each of the aforementioned reproduction shakers that we have investigated, it appears that these cased Tomato forms had been converted (from a lidded box or perfume, etc.) to salt/pepper shakers (probably) by a previous seller.

Also, of momentous importance is the fact that all of the reproduced Tomato forms that have been unearthed so far, are essentially in mint condition and contain no Mt. Washington type of HP exterior surface decorations. Any application of modern HP decoration would be a dead giveaway to any experienced collector. The original Mt. Washington enamels were a special formulated type of paint that required additional kiln firing to set the paint; a very expensive process in terms of today's artists and the labor costs involved.

Therefore, as a result of their unique appearance and design, it is readily understandable why these little reproduction cuties present quite a striking appearance and can create a considerable purchasing dilemma to both beginning and advanced salt shaker collectors. If one is discovered for sale, the asking price will probably be high. However, your purchasing decision is simple! The authentic Mt. Washington Tomato salt shaker was not produced in cased glass.

As a twentieth century collectible, these cased forms do have value as long as they are properly represented and are not being offered as authentic Mt. Washington Tomato shakers from the Victorian era.

It has been concluded that these repro cased glass Tomatoes are of reasonably good quality; probably imported from Europe during 1950s or 1960s. Thus, while the aforementioned cased shakers have the general Tomato shape, authentic Mt. Washington/Pairpoint shakers they are not!

Imitation Glass Salt Shaker Examples

The Argonaut Shell (Argonaut) pattern was abundantly reissued by L. G. Wright circa 1969 from old original Northwood molds in the toothpick, salt shaker, tumbler, sauce dish, butter dish, compote, creamer, sugar bowl, as well as other types of bowls such as a master berry etc.

Most of the aforesaid pieces were done in flat colored custard, pale blue opalescent, and clear glass forms. Much of the custard was not decorated with gold; those pieces that do have a gold coloration are a dead giveaway because a cold, unfired type of paint was used.

In 1993 we ran across two dealers that had a show booth full of various Wright produced colored custard pieces that didn't seem to realize that their items were not genuine Northwood glass. Everything was being offered for sale at a premium price. One of the salt shakers contained an embossed underlined "N" that was attached to an enclosing circle by an additional line giving it a deformed "W appearance. In an attempt to sell the shaker, considerable verbiage was expended in trying to convince us that the shaker was a signed Northwood piece. We simply told them that their custard colored pieces were not authentic and walked away.

We are illustrating a 2⅞" tall imitation L. G. Wright (undecorated) Argonaut custard salt shaker. For more detail relative to an authentic Northwood Argonaut shaker refer to our Vol. II, page 168.

Argonaut Shell

Authors' collection

Rathbun collection

These chocolate glass shakers were produced by Westmoreland for the L. G. Wright firm circa 1970s from old Northwood molds that Cy Wright acquired during the 1930s. Of course, the Argonaut Shell pattern was never originally produced by the Northwood factories in chocolate glass. Each shaker is 3" tall.[2]

Bulging Three Petal

Authors' collection

Numerous reproductions of this Consolidated Lamp and Glass Company pattern began appearing during the 1960s. What initially flagged their existence to us was the fact that suddenly we would see at least one or two dealers that had this pattern for sale at major antique shows in cased pink, blue, yellow, and green colors. The overall quality of these sets is excellent and since 30 to 40 years have gone by, the reproductions have now become widely disbursed into various collections throughout the country.

To us, the most surprising thing was that (when queried) a high percentage of the selling dealers did not seem to realize that they were selling reproduction shakers and condiment sets with the companion dome-shaped matching pattern glass base.[3]

The Bulging Three Petal pattern was originally produced in both cased and single layered homogeneous glass. Due to the exceptional quality of the cased reproductions, the primary method of identifying the authentic shakers is to look for random intaglio chipping in between the cased layers along the threaded top edge. The cased reproduction shakers are smooth and evenly polished throughout their top cased glass edges.

Unfortunately, there were (and still are) sellers that will have authentic, top chipped, shakers ground off smooth for aesthetic reasons before offering them for sale. A major mistake!

The authentic single layer homogeneous shakers contain normal factory produced fine edge chipping around their threaded tops; caused from being snapped off the pontil rod by the gaffer.

As an alternate insight, we are illustrating a pair of yellow cased shakers showing a side-by-side comparison of an authentic shaker (left) versus a reproduction (right). By close visual comparison the reader can see a slight size difference between the top bulging petal of each shaker.

Realistically, the average potential purchaser would be hard pressed to make a decision with nothing to compare against. However, the pictured authentic shaker also contains the intaglio chipping previously described.

It is our opinion that the reason that this pattern has not enjoyed much higher monetary appreciation over the years is because of the numerous previously discussed reproductions that have been produced and sold. These quality reproductions do have value; but it is our policy not to get involved in pricing imitation glassware. The purchasing decision is up to the reader!

Cane Woven

In our Vol. II salt shaker book we illustrated an authentic "Cane Woven" custard glass shaker produced by the Coudersport Tile & Ornamental Glass Co. factory.[4] Within our pattern descriptive verbiage we stated that it had been stipulated by Peterson that this pattern had been reproduced in Japan.

We have subsequently verified that this shaker has been reproduced in Japan because we have acquired one of the imitation shakers in our collection with the bottom containing a "Made in Japan" paper label.

Lockwood collection

A frosted cased, yellow/orange colored reproduction (left) beside a homogeneous bright pink colored authentic shaker (right). The exterior acid etched glass layer of the reproduction is relatively thin. The top opening of the reproduction is larger; which is clearly revealed by the size of the metal top.

Authors' collection

A pair of the same color cased glass reproductions having identical metal tops. With tops removed. the reproduction shakers have the same 2½" height as the authentic shakers.

Cockle Shell

The authentic Mt. Washington/Pairpoint art glass "Cockle Shell" shaker has always been a difficult pattern to acquire. The collectibility is high and today's market place retail value continues to soar as various advanced collectors attempt to seek out one (or two) that are available for purchase.

Within the last twelve months (1996 – 97) we have become aware that this pattern has been reproduced in a 4¾" tall x 4" wide light blue thick glass with a threaded top opening. Our illustrative photograph was provide by AAGSSCS member Dean Armstrong.

However, any collector/dealer that has ever seen or handled an authentic "Cockle Shell" shaker is aware that these thin delicate shakers were specifically designed to utilize a special shell-shaped, sterling silver push-on top; and that their glass top opening is not threaded.[5] There is also the fact that the authentic shakers contained quality HP exterior surface decoration. We say "exterior" because none have ever been seen (or reported) in "Napoli" decorated art glass.

Any modern HP decorative application to an imitation shaker will raise an instant repro caution flag, to a serious collector, because the original Mt. Washington/Pairpoint paints were a special formulated type that necessitated additional kiln firings to achieve proper paint brilliance and adherence; a very expensive process in terms of today's labor and artist costs.

A question that is often asked by collectors is why the salt, pepper, and sugar "Cockle Shell" shakers are usually found without a holding support stand? The answer is contained within Catalog No. 10 dated 1894 by the Pairpoint Mfg Company. On page 12 there is a pair of salt and pepper "Cockle Shell" shakers being offered for sale within a plush lined box for 92 cents. The availability of an original Pairpoint silver-plated holding stand containing these shakers is not advertised or mentioned in the aforesaid catalog.

After our many years of specialization and research, it is both reasonable and logical that the large "Cockle Shell" sugar shaker was also sold in the same manner. So far, no one has ever verified the existence of any type of original Pairpoint stand that was designed to hold a "Cockle Shell" sugar shaker.

Armstrong collection

Reproduction "Cockle Shell" pattern with threaded glass top opening

No. 234. Assorted Decorated Glass.
Per Set, $ .92

1894 Pairpoint Mfg. Co. Catalog ad showing "Cockle Shell" shakers for sale within a plush lined box.

McElderry collection

Authentic Mt. Washington/Pairpoint salt and pepper shakers retained within a fake silver-plated holding stand. This set sold at a prominent Midwest auction house for $900.00 during 1995.

McElderry collection

McElderry collection

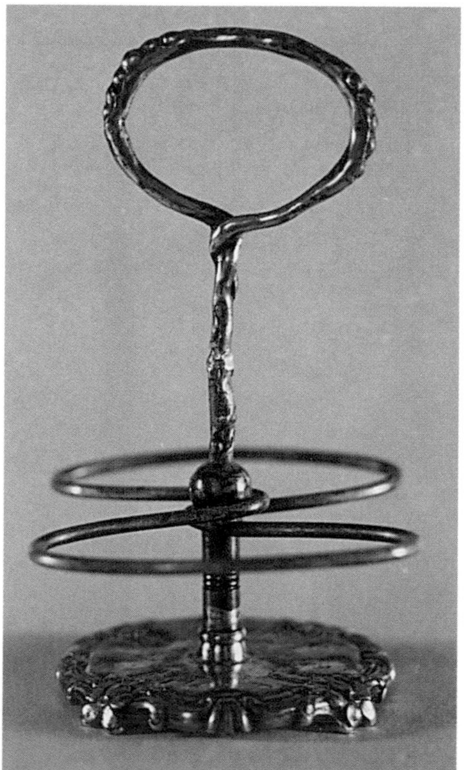

Authentic "Cockle Shell" shakers and Pairpoint holding stand

Fake Glass Bearded Columbus Salt Shaker

Fostoria Museum collection

Fostoria Museum collection

Fostoria Museum collection

Columbus, Bearded: Opaque white opalware, mold blown. The reader is looking at various views of an authentic Bearded Columbus shaker bust that has been changed into a fake by the addition of painted light brown hair, a reddish orange coat of mail, and a blue painted supporting base along with blue eyes. A fake is defined as "changing an item from its original form for the insidious purpose of increasing value." When this shaker was originally produced by the Novelty Glass Co. circa 1892, it was plain basic opalware (milk glass) with a gilt goofus colored paint applied to the beard, mustache, and religious embossed necklace cross.[6] Whoever applied the aforementioned colored paints didn't bother to remove the original gilt paint that still remained on the shaker. As a result, it can be seen at various locations penetrating through the colored paints that have been added. This fake colored piece is a good conversation piece with a seriously impacted monetary value. We brought the existence of this fake shaker to the attention of the Fostoria Glass Museum, Fostoria, Ohio. As a result, the museum has acquired it from the dealers that had it for sale and we presume that it is now available for public viewing.

"Elephant, tall" Pattern (Description of Original Authentic Shaker)

Lockwood collection

Elephant, Tall: Translucent clear, lightweight glass, mold blown (see our illustration). The pattern name describes this unusual shakers form. The translucent effect is caused by a busy pattern that depicts a standing elephant fully clothed in coat tails with hands in pockets standing on a platform. This appears to be one of those early candy containers that was configured for dual usage; candy first, and later as a salt or pepper condiment dispenser. This ware is also sought after by figurine bottle collectors. The shaker is pictured in the Peterson Salt Shaker book on page 160-D. Circa 1925 – 1935. 4⅞" tall. Rare! **$350.00 – 385.00.**

Fake Elephant, Tall Shaker

Lesley and Dick Harris provided us with an authentic "Tall Elephant" shaker that has been turned into a fake by the application of gray, brown, and black enamel paint (see our illustration). The striking coloration perhaps reflects a more quaint and picturesque looking shaker. Unfortunately, the monetary value of what was once an original piece has been seriously impacted. Since this shaker pattern is quite a rarity, not too many painted pieces are likely to turn up. It is unfortunate that the unscrupulous seem to be willing to go to such extreme lengths to create the illusion of a super rare piece in hopes of obtaining a higher profit from an inexperienced purchaser.

Harris collection

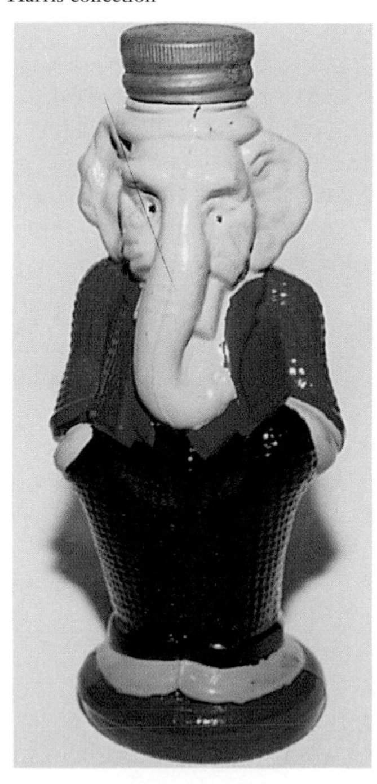

Five Lobe, Lustred

We created the aforesaid pattern name for this piece. We are not calling it a salt shaker since it did not have a two-piece perforated top attached to the top opening when it was purchased. This doesn't mean that one couldn't be emplaced. Fortunately it can't be designated as a Tomato type shaker since it does not have six lobes.

One can only speculate as to the purpose of its appearance. We say this because the piece contains random dark colored contaminates within the glass batch used to originate it.

Our deductive reasoning indicates that the illustrated (attempted) gold lustrous effect emanated from a bottom of the learning curve beginner working with a transparent yellow glass batch. To say it another way, the overall craftsmanship is dreadful. We are appreciative of Lesley and Dick Harris bringing this 2⅝" tall item to our attention so that it can be permanently flagged for our readers. Hopefully, it is only one of a kind! We certainly have never seen anything exactly like it before.

Harris collection

Harris collection

Guttate

The original, authentic, Consolidated Lamp & Glass Co. Guttate shaker pattern is from 1894. The pattern was named by S. T. Millard. The unusual title means "in the form of drops."

We first began seeing reproductions of this pattern in salt shakers during the early 1970s. The early 3" tall repros are in a triple cased, pale, washed-out frosted pink. The glass is thick, heavy, and of a larger maximum circumference; the threaded top edge cased layers are ground down smooth.

By the late 1970s a taller 3¼" triple cased, brighter colored, frosted pink version appeared, having the same general previously described characteristics, except that it used a two-piece metal chromed top.

Illustrated from the McElderry collection is an aforementioned late 1970s frosted pink cased reproduction version (right) beside an original, authentic, 3" tall pink and white variegated shaker (left). The tops have been removed from both shakers. The authentic shaker contains normal top edge roughness; the reproduction top edges have been ground off smooth.

McElderry collection

Authors' collection

Illustrated is another 3" tall frosted pink triple cased reproduction (left) beside a 2⅞" tall pink triple cased authentic shaker (right) from our collection. The authentic shaker's inside layer is white, middle layer pink, and the outer layer is thin and clear. The reproduction is considerably heavier than the authentic due to thick heavy cased layers and the threaded top edge has been ground very smooth and even. Our authentic shaker contains top edge chipping within the center threaded edging.

Authentic Holly Amber Glass

The following illustrations verify the fact that the Indiana Tumbler and Goblet Company was unable to produce consistent coloration control of their various Holly Amber (Golden Agate) glass forms. Obviously, absolute recognition of original authentic pieces has to be based upon more than specific color knowledge and experience.

Authors' collection

All three Holly Amber shakers are from the Authors' collection. To date, the salt and pepper shakers have not been reproduced. Due to rarity, color variance does not effect retail value.

Kelsay collection

Kelsay collection

The two illustrated Holly Amber condiment sets are from the Fred Kelsay collection. Note the color and opalescence difference between the two identical sets. No doubt, today's Holly Amber collectors would be happy to purchase either set. The problem is being able to find a complete set for sale. If the factory at Greentown, Indiana, hadn't burned down after less than a year of Holly Amber production, a solution to more consistent color control might have been found.

Holly Amber
1994 Selling Values (From Kelsay collection)

Compote, 7½"d., $1,000.00.

Water pitcher, $2,800.00. 4 tumblers, $450.00 each.

Bowl, 8½"d., $600.00. Sauce dish, 4½"d., $250.00 each.

Spooner, $650.00.

Butter dish, $150.00.

Nappie, handled, $500.00.

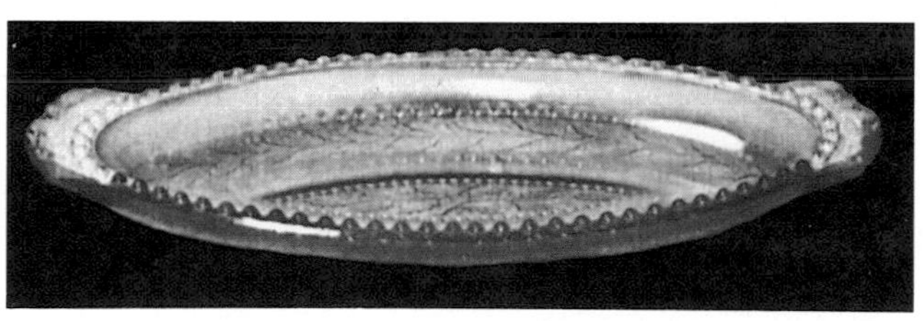

Pickle dish, two handles, $300.00.

Small toothpick, $375.00.

Homestead

This pressed glass pattern was produced during the 1880s by Bryce, Highbee & Company, Pittsburgh, Pennsylvania. This is the OMN for this pattern, apparently selected due to the fact that Homestead Glass Works was an alternate name for this factory.[7]

The pattern's principal focal point is the detailed scrolled handles that are attached to the various forms that were produced. While some of the larger items contain an engraved leaf on the front and back, all the shakers that we have observed over the years lack such engraving; no doubt because of their physical size of 2⅞" tall.

We are illustrating an authentic clear shaker (left) versus a reproduction shaker with frosted handles (right). In addition to the frosted handles, the repro scrolled handles lack detailed clarity, particularly on the lower protruding scrolls.

A. G. Peterson in his 1970 salt shaker book indicates the Homestead shakers are very scarce. We don't know which glasshouse reproduced this ware. Also, there are no indications in antique glass literature that the original pattern was produced in color.

Lockwood collection

Inverted Fan and Feather

Around the mid-1960s, this pattern was produced in a toothpick by the St. Clair Glass Works. They manufactured this item in pink slag, custard, and variety of other colors.

However, the initial color appearance of the aforesaid custard and pink slag toothpick is pallid, wan, and lacks proper color intensity. An experienced toothpick collector is not likely to be taken in by this ware. Of course, a beginner's purchasing reaction might be otherwise.

During the late 1970s, St. Clair sold their Inverted Fan & Feather imitation molds to the Summit Art Glass Co., Rootstown, Ohio. As a result, Summit produced and distributed Inverted Fan & Feather salt and pepper shakers that began appearing in a custard color at shows and flea markets during the early 1980s.

We don't understand why the illustrated 3" tall shaker that Summit produced ever got highlighted in antique glass literature as an Inverted Fan & Feather reproduction. They clearly do not resemble the authentic Northwood pattern in terms of shape, size, or pattern configuration.[8] Any collector that has ever seen an authentic shaker in this pattern would not be fooled or confused.

Authors' collection

Paneled Shell

Illustrated is a photo showing a side-by-side comparison of a genuine authentic, blue homogeneous, Consolidate Lamp & Glass Co. "Paneled Shell" shaker (left) versus a cranberry reproduction (right). The repro was produced by Fenton Art Glass circa 1990, and, the bottom of the cranberry reproduction has a Fenton paper label attached. The authentic shaker is circa 1894 – 1900.

We purchased the repro from an authorized Fenton distributor's stock that was being offered for sale to the public. The pattern mold that produced this reproduction is of excellent quality and detail; as is the handmade gaffer craftwork that produced it.

If the average collector found this shaker in a dealer's booth with an old top and the Fenton label missing it would at least create some self deliberation as to whether (or not) it was a genuine item. An inexperienced collector would probably buy it as an authentic piece.

To demonstrate one of the methods that should be used while evaluating an old mold blown shaker, we are also providing a side-by-side photo of the top threaded portion of an authentic green "Paneled Shell" shaker beside the top part of the Fenton reproduction. The reader can readily discern the normally found Victorian era factory chipping along the top edge of the green piece versus the ground-off smooth top edge of the Fenton reproduction.

Authors' collection

Authors' collection

"Paneled Shell" threaded top edge comparisons

Paneled Sprig

The "Paneled Sprig" pattern name was created by Heacock.[9] It was among the first group of patterns produced circa 1896 by Harry Northwood at his Indiana, Pennsylvania, plant in decorated opalware, emerald green, and later in ruby. Earlier colors of Rubina and blue with white speckling were made by the Northwood factory at Ellwood City, Pennsylvania.[10]

Mildred and I bought a pair of cranberry reissues around 1980 that were undoubtedly made from original Northwood molds acquired by L. G. Wright. About 10 years later we purchased another reissue in emerald green glass.

We are illustrating an emerald green reissue (left) alongside an authentic cranberry colored shaker (right) that has a smaller neck opening along with top edge chipping from having been broken off from the pontil rod. The top edge of the green shaker has been ground off smooth and has a larger opening.

McElderry collection

"Priscilla," Fostoria's Reproduction by L. G. Wright

Authors' collection

Reproduction

Authors' collection

Authentic

The original, authentic, "Fostoria's Priscilla" shaker was made by The Fostoria Glass Co., Moundsville, West Virginia, circa 1898. The pattern was patented in 1899 as their No. 30047. However, it was called "Priscilla" at the factory.[11] The six vertical panel design consists of a dainty scrolling and beading (see our illustration). This ware was originally produced in clear, green, and yellow opaque. The authentic shaker is 3" tall with fine threaded top edge chipping. The top opening has ⅞" diameter. The reproduction has the same top diameter but it is a much heavier thick glass and the top threaded edge has been ground down smooth. Our repro illustration has a cranberry stained spatter applied to the inside surface. The biggest difference is in a side-by-side embossed pattern comparison. The repro has what looks more like a hanging leaf and the upper scroll and beading have a completely different appearance. Also, the reproduction has a much larger bulbous shape. The repro base diameter is 1¼"; the authentic shaker base diameter is 1".

Refrigerator

This unusual (and highly collectible) ware (circa 1925 – 35) is configured in the form the early General Electric refrigerator of the late 1920s. These table condiment shakers were given as a gift to the consumers that purchased one of the GE appliances along with a matching lidded sugar. The original salt and pepper contained a round, black GE paper label within a recessed spot at the top of the embossed refrigerator door (see illustration). All three rare authentic (original) pieces have a top that portrays the metal spiral coil that is present on the early functional GE refrigerators. The separately illustrated recent reproduction (from the Harris collection) lacks both the top coil and paper label recessed spot on the door. The authentic shakers are 2⅞" tall; the matching sugar is 3⅝" tall to the top of the removable lid; reproduction shaker, 2¾" tall. Finding a salt and pepper with the black GE marked paper label(s) present is indeed a rarity today.

Harris collection

Reproduction

Authors' collection

Authentic refrigerator

Rose Viking

The original New Martinsville Glass Manufacturing Company's "Rose Viking" shaker appears in their 1904 catalog as their "No. 61 salt" which represents the original manufacturer's name for it.

Arthur Peterson in his 1970 salt shaker book states that the "Rose Viking" is a late pattern of the Viking Glass Company. However, the Viking Glass Co. was not formed until 1944 at the same New Martinsville, West Virginia, factory site. Obviously, the "No. 61 salt" is a New Martinsville Glass Manufacturing Company pattern.

Historical research has disclosed that all of the old original New Martinsville molds were used until World War II at which time they were all melted down and the iron metal sold off. However, two of the original molds were retained; one of which was the "Rose Viking" shaker pattern of which reissues were made in clear and colored glass by Viking but not in opaque glass.[12]

The 4¼" tall imitation glass shaker that we are illustrating is a clear glass reproduction shaker (not a reissue) that has been stained inside to resemble Reverse Amberina. The glass is excessively thick and the threaded top edge has been ground off smooth. We estimate the shaker to be between 10 and 15 years old. The authentic "No. 61 salt" (Rose Viking) was not produced in this glass coloration.[13]

Authors' collection

"Swirl, Opalescent" Reproduction by L. G. Wright

The original, authentic, Hobb's, Brockunier "Opalescent Swirl" shaker[14] forms have a much thinner glass and the threaded top edge was not ground down smooth; the threaded opening is 1" in diameter. The repro opening is ⅝" in diameter with the thick top edging ground down smooth. Another obvious difference is the poor control of the swirled opalescent striping; the white opalescence is smeared over into adjacent stripes at various spots on the repro shaker. For reader discernment we are illustrating two views of the reproduction shaker.

Rathbun collection

Both reproduction and authentic are 3⅜" tall.

Rathbun collection

Teardrop, Bulging
Reproduction Condiment Set

In our Vol. II book we alerted our readers to the fact that Fenton had reproduced this pattern circa the mid 1950s in opaque white, yellow, and blue.[15]

During our 1994 visit with Frank Fenton, we obtained his permission to photograph the illustrated condiment set in the yellow color while it was on display in the Fenton Factory Museum. This ware is now 40+ years old and highly collectible to the many Fenton glass collectors that include today's market place.

As is the case with all Fenton glass, the quality is outstanding. Of course, this pattern was originally produced by Dithridge & Co. of Pittsburgh, Pennsylvania, circa 1894 – 1901 in the aforementioned same opaque colors plus pink and custard.

Fenton collection

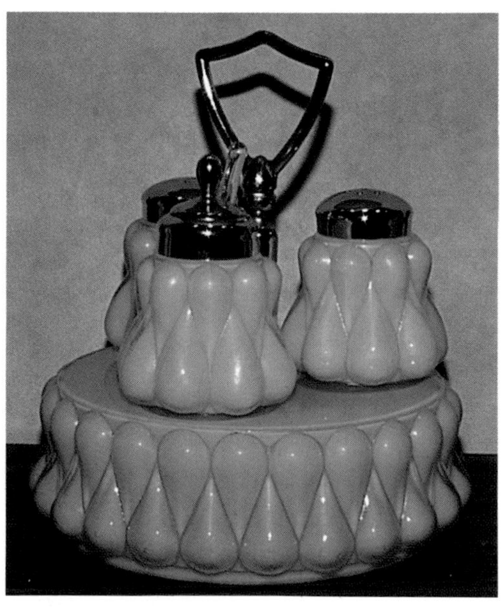

Tulip Wave Crest "Opal Atomizers"
(fake salt shaker)

Rather than list these pieces within the C. F. Monroe section of this book, we felt it would be more appropriate to illustrate them as imitation salt and pepper shakers when a two-piece metal salt shaker top has been attached. The authentic Monroe "Tulip" shakers have threaded glass tops and do not require a two-piece metal top.

We have observed these extended neck Wave Crest pieces, in the C. F. Monroe "Tulip" pattern,[16] within at least two salt shaker collections. Obviously, if such an atomizer has been reconfigured to be offered for sale as a salt shaker it becomes a fake glass form.

Subsequent investigation has revealed that one advanced Wave Crest collector has one of these "Tulip"' forms with the original atomizer and squeeze bulb attached which is what the item was originally designed function as.

During the Victorian era two-piece metal salt and pepper tops were designed to fit a wide variety of condiment dispenser top openings. Therefore, it is not too difficult to procure a two-piece top that can be emplaced upon this ware. This particular pattern is rare as an atomizer; so, if it is converted to a salt shaker, the collectibility factor rises accordingly along with an associated higher retail price.

In the case of the pair we are illustrating, the owner purchased them with the tops missing and thought that they might be salt and pepper shakers. It took a considerable amount of investigation to establish the actually intended function of these non-threaded pieces.[17]

McElderry collection

Imitation Victorian Era Glass Cruets

Victorian oil or vinegar cruets were first introduced in America during the 1880s and reached the peak of their popularity around 1900. Unfortunately, they have been heavily imitated primarily by L. G. Wright during the 1960s and early 1970s.

Because of the purchasing cost that is involved, special study should be undertaken by the collector/dealer to lessen the chance of buying reproduced/look alike pieces. Wright purchased many of the old original Northwood, Dugan, and Diamond molds and issued special contracts to Westmoreland, Fenton, etc. to have excellent reproductions made. Due to the quality of these imitations, caution is the word if anyone intends to collect/deal in this type of glassware.

One of the characteristics that can be used to determine authenticity of a Victorian cruet relates to the fact that the majority of old cruets will be found to have tiny cracks on their applied handles that are called "heat checks." Many collectors accept them as not having an impact upon a cruet's value since they were sold this way by the various producing factories. They can be identified by the fact that these checks are usually horizontal or straight lined at a slight angle. Such separations will appear on the handle and not where the handle attaches to the cruet neck. Since most of these types of cruets are near (or over) 100 years old, one should view a perfect cruet as suspect and subject it to further scrutiny and investigation.

The lack of the presence of the original stopper has an impact upon its monetary value; substitute stoppers can devalue an otherwise perfect cruet by as much as 40%. Almost all old American glass cruet stoppers have been found to be either cut or pressed (not blown). The most research involving original stopper identification was done by William Heacock in his *Encyclopedia of Colored Pattern Glass, Book 6.*

Original Northwood cruet stoppers were usually high shanked pressed faceted pieces. However, a short shanked stopper in the shape of a pagoda was used on the taller cruets such as the "S Repeat," "Everglades," and "Wild Bouquet" patterns.

Hobbs, Brockunier used a cut crystal or colored faceted stopper. Examples are the "Wheeling Peachblow" and "Satina Swirl" pattern cruets.

When Bill Heacock published his Book #6 (H-6), he was puzzled as to what form comprised the original stopper for the rare "Klondike" cruet?[18] Thanks to the detailed research by Don E. Smith, it has been confirmed that it is a solid, round ball-shaped stopper.[19] In his 1973 book *More Cruets Only*, Dean L. Murray color illustrates the correct stopper in a "Klondike" cruet shown on the second color page after the pattern index.

We have presented the aforementioned example to further highlight the monetary importance that collector/dealers attach to the presence of an original cruet stopper.

The collector should acquire speciality books written about Victorian cruets and study the republished trade and catalog ads they contain which show what the various original cruet glass stoppers looked like. Such knowledge is an excellent way to help avoid a bad purchase.

While there have been reports that new reproduction stoppers were made in new custard and chocolate glass in the Northwood faceted style during the late 1970s, we have never seen any of them (if they exist) nor have we talked with any collectors or dealers that have.

Authors' collection

This is a rare "Libbey Maize" cruet. However, the stopper is not original. Therefore, the market value should be reduced by 30% to 40%. The proper original has the same corn pattern that is present on the cruet body.

Authors' collection

Northwood wine decanter in "S-Repeat" pattern illustrating the original short-shanked pagoda stopper used on the taller cruets and decanters. Decanter is 11¾" tall including stopper. Stopper, 4⅝" in length.

Imitation Victorian Era Sugar Shakers

Sugar shakers (as they are known to current collectors) were originally called a "sugar sifter" or "sugar duster." The first shaker that we acquired (30 or more years ago) was a satinized, hand-decorated, circa 1895 "Gillender Melon." Our art glass dealer friend, Victor Buck, referred to it as a muffineer. However, in today's collecting universe the term sugar shaker encompasses all of the aforementioned titles.

Various art and pattern glass types of this ware began appearing during the early 1880s and by about 1905 had been replaced by the more utilitarian clear pressed glass and china shakers. From time to time, a few sugar shakers can also be found in cut glass patterns.

Research indicates that sugar shakers never had much practical application in the Victorian kitchen and therefore were not subjected to the rigorous wear and tear that other kitchen and table glassware items experienced, such as salt and pepper shakers for example. With the exception of occasional rusty tops, the glass bodies are generally found to be in very good to excellent condition because this ware was soon relegated to exile on the shelf of the family display cabinet for the subsequent purpose of visual enjoyment.

Because of the aforesaid relatively good physical condition and lack of random wear marks, the beginner or less experienced collector is more likely to purchase one of the quality reissues or reproductions made (for example) in such patterns as Cosmos, Opalescent Daisy and Fern, Coinspot, Nine Panel, Venetian Diamond, etc.

Beginning in the 1950s and subsequent years, there have been numerous imitations of this ware produced primarily by L. G. Wright from old original molds. Over time, we have obtained several examples in Mildred's sugar shaker collection that she deliberately purchased for comparative purposes against old authentic original patterns.

One of the better defenses against the sugar shaker repros and reissues is the application of what we call the thickness test. Antique sugar shakers were mostly mold blown items and have thin sides. In addition, they were snapped off at the top of the pontil rod by the gaffer which resulted in rough or fine-chipped top threaded edges.

This regular factory production technique retained the fine chipping because it would be hidden by each shaker's metal top. To save labor costs these shakers were sold to the Victorian customers in this condition just as salt and pepper shakers were. Sugar shakers that are offered for sale containing thick sides and ground off top glass rims are usually not old authentic pieces.

Among the various imitation sugar shakers we are illustrating is a Northwood sugar shaker with a companion lid containing a permanently attached rotary agitator that was purchased by AAGSSCS member, Mr. Scott Beale. It was sold to him as part of an authentic blue translucent glass "Leaf Mold" sugar shaker. Mr. Beale is a highly experienced art and pattern glass collector and dealer. However, he deliberately purchased the shaker with subsequent investigation in mind.

Of course, Scott had never heard of any Victorian produced sugar shakers utilizing any type of lid mounted mechanical agitator. Upon completion of his own personal investigation, he submitted the shaker and agitator to Mildred and I for comment and opinion.

In the course of our personal investigation, we involved very experienced collectors and dealers Dick Krauss, Tom Neale, and metallurgist Harold Coalmer. Harold is also an advanced art and pattern glass collec-

Beale collection

Authentic Northwood "Leaf Mold" sugar shaker with fake lid. The lid would be authentic except that it has a permanently attached fake metal agitator underneath it.

Beale collection

Sugar shaker lid with fake agitator attached

tor. With great personal interest he subjected the lid and agitator to detailed testing and analysis.

After comprehensive and collective group investigation and communication, the bottom line is everyone agreed that someone had gone to a lot of trouble to create a fake rotary agitator within an authentic Northwood sugar shaker lid.

In addition, no one was able to find any existing antique sugar shaker literature, catalogs, or trade publications that documented the production of lid mounted mechanical agitators in sugar shakers during the Victorian era.

While none of the aforesaid individuals, that became a part of the investigation, believed that mechanical agitators were ever produced for sugar shakers, the fact that one had turned up was quite unique. Since no one had ever seen or heard of such agitator usage before, it was an interesting challenge; the results of which should be recorded for both current and future collectors and dealers to be aware of.

Maize Sugar Shaker Reproduction

Authors' collection

Side by side comparison of reproduction "Maize" sugar shaker (left) with authentic "Maize" sugar shaker (right)

The L. G. Wright reproduction is pink cased; the authentic circa 1889 Libbey "Maize" shaker is homogeneous light colored ivory with HP embossed corn-shaped leaves. The reproduction has more center bulging than the authentic original.

According to Dorothy Hammond, during the 1960s L. G. Wright produced a "Maize" pickle jar, water pitcher, lamps in various sizes, rose bowl, tumbler, vases, covered candy dish, and salt and pepper shakers all in cased glass in the colors pink, rose, white, amber, and light and dark blue.[20] We have never seen any of the aforementioned reproduction salt and pepper shakers.

Nine Panel "Coinspot"

Authors' collection

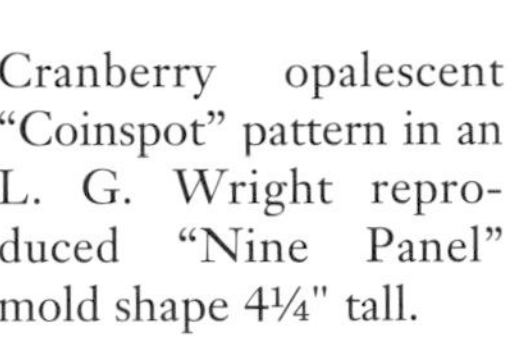

Cranberry opalescent "Coinspot" pattern in an L. G. Wright reproduced "Nine Panel" mold shape 4¼" tall.

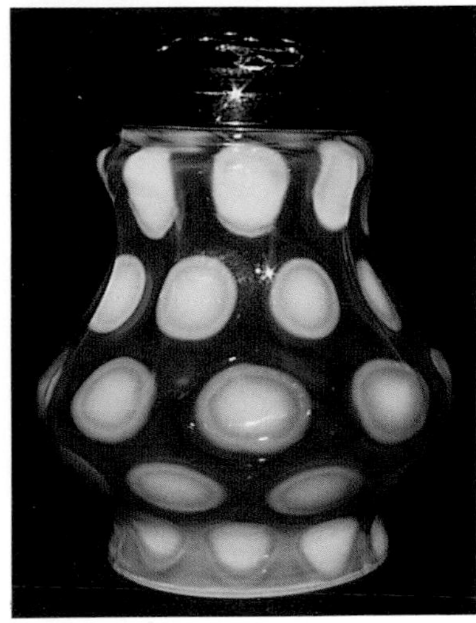

The "Nine Panel" mold shape was used by Cy Wright in several cranberry opalescent patterns.[21] Beginning in the 1930s, he built his business involving the sale of reproductions.

Our illustrated "Coinspot" pattern will not pass the thickness test. The glass is quite heavy, including the sides and base. The top opening edges have been ground-off smooth. The dark oxidized top was originally chrome plated. The shaker is from the 1960s as part of a private Wright contract with Fenton Art Glass. As a result the glass quality is excellent.

Daisy and Fern

According to Heacock,[22] the vast quantity of L. G. Wright reproductions of Daisy and Fern, from both old original Northwood/ National Glass/Dugan molds plus, other contemporary mold shapes, has

Authors' collection

Cranberry opalescent "Daisy & Fern" pattern in an L. G. Wright reproduced "Nine Panel" mold shape

essentially caused this to be a perilous pattern to collect by opalescent glass collectors.

All items in yellow opalescent or with a satinized finish are reproductions. The aforesaid old original "Daisy & Fern" molds were purchased by Cy Wright during the 1930s and he had them massively produced for his firm by Fenton.

Our illustrated sugar would not pass the thickness test; the glass sides are thick, heavy, and the top edge opening has been ground-off smooth. However, the brass-plated top is an old one.

Three Face

Authors' collection

This is a look alike copy of the "Three Face" pattern that was designed and patented by John E. Miller on June 18, 1878. No sugar shaker was ever originally produced in this pattern.

The 4½" tall illustrated shaker was purchased by Mildred during the mid-1980s at an antique show. An honest dealer sold it at a reasonable price and made no attempt to represent it as being old. The glass quality is excellent and today it apparently has a high collectibility factor because one is seldom seen for sale anymore.

Imitation Glass Toothpick Holders

According to the National Toothpick Holder Collectors Society (NTHCS) there are thousands of toothpick holder collectors throughout America. The various types cross all collection categories from glass and ceramic to wood. In terms of glassware, we have been able to trace these little cuties in art and pattern glass to as early as 1880, with the majority having been produced from 1885 to 1907.

Unfortunately, toothpicks are first in the antique glassware field when it comes to imitations. Anyone planning to collect or deal in this Victorian glassware category had better belong to the NTHCS rather than trying to go it alone. The reason toothpicks have attained this reputation within the trade is tied directly to their lower cost to manufacture.

It is essential that the collector become knowledgeable as to what colors each pattern was originally produced in. The field of toothpicks is rampant with colors that old original pieces were never made in. Use magnification assistance to check for wear marks which usually appear around the base or top rim in a random non-symmetrical fashion. Be on the lookout for ground down salt shakers. The marks left by a grinding/buffing wheel will be readily apparent by use of a 10 power magnification eye loop. If a piece looks new to you, it most likely is a reproduction or look alike. Do not hesitate to ask the seller if he/she will provide you with a right of return privilege in writing. If you get a negative answer, walk away! There is not much point in spending money when you are not sure what you will be buying.

Never purchase art glass toothpicks without dealer certification because large dollar sums are usually involved. Old authentic art glass toothpicks were produced in very limited quantities and are seldom available for purchase anymore.

We can say without hesitation that all art and most pattern glass toothpick categories have been imitated at one time or another. Some pieces are so badly done that their appearance arouses immediate suspicion; others, require special expertise to spot.

Beginning in the late 1960s, certain forms of Holly Amber (Golden Agate) art glass have plagued collectors with some very good reproductions issued by the St. Clair Glass Co. of Elwood, Indiana. There are four-pieces involved: toothpick, tumbler, sauce dish, and mug.

As a prominent example, many advanced collectors and dealers have real problems in distinguishing the old authentic toothpick from the St. Clair reproduction. One of the reasons is due to the fact that nonuniform/irregular opalescent splotching is commonplace on genuine Holly Amber pieces which was caused by difficulties encountered in obtaining consistent factory production color control results.

Holly Amber glass was produced in 1903 by The Indiana Tumbler and Goblet Co., Greentown, Indiana, from a basic amber colored glass batch made sensitive to caloric changes. After the article had been pressed, it was reheated so that the raised portion of the design struck an opalescent coloring. The extensive grayish-white color variations thus created were caused by uneven (gradual) cooling within the Lehr ovens. The phenomena is particularly noticeable on the forms containing individual beaded parts such as the toothpicks and salt and pepper shakers.

Where you have a situation in which no single form (such as a toothpick) may have the same visual level of opalescent coloring when compared against another like form, knowledge of the glass itself cannot always be the sole determinate in solving a reproduction/reissue dilemma.

Not to worry! If a Holly Amber toothpick being considered for purchase first passes your glass appearance evaluation, an old, authentic toothpick can be further determined by counting the number of base beads. An old original will have 36; the reproduction will contain 38.

During the late 1970s, Summit Art Glass Co., Rootstown, Ohio, acquired various new and old original Holly Amber molds from St. Clair Glass and began producing look alikes of the Holly Amber pattern in a wide range of colors, including efforts to replicate the Golden Agate color. This ware existed in the antique market throughout the 1980s. In most instances the Holly Amber coloring was substandard and did not deceive most Holly Amber collectors. A less experienced collector will be wise to get written dealer authentication of a purchase.

All "toothpickers" (as they call themselves) should obtain the various toothpick books written by William Heacock, the NTHCS, and Mark Boultinghouse. These books will provide excellent guidance for both the beginner and advanced toothpick collector.

Holly Amber

Harris collection

Repro, 2⅜" tall — Authentic, 2½" tall

Summit Art Glass Holly Amber repro (left); Authentic Holly Amber toothpick (right). Repro has 38 base beads; authentic Greentown Holly Amber has 36 base beads.

Witt collection

Summit Art Glass repro (left); Summit Produced Vaseline look alike pedestal toothpick (right); 4⅛" tall. Metal pedestal is attached by an external adhesive.

Croesus

Authors' collection

Side-by-side view of an authentic "Croesus" (right) versus a look alike "Slag Croesus" (left): The authentic amethyst toothpick has a 2" opening; the look alike opening is 2½". The Riverside Glass Factory never produced one in a slag. Also, the slag toothpick has a scalloped top rim.

Inverted Fan and Feather

Authors' collection

Reproduction Pink Slag "Inverted Fan & Feather" toothpick made during the late 1960s by St Clair Glass Works, Ellwood, Indiana: Better coloration than the toothpicks made by Northwood.

Bead Swag

Authors' collection

Look alike "Bead Swag" custard toothpick (center) between two authentic Heisey "Bead Swag" salt shakers: Heisey did not produce a custard toothpick in this pattern. Our illustrated custard toothpick was made by Mosser Glass, Inc., Cambridge, Ohio.

Tulip

Lockwood collection

C. F. Monroe "Tulip Pattern: Authentic C. F. Monroe "Wave Crest" shaker (left); fake toothpick created by cutting off and grinding down a shaker of the same "Wave Crest" pattern (right).

This fake toothpick was created by cutting and grinding down a C. F. Monroe "Tulip" pattern "Wave Crest" salt shaker. Monroe did not produce a toothpick in this pattern.

Authors' collection

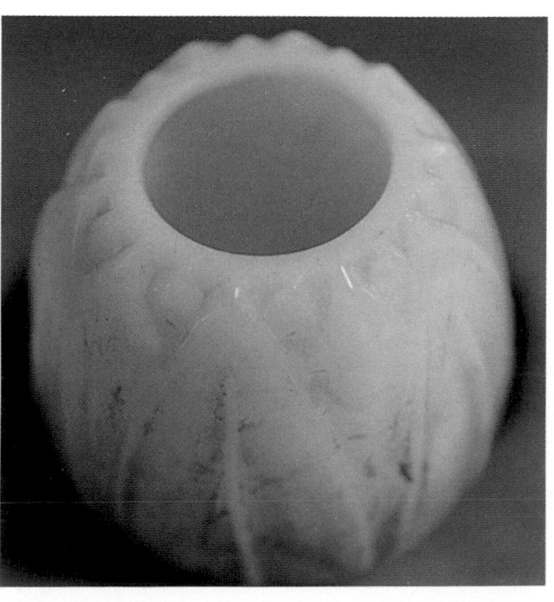

Glass Types & Associated Terminology

Our reader correspondence indicates that in some instances a considerable amount of confusion still abounds involving the specific recognition, identification, and composition of the various types of antique glass salt shakers that can be acquired by collectors. As a result, we believe that it is appropriate to include additional discussion of certain specialized vocabulary and idioms used to describe the various types of glass contained in our books. In our (Vol. II) we presented some limited specific glass terminology using a very concise, descriptive text; perhaps some of our previous explanations were a bit too brief.

The following represents an effort to further enhance readers' education and comprehension relative to some of the various types of glass that may be encountered:

Amberina Glass – A homogeneous heat sensitive glass mixture containing a small amount of gold in solution that was colloidally mixed in a transparent amber glass batch. Patented by Joseph Locke on July 24, 1883, for the New England Glass Co. A normal configuration shades from deep red to amber at the bottom. Coloration is brought about by reheating a piece at the glory hole. If the coloration sequence is reversed, it is referred to as Reverse Amberina. The market collectibility and monetary value of Amberina art glass is determined by the amount of fuchsia-red coloring that is present on a piece and the measurement in length/distance of this type of coloration.

Bluina Glass – Flashed glass that shades from light or dark blue to clear (uncolored) glass.

Blurina Glass – Flashed glass that is shaded from light blue to ruby or dark cranberry. Seldom found in salt shakers and therefore highly collectible.

Cased Glass – Any blown article containing two or more uniform successive layers of glass incorporated into one over an inner core. Sometimes referred to as "layered glass." This type of glass is made up of relatively thick individual layers as opposed to the single thin layer found on flashed ware.

Cut Overlay Glass – A casing of one colored glass over another that is then cut through to produce various pattern effects. Produced from a blank of homogeneous colored glass that has been overlaid with one or more additional uniform colored glass layers.

Flashed, Flashing – Coated with another color. True flashing on glass consists of a very thin coating fixed by fire but subject to wearing off over time. Such glass generally has only two layers; one colored, the other usually clear (uncolored). Various production processes have been used by the glass industry in the manufacture of flashed glass.

An original method involved dipping a gathered glass bulb into a pot of contrasting clear or colored glass. As the desired shape is expanded (blown), the colored layer becomes lighter in color and thinner (especially if it involves the outside layer).

An alternate method was to start with a small pear-shaped bulb of colored glass, let it cool down, and then blow another clear layer on the inside.

Still, other glass factories simply attached strips of colored glass on the outside of a clear hot bulb and reheated the combination. By the use of special tools the colored layer was then spread over the outside. The aforesaid methods are the more typical processes that were utilized; however, additional flashing process methodologies were also employed.

There is little doubt that the popular acceptance of Joseph Locke's July 24, 1883, patented heat sensitive Amberina glassware brought on a competitive accelerated appearance of flashed ware from various American and European glass factories. While patents for discrete flashed ware processes were issued as early as 1814 in Europe, American patents involving differing manufacturing methods began appearing in the mid-1880s. It is apparent that each specific production process used was generally contingent upon the projected production costs involved. Also, the article size to be produced often dictated the selection of which process would be implemented.

Green Opaque Art Glass – A type of homogeneous green opaque glassware produced by adding copper oxide to an opal glass mix. Produced by the New England Glass Co., Cambridge, Massachusetts. The various glass shapes produced will be found to contain a mottled blue metallic stain usually around the top or midsection adjacent to a wavy band of gold. The salt shakers are quite rare and are very difficult to find with the blue staining intact.

Holly Amber Art Glass – A translucent rich golden amber glass with stylized holly leaves and berries having onyx-like color of an opalescent nature. A product originally produced by Jacob Rosenthal while employed by the Indiana Tumbler & Goblet Co. at Greentown, Indiana, during 1903 that was produced for less than a year, it is a pattern glass that has attained an art glass classification due to its rarity. The salt shakers are very rare. Opalescent color control process problems resulted in various light and dark Holly Amber pieces that were produced and sold to the consumer.

Homogeneous Colored Glass – This terminology refers to a glass mix containing certain minerals that result in a uniform color throughout from one surface to the other. Opalware (milk glass) is an excellent example of a homogeneous white colored glass.

Iridescent Art Glass – Glassware produced by various "in-the mix" ingredients that has a visual "lustred effect" with varied colored density on certain multicolored ware. The early type lustred wares are mirror-like in appearance. Lustred ware of the later Art Nouveau period has a more soft luminous sheen such as those produced by Tiffany Furnaces in plain gold or blue iridescent glass. Arthur J. Nash developed a lustre (for Tiffany) that closely approximated the nacreous (iridescent) finish found on ancient glass that has been exposed to the corrosive elements of the earth and atmosphere.

This type of iridescent glassware was manufactured at least two decades prior to the production of the type of iridescent glass known today as carnival glass which was produced by an entirely different methodology.

Iridescent Carnival Glass – A title assigned by early twentieth century collectors to a type of iridescent glassware that was given away as prizes at carnivals and fairs. This glassware is produced by the application of thin sprayed-on chemical solutions of metallic salts, such as iron or tin chlorides, to an already formed glass piece which was subsequently reheated to accept appropriate chemical sprays that would produce a desired surface coloration. The carnival iridescence is created by the chemical spray; not by the reheating process. Glass workers often referred to this type of glass as "doped ware."

The Fenton Art Glass Company is credited with being the first glass factory to enter the consumer market place with production quantities of this type of iridescent ware during 1907. However, there is abundant research evidence that prototype forms of this glass were innovated by other glass factory chemists as early as 1902. Some of these early experimental pieces have since found their way into some of today's carnival glass collections creating an occasional enigma as to when and where such pieces were produced. Very few antique salt shaker patterns were initially produced in early carnival glass.

Ivrene – Produced primarily during the 1920s by Frederick Carder at the Steuben Glass Works, Corning, New York. Sometimes erroneously referred to as "white aurene." This is the closest that Carder ever came to making a milk white glass. The whitish glass has an iridescent surface and is translucent. The glass batch contained feldspar and cryolite. The iridescence was produced by the use of stannous chloride spray applied at the fire; the technique was very similar to that used to create aurene and verre de soie glassware.

Loetz Glass – Manufactured in Austria. This glasshouse is primarily noted for the production of an iridescent art glass that is very similar in shape and surface colors to what was produced by such fine American glass factories as Tiffany and Frederick Carder Steuben. Small items are rarely found signed with the pair of crossed arrows in a circle containing the word(s) "Loetz," "Loetz-Austria," or "Austria." Generally speaking, the majority of the Loetz larger art glass pieces will also be found unsigned. A visual characteristic of this type of glass is the fact that the decoration seems to stand out on the surface. In the case of Tiffany glass, decoration seems to be coming from within the glass itself. This type of decorative phenomena can sometimes be used as an important aid in the identification of unsigned Loetz pieces. Salt shakers were apparently only produced by way of special customer orders at Loetz and are quite rare.

Marbleized/Slag/Variegated Glassware – Each of these descriptive adjectives are used interchangeably today by collectors/dealers. The terms refer to glassware that has impressive color streaking variations produced by the incomplete mixing of colors within a glass batch. The various visual effects produced usually involve blown glass items and are very much sought after by collectors.

Opalescent Glass – Glassware containing raised white colored designs on their surfaces. The creation of this ware involved the coating of a colored glass bulb with a sensitive crystal glass containing bone ash and arsenic which was then blown into a pattern mold to create the desired raised decoration on its exterior surface. After being slightly cooled, the piece was reheated at the glory hole. The raised designs, having cooled below a glowing red temperature, were reheated; thus creating an opalescent white color response.

Opalware Glass – Often referred to as milk glass by today's collectors. However, it was catalogued and advertised as opal ware during the Victorian era and for many years thereafter. It is an opaque glass produced by adding special materials such as fluorspar or other fluorine derivatives to the batch. The finish can be glossy or satin.

Peachblow Glassware – There are three principal types of Victorian era Peachblow glassware made by American glass factories. Two additional types were made by European factories:

Mt. Washington Peachblow

The tradename papers for Peachblow – Peach Skin

glassware were filed by Frederick S. Shirley on July 20, 1886. The ware consists of a single layered, heat sensitive glass that shades from a pink at the top down to a pale blue; when a piece is subjected to an outer surface acid treatment (as most pieces were) the pale blue often takes on a slightly gray cast.

This glass formula is a variation of the patented Mt. Washington Burmese formula. It was created by the addition of cobalt or copper as a colorant in place of the oxide of uranium used to produce Burmese glassware. When the initial glass batch emerges from the furnace it is colored blue; the portion of the piece that is subsequently subjected to refiring at the glory hole causes the blue to change to a pink color. Because this is a single layered homogeneous glass, the color shading is the same on the inside as on the outer surface. The majority of this art glass was produced satinized (acid treated). Both free and mold blown items were made. Exterior decorated pieces are considered to be choice and very rare.

New England Peachblow — aka "Wild Rose"

This ware was patented by Edward D. Libbey on March 2, 1886. A product of the New England Glass Co. that consists of a single layered, homogeneous heat sensitive glass that upon reheating shades from a deep red to a white on the lower portion of a piece. The reheated coloration can be readily observed on both the inner and outer surfaces. On some items, the white will shade off to a light gray.

Wheeling Peachblow — aka "Coral"

A two layered or lined glassware. The outer layer is heat sensitive; and after refiring shades from a golden yellow at the bottom to a fuchsia-red at the top. The inside layer is a white opal glass that was the first part of the piece to be formed by the gaffer. Majority of items produced are glossy, but pieces will be found that have been acid finished. This ware was made in both mold and free blown forms by Hobbs, Brockunier & Co ., Wheeling, West Virginia.

Webb Peachblow

Produced by Thomas Webb & Sons in England. This is a two- or three-layered ware, the outer layer may be clear or frosted. The middle heat sensitive layer often shades from a light pink at the base to a deep rich red at the top. However, there are many rich color variations. The inner layer is an off-colored cream; sometimes with a somewhat greenish hue. This type of art glass was made in both a glossy and acid finish. Quite rare in shakers.

Stevens & Williams Peachblow

Made by Stevens & Williams, Stourbridge, England. This ware is also cased glass and very similar in coloration to the Webb Peachblow. Produced in mostly free blown forms including their salt shakers. Differences in hand-decoration techniques (from that of Webb) is a primary means of identifying this ware.

Peloton Glass – Thin colored filaments of glass randomly applied to a previously shaped glass piece while it is still hot enough for the glass filaments to adhere to it. Patented on October 25, 1880, by Wilhelm Kralik of Neuwelt, Bohemia. No records could be found of a patent having been granted for this type of process in the United States.

Plated Amberina – Originally named "Aurora" by the factory. Patented by E. D. Libbey on June 15, 1886. The patented description text states "hereby a piece of opal or opalescent glass, plated with a gold-ruby mixture, was reheated to develop a deeper color at portions which would blend into the lighter part of glass, not sufficiently reheated to develop any color." When a heat sensitive Amberina batch was used, the color would appear in an Amberina shading. The patent papers also indicated that colored casings of canary, blue, or green could be substituted for the opalescent casing. There is nothing in the patent papers that discussed the ribbed molding pattern effect that is found on the exterior surface of Plated Amberina pieces.

Rigaree – Applied (fused-on) glass ornamentation involving the use of individual pieces of colored or clear glass. Beginning around 1880, this type of embellishment was used by many glass factories, both American and European. Flowers, fruits, and leaves were some of the more attractive applications used. However, during the Art Nouveau era various other innovative rigaree designs were created by the many artistic talented gaffers that worked at the various quality glass factories.

Rose Amber – A descriptive title used by Mt. Washington/Pairpoint for their Amberina art glass due to the fact that The New England Glass Co. had patented this ware prior to Mt. Washington. A pending suit by New England Glass resulted in Mt. Washington agreeing to call their Amberina glassware by the "Rose Amber" title. Refer to Amberina for additional descriptive and technical information.

Rubina Glass – A flashed glassware that shades from a ruby or deep cranberry at the top to a clear crystal at its base; sometimes the direction of shading is vice versa causing collectors to call such glass "Reverse Rubina."

Rubina Verde Glass – Flashed glass that shades from a ruby or dark cranberry at the top to a light green or greenish yellow at the base. It was produced by the same process as Rubina Glass.

Silvered, Silver Deposit, and Metal Encased Glassware – The detailed processes involved in the manufacture of these types of glassware are fully explained by A. C. Revi in *Nineteenth Century Glass* on pages 218 – 230 with excellent illustrative examples of the various types that were produced from 1850 to the turn of the twentieth century. Various patented creative approaches are also explained.

Silvered glass is achieved by application of a mercurial deposit sealed inside the glass and is therefore untarnishable. The various wares that were produced are commonly called mercury glass by todays collectors.

The art glass shakers that we have illustrated in this book involve silver deposit art glass and metal encased ware. Perhaps the best examples we have pictured in silver deposit glass are those produced by Loetz of Austria.

Metal encased glass shakers were first illustrated and discussed by A. G. Peterson in his book *Glass Salt Shakers* p. 31-N and 134; also our 1976 book on pp. 36 and 92. Generally speaking, such ware consists of a clear or colored glass holder encased in metal with a perforated top. In some designs the glass condiment part is removable from the metal holder.

Spangled Glass – Spangled glass denotes calling for "a series of spangles or flakes incorporated into the body of the glass." It is an art glass that was first design patented on November 27, 1883, by William Leighton, Jr. of Wheeling, West Virginia (patent #14,443); followed by his later patent #292,663 dated January 29, 1884. Produced by Hobbs, Brockunier, Wheeling, West Virginia.

A similar process was also employed by The Vasa Murrhina Art Glass Co., at Sandwich, Massachusetts, which began operations during July 1883 and existed for only 18 months thereafter.

Spatterglass – Glassware containing variegated colors applied to a body of opaque white or colored glass. Produced in the same manner as spangled ware but does not contain either metallic or mica flakes added thereto.

An American patent for producing a type of spatterglass was awarded on August 1, 1893, to John S. Irwin of Saltsburg, Pennsylvania, Patent office records indicate that it is one of the very few patents granted for the manufacture of this type of glass in the United States.

Stained Glass – This involved the art of painting on all or part of a smooth glass surface with a colored fluid. Staining could be applied as a spray, by dipping, or with a brush to a moderately hot glass and then firing it to bake on the color.

Such special American companies as the Oriental Glass Co. and Pioneer Glass Co. of Pittsburgh, Pennsylvania, specialized in doing contract staining work for various glass factories in the Pittsburgh area. The most popular stained color was ruby. Also, they purchased clear glass articles from various manufacturers and distributors which were then stained and sold on the open market. The aforesaid firms are just two examples of such specialized businesses that performed glass staining for Victorian era glass factories.

Stained glass items involving souvenir inscriptions or small decorations in ruby and other colors were easy to create by removing portions of a stained surface prior to setting the stain by baking. Various pattern glass shakers such as "Punty Band," "Button Arches," "Diamond with Peg," "Ruby Thumbprint," and "Kings Crown," etc. are excellent examples of this relatively simple and cost effective staining process. Ruby stained glass enjoys a high collectibility factor among today's collectors.

Vasa Murrhina Art Glass – A patent (#301,100) calling for mica coated with silver, gold, copper, or nickel applied to the hot glass in which reheating caused the glass to flow over the mica and form a transparent outer layer was issued on July 1, 1884, to John C. DeVoy who assigned the patent to the Vasa Murrhina Art Glass Co. of Sandwich, Massachusetts.

These art glass types are unique, highly collectible, and difficult to find in salt shakers. Similar type ware was also produced in various shapes by English glass factories from discrete patented processes beginning around 1878.

Vaseline/Uranium Glass – A transparent (sometimes translucent) glass that fluoresces yellow-green when exposed to ultraviolet (black) light. Early glass workers referred to this type of wares as uranium or canary glass. The jargon "vaseline" has been created by contemporary collectors and is generally recognized within today's glass market place. The aforesaid fluorescence reaction is due to the glass content having a uranium oxide compound. Translucence (when present) is created by acid treatment or grit blasting of the glass surface.

Notes

Outstanding Historical Glass Salt Shaker Rarities

[1]For additional Dewey commemorative figurals refer to *Greentown in Color* by Ralph and Louise Boyd, Items 220, 222; also *Milk Glass* by Belknap, p.175.

[2]Refer to our special write-up on General Shafter.

[3]See *Fostoria, Ohio Glass II* by Melvin Murray, p.33, 34 – 35.

[4]See *Glass Salt Shakers* by Peterson p.131 and 162-E.

[5]Gen. Shafter historical research provided by Dick Krauss.

Adams Company

[1]Refer to H-7, p.129

Atterbury & Company

[1]Refer to *Glass Patents and Patterns* by Peterson, p.20.

Beaumont Glass Company

[1]Refer to H-5, pages 15 and 61.

[2]Refer to H-1 pages 34 and 54.

[3]Refer to Kamm 8, 37.

[4]For more details refer to H-2, p. 45; H-3, p. 41; H-6, p.41.

The Bellaire Goblet Company

[1]Refer to *Findlay Pattern Glass* by Don Smith, p.10; also *Pattern Glass* by McCain, p. 4.

[2]See Kamm 5, p.140; H-3, p.58 & 59; our Vol. II, p.30.

Boston & Sandwich Glass Company

[1]See *The Glass Industry in Sandwich* Vol. 1, p.302 by Barlow & Kaiser.

[2]See *The Glass Industry in Sandwich* Vol. 1, p.300 by Barlow & Kaiser. Also Vol 4, page 290.

[3]*The Glass Industry in Sandwich*. Vol. 1, p.292 by Barlow & Kaiser.

[4]*Glass Industry in Sandwich* by Barlow & Kaiser, Vol. 1, p.180.

[5]*Glass Industry in Sandwich* by Barlow & Kaiser. Vol. 4, p.228.

[6]*Glass Industry in Sandwich* by Barlow & Kaiser, Vol. 4, p.229.

[7]*The Glass Industry in Sandwich* by Barlow & Kaiser, Vol. 4, p.291.

[8]*The Glass Industry in Sandwich* by Barlow and Kaiser; Vol. 1, p.302.

[9]*The Pairpoint Glass Story* by Geo. C. Avila, p.6, plate 7.

[10]*The Pairpoint Glass Story* by Geo. C. Avila, p.61 – 63.

[11]*Pairpoint Glass* by L.E. Padgett, p.51.

Bryce, Higbee & Company

[1]See H-7, p.9, 10, 116, 117.

[2]See Kamm 8, 17, and pl.38; McCain, pl.61.

Buckeye Glass Company

[1]Refer to our Vol. II, p.33.

[2]Refer to H-6, p.12.

[3]Refer to H-1, fig 248; H-3, p.37 for additional details.

Cambridge Glass

[1]Refer to 1930 – 1933 Cambridge catalogs published by the National Cambridge Collectors, Inc., p.33 – 7.

[2]Refer to 1930 Cambridge catalog reproduced in 1976 by National Cambridge Collectors, Inc. catalog illus. #1266.

[3]Refer to pages 32-19 & 33-19. Same 1930 Cambridge catalog.

[4]Ref. *The Cambridge Glass Book* by Harold and Judy Bennett.

[5]Refer to H-7, p.219.

The Central Glass Company

[1]Refer to Kamm 8, p.33; Peterson 27-M.

Challinor, Taylor & Company

[1]See *Tarentum Glass* by Lucas, p.117.

[2]Refer to *Tarentum Pattern Glass* by Lucas, p.75 – 77, pl.137B.

Consolidated Lamp & Glass Company

[1]Refer to our Imitation Glassware section.

[2]Refer to *Old Pattern Glass According to Heacock*, p.8,9.

[3]See our Vol. II, p.43 & 292 Color Addendum.

[4]See *Old Pattern Glass* by Heacock, p.181.

Cooperative Flint Glass Company

[1]Refer to H-7, p.206 for a trade ad of this pattern.

[2]Refer to Kamm 5, p.103.

[3]Refer to Kamm 5, p.103.

Crystal Glass Company

[1]Refer to *Glass Salt Shakers* by Peterson; p.21-E and 119.

[2]Refer to Kamm 4, page 6; *Pattern Glass* by McCain, plate 178.

Dalzell, Gilmore and Leighton Company

[1]Reference *Findlay Glass* by Measell & Smith, p.101.

[2]Refer to our Vol. II, p.55 and 56.

Dalzell Viking Corporation

[1]Refer to *Glass Salt Shakers* by Peterson, p.163-P.

Dithridge & Company

[1]Refer to "Leaf, Double," in our Vol. II p.65

[2]Refer to our Vol. II, pg.69 and 70.

[3]Refer to our Vol. II, pg.82 and 85.

[4]Refer to *Glass Collectors Digest* Feb./Mar. 97, p.85 and April/May 97, p.36.

Duncan & Miller Glass Company

[1]Refer to H-7, p.79.

George Duncan & Sons

[1]See *U.S. Glass* by Heacock & Bickenheuser, p.99.

[2]See *U.S. Glass* by Heacock & Bickenheuser, p. 15.

[3]Refer to Kamm 8, p.44; McCain's *Pattern Glass*, pl. 93.

[4]Ref. *American Pressed Glass & Figure Bottles* by Revi, p.144 and 145.

Eagle Glass & Manufacturing Company

[1]Refer to *Glass Salt Shakers* by Peterson, p.164.

[2]See our Vol. II, p.74.
[3]Refer to *Milk Glass Addenda* by Warman, pl. 142.

Fenton Art Glass Company
[1]See Caught in the Butterfly Net p.76, Fig. 122.
[2]Refer to our Vol. II, p.104.
[3]Refer to *Fenton Glass, 3rd 25 years* page 66.
[4]Refer to *Fenton Glass, The 3rd 25 Years*, p.108.
[5]Refer to *Fenton Glass, The 2nd 25 Years*, p.45.
[6]Refer to our Vol. II, p.84.
[7]See *Glass Salt Shakers* by Peterson; Art Glass plate and p.146.
[8]See our Vol. II, p.83 "Swirl, Fenton."
[9]Refer to our Vol. II, pages 82 and 85.
[10]Refer to our Vol. II, p.68.

The Findlay Flint Glass Company
[1]Refer to *Rare & Unlisted Toothpick Holders* by Heacock, p.10; also *Findlay Pattern Glass* by Don E. Smith, Chapter V beginning on p.30.
[2]See *Collecting Glass* Vol. 1 by Heacock, p.23.

Fostoria Glass Company
[1]Refer to *Glass Patents & Patterns* by Peterson, p.195.
[2]See Kamm 8, p.49 and plate 100.
[3]Refer to H - 7. p.144; also K3 – 94.
[4]Refer to *Salt Dishes* by C. W. Brown, fig. 1121.
[5]Refer to H-3, p.46.

Fostoria Shade and Lamp Company
[1]Refer to our Vol. II, p.90 and 282.

Greensburg Glass Company
[1]See Kamm 5, p.47.
[2]See Kamm 8, p.164.

The A.H. Heisey Glass Company
[1]Ref. Kamm 4, p.98.
[2]Refer to *Collector's Encyclopedia of Heisey Glass* by Bredehoft, pp.124 and 125 for more detailed pattern information.
[3]Refer to our Vol. II, p.93 for additional details.

The Helmschmied Manufacturing Company
[1]Refer to *American Art Nouveau Glass*, Appendix D. by A. C. Revi.

Hobbs, Brockunier & Company
[1]Ref. *The Glass Industry in Sandwich* by Barlow & Kaiser Vol.1, p.302.
[2]Ref. *The Glass Industry in Sandwich* by Barlow & Kaiser Vol. 4, p.137.
[3]Ref. *The Glass Industry in Sandwich* by Barlow & Kaiser Vol. 4, p.138.
[4]Also refer to H-3, pp.55 and 67.
[5]Refer to H-3, page 32.
[6]Ref. H-6, pgs.41 and 56.
[7]Refer to H-9, p.60; H-2, p.45 for more detail.
[8]Ref. H -3, p.45.

The Imperial Glass Company
[1]Refer to Kamm 7, p.208 and pl. 108.
[2]Refer to our Vol. II, p.256; also Kamm 7, p.131.

Indiana Tumbler & Goblet Company
[1]Refer to *Greentown Glass* by Measell, p.76, 77 and Pl 164. Also, *Glass Salt Shakers'* by Peterson, p.168-B.
[2]See *Greentown Glass* by J. Measell, p.58 and 59.

The Jefferson Glass Company
[1]Refer to our Vol. II, page 106.
[2]See Heacock 3, page 63 for Jefferson Catalog ad.

D.C. Jenkins Glass Company
[1]Refer to Kamm 2, p.26; also *Pattern Glass Preview*, issue No. 1 by Bill Heacock.

Libbey Glass Company
[1]See *Libbey Glass* by Carl U. Fauster, pages 25 and 226.
[2]See *Dugan/Diamond* by Heacock, Measell & Wiggins, page 121.

Loetz Witwe, Klostermuhle
[1]See *Art Glass Nouveau* by Grover, p.206. Also *Nineteenth Century Glass, 1967 Revised Edition* by A.C. Revi pages 224 – 230 for silver deposit & metal encased glassware.

McKee Glass Company
[1]Refer to Kamm 1, p.73; Peterson 159-L.
[2]Refer to our Vol. II, page 114.
[3]Refer to H-7, p.123.
[4]See *The Complete Book of McKee Glass* by Stout, p.212.
[5]Ref. *Complete Book of McKee Glass* by Stout, p.212.
[6]Ref. *Much More Early American Pattern Glass* by Metz, p.154 #1907.
[7]See *The Complete Book of McKee Glass* by Stout, p.212.
[8]See *Complete McKee Glass* by Stout, p.97 and 211. Also Heacock I, *Toothpick Holders*, p.44 and *Toothpick Holders* by NTHCS, page 9 and 34.
[9]See Kamm 9, p.44.

Model Flint Glass
[1]Refer to our Vol. II, page 118.
[2]Refer to H-9, page 71.

C.F. Monroe
[1]Refer to our Vol. II, p.119.
[2]See *Wave Crest* by Cohen, p.206.
[3]See *Wave Crest Ware 1900-1901 No.6 Catalog*, p.86. Republished by Elsa H. Grimmer in 1978.
[4]See *Glass of C. F. Monroe* by Cohen, p.232.
[5]See *Glass Salt Shakers* by A.G. Peterson; p.39-E and p.145.
[6]See our Vol. II, p.125.
[7]Refer to *Wave Crest* by Cohen, p.30, top row, 5th shaker.

Investigated Facts Relative to Verona Art Glass Produced by Mt. Washington/Pairpoint Circa 1894
[1]See *Confusing Collectibles* by Dorothy Hammond, p.13.,14. *Antique Week* March 23, 1992, issue, front page feature article that addresses phony signatures by Victor Buck and Mildred and Ralph Lechner. *The Black Light Book* by Antique & Collectors Reprod. News, 2nd edition, pages 61, 63.

[2]See "Fine Points To Recognizing Unusual Lines" by Mildred and Ralph Lechner, *Antique Week* Nov. 8, 1993 issue, front page feature article. "Does It Need a Signature to be Verona?" by Mildred and Ralph Lechner, *Antique Week* April 11, 1994, issue, front page feature article.
[3]See *Art Glass Nouveau* by Ray and Lee Grover, p.55 and pl.105.

Mt. Washington/Pairpoint Corp.

[1]Refer to our Vol. II, page 9 for more historical details.
[2]Refer to our Vol. II, p.143.
[3]Refer to our Vol. II, p.212.
[4]Refer to our special write-up on Verona art glass for more analysis profundity.
[5]See our Vol. II, p.151.
[6]See Glass Salt Shakers by Peterson, p.174-K and 147.
[7]Refer to our Vol. II, p.132.
[8]Refer to Peterson 176-M who named this pattern.
[9]See our Vol II, p.133.
[10]See *Rare & Unlisted Toothpick Holders* by Heacock, p.14 fig. 1056.
[11]Refer to 1894 Pairpoint catalog, pages 39 – 41.
[12]See our Vol. II, p.137.
[13]See *Glass Salt Shakers* by Peterson p.59 and 160-R.
[14]See our Vol. II, p.273.
[15]Refer to *More Cruets Only* by Dean L. Murray, top of page 17.
[16]Refer to our Vol. II, p.30 and 32.
[17]Refer to the Glass Type Section in this book.
[18]For more detail see *Pairpoint Glass* by Padgett, p.28.

National Glass Company

[1]Refer to H-1, p.58 trade ad.
[2]See Kamm 3, p.104; *Riverside Glass Works* by Gorham, p.210, 211; Heacock *Rare & Unlisted Toothpicks*, fig. 1199.
[3]Ref. Kamm 5, p.63 and pl.63; also H-7, p.214.

New England Glass Company

[1]See our Vol. II, p. 158 for Agata mfg. process details.
[2]Refer to our Vol. II, pages 157, 159; also our Glass Types section of this book for glass patent details, etc.
[3]For additional details on 2nd grind see our Vol. II, p.161.
[4]See our Vol. II, p.162 for additional details.

The New Martinsville Glass MFG. Company

[1]Refer to *New Martinsville Glass* by Measell, p.58.
[2]Refer to Kamm 3, p.90; Heacock *1,000 Toothpicks*, fig. 628.
[3]Ref. *New Martinsville Glass*, 1900 – 1944 by Measell, pp.17 and 102.

The Nickel Plate Glass Company

[1]Refer to our Vol. II, p.215 for an example of a Libbey Maize mustard that was represented as a salt shaker.

Harry Northwood Glass Patterns

[1]Refer to H-9, p.56 for additional details.
[2]Refer to *Harry Northwood The Early Years*, p.127.
[3]See *Harry Northwood The Early Years* by Heacock, Measell, and Wiggins; p.137, 138, for additional commentaries.
[4]See our Vol. II, p.169 for individual shaker details.
[5]Refer to *Dugan/Diamond* by Heacock, Measell, p.91 for photograph of toothpick and cruet set.
[6]See *Dugan/Diamond* by Heacock, Measell, Wiggins, p.80, fig. 132 – 134.
[7]See *Dugan/Diamond* by Heacock, etc. p.80, fig. 122, 123.
[8]Refer to *Dugan/Diamond* by Heacock, Measell, p.77.
[9]Ref. H-2, pp. 22, 29, 31; also Kamm 2, p.59.
[10]Ref. *Harry Northwood The Wheeling Years* by Heacock, Measell, Wiggins, p.54, 56.
[11]Refer to *Harry Northwood The Early Years* by Heacock, Measell, Wiggins, pp.37, 38, 44, 47, 93 and 109.
[12]Refer to *Glass Salt Shakers* by Peterson, p.140; also see our Vol.II, p.243.
[13]See H-6, pp.33 and 85; also Kamm 5, p.122.
[14]Research data provided by past AAGSSCS president Marilyn Lockwood.
[15]Refer to H-4, p.29.
[16]Refer to *Dugan/Diamond* book by Heacock, Measell & Wiggins, p.35.
[17]See *Glass Salt Shakers* by Peterson, pp.152 & 177.
[18]Refer to *Harry Northwood The Early Years* by Heacock, Measell & Wiggins; pp.43, 68, and 69.

Novelty Glass Company

[1]See Fostoria, Ohio Glass II by Melvin Murray, pp. 33 – 35.
[2]Refer to our Vol. II, pp.23, 235.

Ohio Flint Glass Company

[1]Refer to our Vol. II, p.200.

The Paden City Glass Mfg. Company

[1]See H-6, p.92 for a catalog reprint of this pattern.

Phoenix Glass Company

[1]Refer to H-9, pp. 15 and 16; also *New Martinsville Glass* by Measell, pp. 14 – 17.
[2]Refer to our Vol. II, p.244 for additional details.

H.M. Rio Company

[1]For additional examples see *The Glass of C.F. Monroe* by Cohen, p.173.

Riverside Glass Works

[1]Refer to *Riverside Glass Works* by Gorham, p.80.
[2]Refer to *Riverside Glass Works* by Gorham, p.83.
[3]Refer to *Riverside Glass Works* by C.W. Gorham, p.97.
[4]See our Vol. II, p.179.
[5]See *Riverside Glass Works* by C.W. Gorham, p.196.
[6]Refer to *Riverside Glass Works* by Gorham, pp.244, 245.
[7]Refer to *Riverside Glass Works* by Gorham, p.183 – 187. Also H-1, pp.25, 54.
[8]See *Riverside Glass Works* by C.W. Gorham, p.178 and 182.

[9]Ref. *Riverside Glass Works* by C.W. Gorham, pp.223 – 226.

Tarentum Glass Company

[1]Refer to H-7, p.92.
[2]Refer to H-7. pp. 48 and 175.
[3]Refer to *Tarentum Glass* by Lucas; pp. 336, 341

Tiffin Glass Company

[1]See *Colored Glassware of the Depression Era* by Hazel Marie Weatherman, p.340.

The Thompson Glass Company

[1]For more detail see H-7, pp.56, 205; Kamm 6, pl.40.

The United States Glass Company

[1]Refer to Kamm 6, pl.59; McCain pl.121; H-1, p.15.
[2]Refer to Kamm 4, p.134; H-5, p.156.
[3]Refer to H-5, pp.19 and 176.
[4]See H-5, page 19 for additional information.
[5]Refer to H-7, p.149.
[6]Refer to H-7, p. 189; K6, pl.36.
[7]See H-5, pp. 43 and 150; Kamm 7, p.121.
[8]Refer to H-7, p.197; K6, pl.4.
[9]Ref. H-5, p.156; Kamm 8, p.54; H-1000 TP, fig.721.
[10]Refer to H-5-82a in a condiment set.
[11]Refer to H-5; pp.24, 48, and 166.

Thomas Webb & Sons

[1]Refer to *Nineteenth Century Glass* by Revi, p.38.
[2]Refer to our Glass Types Section for additional detail.
[3]Refer to our Vol. II, p.20.
[4]Refer to our Glass Types Section.

Westmoreland Glass Company

[1]Ref. *Guide to Westmoreland's S&P Shakers* by Grizel (privately published).
[2]Refer to H-7, p.213; Kamm 5, pl.34.

The West Virginia Glass Company

[1]Refer to Kamm 3, p.92.

Potpourri

[1]Refer to Peterson 153-A; also Kamm 5, p.105.
[2]Refer to Peterson 21-H.
[3]Refer to *Glass Salt Shakers* by Peterson, pp.62 and 141.
[4]Reference our Vol. II, p.244.
[5]Ref. *Glass Salt Shakers* by Peterson, pp.31-N and 134.
[6]Ref. our 1976 salt shaker book, pp.36 and 92.
[7]Ref. *Nineteenth Century Glass* by Revi, pp.218 – 230.
[8]Refer to our Vol. II, p.208 for additional details.
[9]Refer to *Milk Glass Today* by Ferson for additional detail.
[10]Refer *Glass Salt Shakers* by Peterson 156-T and p.124.
[11]Refer to our Glass Types section for more spangled glass detail.
[12]See our Vol. II, pp.135 and 215 for process details.
[13]Refer to *Nineteenth Century Glass* by Revi, pp.61, 62, and 64 for various creative craquelle process details.
[14]Refer to *Harry Northwood The Early Years,* by Heacock, Measell & Wiggins; pp. 58, 60, 61, and 31.
[15]Refer to our Glass Types Section relative to Amberina art glass and value determination.
[16]Refer to our Vol. II, p. 221.
[17]Ref. *Milk Glass Addenda* by Warman, pl.,143A.
[18]Refer to Kamm 6, p.44.
[19]Refer to *Milk Glass Addenda* by Warman, pl.134D.
[20]Refer to *Goblets II* by Millard, pl.163.
[21]Refer to *1000 Toothpicks* by Heacock, pp.32 and 58.
[22]Refer to Kamm 4, p.58; Also, *Pattern Glass* by McCain, p.251.
[23]See *Glass Salt Shakers* by Peterson pp. 131 and 162-E.
[24]Gen. Shafter historical research provided by Dick Krauss.
[25]Refer to our Vol. II, pp.231 and 275.
[26]Refer to H-7, pp.127, 128.
[27]Refer to our Glass Types section.
[28]See *Rare and Unlisted Toothpicks* by Heacock, fig. 1029.
[29]Ref. *Miniature Lamps* by Smith, p.96.
[30]See our Vol. II, pp.128 and 201.
[31]Refer to our Vol. II, p.92.
[32]Refer to Peterson 165-K and 136.
[33]Refer to our Vol. II, p.92.
[34]See our Vol. II, p.218 for additional data on this type shaker.
[35]Pattern name by Peterson; see *Glass Salt Shakers* 167H.
[36]Refer to our Vol. II, p.32.
[37]Refer to *The Glass Industry in Sandwich* Vol. II by Barlow and Kaiser, p.310.
[38]Refer to Peterson pp.35-G and 140.
[39]Ref. *Nineteenth Century Glass* by Revi p.220.
[40]Refer to *Fenton Glass The Second 25 Years* by Heacock, p.27.
[41]Refer to H-9, pp. 41 – 45 inclusive.
[42]See our Vol. II, p.133.
[43]Refer to *Milk Glass Addenda* by Warman, pl.142.
[44]Ref. H-7, p.146; *H-Collection Glass* Vol. II, p.76.
[45]See *The Glass Industry In Sandwich* by Barlow and Kaiser, Chapter 14, pp. 277 – 297.
[46]Refer to Peterson 40-J.
[47]See *19th Century Glass* by Revi, p.55.
[48]Refer to Peterson 42-D and page 149.
[49]See our Vol. 2, p.261 for more pattern details.
[50]Refer to Glass Salt Shakers by Peterson; p.149, 175P.
[51]Ref. *Milk Glass Addenda* by Warman, pl.126B.
[52]Refer to *Glass Salt Shakers* by Peterson p.42-N and 150.
[53]Refer to *The Glass Industry in Sandwich* by Barlow & Kaiser, Vol. 2, p.103 – 105.
[54]Refer to *American Pressed Glass* by Revi. p.445 which gives various pages involving this pattern.
[55]Refer to *Rare & Unlisted Toothpicks* by Heacock, fig. 1316.
[56]See our Vol. II, p.262 for a similar shaker.
[57]Ref. H-7, p.21.

Reproductions, Look Alikes, Reissues and Fakes

[1]Refer to our Vol. II pp. 10 and 11 for dual mold details.

[2]Refer to the Aug./Sept. 1992 issue of *Glass Collect. Digest*, p.6.

[3]Refer to our Vol. II, p.42 for a red, single layered shaker and a fake yellow cased condiment set with phony handle.

[4]Refer to our Vol. II, p.53.

[5]Refer to our Vol. II, p.134 for additional details.

[6]Refer to our write-up on the Novelty Glass Co., p.144 of this book for more details.

[7]Refer to Kamm 8, p.2 and Plates 18 and 19.

[8]Refer to *Glass Salt Shakers* by Peterson, p.31 – 9 or our Vol. II, p.172 for custard and pink slag colors.

[9]Refer to *Old Pattern Glass According to Heacock*, pp. 115 – 117 for additional details.

[10]Refer to *Dugan/Diamond* by Heacock, Measell & Wiggins, p.14.

[11]Refer to Kamm 8, p.50; also H-1, p.50.

[12]Refer to *The New Martinsville Glass Story* by Miller, p.15.

[13]For additional details refer to our Vol. II, p.166.

[14]Refer to our Vol. II, p.99 for authentic Hobbs shakers.

[15]For additional detail refer to our Vol. II, p.68.

[16]Refer to our Vol. II, p.126 for an overview of the Monroe "Tulip" salt/pepper shakers.

[17]Refer to 1900-1901 C. F. Mornoe catalog No.6 published by Elsa Grimmer for various extended neck opal itemizers and their associated hardware.

[18]Sec H-6. p.32.

[19]See *Findlay Pattern Glass* by Smith, p.123, row 2, 3rd stopper shard.

[20]Refer to *Confusing Collectibles* by Dorothy Hammond, published in 1969 by Mid-America Book Co., Leon, Iowa; p.31.

[21]Refer to H-9, *Cranberry Opalescent from A to Z*, pages 108 and 109.

[22]Refer to H-9, *Cranberry Opalescent From A to Z*, p.47

Bibliography

Antique Collectors Reproductions News. *Black Light Book.* Des Moines, Iowa.

Archer, Douglas. *Imperial Glass Co.* (catalog reprint). Collector Books, Paducah, KY.

Baldwin, Gary & Carno, Lee. *Moser – Artistry In Glass 1857 – 1938.* Antique Publ., Marietta, Ohio.

Barlow, R. E. & Kaiser, J. E. *The Glass Industry in Sandwich, Volumes 1,2,3& 4.* Barlow/Kaiser Publishing Co. Windham, New Hampshire.

Barnett, Jerry. *Paden City – The Color Co.* Stevens Publishing Co., Astoria, IL (out of print).

Boyd, Ralph & Louise. *Greentown in Color*, Modlin Printing Co., Marion, Idaho (out of print).

Bredehoft, Neila. *Heisey Glass (1925 – 1938).* Collector Books, Paducah, KY.

Fauster, Carl U. *Libbey Glass.* Len Beach Press, Toledo, OH.

Gardner, Paul V. *The Glass of Frederick Carder.* Crown Publ. Inc., NY (1971 – 2nd Edition).

Gorham, C. W. *Riverside Glass Works* (1995). Privately published.

Heacock, William. *Fenton Books 1, 2, & 3.* Antique Publ. Marietta. OH.

____. *1,000 Toothpick Holders.* 1977: Richardson Printing Co., Marietta, OH (out of print).

____. *Encyclopedia of Victorian Colored Pattern Glass: Volumes 1 thru 7.* Antique Publications, Marietta, OH.

____. *Old Pattern Glass.* Antique Publ., Marietta, OH (out of print).

____. *Collecting Glass: Vol. 1,2,& 3.* Antique Publ., Marietta, OH.

____. *The Glass Collector Vol. 1 thru 6.* Antique Publ., Marietta, OH.

Heacock, William & Gamble, William. *Encyclopedia of Victorian Colored Pattern Glass, Cranberry Opalescent from A to Z – Vol. 9.*

Heacock, William; Measell, James; Wiggins, Barry. *Harry Northwood The Early Years 1881 – 1900.* Antique Publ., Marietta, OH.

____. *Harry Northwood The Wheeling Years 1901 – 1925.* Antique Publ., Marietta, OH.

____. *Dugan/Diamond.* Antique Publ., Marietta, OH.

Kamm, Minnie W. – *Pattern Glass.* 8 books (out of print).

Lechner, Mildred & Ralph. *The World of Salt Shakers.* 1976 paper back: Collector Books, Paducah, KY (out of print).

____. *The World of Salt Shakers, Vol. II*, Collector Books, Paducah, KY.

McKearin, A. E. – *American Glass.* Crown Publishers, NY.

Measell, James & Don E. Smith. *Findlay Glass.* Antique Publ. Marietta, OH.

Measell, James. *New Martinsville Glass, 1900 – 1944.* Antique Publ., Marietta, OH.

____. *Greentown Glass.* Grand Rapids, MI Public Museum.

Millard, S. T. *Opaque Glass* (3rd edition, 1953). Central Press, Topeka, Kansas (out of print).

Miller, Everett & Addie. *New Martinsville Glass Story.* Richardson Printing Co., Marietta, OH (out of print).

Murray, Dean L. *More Cruets Only* (1973). Kilgore Graphics, Inc. Phoenix, Arizona.

Murray, Melvin L. *Fostoria, Ohio Glass II (1992).* Privately published by the author – 425 West Ridge Dr., Fostoria, OH 44830.

Peterson, A. G. *Glass Patents & Patterns (1973).* Celery City Printing Co., Sanford FL: (out of print).

____. *Glass Salt Shakers: 1000 Patterns (1970).* Wallace-Homestead, Des Moines, IA (out of print).

Revi, A. C. *American Art Nouveau Glass.* Crown Publ. Inc., NY.

____. *American Pressed Glass & Figure Bottles.* Crown Publ. Inc., NY.

____. *Nineteenth Century Glass.* Crown Publ. Inc., NY.

____. *Spinning Wheel's Collectible Glass.* Castle Books, Secaucas, NJ (out of print).

Shuman, John A. *American Art Glass.* Collector Books, Paducah, KY.

Stout, Sandra. *Complete Book of McKee Glass* (1972). The Trojan Press, North Kansas City, Missouri (out of print).

____. *Three Books on Depression Glass.* Wallace-Homestead, Des Moines, IA (out of print).

Weatherman, Hazel. *Colored Glassware of The Depression Era 2.* Privately published (out of print).

Special Bibliography References

The following publications describe/illustrate the three types of Mt. Washington/Pairpoint clear and colored glass blanks and forms that comprise "Verona" style motif decoration:

American Art Glass by John A. Shuman, III, page 113 (3 photo illustrations) and page 48 (descriptive verbiage).

Antiques & Collecting Magazine, Dec. 1991, contains an advertisement by Bookside Antiques, Louis O. St. Aubin, Jr., #5 illustration and written details.

James D. Julia, Inc. Dec. 3, 1991 Glass & Lamp Auction catalog page 57, item 233, describes a clear Verona glass tankard pitcher decorated in shades of purple and blue pansies with gold highlights.

Mt. Washington Art Glass Review, Volume 1, No. 2 dated December 1992, page 29. Published by the Mt. Washington Art Glass Society, bottom of the page, left-hand illustration.

Pattern Index

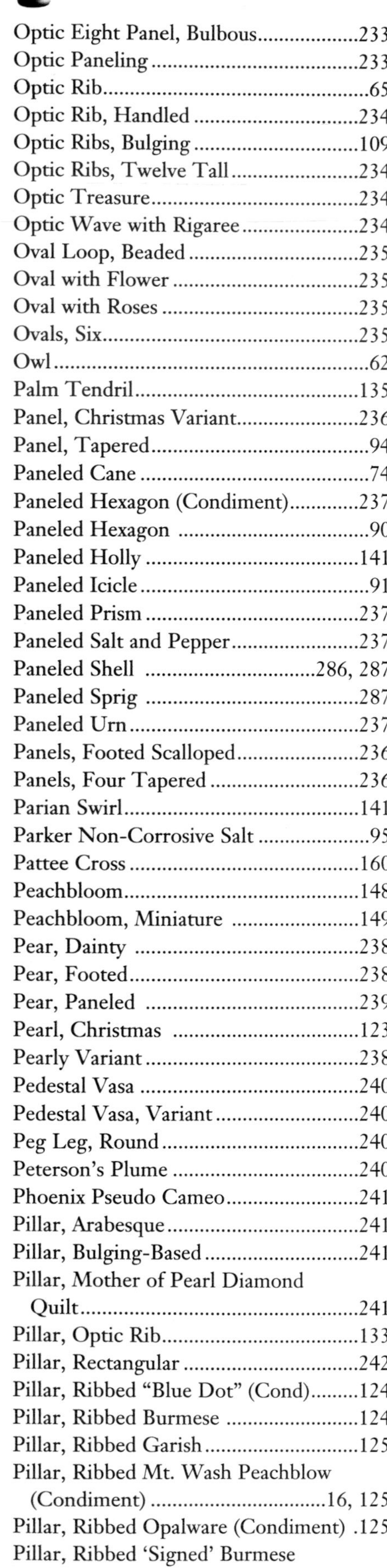

Schroeder's ANTIQUES Price Guide

. . . is the #1 best-selling antiques & collectibles value guide on the market today, and here's why . . .

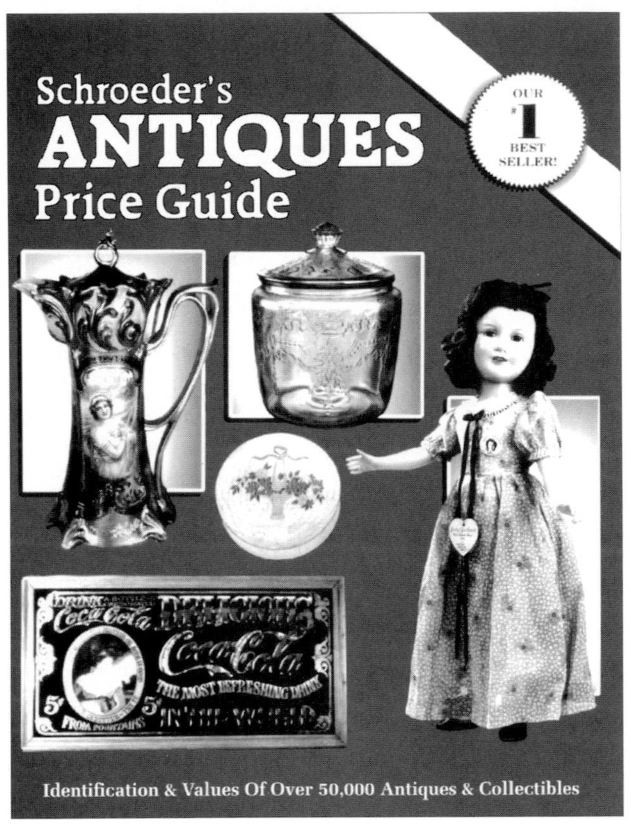

8½ x 11, 608 Pages, $12.95

- *More than 300 advisors, well-known dealers, and top-notch collectors work together with our editors to bring you accurate information regarding pricing and identification.*

- *More than 45,000 items in almost 500 categories are listed along with hundreds of sharp original photos that illustrate not only the rare and unusual, but the common, popular collectibles as well.*

- *Each large close-up shot shows important details clearly. Every subject is represented with histories and background information, a feature not found in any of our competitors' publications.*

- *Our editors keep abreast of newly developing trends, often adding several new categories a year as the need arises.*

If it merits the interest of today's collector, you'll find it in *Schroeder's*. And you can feel confident that the information we publish is up to date and accurate. Our advisors thoroughly check each category to spot inconsistencies, listings that may not be entirely reflective of market dealings, and lines too vague to be of merit. Only the best of the lot remains for publication.

Without doubt, you'll find
SCHROEDER'S ANTIQUES PRICE GUIDE
the only one to buy for
reliable information and values.